Wagner's *Parsifal*

VERITAS

Series Introduction

". . . the truth will set you free." (John 8:32)

In much contemporary discourse, Pilate's question has been taken to mark the absolute boundary of human thought. Beyond this boundary, it is often suggested, is an intellectual hinterland into which we must not venture. This terrain is an agnosticism of thought: because truth cannot be possessed, it must not be spoken. Thus, it is argued that the defenders of "truth" in our day are often traffickers in ideology, merchants of counterfeits, or anti-liberal. They are, because it is somewhat taken for granted that Nietzsche's word is final: truth is the domain of tyranny.

Is this indeed the case, or might another vision of truth offer itself? The ancient Greeks named the love of wisdom as *philia*, or friendship. The one who would become wise, they argued, would be a "friend of truth." For both philosophy and theology might be conceived as schools in the friendship of truth, as a kind of relation. For like friendship, truth is as much discovered as it is made. If truth is then so elusive, if its domain is *terra incognita*, perhaps this is because it arrives to us—unannounced—as gift, as a person, and not some thing.

The aim of the Veritas book series is to publish incisive and original current scholarly work that inhabits "the between" and "the beyond" of theology and philosophy. These volumes will all share a common aspiration to transcend the institutional divorce in which these two disciplines often find themselves, and to engage questions of pressing concern to both philosophers and theologians in such a way as to reinvigorate both disciples with a kind of interdisciplinary desire, often so absent in contemporary academe. In a word, these volumes represent collective efforts in the befriending of truth, doing so beyond the simulacra of pretend tolerance, the violent, yet insipid reasoning of liberalism that asks with Pilate, "What is truth?"—expecting a consensus of non-commitment; one that encourages the commodification of the mind, now sedated by the civil service of career, ministered by the frightened patrons of position.

The series will therefore consist of two "wings": (1) original monographs; and (2) essay collections on a range of topics in theology and philosophy. The latter will principally by the products of the annual conferences of the Centre of Theology and Philosophy (www.theologyphilosophycentre.co.uk).

Conor Cunningham
Eric Austin Lee
Series editors

Wagner's *Parsifal*

An Appreciation in the Light of his Theological Journey

RICHARD H. BELL

CASCADE *Books* · Eugene, Oregon

WAGNER'S *PARSIFAL*
An Appreciation in the Light of His Theological Journey

Veritas Series 10

Cascade Books
An Imprint of Wipf and Stock Publishers
199 W. 8th Ave., Suite 3
Eugene, OR 97401

www.wipfandstock.com

ISBN 13: 978-1-62032-885-9

Cataloging-in-Publication data:

Bell, Richard H., 1954–.

    Wagner's *Parsifal* : an appreciation in the light of his theological journey / Richard H. Bell, with a foreword by Roger Allen.

    Veritas Series 10

    xx + 380 p.; 23 cm—Includes bibliographical references and index.

    ISBN 13: 978-1-62032-885-9

    1. Wagner, Richard, 1813–1833. Parsifal. 2. Music—Religious aspects. 3. Theology. I. Allen, Roger. II Series. III. Title.

ML410.W17 B45 2013

Manufactured in the USA.

Ed Ball

9 August 1952 – 19 January 2011

In memoriam

Table of Contents

List of Musical Examples

Foreword

One of the most vigorously debated aspects of Wagner's Parsifal is to what extent it is, if at all, a Christian work? Does it contain any kind of Christian message? Does it, as the subtitle of this study suggests, represent the culmination of a theological journey, or is Wagner's use of sacred imagery and ecclesiastical ritual simply a self-serving dramaturgical device? What is beyond doubt is that Wagner was deeply fascinated by and made telling use of Christian symbolism and metaphor in his creative work; and that the idea of the mythical and historical figure of Jesus was central to his thought and gained in importance towards the end of his life. These are the broad perspectives from which Richard Bell offers new interdisciplinary insights into Parsifal in this widely researched and thought provoking study.

Richard Bell has done Wagner scholarship an enduring service. Wagner's theology is an aspect of the composer's intellectual universe that is seldom even acknowledged, let alone researched or understood; yet as Professor Bell demonstrates beyond any doubt, it is crucial to an understanding of Parsifal. Drawing on an extensive knowledge of primary and secondary sources, Bell considers the extraordinary depth and breadth of Wagner's reading, in particular his detailed knowledge of the New Testament and his grounding in the traditions and practices of Lutheran Protestantism. Bell is an eloquent and sure-footed guide through the labyrinth of theological and philosophical discourses that nourished Wagner's final opera. Issues of Christology and to what extent the person and work of Christ were at the centre of Wagner's theological concern are considered in depth together with, inter alia, the ideas of compassion and regeneration that were to result in the paradox of divine suffering and the renewal of nature existing in a single day in the Act III Good Friday scene.

This study will inform and provoke in equal measure. It does not shy away from the inevitable controversies engendered by any discussion of Parsifal and the associated Prose Works written about the time of the opera's composition. Three examples will serve for many. Bell's critical examination of the late "Regeneration" essays, especially Religion and Art and its supplements, questions the widely accepted notion that Wagner's late thought is dominated by a pernicious racist ideology. Controversial new perspectives are offered on the issues arising from Wagner's anti-Semitism: e.g., the support given to Wagner's assertion that Judaism has been superseded and that the way of salvation for Jewish people is through faith in Christ will not find many adherents today—even if he did, as Bell claims, have the New Testament on his side! The notion that the music of Parsifal's closing moments is "so exalted as to bring to our consciousness 'dogma free' Christian truth" raises serious aesthetic difficulties. (An alternative view is that the general wash of sound with which Parsifal ends comes dangerously close to kitsch!) These and other claims in the book will fuel debates surrounding Parsifal for years to come.

Richard Bell wisely avoids any detailed discussion on what might or might not have been the nature of Wagner's personal faith. Rather he demonstrates beyond empirical doubt that Parsifal is the distillation of a lifetime's creative experience and reflection on the philosophical and theological issues of the age realized in music of hypnotic fascination. Parsifal is presented here in essence as a synthesis of the Old Testament mythology of creation and the New Testament theology of the cross. The achievement of this study is that in identifying this as the culmination of Wagner's theological journey it moves on from the ideological issues that have dominated recent, and not so recent, discourses surrounding the opera into broader interdisciplinary territory. To what extent Parsifal promotes the explicitly Christian message determined by Bell must be open to question and will undoubtedly be challenged; but in engaging with these debates we can enhance our knowledge and add a new dimension to our understanding of one of the most elusive yet continually fascinating conceptions ever to possess the human imagination.

Roger Allen
Fellow and Tutor in Music and Dean of St Peter's College, Oxford

October 2013

Preface

"The auditorium grows completely dark. A breathless hush falls. Like a voice from another world, the first expansive theme of the prelude begins. This impression is unlike anything else, and is ineradicable."[1]

Experiencing *Parsifal* in Bayreuth can be an unforgettable experience. And wherever it is experienced, many find themselves in exactly the same state as Parsifal at the end of Act I: transfixed, but also completely puzzled. Parsifal has witnessed the ceremony of the grail where the redeemer is manifest to and lives in the knights of the grail, and when Gurnemanz asks him "Do you know what you have seen?" ("Weißt du, was du sah'st?") all he can do is press his hands against his heart and shake his head.[2] Likewise, after experiencing Parsifal we know something profound has happened, but often it is impossible to articulate what we have seen.[3]

My purpose in writing this book is partly an attempt to answer Gurnemanz's question, focussing on the theological aspect. I am not remotely suggesting that the whole "message" of *Parsifal* can be expressed in words; the "message" is in many ways "ineffable" and we will often have to respond, like Parsifal, by pressing our hands against our heart. But I am convinced that the experience of *Parsifal* can be enhanced by analyzing the artwork in the light of the composer's intellectual, artistic, and theological journey. *Parsifal* was Wagner's "last card"[4] where he was bringing together much that

1. Weingartner, *Lebenserinnerungen*, 165, quoted and translated in Barth, Mack, and Voss, *Wagner*, 242.

2. *WagPS* 154–55.

3. Even Patrice Chéreau said he could never do a production of *Parsifal* because he "did not understand anything about Parsifal"; he therefore declined a request of Pierre Boulez to produce *Parsifal* in Bayreuth ("Lebrecht interview on Radio 3, 6 September 2010).

4. *CD* 28 March 1881: "Gobineau says the Germans were the last card Nature had to play—Parsifal is my last card."

went before and, in the light of his failing health and approaching death, he was clearly seeking "closure."[5]

My focus in trying to understand the work is to offer a theological appreciation. As I first engaged in this exercise, I think I could be accused of subjecting this great work of art to a theological "procrustean bed," constantly asking whether the work conforms to the "catholic and apostolic faith" (for me this essentially means the Protestant, especially Lutheran forms of theological confession). Although my book will involve some sort of critical engagement, asking whether *Parsifal* coheres or even agrees with Christian theology, I hope to go beyond this and see where the artwork takes us. Truly appreciating *Parsifal* is a self-involving enterprise and, like self-involving theology,[6] takes us on an existential journey. I have heard it said that *Parsifal* is a problematic work because it is difficult to identify with any of the characters. How can we identify with a guilt laden king (Amfortas), an old celibate knight (but a knight, Gurnemanz, who does not even engage in fighting), a castrated magician (Klingsor), and a wild composite sphinx-like creature who flies through time (Kundry)? However, there is a figure we are perhaps meant to identify with: Parsifal himself. And by identifying with him we may well discover a life-changing existential journey.

---

5. See the comments of John Deathridge, broadcast on Radio 3, 7 May 2013.
6. Cf. Evans, *Self-Involvement*.

Acknowledgements

The origins of this book go back to a lecture I gave to the Postgraduate Study Day for students of theology and religious studies at the University of Nottingham in November 2006 on "Schopenhauer and Art" with a focus on Wagner's *Parsifal*. But my thinking on *Parsifal* really started to crystallize when I gave a paper "Union with 'Christ' in Wagner's *Parsifal*" in November 2009 to the Oxford seminar group "The Bible in Art, Music and Literature," organized by Christine Joynes and Christopher Rowland. The work was developed through two further papers I gave in 2011 (I am grateful to Nanette Nielsen for inviting me to give them): first, a paper given to the Music and Philosophy conference held at King's College London on "The Miracle of Conversion in Wagner's *Religion and Art* and *Parsifal*"; second, a paper given to the Nottingham Centre for Music on Stage and Screen (MOSS) on "Sex, Sin, and Suffering in *Parsifal*". The book then finally began to take shape in a module I taught at the University of Nottingham on the theology of *Parsifal* and I am grateful to the University for allowing me teach this adventurous module and to my students for their enthusiasm, industry, and great sense of fun.

I am grateful to Nanette Nielsen, David Duckworth, Philip Goodchild, Maria Forsberg, and Jack Bell for reading through parts of the book and to Christoph Ochs for discussions about Wagner's German. I particularly thank Peter Watts for many stimulating conversations about music and theology, and for being so generous with his time (in the middle of his own busy schedule) in helping me with computer issues. I thank the University of Nottingham library for allowing me to borrow a large number of books and the music department of the Bodleian library, Oxford. My visits to the Nationalarchiv der Richard Wagner-Stiftung/Richard Wagner Gedenkstätte were especially valuable and I thank Frau Kristine Unger for all her help. I also thank the Kartenbüro for enabling me to experience Stephan Herheim's remarkable production of *Parsifal* and the staff of the Hotel Goldener Anker, especially the proprietor Frau Eva Graf, for making my visits to Bayreuth so enjoyable.

Finally I thank the staff of Cascade Books, especially Robin Parry, for the way they so efficiently helped bringing this work to publication.

Abbreviations

Introduction

Abbreviations follow the *SBL Handbook of Style*. References to *Parsifal* are either made to the Act and measure (e.g., Act I measures 1–7 is expressed as I.1–7) or to the page number in the libretto given in the edition and translation of Lionel Salter (*WagPS* 92). References to Wolfram's *Parzival* are given either to the Middle High German references (e.g., 1.1–9) or to Hatto's translation (e.g., *WolPH* 292). References to *Willehalm* are to the translation of Gibbs and Johnson (*WolWGJ* 25). Unless otherwise indicated, all Bible quotations in English are taken from the *New Revised Standard Version*. Quotations of the German of Wagner's prose works are taken from *Gesammelte Schriften und Dichtungen* (*GSD*) but where available I have also given the reference to *Dichtungen und Schriften: Jubiläumsausgabe* (*JA*), which uses modernized spellings and script.

Unless otherwise stated, all emphasis is that given in the source.

ASSW	*Arthur Schopenhauer Sämtliche Werke, textkritisch bearbeitet von Wolfgang Frhr. von Löhneysen.* 5 vols. 1968. Reprint. Darmstadt: Wissenschaftliche Buchgesellschaft, 2004.
BBH-K	*Bremer Biblische Hand-Konkordanz.* Stuttgart: Anker/Christlichen Verlagshaus, 1979.
BB	Joachim Bergfeld, editor. *The Diary of Richard Wagner 1865–1882: The Brown Book.* Translated by George Bird. London: Victor Gollanz, 1980.

BSELK   *Bekenntnisschriften der evangelisch-lutherischen Kirche.* 10th ed. Göttingen: Vandenhoeck & Ruprecht, 1986.

CD   Martin Gregor-Dellin and Dietrich Mack, editors. *Cosima Wagner's Diaries.* 2 vols. Translated by Geoffrey Skelton. New York: Harcourt Brace, 1978–80.

CT   Martin Gregor-Dellin and Dietrich Mack, editors. *Cosima Wagner: Die Tagebücher.* 2 vols. München/ Zürich: R. Piper, 1976.

DEAP   Martin Geck and Egon Voss, editors. *Dokumente zur Entstehung und ersten Aufführung des Bühnenweihfestspiels Parsifal.* SW 30. Mainz: B. Schott, 1970.

DBE2   *Deutsche Biographische Enzyklopädie.* 2nd ed. München: K. G. Saur, 2005–8.

DCT   Alan Richardson, editor. *A Dictionary of Christian Theology.* London: SCM, 1969.

DTB   Isolde Vetter and Egon Voss, editors. *Dokumente und Texte zu unvollendeten Bühnenwerken.* SW 31. Mainz: B. Schott, 2005.

FTG   Lionel Friend. "Thematic Guide". In *P:OOG*, 95–104.

GSD   Richard Wagner. *Gesammelte Schriften und Dichtungen.* 10 vols. 3rd ed. Leipzig: E. W. Fritzsch, 1897.

JA   Richard Wagner. *Dichtungen und Schriften: Jubiläumsausgabe.* 10 vols. Edited by Dieter Borchmeyer. Frankfurt am Main: Insel, 1983.

KB   Otto Strobel, editor. *König Ludwig II. und Richard Wagner: Briefwechsel.* 5 vols. Karlsruhe: G. Braun, 1936–39.

KGB   Giorgio Colli and Mazzino Montinari, editors. *Friedrich Nietzsche Briefwechsel: Kritische Gesamtausgabe.* 25 vols. Berlin: de Gruyter, 1975–2004.

KGW

Giorgio Colli and Mazzino Montinari, editors. *Friedrich Nietzsche Werke: Kritische Gesamtausgabe.* 42 vols. Berlin: de Gruyter, 1967–.

KSA

Giorgio Colli and Mazzino Montinari, editors. *Friedrich Nietzsche, Sämtliche Werke: Kritische Studienausgabe.* 15 vols. Berlin: de Gruyter, 1999.

LchI

Engelbert Kirschbaum, editor. *Lexikon der christlichen Ikonographie.* 5 vols. Freiburg: Herder 1968.

LW

J. Pelikan and H. T. Lehmann, editors. *Luther Works.* 55 vols. Philadelphia: Fortress, 1943–86.

Mein Leben

Richard Wagner. *Mein Leben.* 2 vols. 1963. Reprint. Edited by Martin Gregor-Dellin. München: Paul List, 1969.

MGG

Ludwig Finscher, editor. *Musik in Geschichte und Gegenwart.* 29 vols. Stuttgart: J. B. Metler, 1994–2008.

My Life

Richard Wagner. *My Life.* Translated by Andrew Gray. Edited by Mary Whittall. Cambridge: Cambridge University Press, 1983.

NDCT

Alan Richardson and John Bowden, editors. *A New Dictionary of Christian Theology.* London: SCM, 1983.

NPNF1

Philip Schaff, editor. *Nicene and Post-Nicene Fathers: First Series.* 14 vols. 1890–1900. Reprint. Peabody, MA: Hendrickson 1994.

NWSEB

Dieter Borchmeyer and Jörg Salaquarda, editors. *Nietzsche und Wagner: Stationen einer epochalen Begegnung.* 2 vols. Frankfurt am Main: Insel, 1994.

P:OOG

Parsifal: Overture Opera Guides. London: Oneworld Classics, 2011.

PP

Arthur Schopenhauer. *Parerga and Paralipomena.* 2 vols. 1974. Reprint. Translated by E. F. J. Payne. Oxford: Clarendon, 2000.

PW

Richard Wagner's Prose Works. Translated by William Ashton Ellis. 8 vols. New York: Broude Brothers, 1892–99.

SB

Richard Wagner: Sämtliche Briefe. Edited by Gertrud Strobel and Werner Wolf (vols. 1–5),

	Hans-Joachim Bauer and Johannes Forner (vols. 6–8), Klaus Burmeister and Johannes Forner (vol. 9), Andreas Mielke (vols. 10, 14–15), Andreas Mielke and Isabel Kraft (vol. 18), Martin Dürrer and Isabel Kraft (vols. 11–13, 16–17, 22), Margret Jestremski (vol. 19) (Leipzig: Deutscher Verlag für Musik, 1967–2000 (vols. 1–9); Wiesbaden, Leipzig, and Paris: Breitkopf & Härtel, 2000– (vols. 10–))
SL	Spencer, Stewart, and Barry Millington, translators and editors. *Selected Letters of Richard Wagner*. New York/London: W.W. Norton, 1987.
SW	*Richard Wagner Sämtliche Werke*. 31 vols (projected). Mainz: B. Schott, 1970–.
WA	*D. Martin Luthers Werke, kritische Gesamtausgabe*. Weimar: Hermann Böhlaus, 1883–
WagPS	Lionel Salter. "Libretto." In *P:OOG*, 105–237.
WagRS	Stewart Spencer. "The Ring of the Nibelung." In *Wagner's Ring of the Nibelung: A Companion*, edited by Stewart Spencer and Barry Millington, 53–372. 1993. Reprint. London: Thames & Hudson, 2010.
WagTS	*Libretto for Richard Wagner's Tristan and Isolde*. Translated by Lionel Salter. Booklet accompanying the Compact Disk recording, conducted by Leonard Bernstein, Philips, 1993.
WolPH	Wolfram von Eschenbach. *Parzival*. Translated by A. T. Hatto 1980. Reprint. Harmondsworth, UK: Penguin, 2004.
WolWGJ	Wolfram von Eschenbach. *Willehalm*. Translated by Marion E. Gibbs and Sidney M. Johnson. Harmondsworth, UK: Penguin, 1984.
WWR	Arthur Schopenhauer. *The World as Will and Representation*. 2 vols. Translated by E. F. J. Payne. 1958. Reprint. New York: Dover, 1966.
WWV	John Deathridge, Martin Geck, and Egon Voss, editors. *Wagner-Werk-Verzeichnis: Verzeichnis der musikalischen Werke Richard Wagners und ihrer Quellen*. Mainz: B. Schott, 1986–87.

1

How Can Wagner Inform
the Christian Theologian?

Introduction

I START ON A positive note. Wagner has composed music of inexpressible beauty that has given joy, comfort, and pleasure to countless people. Debussy described *Parsifal* as "one of the finest monuments in sound ever to have been raised to the everlasting glory of music."[1] Wagner's art has inspired painters, poets, novelist, dramatists, and, of course, composers. Restricting ourselves to composers alone, and only a small handful, if it were not for Wagner we would not have the composers Bruckner, Mahler, Strauss, Schönberg, Sibelius, and Elgar as we now know them. In view of this I have a sense of profound gratitude that the composer Wagner was given to us. One could add that the Christian theologian should be especially grateful for not only has such wonderful music been given to us, but also Wagner's stage works are rich in theology, and time and again in his writing and conversation he stressed the fundamental importance of Jesus' self-sacrifice and that "the true task is to glorify the pure figure of Christ."[2]

There has been a steady stream of theologians who have offered a grateful appreciation of Wagner's art.[3] However, the greeting Wagner has

---

1. Quoted in Millington, *Sorcerer*, 233.

2. *CD* 13 January 1880.

3. Among well-known theologians who expressed their appreciation were Albert Schweitzer (*Denken*, 23–24, 108–10); Dietrich Bonhoeffer (Bethge, *Bonhoeffer*, 127);

received from theologians often matches in its rancor Alberich's "fond fare-well" ("Liebesgruß") as he leaves the stage in Scene 4 of *Das Rheingold*.[4] Consider the following examples. The entry on "Wagner" in the *New Catholic Encyclopedia* begins thus: "Wagner was the supreme egoist, living luxuriously off his friends' largesse, intriguing against his opponents, dallying with inaccessible women. At the same time, in his pseudophilosophic writings . . . as in his librettos, he posited a clean world populated by a purified, redeemed humanity (his *Volk*), unfettered by law and religious dogma."[5] One of the most influential Protestants of the twentieth century, Karl Barth, described Wagner as "dreadful" ("greulich").[6] Margaret Brearley in an article on Hitler and Wagner often brackets the two together and concludes that "in the case of both Wagner and Hitler evil was cloaked in religious garb."[7] And there are non-theologians who, in assessing the "Christian" character of Wagner and his art, have been hardly more flattering. So regarding Wagner's final stage work, Gutman declares: "*Parsifal* is not only un-Christian, it is anti-Christian."[8] Köhler, who considers Wagner a "confirmed atheist,"[9] finds his person and art questionable and, like Brearley, sees him as Hitler's inspiration.[10] There has been no shortage of extremely negative views of Wagner's personality and a good proportion of those who attack his person also find his art fundamentally evil.

Hans Küng ("Theology for Our Time"). See also Forsyth, "Pessimism"; Forsyth, "Wagner's 'Parsifal'"; Hébert, *Sentiment*; Steinacker, *Wagner*; Hans Hübner, *Erlösung*. There have also been some fine theological appreciations by non-theologians, e.g., Beckett, *Parsifal*; Scruton, *Death-Devoted Heart*; Borchmeyer, *Ahasvers Wandlungen*, and Kienzle, *Religion und Philosophie*.

4. *WagRS*, 106.

5. Beaufils and Evans, "Wagner," 604. The second edition is unchanged apart from an updated bibliography.

6. Barth, *Protestantische Theologie*, 514 (Barth, *Rousseau to Ritschl*, 388). The context for this comment is Nietzsche's attack on David Friedrich Strauß: "In this poor Strauss really seems to have chosen the better part, as against Nietzsche, who, as is well known, was the helpless slave of the dreadful Wagner at the time of his great deriding of Strauss." Nietzsche's attack on Strauß is generally considered poor (Hübner, *Nietzsche*, 85) but it is unclear why Wagner should take any blame for this (unless it was simply because Wagner disliked Strauß also). Barth's negative of view of Wagner in his 1947 publication is best considered an irrational outburst and contrasts with the youthful Barth who praised *Tannhäuser* as a piece of "powerful preaching" (Busch, *Barth*, 30).

7. Brearley, "Hitler and Wagner," 19. Her views are adopted by the former Bishop of Oxford, Richard Harries, *After the Evil*, 14–16.

8. Gutman, *Wagner*, 431.

9. Köhler, *Titans*, 560.

10. Köhler, *Wagner's Hitler*.

It can therefore come as no surprise that when I have confessed my love and admiration for the works of Wagner, especially in Christian circles, I have usually received reactions ranging from a wry smile to explicit disapproval. For how can a figure like Wagner, the "antisemite,"[11] the philanderer,[12] the megalomaniac,[13] and "inveterate scrounger"[14] be considered compatible with Christian faith? Further, do not the works themselves contain unseemly stories? The agnostic philosopher Schopenhauer was shocked by the immorality of the Volsung twins Siegmund and Sieglinde and their treatment of Hunding in *Die Walküre* and Siegfried's attitude to Mime in *Siegfried*. In the margin of the *Ring* libretto, which Wagner had sent him,[15] he wrote right across the upper margin of pages 42–43 "One can put morals on one side; but one should not slap them in the face."[16] After Sieglinde's words "were my arms to enfold the hero" ("umfing' den Helden mein Arm")[17] he reduces her sentiments to: "Go and murder my husband";[18] and after Sieglinde's words "How broad is your brow, the scrollwork of veins entwines in your temples!" ("Wie dir die Stirn so offen steht, der Adern Geäst in den Schläfen sich schlingt")[19] he writes: "This is infamous" ("Es ist infam.")[20] At the end of

11. Throughout this work I use the forms "antisemite" and "antisemitism" rather than "anti-semite" and "anti-semitism." For my rationale, see chapter 9 below.

12. See section 2 below.

13. He was so described by Franz Strauss (who played first horn for the 1882 performances of *Parsifal*) and by the pianist Andreas Schiff, who believes the megalomania also comes over in the music.

14. Cf. Millington, *Sorcerer*, 133, who then radically qualifies this conventional image of the composer (141–47).

15. See *My Life*, 510 (*Mein Leben* 2:523): "I felt impelled to send the esteemed philosopher a copy of my Nibelung poem; I appended to the title in my own hand only the words 'With admiration' (aus Verehrung), without any other communication." This account is corroborated by Schopenhauer's letter to Julius Frauenstädt, 30 December 1854 (Hübscher, *Schopenhauer Briefe*, 357) with the minor "correction" "aus Verehrung und Dankbarkeit."

16. Otto, *Wagner*, 170: "Man kann die Moral vergessen; aber man soll sie nicht maulschellieren" (in reference to the encounter between Siegmund and Sieglinde, Act I).

17. *WagRS* 134.

18. Otto, *Wagner*, 171 (the English here is Schopenhauer's).

19. *WagPS* 136.

20. Otto, *Wagner*, 171. Schopenhauer's shock about *Die Walküre* Act I is again emphasized in the witness of Karl Heblers (cited by Dr. Felix Gotthelf). Although he was impressed by Wagner's poetic gifts in the *Ring*, he said: "Das Gedicht enthalte übrigens Unmoralisches: Eine Frau gebe dem Feinde ihres Mannes, der jenen gastfreundlich aufgenommen, Waffen in die Hand, je sich selbst gebe sie ihm hin, in welcher Hinsicht es zum Äußersten komme, wo es dann heiße: 'Der Vorhang fällt schnell'. Die Poesie solle nicht moralisieren, aber auch nicht unmoralisch sein" (Otto, *Wagner*, 170).

Siegfried Act I Scene I (as Siegfried tells Mime that he will leave him) he wrote "scandalous ingratitude, villainous morals" ("Empörender Undank, maulschellierte Moral.")[21] I suspect Schopenhauer found *Die Walküre* particularly distasteful because Wagner not only portrays immorality but presents it such that we sympathize with the Volsung twins who not only commit incest but know they are doing so![22] If Paul entreats the Philippian Christians: "whatever is true, whatever is honourable, whatever is just, whatever is pure, whatever is pleasing, whatever is commendable, if there is any excellence and if there is anything worthy of praise, think about these things" (Phil 4:8), why do some Christians go to the theatre to experience works such as the *Ring* with its portrayal of adultery, incest, and murder?

Over the years I have pondered how to respond to all this. One way is to say that I have to accept that Wagner's works contain an alien and unacceptable ideology and simply get on and enjoy them.[23] Barry Emslie even goes to the point of saying that Wagner's antisemitism and racism "were to him sources of inspiration"[24] and concludes that "we will never be able to appreciate, to enjoy properly, the full aesthetic and intellectual experience of the complete Wagner oeuvre unless we accept that it violates the stringent rules of respectable moral catechisms. How the individual handles this is entirely his or her own problem."[25]

A second strategy is to say that everyone, Christian or not, has a dark side, and Wagner's music, by a strange psychological process, helps us deal with that side.[26] Should not the Christian acknowledge this "darker side" of their personhood? Having acknowledged it can one not try to deal with it through the artworks of Wagner? Many of his stage works are, after all, like "animated textbooks of psychoanalysis";[27] further, through experiencing them we come to terms with this darker side and the strange interaction

21. Otto, *Wagner*, 171.

22. Contrast Shakespeare's *Hamlet* where we hardly sympathize with the particular immorality of Claudius and Gertrude (Schopenhauer was a great admirer of the playwright).

23. Cf. Deathridge, "Strange Love."

24. Emslie, "Race, Nation, Culture," 18.

25. Ibid., 19.

26. Magee, *Aspects*, 41–42, argues that the particular "magic" of Wagner's music explains why it appeals to "the emotionally isolated or repressed." He gives as examples Nietzsche, Proust "living alone in his cork-lined room," Albert Schweitzer, Bernard Shaw, Richard Strauss, Mahler, Schönberg, and Bruckner. Although Magee may be on to something here, the idea that the Wagnerian audience is full of emotional cripples needs to be radically re-thought.

27. Magee, *Aspects*, 36.

of the singer's voice of the "ego" and the orchestral "id"[28] brings us to a self-understanding and self-transformation that few other artworks can achieve. Wagner, who anticipated so many insights of Freud and Jung, can function as our therapist;[29] and we have the most beautiful music thrown in as an added extra!

A third strategy is to ask whether Wagner, both the person and the work, are as "bad" as is often made out and whether he can in fact make an important contribution to Christian theology and even promote a Christian holiness. Ironically the *Ring* with its "pagan" background can be seen as a Christian reflection on original sin.[30] The *Ring* does indeed contain "immoral stories" but the Old Testament contains material that is even grimmer[31] and both can prepare for and even anticipate the Christian gospel. If one is to search for Christian theology in Wagner the obvious work to consider is *Parsifal*. As we shall see, various arguments have been advanced to question the Christian character of the work.[32] But those who argue it is *not* a Christian work are, I believe, evading the obvious.[33] I suggest that it is not only possible to integrate *Parsifal* into a Christian theological outlook but also to study *Parsifal* such that it presents some distinctive theological insights.

Over the years I have moved towards this third strategy (but also seeing the value in the second). I will, throughout this work, argue that *Parsifal* is in many ways a "Christian" work even though there are some "unorthodox" elements in it. I will also argue that it has affinities to earlier works in the Wagnerian canon, not just with those having a "Christian" ambience such as *Tannhäuser*, *Lohengrin* and *Meistersinger* but also with those works having more "pagan" elements (at least on the surface) such as the *Ring* and *Tristan und Isolde*.[34]

28. Cf. Magee, *Aspects*, 37.

29. Perhaps it is not accidental that of all the professions represented in the audience of Bayreuth, medicine, according to Siegfried Wagner, was the foremost (Cormack, "Faithful," 42). See also below on Ellis, the translator of Wagner's prose works.

30. Cf. Scruton, "Quest," 15. Note also the comments of Gabriel Fauré in a letter written to his wife on 6 August 1896: "The Tetralogy is packed with philosophy and symbolism that merely serve to demonstrate our poverty, our emptiness. When it comes to an end it leaves one convinced of universal misery, eternal suffering and that is all! It is penitence in the noblest meaning of the word, it is almost contrition" (Hartford, *Bayreuth*, 223).

31. Consider, for example, the story of the Levite's concubine (Judg 19).

32. See, for example, Tanner, "Total Work of Art," 205–18; Magee, *Wagner and Philosophy*, 278–85.

33. This is a point made by Domingo (Matheopoulos, *Domingo*, 211).

34. Cosima in her entry for 6 October 1882 records her husband as saying

But I image there are many who question whether Wagner can promote a Christian theology in view of their perception of the moral quality of the man. It is therefore to this issue that I now turn.

Fair and Unfair Criticism of Wagner

Few artists have been subjected to such intense public scrutiny as Wagner. He has been judged on the basis of letters, private utterances, and even his dreams.[35] Further, there is a "strangeness of the hostility" towards the composer[36] that makes a rational assessment of his person difficult. But since his moral failings could be considered a "stumbling block" to the whole aim of his work, I turn to three criticisms levelled at him: his sexual morals, his antisemitism, and his racism.

Many Christians would wish to judge Wagner by a strict standard of sexual ethics as put forward in the New Testament. By this standard he certainly falls well short, as we all do. One could also add that he appeared to show very little remorse for the pain he did cause through his sexual misadventures. But I should also add that Wagner's promiscuity has been greatly exaggerated and in fact one can say that "he was far more loyal to each of his two wives than the typical man in his generation."[37] But there was a most painful episode upon which one must reflect in assessing Wagner's character. On the very day Hans von Bülow started the first rehearsals for *Tristan und Isolde* on 10 April 1865, his wife Cosima gave birth to Wagner's child Isolde! Von Bülow was devastated by Cosima's affair with Wagner. The testimony of the domestic servant Anna Mrázek is heart wrenching. She tells of how in the Villa Pellet von Bülow discovered that his wife had gone into Wagner's bedroom; he tried to enter but found the door blocked.

"*Tannhäuser, Tristan*, and *Parsifal* belong together." I will argue in subsequent chapters that *Parsifal* also has strong links to the *Ring* and that one problem with Nietzsche's criticism of *Parsifal* is that he isolated it from Wagner's other dramas.

35. In an otherwise well researched study, Lobenstein-Reichmann, *Chamberlain*, 560, writes that Wagner "attacks" the Jews as "*worms*" ("*Gewürm*"), referring to CD 20 July 1881. It is worth quoting Cosima's entry: "R. had a somewhat restless night, he dreamed first of all that I did not love him, then that he was surrounded by Jews who turned into worms."

36. Tanner, *Wagner*, 16.

37. Millington, *Sorcerer*, 138. He does go on to clarify and perhaps qualify this. Wagner's affair with Jessie Laussot in 1850 was both an offense to her husband and to Minna (although Millington says it was "but a further nail in the coffin of a marriage that was already in a terminal condition," 139). Further, he had an infatuation with Judith Gautier during his marriage to Cosima, his second wife (see chapter 8 below).

Returning to his room, "he threw himself on the ground, beat on the floor and with his hands and feet like a madman, and cried and even screamed."[38]

I will have occasion to put the other side of Wagner's character a little later but for now it is worth mentioning that Cosima's marriage to von Bülow was unhappy. A passage from Cosima's diary tells of her guilt about leaving Hans (a theme which frequently appears in her diary) but also of their disastrous relationship: "My grieving about Hans—never expressed aloud—R. guesses, and it makes him sad. He recalls scenes, at which he was present, when Hans struck me, and says he was horrified at the calm indifference with which I had borne this. Very painful feelings."[39] There were a whole catalogue of problems in her marriage to von Bülow[40] and perhaps these words of Millington may make us feel slightly better about this love-triangle: "It rapidly became apparent to all parties concerned—including Bülow himself—that Cosima belonged not with him, but with Wagner. 'Wife-stealing' is hardly an appropriate term to describe what all the participants themselves regarded as a rational reordering of an anomalous situation."[41] It is the case that Richard and Cosima had a remarkably fruitful marriage and that von Bülow did remarry,[42] but the story of Wagner's affair with Cosima is likely to make many uncomfortable in the extreme; and it certainly made Cosima uncomfortable to the very end of her life.[43]

The second issue of "antisemitism" is complex and will be considered in detail in chapter 9 below. But for now I will make two basic points. First, Wagner's antisemitism was very different to that of the national socialists. There is a leap from Wagner to Chamberlain[44] and an even bigger one from

---

38. Hilmes, *Herrin Des Hügels*, 114. This testimony was given to the court in Munich (20 May 1914) in relation to the paternity of Isolde von Bülow (see below).

39. *CD* 11 July 1869.

40. E.g., because of "crippling neuralgic pains and black moods of despair" he would "lash out with sharp tongue, subjecting all around him to humiliating sarcasm." Further, he was "monstrously insensitive" (Millington, *Sorcerer*, 127–28).

41. Millington, *Sorcerer*, 128.

42. On 29 July 1882, three days after the first performance of *Parsifal*, von Bülow married Marie Schanzer. Although their first months were a "vale of tears," "in his union with Marie, Bülow found much contentment" (Walker, *Hans von Bülow*, 308–9).

43. Her guilt at leaving von Bülow is frequently mentioned in her diaries. It is significant that her last words referred to Hans von Bülow: "Verzeih!" ("sorry") (Hilmes, *Herrin Des Hügels*, 431, quoting Friedelind Wagner, *Nacht über Bayreuth*, 56).

44. For a contrary view, see Lobenstein-Reichmann, *Chamberlain*, 567. Note, however, that Chamberlain himself pointed to the gulf between Wagner's thought and his own discussion of "race" (Allen, "Consecration of the House," 263–72). See chapter 9 below for further discussion.

Chamberlain to Hitler.[45] Secondly, Wagner worked closely with Jewish artists, and they had great affection for him,[46] something based not just on his musical stature but also on Wagner's genuine concern and emotional support for them. That he had such close relationships may suggest that to some extent his antisemitism was a theoretical ideology.

The third issue is "racism." Although in some quarters it has been denied that Wagner was a racist, there is quite a lot of evidence that he has to be so considered, although his views are complex and often contradictory. In chapter 6 below I will consider in some detail his 1881 essay *Heroism and Christianity*, but for now, I simply quote Cosima's entry for 16 October 1882: "We come back to the subject of race, wondering which theory is right, Schop[enhauer]'s or Gobineau's. R. feels they can be reconciled: a human being who is born black, urged toward the heights, becomes white and at the same time a different creature."[47] Although such comments may shock twenty-first-century ears, "racist" views were widely held during this time, and in fact were particularly widespread in German idealism.

Wagner as a human being did have serious shortcomings but since much literature thrives on portraying him as some sort of "monster"[48] I simply make a plea for a sense of proportion. And if theologians such as Karl Barth call Wagner "dreadful," let it be recognized that this epithet can be applied in one way or another to most human beings, including Barth himself.[49] Further, Wagner never claimed to be a saint and at least one can say instances of hypocrisy are relatively rare; two such instances

45. Chamberlain would be horrified if he lived to see the holocaust (he died in 1927). Note also that Hitler was critical of his positive view of Christianity: "In my view, H. S. Chamberlain was mistaken in regarding Christianity as a reality upon the spiritual level." Indeed Hitler had an extremely negative view of Christianity, believing it to be "an invention of sick brains." "[O]ne could imagine nothing more senseless, nor any more indecent way of turning the idea of the Godhead into a mockery" (Roper, *Hitler's Table Talk*, 144).

46. See chapter 9 below where I discuss his Jewish fellow workers such as Hermann Levi and Joseph Rubinstein.

47. *CD* 16 October 1882.

48. See, e.g., Rabbi Julia Neuberger comment in her preface to Gottfried Wagner, *Wolf*, 12, that the book "will upset the very considerable number of anglophone Wagnerians, who have tried to close their eyes to the monster who was their musical hero, the fine artist and pig of a man who was able to put some of his more unpleasant ideas into his music."

49. See Busch, *Barth*, 186.

being "preaching compassion"[50] and vegetarianism.[51] In fact, he despised hypocrisy and in *A Communication to My Friends* (coming from 1851, a time when he had moved away from Christianity), he writes that when he considered taking his own life he was acting more as an "honest Christian" in wishing to escape "the worthlessness of the modern world" than those who "with smug impertinence" were upbraiding him for his "lapse from Christianity."[52]

Since so much is made of Wagner's failings, I would like to even the balance by saying some kind words about Wagner's character. The first I want to mention is that he was in many respects a wonderful father.[53] Secondly, despite his flirtations with other women (e.g., Judith Gautier) he was a loving husband to Cosima,[54] who was clearly not a very easy person to live with.[55] Thirdly, he bore with great stoicism and dignity the many attacks of

50. See *CD* 19 January 1879. "At supper yesterday he talked about an article in the *Illustrirte Zeitung*, 'The Elk Fighting the Wolves,' and said it had taught him some very curious things—how in Nature even the most heroic must perish, men as well as animals, 'and what remain are the rats and mice—the Jews.'—I told him that I had seen Friend Wolz[ogen]'s two sisters-in-law in the mental hospital, and he talks with horror of the maintenance of such poor creatures, 'which uses up the energies of the healthy and the good.'" As well as being shocking comments (even taking into consideration that he was in a poor physical and psychological state, having slept badly and suffering from chest congestion), they hardly match the ideas of "compassion" ("Mitleid") that he was "preaching" in *Parsifal*.

51. Wagner was critical of meat eating in *Religion and Art* (*PW* 6:226–27) and in *Against Vivisection* (*PW* 6:201–2). However, as Taylor, *Wagner*, 231, remarks, "Wagner's vegetarianism proved to be just one more of his passing humours." After a few weeks of a vegetarian diet he exclaimed: "How can I produce any decent ideas as long as I'm only stuffing myself with grass?" Note also the observation of Felix Weingartner on his visit to Wahnfried in 1882: "For a short time he withdrew into the next room where some food was served to him. A glance at the dish set before him showed that he did not put into practice the vegetarian principles which he advocated" (Hartford, *Bayreuth*, 134).

52. *PW* 1:350; *GSD* 4:304; *JA* 6:281.

53. See Siegfried Wagner's recollections of his father in Spencer, *Wagner Remembered*, 271–74. One can add that he accepted Minna's daughter, Natalie, as his own as well as Cosima's children from Hans von Bülow (Daniela and Blandine). One also wonders how Wagner would turn in his grave at Cosima's treatment of Isolde (Hilmes, *Herrin Des Hügels*, 382–93). His great love for Isolde, his first child, is reflected in a poem he composed for her fifteenth birthday: "Fifteen years ago you were born: / The whole world pricked up its ears; / Others wanted *Tristan und Isolde*—/ but all I wished for and wanted / Was a little daughter: Isolde! / May she now live a thousand years, / And *Tristan and Isolde* also." This poem is on a sheet inserted in Cosima's diary for the 10 April 1880 entry.

54. The best known story of his devotion is the surprise performance of the *Tribschen Idyll* on her birthday, recalled in *CD* 25 December 1870.

55. Although Cosima was highly intelligent and was in many ways Wagner's ideal conversation partner, she clearly did not satisfy many of her husband's needs, including

his opponents.[56] Fourthly, he showed great kindness to friends and fellow workers and was a great inspiration to his musicians and singers,[57] including those who were Jewish.[58] Fifthly, he could be great company and had a wonderful sense of humor, his best side often coming over in his work as theatre director.[59] Sixthly, although he has been accused of showing remarkably little gratitude to those who helped him, even biting the hand that fed him,[60] he could show enormous gratitude to his fellow workers, including quite ordinary people.[61] Seventhly, he loved animals!

These positive traits may be considered little compensation for his sexual morals, his antisemitism, and his racism. Wagner had his faults; but nevertheless he can make his theological contribution. Although one should always bear in mind Jesus' words that prophets are to be judged by "their fruits,"[62] the theological contribution of the "prophet" is ultimately independent of his holiness, a point made vividly by Martin Luther.[63] And in this connection, it is worth stressing that Martin Luther made many more intemperate comments than Wagner, and some of his utterances had

---

sexual needs. Her diaries witness to her lack of interest in sex. See, e.g., her entries for 16 May 1870 (she was then thirty-three years old): "If only we could curb passion—if only it could be banished from our lives! Its approach now grieves me, as it were the death of love." This may explain her comments made six months later (12 November 1870): "I am in a permanent state of inward contemplation; I think I am ripe for a convent."

56. One thinks especially of Nietzsche's savage attacks. Only on few occasions did Wagner attack Nietzsche in return.

57. See the comments of the painter Friedrich Pecht in Spencer, *Wagner Remembered*, 176.

58. See chapter 9 below.

59. See, e.g., Neumann, *Recollections*, 9–14.

60. I am particularly thinking of his attitude to Meyerbeer.

61. See public announcement in the *Bayreuther Tagblatt* (5 September 1882) expressing his "heartfelt thanks to fellow citizens" for their part in making the performances of *Parsifal* a success (Barth, Mack, and Voss, *Wagner*, 242–43).

62. Jesus says that false prophets will be known "by their fruits" (Matt 7:15a), by which is meant their deeds, not the consequences of their deeds (Luz, *Matthäus I*, 526).

63. See his "Preface to Epistles of James and Jude": "Whatever does not teach Christ is not (yet) apostolic, even though St. Peter or St. Paul does the teaching. Again, whatever preaches Christ would be apostolic, even if Judas, Annas, Pilate, and Herod were doing it" (*LW* 35:396; Heinrich Bornkamm, *Vorreden*, 216–17: "Was Christum nicht lehret, das ist nicht apostolisch, wenn's gleich S. Petrus oder S. Paulus lehrete. Wiederum, was Christum predigt, das ist apostolisch, wenn's gleich Judas, Hannas, Pilatus und Herodes täte.")

devastating human consequences,[64] yet many theologians recognize him as one of the greatest figures of Christendom.

An Outline of Wagner's Theological Contribution

The first theological contribution Wagner makes is his presentation and understanding of the human predicament. This certainly includes a reflection on the Christian view of sin but it also encompasses the helplessness and suffering of the human being. This helplessness is perhaps best seen in *Parsifal* through the person of Kundry. In her very first entry in Act II she sings in a broken form of her anguish: "Oh! Oh! Deep night! Frenzy! O rage! O misery! Sleep . . . sleep . . . deep sleep! Death!"[65] Later in Act II she expresses her total desperation just before she speaks of how she laughed at Christ. "Oh! If you knew the curse which afflicts me, asleep and awake, in death and life, pain and laughter, newly steeled to new affliction, endlessly through this existence!"[66] Human suffering is expressed eloquently through the physical, mental, and spiritual torment of Amfortas; and it is seen, rather paradoxically, in Parsifal's response to Kundry's kiss, where he participates in the agony of Amfortas ("Amfortas! The wound! The wound! It burns within my heart.")[67]

Secondly, related to this human helplessness and suffering is the suffering and the death of Christ. This is expressed as the ultimate identification of God with humanity; indeed one can view Wagner's understanding of God as concentrated in the person of Christ the redeemer. His sufferings

---

64. At the risk of putting readers off both Luther (as well as Wagner) I take two examples. First, his comments on the peasants' revolt resulted in a terrible slaughter. Secondly, in his tract "On the Jews and Their Lies" he offers the following advice: "set fire to their synagogues or schools"; "their houses also be razed and destroyed"; "prayer books and Talmudic writings . . . be taken from them"; "rabbis be forbidden to teach henceforth on pain of life and limb"; "safe-conduct on the highways be abolished completely for the Jews"; that "usury be prohibited, and that all cash and treasure of silver and gold be taken from them"; "putting a flail, an ax, a hoe, a spade, a distaff, or a spindle into the hands of young strong Jews and Jewesses and letting them earn their bread in the sweat of their brow" (*LW* 47:268–72). For further discussion of this text, see Bell, *Irrevocable Call*, 350–52.

65. *WagPS* 158–59: "Ach! Ach! Tiefe Nacht! Wahnsinn! Oh! Wut! Ach! Jammer! Schlaf . . . schlaf . . . Tiefer Schlaf! Tod!"

66. *WagPS* 198–99: "Oh! Kennst du den Fluch, der mich durch Schlaf und Wachen, durch Tod und Leben, Pein und Lachen, zu neuem Leiden neu gestählt, endlos durch das Dasein quält!"

67. *WagPS* 195–96: "Amfortas! Die Wunde! Die Wunde! Sie brennt in meinem Herzen!"

are expressed throughout the work, starting in the prelude to Act I, which introduces the "saviour's lament" ("Heilandsklage") and right through to Act III where the drama climaxes in the "Good Friday Magic" ("Karfreitagszauber.") Indeed the whole stage work, as well as passages in his letters and theoretical writings, present what could be called Wagner's "Theology of Good Friday."

Thirdly, the sufferings and death of Christ are not simply presented as events "outside us." Wagner presents Christ as identifying with all suffering, and conversely human beings participate in Christ. This idea of union in *Parsifal* results in a thorough regeneration of the human person from within (and contrasts with *Tannhäuser* where redemption is mere absolution received from without).[68]

Fourthly, Wagner's vision of regeneration extends well beyond the human realm: Christ's atoning work comes to affect the whole created realm, a view that is so eloquently expressed in the "Good Friday Magic."

Fifthly, the stage work reflects on the perennial questions of free will and predestination. This is not so obvious but can be discerned in the way Wagner combines music and text and in the relationship of the stage work to his theoretical writings such as *Religion and Art.*

Sixthly, *Parsifal* raises the thorny issue of the relationship of the Christian redemption to the Old Testament. Wagner was in many respects a Marcionite and, like Marcion, he addresses directly what he perceives to be the problem of the Old Testament. But alongside his critique of the Old Testament we find also occasional appreciation of Jewish mysticism.

Seventhly, *Parsifal* raises intriguing questions about sexual love and we find Wagner bringing together concerns about sex, death, and redemption in what one could term a theological psychoanalysis. All this comes to a head in Parsifal's encounter with Kundry in Act II.[69]

These are the sorts of theological themes that will arise. But how then does Wagner "do theology" and how can we discern his theological intentions? I mention four ways.

First Wagner does theology through myth, not only through biblical myths but also through those of the holy grail. Through an appropriation and development of such myths he engages in a work of profound mythogenesis. This can be discerned in how he develops Genesis 1–3 and his main source, Wolfram von Eschenbach's *Parzival.*

---

68. Forsyth, "Wagner's 'Parsifal,'" 255.

69. See, e.g., the reflection on this scene in *CD* 8 Dec 1869: "Talked about Parcival, the first kiss of love, premonition of death."

Secondly, music is a fundamental means by which Wagner does theology. He captures the emotional mood of a person or the fundamental nature of a concept or idea through his use of and development of leitmotifs. For example, the suffering of Amfortas is expressed through the descending motif on 'cellos and double basses together with the hesitating syncopation of first and second violins and violas (I.264–68).[70] The idea of "faith" is expressed by a leitmotif that sometimes appears in its "dogmatic" form (see its first bold appearance in the Prelude to Act I)[71] and sometimes in a gentle form.[72] Further he manages to present "faith" using the grail theme by both reversing it and sometimes by giving the characteristic sixths of the Dresden Amen.[73] Another example can be seen in his development of the love feast motif. At the beginning of the Prelude to Act I and in many other instances he gives a motif that rises and falls forming a slow arc and containing the themes of pain and spear (e.g., I.1–6).[74] But at the end of the work we simply have the rising part of the motif, signifying that the love feast now concerns the redeemed state of humanity (III.1137–41).[75]

Another way Wagner expresses theology through music is by his use of particular keys that, one could argue, have certain "moods" or associations. This is a controversial topic and one could object that keys having particular moods is meaningless in a world of equal temperament and in view of the fact that the frequency of "concert pitch" has changed over the centuries. In response to this one can say that for particular instruments certain keys do have a particular "mood."[76] Secondly, and this is partly related to the first point, once certain composers employ certain keys with particular associations, others are going to follow. A good example here is the key of D minor, used by Beethoven at the beginning of the Ninth Symphony and then employed by Wagner for the opening of *Der fliegende Holländer*,[77] and

70. I.366–69. Such referencing is to the Act and measures.

71. I.44–55.

72. I.59–65 (Prelude) or III.608–21 (Kundry's baptism).

73. I.59–63.

74. This theme is given in chapter 5 below (example 2).

75. See *FTG* themes 1–2.

76. Obvious examples are keys where "open strings" can be employed and the keys used for baroque trumpets.

77. Wagner writes of the Ninth Symphony that "[t]he first movement appears to be found on a titanic struggle of the soul, athirst for Joy, against the veto of that hostile power which rears itself 'twixt us and earthly happiness" (*PW* 7:247), a mood not too dissimilar to his overture (cf. his explanatory programme, *PW* 3:228–29). There are also other well-known musical similarities in the opening of these two works (absence of the thirds; number of repeated notes in the tremelo before the entry of the main theme).

by Bruckner for the opening of his own Ninth Symphony. Ab major had associations for Wagner, being the key in which *Parsifal* opens and closes[78] and associated with the "night," as in *Tristan* Act II. It may be fanciful to go on to claim that the key of Ab is "the voice of the deepest inwardness" ("die Stimme der tiefsten Innerlichkeit").[79] But nevertheless for Wagner certain keys did have certain moods and associations, and thereby he is able to convey a particular mood, even a theological one. A good example is his use of B minor, which opens and closes Act II. This is a key that in the eighteenth and nineteenth centuries was associated with a particular "Affekt." For Beethoven it was the "dark key" ("schwarze Tonart") and Wagner uses it as an "iconic key" for the Dutchman, Hagan, and for Alberich's curse, and in *Parsifal* Act II for the sorcerer Klingsor.[80]

The third way Wagner does theology, and this is his most significant contribution, is how he relates the music to the text to produce what is fundamental, the drama; and it is primarily through this drama that Wagner "does his theology." One of the most striking examples is Kundry's recollection of how she mocked Christ as he hung on the cross, a passage that will be studied in some detail in chapter 5. Wagner's theological insight here in his remarkable marriage of music and text cannot be "translated" into any other language. But nevertheless in this my work of words (with musical examples) I will endeavor to explain how Wagner expresses his theology through the drama of *Parsifal*.

The fourth way he does theology is the more conventional and straightforward route: through his writings. Although Wagner's true genius is manifest in his stage works, some profound ideas can be found in his prose writings. Generally speaking he expresses these ideas most clearly in his letters[81] and these can be a real pleasure to read. But following his argument in his essays can often be hard work in view of the difficult prose

---

78. It is the key Beethoven uses in the second movements of his *Pathétique* Sonata and Fifth Symphony, and for his Opus 110 Piano Sonata. Note also that Wagner chose the key of Ab major for a number of his piano works: the Sonata of 1853 (WWV 85) dedicated to Mathilde Wesendonck, *Theme in Ab major* composed around 1858 (revised 1881) (WWV 93), and *Arrival at the House of the Black Swan* (WWV 95), whose "charged atmosphere recalls *Tristan und Isolde*" (Millington, "Music," 320).

79. See Meyer, *Gralsgeschichte*, 381. Cf. Mickisch, *Parsifal*, who speaks of "outer darkness but inner light." Meyer refers to Beckh, *Tonart*, who went to the point of relating the twelve major and minor keys to the zodiac. Something similar is found in Mickisch, *Tonarten*.

80. Abbate, "Words and Music," 58.

81. As Spencer, "Letters," 190, points out Wagner was "an indefatigable correspondent," the surviving corpus running to between ten and twelve thousand letters.

style;[82] nevertheless they deserve a careful reading since he makes many creative suggestions that not only throw light on *Parsifal* but also give the theologian and philosopher many leads to follow through. Provided one bears in mind that he writes as an artist, one can overlook any deficit in theological and philosophical rigor.

If this is how Wagner "does theology" how can *we* "do theology" by reflecting on his art? As indicated in the preface, one option is to judge the work by "orthodox" Christian doctrine, seeing how it measures up to teaching on the doctrine of God and salvation. One obvious problem is which particular "orthodox" standpoint to adopt. Further, if one judges *Parsifal* using some pre-conceived theological framework, it is inevitable that the art-work will be "violated." Although I will at various points ask how the ideas in *Parsifal* cohere with Christian theology the approach I adopt is to appreciate the work "on its own terms" and to receive the drama positively and see where this leads us. Some of the things that do emerge may be uncomfortable for many Christians but I think they deserve our serious attention.

---

82. In the discussion I have used the English translation of William Ashton Ellis with occasional modification; I have also kept to the translation of the titles with the exception of *What Boots This Knowledge?* which I refer to as *What Use Is This Knowledge?*. Ellis (1852–1919) trained as a surgeon and physician but for much of his working life devoted more time to Wagner (translating the prose works 1891–99; editing *Der Meister* 1888–95; writing a biography of Wagner, etc.) than to medicine. Indeed he did not practice medicine for the whole period 1887 to 1915. A list of Ellis' publications (together with a valuable discussion of his work on Wagner) is given by Cormack, "Faithful," 9–11. Despite being frequently criticized his translations are still widely used and cited and do capture something of the mood of the original German (cf. Deathridge in *Family Letters*, xliii). Ellis gave a paper on Wagner's prose for the Musical Association (13 December 1892) that included discussions on translating Wagner, on those who had previously attempted it, and on the influences on his style of prose. After a very thoughtful paper, there was little helpful debate. Shaw's negative comments about Brahms moved the discussion away from Wagner's prose, which, understandably, Ellis found frustrating ("Prose," 32).

2

Background to *Parsifal* I
Development of Wagner's Thought

Introduction

Wagner relates in his autobiography that he read Wolfram von Eschenbach's *Parzival* in summer 1845[1] and, as we will see in chapter 3 below, there is evidence he may have read the work earlier and probably knew some of the *Parzival* traditions as early as 1840. However, his stage work *Parsifal* was not completed until 1882. This then gives a period of thirty-seven years (perhaps even longer) between the reading of his main source and the completion of *Parsifal*. Not surprisingly, over such a period of time Wagner's views changed. In this chapter I will first sketch the changes in his views on politics and music and drama. I will then move on to a detailed examination of the development of his theological views and how these relate to the development of his philosophical views (his theology and philosophy are inseparable).

Politics

The young Wagner had high ideals of political revolution. As a young Hegelian and disciple of Feuerbach he took part in the Dresden revolution of

---

1. *My Life* 302; *Mein Leben* 1:315.

16

May 1849. This took place when he was starting to work on the *Ring*, which in many ways is concerned with the destruction of "old regimes" and the starting afresh of a "new order,"[2] and it is significant that one of his companions in the uprising was the anarchist Mikhail Bakunin.[3] From about 1848 Wagner's aim was to overthrow the aristocracy (but not the monarchy)[4] and to radically reform the artistic life in Dresden. By April 1849 his views seem to have become more extreme[5] and having taken part in the failed revolution of May he fled Dresden and eventually went into exile in Switzerland. The extreme views he held in 1848–49 were later given up. Indeed he came to express serious doubts as to whether political revolution could actually bring about the changes he desired. He turned to a more politically conservative position (and after being "rescued" from financial disaster by King Ludwig II he had to downplay his earlier revolutionary activities). Later in life Wagner became disillusioned with politics and although he had great hopes for the new German Reich, established in 1871 after the Franco-Prussian war, he became highly critical of Bismarck and his policies.

The fundamental change in his political persuasion is in many ways related to the change in his philosophical outlook. The young Hegelian and disciple of Feuerbach became, it is said, a fervent disciple of Schopenhauer in 1854.[6] The nature of this "conversion," if it was indeed a conversion, has

2. On "Wagner, Feuerbach and the Future," see Magee, *Wagner and Philosophy*, 48–67.

3. Bakunin was personally acquainted with Marx and Engels and it is highly likely that Wagner came to know of Marx's teaching through Bakunin (cf. Millington, *Wagner*, 37). George Bernard Shaw saw Bakunin as one of the inspirations for the figure of Siegfried (Laurence, *Shaw's Music III*, 457–58).

4. See his article *How Do Republican Endeavours Stand in Relation to the Monarchy?* (*PW* 4:136–45).

5. See Wagner's anonymous article "The Revolution" written for the *Volksblätter* (Dresden 8 April 1849): "I [Revolution] will destroy the domination of one over the other . . . of the material over the spiritual, I will shatter the power of the mighty, of the law and of property. Man's master shall be his *own* will, his *own* desire and his only law, his *own* strength his only property, *for only the free man is holy and there is naught higher than he*. Let there be an end to the wrong that gives one man power over millions . . . *and since all are equal I shall destroy all dominion of one over the other*" (Barth, Mack, and Voss, *Wagner*, 172).

6. That he distances himself from Hegel and Feuerbach seems clear from his writings (although, as we shall see, he did not altogether abandon them). Although *Art and Revolution* was originally dedicated to Feuerbach, when Wagner came to write an introduction to the 1872 edition of his works he wrote: "Actively aroused by the perusal of some of *Ludwig Feuerbach's* essays, I had borrowed various terms of abstract nomenclature and applied them to artistic ideals with which they could not always closely harmonise. In thus doing, I gave myself up without critical deliberation to the guidance of a brilliant writer, who approached most nearly to my reigning frame of mind, in that

been a matter of dispute, and I will deal with this below when I discuss the development of this theological and philosophical views.

Opera and Drama

Taking the ten stage works of the "Wagnerian canon," the significant change in his views regarding opera and drama occurred between the third, *Lohengrin*, and the fourth, *Das Rheingold*. After composing *Lohengrin* (1848), he turned his attention to writing theoretical "essays." One of the most significant (and most lengthy) was *Opera and Drama* of 1852.[7] One of the central ideas put forward here was that music should serve the drama (and we see the outworking of this principle especially in *Das Rheingold*). Wagner's discussion of the roles of "music" and "drama" has often been misunderstood in terms of music and *text*, music and *libretto*. Therefore Wagner's view expressed in *Opera and Drama* has often been misunderstood as the music serving the *text*.[8] But for Wagner "drama" refers not to the libretto but to the visible stage action; this is made clear in his essay *Beethoven* of 1870 where he distinguishes between the "dramatic poem" and "the drama we see taking place before our eyes," the latter being "the visible counterpart of Music, where word and speech belong no more to the poet's thought, but solely to the action."[9]

The idea that the text was the key thing has often been derived from the fact that Wagner first wrote the libretto and then the music. It is also further assumed that because the libretti were published separately the music was written to fit the words. In fact, as Borchmeyer points out, "many were the times [Wagner] suffered scruples about publishing his texts before setting them to music."[10] Borchmeyer underlines the fact that the "poetry"

---

he bade farewell to Philosophy (in which he fancied he detected naught by masked Theology) and took refuge in a conception of man's nature in which I thought I clearly recognised my own ideal of artistic manhood" (*PW* 1:25; *GSD* 3:3).

7. Note, however, that some extracts were printed already in 1851 (Kühnel, "Prose Writings," 642).

8. One reason for this misunderstanding may be the way music and text are combined in *Das Rheingold*. Often the music changes quite abruptly and this may be seen as an attempt to "fit the text."

9. *PW* 5:112; *GSD* 9:111–12; *JA* 9:94. See also Dahlhaus, *Music Dramas*, 156.

10. Borchmeyer, *Theory and Theatre*, x. So Wagner writes in his *Epilogue to the "Nibelung's Ring"*: "I had the completed poem printed at my own expense, in a very small number of copies, and sent them to my closer and more distant acquaintances. My disinclination to having it regarded and judged as a literary product was so pronounced, that I expressly safeguarded myself against this in a short preface . . . " [*PW* 3:260 (modified); *GSD* 6:260–61; *JA* 3:339].

should not be seen apart from the music by quoting what Nietzsche wrote in "Richard Wagner in Bayreuth," the fourth of his *Untimely Meditations*, written in July 1876, one month before the first festival. After speaking of the power of the two worlds of poetic language and music, worlds that are "as disparate in form, colour and articulation as they are in soul,"[11] Nietzsche comments: "Where this rarest of powers expresses itself, censure of individual excesses and singularities, or of the more frequent obscurities of expression and thought, will always be no more than petty and unfruitful. . . . Before all, however, no one who reflects on Wagner as poet and sculptor of language should forget that none of the Wagnerian dramas is intended to be read, and thus they must not be importuned with the demands presented to the spoken drama."[12]

So we have this change between *Lohengrin* and *Das Rheingold* that music serves the drama. But there was another change and this is related to his discovery of Schopenhauer in 1854. Schopenhauer believed that music was the greatest of all arts and reflected the most fundamental reality, the "world-will," the noumenal world. This led Wagner to believe that music was actually the driving force behind the drama and even "gives birth" to the "drama" ("tragedy" in the case of *Tristan*).[13] Or, as Wagner expressed it in an essay written in 1872, *On the Name Musikdrama*, his dramas were "*deeds of music that have become visible*" ("*ersichtlich gewordene Thaten der Musik.*")[14] Therefore, although some of the stories about the genesis of his works may seem fanciful (and unhistorical), one could nevertheless make a case that the original inspiration came from a musical "idea."[15]

This Schopenhauerian idea that music gives birth to the drama is seen supremely in *Tristan und Isolde* and in *Parsifal*. But Wagner seemed to hold "Schopenhauerian" ideas before he read Schopenhauer, as is suggested by A

---

11. Nietzsche writes that anyone reading the poems *Tristan* and *Meistersinger* will ask: "wie es nämlich möglich war, über zwei Welten, so verschieden an Form, Farbe, Fügung, als an Seele, schöpferisch zu gebieten. Diess ist das Mächtigste an der Wagnerischen Begabung, Etwas, das—allein dem grossen Meister gelingen wird . . ." (*KSA* 1:487; Nietzsche, *Meditations*, 238).

12. Ibid. *KSA* 1:487–88: "Wo eine solche allerseltenste Macht sich äussert, wird der Tadel immer nur kleinlich und unfruchtbar bleiben . . . Vor allem aber sollte niemand, der über Wagner, den Dichter und Sprachbildner, nachdenkt, vergessen, dass keines der Wagnerischen Dramen bestimmt ist gelesen zu werden und also nicht mit den Forderungen behelligt werden darf, welche an das Wortdrama gestellt werden."

13. Such views were taken up by Nietzsche in *The Birth of Tragedy* (*KSA* 1:9–156).

14. *PW* 5:303 (modified); *GSD* 9:306; JA 9:276. A similar expression is used in his essay *Beethoven* of 1870 (see chapter 11 below). Note that Nietzsche's *Birth of Tragedy* was also published in 1872 and contains a similar idea.

15. See the discussion in chapter 11 below.

Communication to My Friends (July/August 1851): "What I beheld, I now looked at solely with the eyes of Music (aus dem Geiste der Musik); though not of *that* music whose formal maxims might have held me still embarrassed for expression, but of the music which I had within my heart, and wherein I might express myself as in a mother tongue."[16] Therefore, already in 1851 he thought that the wellspring of his stage works was to be found in this "music within the heart."

Theology and Philosophy

In discussing the developments in his theological and philosophical thinking over those thirty-seven years from 1845 to 1882 I will focus on his theology and then relate it to his corresponding philosophical outlook.

The changes in his theological views should not be exaggerated since positive references can be found to Christianity throughout his prose works composed during these years.[17] But on the whole he seems to have had a growing and deepening appreciation of Christianity. The roots of what I call his Christian faith[18] can be found in his childhood, especially through the influence of his mother and particularly of Pastor Wetzel of Possendorf.[19] He speaks of how as a boy he "had gazed with painful longing at the altarpiece of the [Dresden] Kreuzkirche . . . yearning to take the place of Our Saviour on the cross."[20] To such pietist mysticism[21] was then added a romantic fascination with Catholic mythology. He tells of a visit to Prague when he was thirteen that "exercised a poetic charm" on him, and speaks of the "ubiquitous signs of Catholicism, the many chapels and pictures of saints"

16. *PW* 1:365; *GSD* 4:318–19; *JA* 6:297. Again note the similarity, this time to the title, of *Birth of Tragedy out of the Spirit of Music* ("aus dem Geiste der Musik"). The title for the edition of 1886 was changed to *Die Geburt der Tragödie. Oder: Griechentum und Pessimismus.*

17. Ellis in *PW* 6:xxix–xxx, cites a number of texts from 1848 onwards and concludes: "I can see no alteration in his attitude toward the Christian religion itself" (xxx). This, we will see, is too simplistic.

18. As we will see, many have doubted whether he had such a "faith."

19. According to Cosima's entry for 13 May 1874, Wagner remembered him as "a splendid man" and also had fond memories of his curate, Heine. He speaks enthusiastically about his education under Pastor Wetzel in his autobiography (*My Life* 5–6; *Mein Leben* 1:12–13).

20. *My Life* 20; *Mein Leben* 1:27.

21. Kienzle, *Religion und Philosophie*, 22, writes: "Diese intensive Empathie mit der christlichen Passion erinnert an die Mystik des Pietismus, wie sie auch in der religiösen Lyrik der Romantik—von allem bei Novalis—gestaltet ist."

that "always combined to produce a strangely exhilarating impression."[22] Kienzle comments that this encounter with Catholicism was the first and perhaps the decisive encounter Wagner had with lived mythology.[23] It is true that Wagner had doubts about Christianity in his teens but this was mainly caused by losing respect for the clergyman who led Wagner's confirmation classes.[24] Nevertheless, he adds this:

> How I really felt, however, was revealed to me, almost to my own dismay, when I walked with fellow confirmands in procession to the altar, and the choir, organ, and singing burst forth at the partaking of holy communion. The shudder of emotion with which I received the bread and wine remained so unforgettable to me that in order not to spoil this impression I never again went to communion, which was easy for me because such participation is not compulsory among Protestants.[25]

In fact, later in life Wagner did attend Communion (although it is difficult to ascertain how often!)[26] and it was a rite that came to be especially important as he composed the music for *Parsifal*.[27]

Such childhood influences were clearly very important for Wagner. And before leaving his early years and jumping to the 1840s (for which we have a lot of evidence on which to draw), I should mentioned the influences of his uncle Adolf. He lived in Leipzig and had studied with Fichte and Schelling but had come to be influenced above all by Hegel. This no doubt thrust Wagner himself into a study of Hegel. In addition there was the influence of a friend of his uncle, Christian Hermann Weisse. This

22. *My Life* 17; *Mein Leben* 1:23.

23. Kienzle, *Religion und Philosophie*, 23: "Für Wagner bedeutete die Begegnung mit dem Katholizismus die erste und vielleicht entscheidende Berührung mit *gelebter Mythologie.*"

24. *My Life* 20; *Mein Leben* 1:27.

25. *My Life* 21; *Mein Leben* 1:27.

26. Cosima's diaries often mention her going to Communion with her children but her husband staying at home. See, e.g., *CD* 26 March 1875. This was both a Good Friday and the first Communion of Daniela (her eldest daughter with von Bülow).

27. Note that the dictation of *Mein Leben* started on 17 July 1865 and within a week Cosima had already filled forty sides (see Martin Gregor Dellin's "Afterword," *My Life* 741, 746). By 18 May 1866 she had prepared a fair copy of the first part of the manuscript (see her letter to King Ludwig). By October 1866 they had reached the time when the *Faust* Overture had been written (1839–40). Therefore his comments "I never went again to communion" are only relevant up until 1865–66. The final part (Part Four, covering 1861–64) was begun 10 January 1876 and completed in 1880. The autobiography ends in May 1864 when Wagner received the invitation from Ludwig that was to transform his fortunes.

philosopher was a pupil of Hegel and in 1830 published his *System der Ästhetik*, "interpreting art along dialectical lines and acclaiming love as its supreme expression."[28] According to his autobiography, Wagner attended two or three of his lectures in Leipzig; more significant is that he met Weisse at his uncle's home and he writes: "I had listened to a conversation between these two men about philosophy and philosophers, which impressed me very deeply."[29] In view of the influence of his uncle Adolf (and Weisse), Köhler writes that Wagner "assimilated Hegel's world view long before he studied the philosopher's main works during his final years in Dresden."[30] Further, through his uncle and Weisse, he was familiar with the speculative philosophy of Schelling:[31] his uncle had attended Schelling's lectures in Jena[32] and Weisse was influenced by Schelling.

We now come to those Dresden years and beyond. As indicated above we have a considerable body of evidence on which to draw. It is difficult to divide up his theological development into simple, well-defined stages; but nevertheless I think four stages can be discerned. The first is his view in the 1840s and associated with his first three "canonical" operas; the second is his view of 1849–54 when he embarked on his new understanding of music and drama, as mentioned above; the third is associated with his discovery of Schopenhauer in 1854; and the fourth is the period of 1873–83 when he engaged in new and sometimes intense theological study.

In the first stage in the 1840s we find a Christian piety that sometimes borders on the profound. In 1843 he wrote some reflections on a performance of Mendelssohn's oratorio *Saint Paul*, possibly intended for

28. Köhler, *Titans*, 256.

29. *My Life* 54. Weisse was subsequently to turn his attention to the New Testament. He was impressed by Strauß's *Leben Jesu* (which Wagner also studied), which propelled him to the "reconstruction of the historical picture of Christ." But he realized that in order to do this he must explain the relationship of the Synoptic Gospels to each other. This he did in his 1,157 page work *Die evangelische Geschichte*, thereby coming to be the first to develop the now widely accepted two-source hypothesis (Kümmel, *Investigation*, 149–51). The most significant thing about Weisse's portrayal of Jesus is that he removed eschatology from Jesus' teaching (see chapter 10 below).

30. Köhler, *Titans*, 256.

31. *My Life* 429 (*Mein Leben* 1:422) may underestimate Schelling's influence: "None of my Leipzig professors had been able to hold my attention with their lectures on basic philosophy and logic. I had later obtained Schelling's *System of Trannscendental Idealism*, which I had been recommended by Gustav Schlesinger, a friend of Laube, but upon reading even its first few pages had scratched by head in vain to make anything of it . . ."

32. Further, Köhler, *Titans*, 296, points out that the philosopher Johann Arnold Canne, his uncle's friend, was influenced by Schelling's work on myth and even wrote an "Overview" of Canne's "Mythological System" as a supplement to one of his books.

a Dresden newspaper, but never published. He wrote that he was greatly impressed by the work but regretted

> that such an oratorio cannot be wholly grafted on our Protestant church-service, as that would be the only way for its true meaning to pass into the hearts of all believers; whereas without this basis, and especially in the concert-room, it comes to us more or less as a mere artwork of serious order, and its real religious efficacy can by no means be so salient as would be the case under similar conditions to those under which Sebastian Bach once gave his oratorias to the congregation.[33]

Then from the same period is his *Das Liebesmahl der Apostel* (The Love Feast of the Apostles; WWV 69), a work premiered in the Frauenkirche on 6 July 1843 (during the Dresden summer festival).[34] In a letter to his sister Cäcilie he described this thirty-minute work as "a short oratorio,"[35] although the actual subtitle Wagner gave the work was "eine biblische Szene" ("a biblical scene"). Kirsch considers this "biblical scene" to be an extreme example of what Liszt called "music between theatre and church" ("Musik zwischen Theater und Kirche").[36] Wagner told his younger sister Cäcilie: "There has never been anything like it in any other church."[37] But thirty-six years later he described it disparagingly as "a sort of Ammergau play" ("eine Art Ammergauerspiel").[38] Elements of the work are in fact taken up in *Parsifal*.[39]

---

33. *PW* 8:279–80. Kühnel, "Prose Writings," 574, appears to suggest that Wagner simply wrote this in order to gain Mendelssohn's favor. He notes that in Wagner's very first publication, *On German Opera*, he viewed the oratorio as anachronistic since "no one believes any longer in either their contents or their forms" (*PW* 8:58). However, he appears to have changed his mind since Mendelssohn "thus shewed us in all perfection a work which is a witness to the highest bloom of art, and fills us with just pride that it should have been fashioned in the age wherein we live" (*PW* 8:279).

34. The score is available in *SW* 16:330–403. For the "Prosaentwurf" ("prose draft") see *SW* 16:171–72 (English translation in *PW* 8:280–82). Here it is entitled *Das Gastmahl der Apostel* and dated 21 April 1843. Ellis remarks that it "differs in but a few words and rhythms from the finished texts of the Liebesmahl" (279). The title of the final version is *Das Liebesmahl der Apostel (Eine biblische Szene für Männerstimmen und großes Orchester)* and was dedicated to the widow of his teacher Theodor Weinlig.

35. Cf. the description of Breig, "Musical Works," 420: "a miniature oratorio." However, it was performed with the vast forces of 1,200 male singers and 100 orchestral players.

36. Kirsch, "Biblische Szene," 175.

37. *SL* 111; *SB* 2:298 (letter of 13 July 1843): "Etwas ähnliches, in einer Kirche—hat noch nirgends u. niemals stattgefunden."

38. *CT* 17 June 1879 (*CD* mistakenly translates "a sort of Oberammergau play.")

39. Breig, "Musical Works," 420–21. See the discussion in chapter 9 below.

If *Das Liebesmahl* can be likened to the passion plays of Oberammergau, perhaps *Parsifal*, which has certain similarities to the earlier work, could be understood as a "mystery drama."[40]

Also to this period belongs Wagner's arrangement of Palestrina's *Stabat Mater* (WWV 79), performed under his direction in Dresden on 8 March 1848,[41] a work that inspired the Prelude to Act I of *Lohengrin*. Palestrina's music, as we shall see in his *Beethoven* essay, was central to Wagner's view of authentic religious music.[42]

More important than all these, although not so clear as to the Christian content, are the first three operas of the "Wagnerian Canon" (composed in the 1840s), all of which display theological insight: *Der fliegende Holländer*, *Tannhäuser*, and *Lohengrin*.[43] Further, in this decade Wagner engaged in some intense study of the New Testament and read recent works of biblical criticism and theology.[44] That Wagner worked intensely on the New Testament in this period finds clear confirmation in that his copy of the New Testament in his Dresden library[45] was heavily marked (usually in the margin).[46] Wagner rarely marked his books (something that can be frustrating for scholarship) and of all his books his New Testament is the most heavily marked.[47] The text is not only marked with lines, but there are Roman numerals I to V in the margin, and these refer to the act of his proposed drama *Jesus of Nazareth* for which that verse was relevant.

We only have "sketches" for this proposed five-act drama *Jesus of Nazareth* but they are quite detailed. They consists of three parts: an outline of the drama, a theological commentary, and finally, going through each Act in turn, he gives systematically (in canonical order)[48] the relevant quotations

---

40. Cf. Mertens, "Middle Ages," 262–66, who discusses *Parsifal* as a drama "From Universal Chivalric Romance to Mystery Play." Stöcker, "Parsifal," 455 (see Zelinsky, *Thema*, 85), likens *Parsifal* performed in Bayreuth to the passion plays of Oberammergau.

41. See Millington, "Music," 323. However, in *My Life* 358 (*Mein Leben* 1:371–72), he claims it was performed in January 1848 together with Bach's *Singet dem Herrn ein neues Lied* and two symphonies, Mozart's D major and Beethoven's *Eroica*.

42. See chapter 11 below.

43. See Hans Hübner, *Erlösung*, 9–54.

44. The most important were Strauß, *Leben* and Feuerbach, *Wesen des Christentums*.

45. Luther's 1545 translation revised by Gersdorf und Espe.

46. I was very fortunate to be able to study his New Testament in the Nationalarchiv der Richard Wagner-Stiftung, Bayreuth.

47. Westernhagen, *Dresdener Bibliothek*, 24: "es ist dasjenige unter seinen Büchern, dessen Text die meisten Anstreichungen am Rande aufweist."

48. This canonical order is stressed by Zegowitz, *Opern*, 191–92.

from the New Testament.[49] The drama, composed between the completion of the libretto for *Siegfried's Death* (*Siegfrieds Tod*) (November 1848) and early 1849,[50] was probably intended as an opera.[51] It displays thoughtful reflections on Christ from a variety of New Testament witnesses with an emphasis on the Gospels and the Pauline corpus. It is often stated that Wagner conceives of Jesus preaching a purely worldly religion of "commonality and communism," advocating "freedom from law and thus liberation from the shackles of the state."[52] One can say (as many do) that Wagner presented Jesus as a "social revolutionary"[53] provided an association is *not* made with Wagner's activities on the barricades of Dresden.[54] He presents a Jesus who preaches love;[55] but he is far from being a merely moralistic teacher (in fact he opposes "law"). His death is seen as a "death of redemption" ("erlö-sungstod," Act III), a "sacrificial death" ("opfertod," Act IV) and the notes accompanying the sketches for the drama suggest a sacramental theology

---

49. For the three sections, see *PW* 8:285–97, 297–323, 323–40; *DTB* 241–46, 248–59, 259–67.

50. See *A Communication to my Friends* (*PW* 1:378; *GSD* 4:331). In *My Life* 389; *Mein Leben* 1:403, he says the drama was "sketched out at year-end"; it is dated 1849 in *BB* 96.

51. Eduard Devrient noted in his diary a visit from Wagner who told him that he had been working on a tragedy "Christus" but had given up on it ("Er sagte, er habe die Zeit her an einer Tragödie 'Christus' gearbeitet, das Unternehmen aber aufgege-ben"; *WWV* 339). Wagner refers to Jesus of Nazareth as a "tragedy" in *My Life* 387 (*Mein Leben* 1:400), and further we have a musical sketch "Jesus in the ship" ("Jesus im Schiffe") that appears to be intended for this work. Cf. the scene in Act II where we read of Jesus teaching the people from the boat ("Jesus, im Schiffe stehend, lehret das Volk.") Ellis in *PW* 8:xv–xvi, believes the work was not intended as a *musical* drama.

52. Kienzle, "A Christian Music Drama?" 84.

53. See, e.g., Barth, Mack, and Voss, *Wagner*, 75. Note that Wagner's revolutionary mindset may be reflected in his change in December 1848 to using a Latin script with virtually no capital letters (*DTB* 241). In the sketches capitals are generally reserved for names, places, titles (e.g., "Messias") and the first letter of sentences.

54. Note that the sketches specifically reject the view that Jesus was a political revo-lutionary. But Millington, *Wagner*, 36, almost suggests he was, believing that Wagner's portrayal of Jesus is supported by "[m]odern scholarship." He refers to Brandon, *Trial*, a work that has not only been severely criticized but whose reconstruction of the trial of Jesus (whereby Jesus was condemned by the Romans as a "zealot" revolutionary) is in direct contradiction to Wagner's drama (see below).

55. E.g., Wagner's version of Rom 3:28 replaces "faith" with "love"; see *DTB* 265: "So halten wir es nun, dass der mensch gerecht werde ohn des gesetzes werk alleine durch die (liebe.)" Luthers translation is: "So halten wir es nu, Das der Mensch gerecht werde on des Gesetzes werck alleine durch den Glauben" (Luther, *Heilige Schrift*, 2274). The love/power themes in the sketches has certain similarities to the *Ring*, but this requires a separate monograph!

and even an (unorthodox) trinitarianism.[56] Wagner's portrayal of the events that led up to Jesus' death, one of the most controversial themes of Gospel studies,[57] follows the Gospel accounts quite closely: the Jews accuse him of claiming to be the Son of God[58] and Pilate is reluctant to put him to death.[59] Although the drama was to end with no resurrection,[60] Jesus "foreshadows his redeeming death and second advent for the liberating of mankind" ("deutet seinen erlösungstod an und seine wiederkunft zur befreiung der menschen").[61] In the "Communion scene" (Act IV) Wagner makes explicit reference to John's Gospel in that after his "sacrificial death" ("opfertod") the Holy Spirit will be sent to those who belong to him. "Jesus' one concern is that at least his disciples shall have learnt to understand him thoroughly: this is to happen through his sacrificial death, after which the Holy Ghost shall be sent to them. (Gosp. John)."[62] This is then realized at the end of the drama: "Peter feels himself inspired with the Holy Spirit: in high enthusiasm he proclaims the fulfilment of Jesus' promise: his words give strength and inspiration to all; he addresses the people,—whoever hears him, presses forward to demand baptism (reception into the community)."[63]

According to his autobiography, the sketches for *Jesus of Nazareth,* were his "last creative project" in Dresden.[64] After the May uprising there begins the second stage in his theological development. Many take this to be a time when Wagner engaged in an extreme critique of "Christianity."

56. *PW* 8:300; *DTB* 249. This trinitarianism is discussed below in chapters 8 and 9.

57. Briefly, some see the Gospels displaying "antisemitism" in that the blame for Jesus' death is placed on the shoulders of the Jews whereas Pilate wishes to absolve himself of his guilt. On the Jews' involvement in Jesus' death, see Bell, *Irrevocable Call,* 72–84.

58. See *PW* 8:295: "When [Jesus] avers that he is son of God,—Caiaphas rends his priestly garments, all the people shout: Crucify him!" (*DTB* 245).

59. *PW* 8:295–96; *DTB* 245–46.

60. Cf. Strauss, *Life,* 709–44. See the further discussion on Strauß and Wagner in chapter 10 below.

61. See Act II (*PW* 8:289; *DTB* 243).

62. *PW* 8:292; *DTB* 244. For this idea in John see John 7:38–39: "As the scripture has said, 'Out of the believer's heart shall flow rivers of living water.' 39 Now he said this about the Spirit, which believers in him were to receive; for as yet there was no Spirit, because Jesus was not yet glorified." This idea of the Spirit being given at Jesus' glorification (i.e., his death) may be reflected in John 19:30: "When Jesus had received the wine, he said, 'It is finished.' Then he bowed his head and gave up his spirit." On the possible link between these passages, see Raymond E. Brown, *John II,* 931.

63. *PW* 8:297; *DTB* 246: "Petrus fühlt sich vom heiligen geist gestärkt: er verkündet in hohem enthusiasmus die erfüllung von Jesus' verheissung; sein wort stärkt und begeistert alles; er redet das volk an,—wer ihn hört, drängt sich hinzu und begehrt die taufe (aufnahme in die Gemeinde)."

64. *My Life* 389; *Mein Leben* 1:403.

In certain respects Wagner did distance himself from Christianity. In *A Communication to My Friends* (1851) he writes that in *Jesus of Nazareth* he wished "to present the nature of Jesus . . . in such a fashion that his self-offering should be the but imperfect utterance of that human instinct which drives the individual into revolt against a loveless whole, into a revolt which the altogether Isolated can certainly only seal by self-destruction; but yet which in this very self-destruction proclaims its own true nature, in that it was not directed to the personal death, but to a disowning of the loveless-ness around."[65] Looking back at this drama he seems to diminish the special status of Jesus.[66]

But sometimes he not only played down Christianity but also attacked it. Was not this religion responsible for the decline in Art?[67] Does one not have to return to the pre-Christian world of Greek tragedy to discover how art should really function? According to some commentators, such was Wagner's negative view towards Christianity. So Magee writes that Wagner "regarded Christian attitudes as misconceived and deleterious";[68] "the young Wagner detested Christian belief—and, specifically, regarded it as inimical to art."[69] However, a careful reading of works such as *Opera and Drama* makes it clear that Wagner's view was by no means so negative and his view of Christianity at this time was ambivalent.[70] The problem Wagner has with Christianity is "stolid dogma" (i.e., "dull dogma," "starren Dogma")[71] and the institutional religion; indeed by "Christianity" Wagner often meant the "church."[72] But concerning the essence of the Christian myth itself, he is generally more positive. Therefore, on the one hand, he can write this: "The enthralling power of the Christian myth consists in its portrayal of a *transfiguration through Death*. The broken, death rapt look of an expiring dear one, who, already past all consciousness, for the last time sends to us the lightning of his glance, exerts on us an impression of the most poignant grief."[73] But, on the other hand, he can make negative comments even about

65. *PW* 1:379–80; *GSD* 4:332; *JA* 6:312.

66. Likewise he wishes to minimize the "Christian" background and imagery of *Lohengrin* (*PW* 1:333–34; *GSD* 4:289–99; *JA* 6:264–74).

67. Magee, *Aspects*, 6, gives a summary of Wagner's view as given in *Opera and Drama*.

68. Magee, *Wagner and Philosophy*, 93.

69. Ibid.

70. See, for example, *PW* 2:157–67; *GSD* 4:35–43; *JA* 7:156–66.

71. *PW* 2:166; *GSD* 4:42; *JA* 7:164.

72. Kienzle, *Religion und Philosophie*, 28.

73. *PW* 2:159; *JA* 7:157. *GSD* 4:36: "Die hinreißende Gewalt des christlichen Mythos auf das Gemüth besteht in der von ihm dargestellten *Verklärung durch den Tod*.

the Christian myth: a little later in *Opera and Drama* he writes: "This dying, with the yearning after it, is the sole true content of the Art which issued from the Christian myth; it utters itself as dread and loathing of actual life, as flight before it,—as longing for death." He then contrasts this with the Greek view.

> For the Greek, Death counted not merely as a natural, but also as an ethical necessity; yet *only as the counterpart of Life*, which *in itself* was the real object of all his viewings, including those of Art. The very actuality and instinctive necessity of Life, determined of themselves the tragic death; which in itself was nothing else but the rounding of a life fulfilled by evolution of the fullest individuality, of a life expended on making tell this individuality. To the Christian, however, death was *in itself* the object. For him, Life had its only consecration (Weihe) and justification (Rechtfertigung) as the preparation for Death, as a yearning for dying. The conscious stripping-off the physical body, achieved with the whole force of Will, the purposed demolition of actual being, was the object of all Christian art; which therefore could only be limned, described, but never *represented*, and least of all in Drama.[74]

There are a number of comments one must make on this important passage. First, Ellis suggests that this argument explains why Wagner abandoned his drama *Jesus of Nazareth*.[75] Secondly, although at this time Wagner considered the Christian myth to be unsuitable for drama, it nevertheless could be represented in music.[76] Thirdly, on discovering Schopenhauer, Wagner was to reverse his views in that Christian views of suffering and death came to be fundamental for his theological outlook.

Der gebrochene todesberauschte Blick eines geliebten Sterbenden, der, zur Erkennung der Wirklichkeit bereits unvermögend, uns mit dem letzten Leuchten seines Glanzes noch einmal berührt, übt einen Eindruck der herzbewältigendsten Wehmuth auf uns aus." Such a "glance" ("Blick,") as we shall see, features in a fundamental point of *Parsifal* Act II, where Kundry speaks of Christ's "Blick" falling on her.

74. *PW* 2:159–60 (modified); *GSD* 4:37; *JA* 7:158.

75. Ellis in *PW* 2:160 n. Note also that Wagner came to see it was impossible for Jesus to be represented as a stage figure.

76. *PW* 2:160–61: "To Music alone, was it reserved to represent this Stuff to the senses also, namely by an outwardly perceptible motion; albeit merely in this wise, that she resolved it altogether into moments of Feeling, into blends of colour without drawing, expiring in the tinted waves of Harmony in like fashion as the dying one dissolves from out the actuality of Life" (*GSD* 4:38; *JA* 7:159). Ellis compares the release of Kundry and Isolde. Compare *Religion and Art* where he considers music to be the best medium to present the truth of the Christian faith (see chapter 11 below).

That Wagner could be negative towards the Christian myth can be seen in the section in *Opera and Drama* where, after discussing this Christian myth, he turns to discuss the myth of the German people, which is "opposed to the Christian myths."[77] This is obviously related to his work on the *Ring*, which can be seen as a remarkable bringing together of Germanic myth and Greek tragedy. This project, which occupied Wagner on and off for twenty-six years (1848–74), takes us into the world of pagan mythology. The *Ring* was written initially under the influence of Feuerbach and the religious mythology does indeed reveal profound truths, but often truths applicable only to the human condition. But to argue that the *Ring* has *only* a message about the human person and has no Christian theological message is far too simplistic.[78] As we shall see, Wotan being limited by making "contracts" such that only a "hero" can reconstitute the world is a "structural parallel" to the Christian myth of God giving a law that condemns humans such that only the sacrificial death of the Son of God can bring redemption. In this connection we will see that the *Ring* can illumine a number of themes of *Parsifal*.

As Wagner started work on the music of *Die Walküre* he made a "discovery" that was to shape the rest of his output and this marks the beginning of the third stage of his theological development. In 1854 the poet Georg Herwegh, who was also living in Zürich as a political refugee, introduced Wagner to Schopenhauer's *The World as Will and Representation*.[79] His first reading of Schopenhauer can be dated to September 1854.[80] The extent of the early influence is seen in a letter to Liszt (16 December 1854): "I have now become exclusively preoccupied with a man who—albeit only in literary form—has entered my lonely life like a gift from heaven. It is *Arthur Schopenhauer*, the greatest philosopher since *Kant*, whose ideas—as he himself puts it—he is the first person to think through to their logical conclusion."[81] He notes that Schopenhauer, "to Germany's shame," had been rediscovered

---

77. *PW* 2:161; *GSD* 4:38; *JA* 7:159.

78. See, e.g., the theological reflections on the *Ring* of Hans Hübner, *Erlösung*, 55–110.

79. One of the coincidences here is that Wilhelm Wiesand, one of the witnesses of Wagner's baptism in the Leipzig Thomaskirche, was a friend of Schopenhauer and in 1818 represented him in his dealings with Brockhaus, who published his magnum opus. Further, Schopenhauer wrote the work when he lived in the Ostraallee in Dresden when the young Richard Geyer was growing up (Köhler, *Titans*, 419). To this one can add that two of Wagner's sisters, Luise and Ottilie, married into the Brockhaus family.

80. See *BB* 104. Note that before actually reading Schopenhauer Wagner may have some inkling of his ideas since the philosopher was discussed in his circle of friends, especially by Georg Herwegh and François Wille at Wille's house at Mariafeld near Zürich (see Spencer and Millington in *SL* 163–64).

81. *SL* 323; *SB* 6:298.

"by an English critic" and adds: "What charlatans all these Hegels etc. are beside him [Schopenhauer]!"[82] This "English critic" was John Oxenford.[83] It is certainly Oxenford who helped make Schopenhauer known. However, it should not be overlooked that Schopenhauer also had German "evangelists" and "apostles."[84]

One of the issues that will occasionally arise in the ensuing discussion is whether Wagner really did come to disassociate himself from Hegel. His comments in this letter to Liszt, rather than being an independent assessment of Hegel, may simply reflect Schopenhauer's own scathing view of his opponent in Berlin[85] (or they could reflect Oxenford's view). A passage in *My Life*, where Wagner praises Schopenhauer for his lucidity and criticizes Hegel for being unclear, suggests that he had in fact read this article. "I had . . . been struck by the verdict of an English critic, who had candidly confessed that his obscure but unconvinced respect for German philosophy had been attributable to its utter incomprehensibility, as represented most recently by the works of Hegel. In reading Schopenhauer, on the other hand, he had suddenly realized that it had not been his dim-wittedness but rather the intentional turgidity in the treatment of philosophical theories which had caused his bafflement."[86] That he read Oxenford is also suggested by a reference to a forty-year neglect of Schopenhauer by "German professors"/"Lumpen von Philosophen" both in the letter to Liszt and in a

82. *SL* 323; *SB* 6:298.

83. The key article was Oxenford, "Iconoclasm," which appeared anonymously in the *Westminster Review*, edited by George Eliot and G. H. Lewes (from 1849 to 1856 George Eliot herself contributed regularly to the journal; see Roberts, *George Eliot*, 10); exactly one year earlier (1 April 1852) appeared Oxenford's review (again it was anonymous) of *Parerga and Paralipomena* (1851) for the *Westminster Review*. His article "Iconoclasm" was translated and then published in the *Vossische Zeitung* in June 1853 (this liberal journal was founded in 1721 but ceased publication in 1934 because of Nazi censorship [Hamann, *Winifred Wagner*, 170]). Schopenhauer was generally pleased with Oxenford's review even though he was termed "this misanthropic sage of Frankfurt" ("Iconoclasm," 407).

84. See Cartwright, *Schopenhauer*, 504–13, 524. Schopenhauer reckoned he had eight "apostles": Friedrich Ludwig Andreas Dorguth (a court judge in Magdeburg), Julius Frauenstädt (Berlin Doctor of Philosophy and private scholar), Johann August Becker (a lawyer in Alzey), Adam Ludwig von Doß (a Munich lawyer), David Asher (a writer, Jewish activist and English teacher in Leipzig), J. Kormann (a Berlin doctor), August Gabriel Kilzer (Frankfurt bank employee), and Ernst Otto Linder (editor of the Berlin *Vossiche Zeitung*).

85. On Schopenhauer's loathing of Hegel see Cartwright, *Schopenhauer*, 366–70.

86. *My Life* 509; *Mein Leben* 2:522.

letter written to Emilie Ritter (29 December 1854) where he also tells of his discovery of Schopenhauer.[87] Compare the opening of Oxenford's article:

> Few, indeed, we venture to assert, will be those of our English readers who are familiar with the name of Arthur Schopenhauer. Fewer still will there be who are aware that the mysterious being owning that name has been working for something like *forty years* to subvert that whole system of German philosophy which has been raised by the university professors since the decease of Immanuel Kant, and that, after his long labour, he has just succeeded in making himself heard . . .[88]

There has been a clear consensus that reading Schopenhauer was of fundamental importance for Wagner. Chamberlain wrote that his discovery of Schopenhauer was "the most important event in his whole life."[89] Likewise Thomas Mann wrote: "His acquaintance with the philosophy of Arthur Schopenhauer was the great event in Wagner's life. No earlier intellectual contact, such as that with Feuerbach, approaches it in personal and historical significance."[90] One can add many other similar assessments of the impact of Schopenhauer.[91] Wagner himself wrote about the impact of Schopenhauer in his letter to Liszt (quoted above) and in his autobiography relates how, after intense work on *Rheingold*, which he finished on September 26 1854, he "became acquainted with a book, the study of which was to assume vast importance" for him.

> I felt myself immediately attracted by it and began studying it at once. . . . I was instantly captivated by the great clarity and manly precision with which the most abstruse metaphysical problems were treated from the beginning. . . . [W]hereas his treatment of aesthetics pleased me immensely, particularly his surprising and significant conception of music, I was alarmed . . . by the moral principles with which he caps the work, for here the annihilation of the will and complete self-abnegation are represented as

87. *SB* 6:310.

88. Oxenford, "Iconoclasm," 388–89 (my emphasis).

89. Chamberlain, *Wagner*, 192, compares the influence of Feuerbach and Schopenhauer on Wagner: "Feuerbach war nur eine vorübergehende Episode, der letzte Widerhall der 'dummen Streiche' der Revolutionszeit; die Bekanntschaft mit Schopenhauer dagegen, diesem 'genialsten der Menschen' (wie Graf Leo Tolstoy ihn nennt), ist das bedeutungsvollste Ereignis in Wagner's ganzem Leben."

90. Mann, "Sufferings and Greatness," 330 (Mann, "Leiden und Größe," 43).

91. See Magee, *Wagner and Philosophy*, 134, who points to the remarks of Newman, Taylor, and Chancellor.

the only true means of redemption from the constricting bonds of individuality in its dealings with the world.[92]

He explains that he read *The World as Will and Representation* four times between his discovery in the Autumn of 1854 and the summer of 1855 and writes: "Its gradual effect on me was extraordinary and, at any rate, decisive for the rest of my life."[93] Wagner's own estimate of its influence is corroborated by so many other things such as the no fewer than 284 times Schopenhauer is mentioned in Cosima's diaries.[94] Wagner was to become the most enthusiastic supporter of Schopenhauer in the last half of the nineteenth century.[95]

Such a "received view" about Wagner's "conversion" to Schopenhauer is summarized by Köhler thus: without Schopenhauer "[t]here would have been no Tristan, no Hans Sachs, no Parsifal."[96] But it is precisely this consensus that Köhler questions. There can be no doubt that Wagner himself very frequently expressed his indebtedness to Schopenhauer. But Köhler provocatively writes: "The reason why he proclaimed his dependence from the rooftops lies in the simple fact that no such dependence existed."[97] So "[i]t was his own thoughts that seethed beneath the Schopenhauerian label."[98] We shall later see that there are a number of problems with Köhler's understanding of this "Schopenhauerian label."[99]

Köhler believes that the only ways Schopenhauer influenced Wagner was that he reinforced his hatred of Jews and his love for dogs! Köhler writes that Wagner "hated the Jews, and Schopenhauer showed him that there was a metaphysical rightness to this. And he was passionately fond of animals, especially dogs, and here too he discovered that his love concealed within it a profound wisdom."[100] It is certainly the case that Schopenhauer reinforced Wagner's dislike of Judaism. There is clear evidence for this in

92. *My Life* 508–9; *Mein Leben* 2:521–22.

93. *My Life* 510; *Mein Leben* 2:523.

94. Millington, *Wagner*, 55. This figure, of course, only covers the period from 1869 to the composer's death in 1883.

95. See chapter 11 below.

96. Köhler, *Titans*, 420.

97. Ibid.

98. Ibid.

99. Later we will have cause to consider some of Köhler's other questionable labelling (e.g., regarding Nietzsche "onanism" signifies "homosexuality"; for Hitler "providence" signifies "Wagner").

100. Köhler, *Titans*, 429.

Wagner's letter to Röckel in April 1855.[101] But was it just on issues of Judaism and dogs that he influenced Wagner? The answer to this has to be *no*. And perhaps the most important way in which Schopenhauer influenced Wagner was to point him back to Kant's distinction between the noumenal and phenomenal worlds, a distinction that was being eroded or destroyed by Kant's successors (Hegel, Fichte, Schelling).[102]

But before looking at the things Wagner and Schopenhauer share, I consider the differences. The first of these regards sexual love and the human person. So Köhler rightly argues that Wagner's view of sexual love flies in the face of Schopenhauer's analysis. Schopenhauer's whole approach in "The Metaphysics of Sexual Love"[103] can be seen as a proto-Darwinian approach to the propagation of the species[104] and is contradicted by the attraction of Tristan to Isolde, Siegmund to Sieglinde, and Siegfried to Brünnhilde.[105] This gap between *Tristan* and Schopenhauer has also been

101. This was written from London to Röckel in prison. See *SB* 7:126: "Ich sehe, daß Du noch ein obstinater Optimist bist, und namentlich, daß Dir das Judenthum mit Deinem Freunde Paulus noch tief in den Gliedern steckt. . . . Freund Sch.[openhauer] half mit seiner enormen Kraft eben nur, den letzten jüdischen Aberglauben auszutreiben." He later criticizes the "optimism" of Judaism in affirming the "will." Later in the letter he writes: "Diese, um jeden Preis durchgesetzte Bejahung ist aber eben das heute zu Tage wieder so übermächtig gewordene Judenthum, in welchem sich die engste und kleinste Weltansicht kundthut, die jemals überhaupt kundgegeben worden" (129). This critique of Judaism as "optimistic" comes from Schopenhauer.

102. Wagner refers to Schopenhauer as "Kant's continuator" in *What Use Is This Knowledge?* (*PW* 6:256; *GSD* 10:257). Related to this destruction of the phenomenal/noumenal distinction in Hegel, Fichte, and Schelling, note these comments in Magee, *Schopenhauer*, 285: "Fichte, Schelling and Hegel all rejected Kant's doctrine of things as existing unconceptualizably in themselves independently of being experienced. As part of this rejection they threw out the empiricist tradition of philosophy entirely, and it is by virtue of this that they are known as idealists. And it is also this more than anything else that differentiates them from Kant and Schopenhauer. Those two, although they were transcendental idealists, were empirical realists, and can therefore not be termed idealists as such."

103. This forms chapter 44 of the second volume of *WWR* 2:531–67.

104. A few months before his death in September 1860 Schopenhauer read an account in the *Times* of Darwin's *On the Origin of Species* (1859) but considered the ideas "shallow empiricism" ("platter Empirismus") and having no relation to his own work (letter to Adam von Doss of 1 March 1860, Hübscher, *Schopenhauer Briefe*, 472). However, the relation of the two thinkers is suggested by Darwin's quotation from "The Metaphysics of Sexual Love" in *The Descent of Man*, 586 (chapter 20) to justify his account of sexual attraction (Cartwright, *Schopenhauer*, 466–67 n. 1). On the ways Schopenhauer does and does not anticipate Darwin, see Young, *Schopenhauer*, 85–87.

105. As an example, see *WWR* 2:542–44 (*ASSW* 2:694–96), where Schopenhauer outlines the basis of attraction: age, health, skeleton, fullness of flesh, beauty of the face. The only one that approximates to Wagner's view of attraction is the last mentioned, especially the "beautiful eyes" (544). On this, see Scruton, *Death-Devoted Heart*, 41–43.

discussed by Scruton: "Wagner accepts Schopenhauer's vision of death as a dissolution of the individual, but he rejects Schopenhauer's theory of the will as the only ultimate reality. On the contrary, the ultimate reality for Wagner is the human individual—the incarnate subject of consciousness as revealed in the look of love."[106]

We do in fact know that Wagner did criticize aspects of Schopenhauer's philosophy, this first explicitly appearing in a letter to Mathilde Wesendonck (1 December 1858) four years after first reading Schopenhauer. Here he questions not only Schopenhauer's view of salvation, but also his fundamental understanding of the relation of the will to the intellect.[107] Further, the work that is supposed to be so thoroughly Schopenhauerian, namely *Tristan und Isolde*, often turns out to be not so after all. This disparity has been analyzed by Scruton, and I consider his two examples, "intentionality" and "erotic love."

The philosophical term "intentionality" is not concerned with our "intentions" but with the way the mind is directed to an "object."[108] Scruton writes: "It is this intentionality that interests Wagner, since it shows that the urge to sacrifice arises from our very existence as free subjects, incarnated in the world of objects and therefore trapped by that world's demands. In desiring Tristan, Isolde finds herself *challenged in her freedom*—such would be a Kantian way of putting it."[109] Related to this "intentionality" in *Tristan und Isolde*, Scruton emphasizes that Schopenhauer's "socio-biology" fails to do justice to Wagner. "Sociobiological theories of the kind first offered by Schopenhauer explain *some* of these phenomena in terms of the underlying reproductive function—but only some. They do not explain (because they are bound to ignore) the peculiar intentionality of desire and its role in our understanding of the human person. Thus socio-biology can explain why

---

106. Scruton, *Death-Devoted Heart*, 190. Compare my idea of the individual "soul" in the noumenal realm, which amounts to a radical modification of Schopenhauer in the light of the gospel (Bell, *Deliver Us from Evil*).

107. See the discussion below in chapter 7.

108. See Magee, *Great Philosophers*, 256 (in discussion with Hubert Dreyfus). Dennett, "Intentionality," points to the origins of intentionality in the Scholastics (from *intendo*, "to point at"), and its revival in the nineteenth century by Franz Brentano, who claimed that it defines the distinction between the mental and the physical: "all and only mental phenomena exhibit intentionality." Brentano's irreducibility thesis (mental phenomena cannot be a species of physical phenomena) has been taken to support the idea that the mind cannot be the brain. But Dennett claims that this is "by no means generally accepted today."

109. Scruton, *Death-Devoted Heart*, 150.

jealous people wish to destroy their rivals, but not why they wish to destroy their faithless lovers."[110]

This brings me to Scruton's second example: Schopenhauer is simply unable to account for the erotic love that is obviously central for Wagner's stage work. Schopenhauer's "conception of death, his negative view of the empirical world, and his theory of the individual are all challenged by erotic love, the meaning of which encompasses life and its continuation."[111] So "erotic love is essentially individualizing: its intentional object is the irreplaceable incarnate subjectivity of the other. . . . What is valued in erotic love is precisely the other person as an individual, and not the impersonal will behind appearances . . ."[112]

Related to the differences regarding erotic love is the disparity regarding "denial of the will." This is surprising since so much secondary literature assumes that this is precisely what Wagner took over from Schopenhauer. However, the differences between the two have been rightly highlighted by Chamberlain, and they will be considered in more detail in chapter 8 below.[113]

In addition to this disparity regarding intentionality and erotic love, one can consider how Wagner clearly contradicts Schopenhauer's denigrating comments about women.[114] Consider these utterances of Schopenhauer: "The most intense sufferings, joys, and manifestations of power do not fall to her lot; but her life should glide along more gently, mildly, and with less importance than man's, without being essentially happier or unhappier."[115] Although Wagner did utter some negative comments about women,[116] the nobility of his heroines such as Senta, Elisabeth, Isolde, Sieglinde, and above all Brünnhilde[117] stands in stark contrast to Schopenhauer's views. Further,

110. Scruton, *Death-Devoted Heart*, 177–78. See also Scruton's further critique of Schopenhauer and why his system fails to explain Isolde's desire to die (148–50).

111. Ibid., 130.

112. Ibid.

113. One fundamental reason why Chamberlain sees the two world views as so different is that one is a poet and the other a metaphysician: "Eine ewig unüberbrückbare Kluft trennt aber dennoch die eine [Weltanschauung] von der anderen; denn die eine ist die Welt durch das Auge eines Dichters, die andere die Welt durch das Auge eines Metaphysikers erblickt" (Chamberlain, *Wagner*, 512–13).

114. Cf. Chamberlain, *Wagner*, 513.

115. *PP* 2:614 (§ 363).

116. See the examples given by Nattiez, *Wagner Androgyne*, 168 (but Wagner's utterances should be seen in the light of general nineteenth-century attitudes to women).

117. Note that it is clear from Cosima's diaries that Wagner read *Parerga and Paralipomena* (although I have found no discussion of "On Women"). He had two editions (the first [1851] and third [1874] of *Parerga and Paralipomena* in his Wahnfried library.

his noble views of women cannot be said to be restricted to the world of Wagner's theatre. He had great respect for his female singers and the fact that he could write such profound letters to his female friends (e.g., Mathilde Wesendonck) showed that he valued the intellect and judgement of women. Hollinrake sums up the disparity between Wagner and Schopenhauer well: "the glorification of erotic passion in *Tristan und Isolde* can be brought into line with Schopenhauer only if it is accepted that the abhorrence which the philosopher expressed in his *Metaphysik der Geschlechtsliebe* (*Metaphysics of Sexual Love*), and in his vitriolic essay *Über die Weiber* (*On Women*), was not meant to be taken at its face value."[118] Although Wagner did express a preference for Schopenhauer on "love" to that of Kant,[119] it may be that ultimately the great philosopher of Königsberg provides a better background for *Tristan*[120] and even for *Parsifal*.[121]

But what are we to say to Köhler's view that the only way Schopenhauer influenced Wagner as in relation to love of dogs and hatred of Judaism? Köhler appeals to Jacob Sulzer's assessment, written in a letter to Mathilde Wesendonck in August 1887 following Wagner's death: "However highly he valued Arthur Schopenhauer he never took over so much as a single

---

Concerning Brünnhilde, Wagner wrote in a letter to Liszt (11 February 1853) "that never has such glorification befallen a woman" ("daß noch nie dem Weibe eine solche Verherrlichung wiederfahren sei"; Wagner, *Briefwechsel zwischen Wagner und Liszt I*, 215; Chamberlain, *Wagner*, 513 n. 2, who refers to this, corrects "wiederfahren" to "widerfahren"). Note also that the so-called "redemption" motif, used first in Act III of *Walküre* immediately after Brünnhilde tells Sieglinde that she bears a child who will become the world's noblest hero and which does not reappear until the closing scene of *Götterdämmerung*, is actually a hymn of praise to Brünnhilde. See Cosima's entry for 23 July 1872 where R. says: "I am glad that I kept back Sieglinde's theme of praise for Brünnhilde, to become as it were a hymn [to the heroine]." Cosima's "Helden" ("heroes") is a mistake; it should read "Heldin" (heroine) (see P. Wapnewski, *Weißt du wie das wird . . . ?*, 309). Also Cosima comments (23 April 1875): "The entire world of the gods, the forces of Nature, the heroes—all serve, as it were, to glorify the noblest of women!"

118. Hollinrake, "Philosophical Outlook," 145.

119. See *CD*: "In the evening he reads me passages from Schopenhauer on love ('Kant spoke of it without practical knowledge'). R. thought it might perhaps repel me, but, on the contrary, I am very moved and uplifted.—R. says, 'Love without children is a sham.'"

120. Passages from "Metaphysics of Sexual Love" do fly in the face of *Tristan* (see, e.g., *WWR* 2:542–44).

121. Wagner possessed a twelve volume edition of Kant in his Wahnfried library (Rosenkranz and Schubert, *Immanuel Kant's sämmtliche Werke*) together with an additional edition of the *Critique of Pure Reason* (Hartenstein, *Immanuel Kant's Kritik der reinen Vernunft*). Some of these volumes must have numbered among Wagner's 1869 Christmas presents (*CD* 5 December 1869)!

comma from his cognitive philosophy."[122] Sulzer's view may reflect his own Hegelianism. But whatever the case, I have strong doubts that it is a correct assessment. As indicated above, I imagine that the phenomenal/noumenal distinction is the crucial thing Wagner took over from Schopenhauer. And although one can argue Schopenhauer simply pointed him back to Kant,[123] the way Wagner later wrote about space, time, causation, and various other issues such as the suffering of the world bears the unmistakable print of the Frankfurt sage.[124]

But although one can speak of the Schopenhauerian influence, it would be a mistake to view the events of autumn 1854 as a Damascus Road experience. There are clear indications that Wagner was a "Schopenhauerian" before discovering Schopenhauer. The first person to recognize this was probably Ellis. One of the first signs of Wagner having Schopenhauerian ideas before reading *The World as Will and Representation* in 1854 is an article *Pasticcio* he wrote in back in 1834![125] Another (and clearer) example is seen in the opening pages of *The Art-Work of the Future* (written in the autumn of 1849): "Nature engenders her myriad forms without caprice or arbitrary aim (absichtlos und unwillkürlich), according to her need (Bedürfnis), and therefore of Necessity (Nothwendigkeit). The same Necessity is the generation and formative force of human life. Only that which is un-capricious and un-arbitrary can spring from a real need; but on Need alone is based the very principle of Life."[126] Ellis comments that this paragraph and the following sections of the chapter show that Wagner's philosophy

---

122. Köhler, *Titans*, 427, who refers to Otto, *Wagner*, 193: "So hoch er Arthur Schopenhauer schätzte, nahm er doch von dessen Erkenntnisphilosophie nie ein Komma in sich auf."

123. I note above how Wagner in *What Use Is This Knowledge?* refers to Schopenhauer as "Kant's continuator" (*PW* 6:256).

124. Concerning space, time, and suffering (and Buddhism), see his letter to Mathilde Wesendonck of August 1860: "Thus my plan for the 'Victors' struck me as being the concluding section of Lohengrin. Here 'Savitri' (Elsa) entirely reaches the level of 'Ananda'. In this way, all the terrible tragedy of life would be attributable to our dislocation in time and space: but since time and space are merely *our* way of perceiving things, but otherwise have no reality, even the greatest tragic pain must be explicable to those who are truly clear-sighted as no more than an individual error: I believe it is so! And, in all truth, it is a question simply of what is pure and noble, something which, in itself, is painless" (*SL* 499; Golther, *Mathilde Wesendonk*, 242).

125. *PW* 8:65–66 (*JA* 5:19): "The essence of dramatic art does not consist in the specific subject or point of view, but in this: that the inner kernel of all human life and action, the Idea, be grasped and brought to show. By this standard alone should dramatic works be judged, their special points of view and subjects being simply regarded as special varieties of this Idea."

126. *PW* 1:69; *GSD* 3:42; *JA* 6:9.

is "self-originated." "Except that Wagner does not employ the term 'Will,' but rather 'Necessity,' the whole scheme is Schopenhauerian from beginning to end, and the gradual evolution of the 'Will's' manifestation, from elementary force to Intellect and Spirit, might have been written by that greatest philosopher of the century."[127] Such a view is also reflected in these comments of Roger Hollinrake: "Wagner's attitude to Schopenhauer, like his attitude to Young Germany, Hegel and the Young Hegelians, was one of imaginative, retrospective identification rather than of literal dependence. If the parities are notable so are the disparities."[128] Further, Wagner himself was aware that Schopenhauer was confirming what he already thought if only on an "unconscious" level. On reading Schopenhauer he writes: "Only now did I understand my own Wotan myself."[129]

But whether or not Wagner was a Schopenhauerian before Schopenhauer, I think he did in fact shape Wagner's philosophical and artistic development and, as I will now focus upon, his theological outlook. Although Schopenhauer has been described as an atheist,[130] he had great admiration for St. Paul, Augustine, and Luther. Further, he deplored a reduction of theology to some system of philosophy.[131] Of the other religions he admired

---

127. *PW* 1:69 n. Note that Ellis believes that Schopenhauer is the greatest philosopher of the century; not many would agree with his assessment.

128. Hollinrake, "Philosophical Outlook," 145.

129. *My Life* 510; *Mein Leben* 2:523.

130. Wagner actually had doubts about such a label for Schopenhauer (*CD* 11 June 1878). See also Irvine, *'Parsifal' and Wagner's Christianity*, 33: "Schopenhauer was *par excellence* the Christian philosopher." Irvine points to §2.48 of the *World as Will*: "There is nothing in which we have to distinguish the kernel from the shell so much as in Christianity. Just because I value this kernel highly, I sometimes treat the shell with little ceremony; yet it is thicker than is often supposed" (*WWR* 2:625; *ASSW* 2:801). However, note the possible problem in that he wishes to equate the kernel of Christianity with that of Brahmanism and Buddhism: "The innermost kernel and spirit of Christianity is identical with that of Brahamism and Buddhism; they all teach a heavy guilt of the human race through its existence itself, only Christianity does not proceed in this respect directly and openly, like those more ancient religions" (*WWR* 2:604; *ASSW* 2:773).

131. He asks: "why should a religion require the suffrage of a philosophy? Indeed, it has everything on its side, revelation, documents, miracles, prophecies, government protection, the highest dignity and eminence, as is due to truth, the consent and reverence of all, a thousand temples in which it is preached and practiced, hosts of sworn priests, and, more than all this, in invaluable prerogatives of being allowed to imprint its doctrines on the mind at the tender age of childhood, whereby they become almost innate ideas. With such an abundance of means at its disposal, still to desire the assent of wretched philosophers it would have to be more covetous, or still to attend to their contradictions it would have to be more apprehensive, than appears compatible with a good conscience" (*WWR* 2:166; *ASSW* 2:214).

Buddhism and Hinduism.[132] There are various entries in Cosima's diaries concerning Schopenhauer's view of Christianity and how Wagner readily accepted this. One aspect was an intense dislike of the Old Testament and a desire to see Christianity rid of its Old Testament roots. Wagner is recorded as saying this in 1878: "That is the curse of Christianity, all this clinging to the Old Testament, such a name: Ephraim! It shows how predominant the Old Testament was, in the beginning presumably in order to impart more authority to the new religion."[133] Although he wished to portray Jesus as a universal figure in his sketches for *Jesus of Nazareth* (1848–49) we do not find there *such* a strong sense of ridding Jesus of his Jewish heritage.[134]

Just as Schopenhauer reinforced his dislike of the Old Testament, so he reinforced his love for St. Paul. Certainly Wagner had an interest in Paul when writing his sketches for *Jesus of Nazareth*[135] and his love of Paul seems to have grown over the years, Schopenhauer perhaps contributing to this. Cosima notes in her entry for 22 March 1874 that she "talked with R. about Paul de Lagarde's essay, in which he comes out strongly against Saint Paul. R. says, 'I was also against him when I knew nothing about him—that was because of my anti-Mendelssohnism.'" Cosima adds: "I do not believe there would be any Christians without Saint Paul, though I think I understand what P. de Lagarde means when he wishes one to be evangelical rather than Christian."[136]

132. Note, however, that he had utter contempt for Islam (*WWR* 2:162; *ASSW* 2:209), a view that may well have influenced Wagner, who speaks of "the majestic foolishness of Mohammedanism" (*CD* 14 February 1881). See further my discussion in chapter 10 on religious pluralism.

133. *CD* 13 November 1878.

134. See *PW* 8:297: "Jesus descended from the house of David, out of which the Redeemer of the Jewish nation was awaited: David's own lineage, however, went back to Adam, the immediate offspring of God, from whom spring all men" (*DTB* 248: "Jesus stammte aus dem geschlecht Davids, aus dem der erlöser des jüdischen volkes erwartet wurde: Davids geschlecht leitete sich aber bis auf Adam, den unmittelbaren sprossen gottes, von dem alle menschen stammen"). Although his Davidic origins were recognized at his baptism, Jesus came to a different conclusion in the desert. "So Jesus brushed aside the House of David: through Adam had he sprung from God, and therefore all men were his brothers" (*PW* 8:298). *DTB* 248: "So warf Jesus die davidische abkunft von sich: durch Adam stammte er von gott, und seine brüder waren nun alle menschen."

135. This is evidenced by the quotations from Paul in the sketches and in his heavily marked New Testament from his Dresden library.

136. The "anti-Mendelssohnism" is presumably referring to the oratorio Saint Paul, which as noted above, Wagner greatly admired at the time he heard it in 1843. However, he came to feel "utter disgust" for Mendelssohn's oratorio. See *CD* 18 January 1879.

To conclude this third phase it may well be that Schopenhauer contributed to Wagner's appreciation of Christianity. The key elements are Schopenhauer's view of suffering and the denial of the will to live, which was exemplified above everything in the cross of Christ. But again this is a reinforcement of a view Wagner already held, as can be seen in the sketches for *Jesus of Nazareth*. And, in addition to this, Schopenhauer's phenomenal/noumenal distinction is something that deeply colored all of Wagner's thinking from 1854 onwards. Schopenhauer was not, as Köhler suggests, a convenient label for Wagner's own thought.[137]

It would be mistaken to suggest that Wagner's view of Christianity remained that of Schopenhauer[138] and this now brings us to the fourth and final stage in Wagner's thought on Christianity. In the years up to the completion of *Parsifal*, Wagner's engagement with Christian theology intensified. This is clear from his reading and his conversations such that with *Parsifal* we have not only Wagner's crowning artistic achievement but also a rich tapestry of theological insight. The main influences that can be discerned in this fourth period are mysticism, a new appreciation of Christian rituals such as baptism and the Eucharist, and an intensified study of Luther. For now I consider briefly the influence of mysticism and of Luther.[139]

Wagner's interest in mysticism can in fact be found earlier. So in the letter to Mathilde Maier of 5 April 1864 he writes: "I have the German Christian mystics in front of me: today it is Tauler."[140] He read not only

137. Köhler, *Titans*, 255–60, argues that it was Hegel who was the key influence even though Wagner hardly admits any such influence. Köhler, among other things, points to Wagner's comment: "The spirit of the universe desired me to have a son by you, and so it arranged things; we ourselves were forced to obey, without understanding why" (*CD* 17 June 1869). He also argues that Nietzsche understood Wagner as a Hegelian. All the relevant references though come from the late Nietzsche after he had fallen out with Wagner (the quotation from *KSA* 1:485 (*Richard Wagner in Bayreuth*), which concerns the *Ring*, does not explicitly refer to Hegel). First there is a quotation from *Beyond Good and Evil* (CUP) (*KSA* 5:185: "welche Hegel in System gebracht, Richard Wagner zuletzt noch in Musik gesetz hat"). Secondly he quotes from *The Case Wagner* (Nietzsche, *Anti-Christ Etc*, 252: "[Wagner] became *Hegel's heir* . . . Music as 'Idea'"; *KSA* 6:36: "Er machte bloss die Nutzanwendung auf die Musik—er erfand sich einen Stil, der 'Unendliches bedeutet',—er wurde der *Erbe Hegel's* . . . Die Musik als 'Idee'"). It is the case that there is much Hegelianism in the pre-Schopenhauer phase and elements of Hegel's philosophy can still be discerned in Wagner work after 1854 but they were combined with a critical adoption of Schopenhauer's worldview.

138. That it so remained is suggested by Magee, *Wagner and Philosophy*, 191–92. See also Dahlhaus, *Music Dramas*, 143, whom Magee quotes.

139. Subsequent chapters will consider the sacraments, a summary being given in chapter 10 below.

140. *SL* 580. This interest in Tauler is corroborated by *My Life* 736; *Mein Leben* 2:752.

Johannes Tauler (c. 1300–61) but also Meister Eckhart (c. 1260–1327), and such study intensified after 1875.[141] In addition to these mystics he was reading August Friedrich Gfrörer,[142] Joseph Görres,[143] and Renan's Saint Paul.[144] But above and beyond all these writers stood the towering figure of Martin Luther. Wagner possessed an eight-volume edition of Luther's works from the sixteenth century[145] together with an eight-volume edition of selected works,[146] a book of hymns,[147] and a book that despite its brevity highlights how important Luther was for Wagner and for his German contemporaries.[148] Luther had links to some of the writers just mentioned: both Tauler and Eckhart have been understood to anticipate a number of Luther's theological ideas[149] and Gfrörer was an ordained Lutheran, although he was to convert in 1853 to Roman Catholicism (much to Wagner's consternation).[150]

141. Kienzle, "A Christian Music Drama?" 108, points to Cosima's entry for 23 September 1875: "In the evening R. opens Meister Eckhart, some sentences occupy our thoughts completely, seeing and hearing, seeing bringing the realization that through knowledge one is bound to attain ignorance—so profound: 'Here I feel at home,' says R." On Eckhart's influence on Wagner, see Aberbach, *Richard Wagner's Religious Ideas*, 194–203.

142. Gfrörer, *Geschichte*.

143. Görres, *Mystik*. This massive work discusses not just what one would usually understand as "Christian mysticism" but also a whole range of issues regarding the "paranormal." Issues include "Mystische Erscheinungen im oberen Menschen und den geistigen Gebieten" (2:135–89) including a section on "Tonkunst"; "Die Ecstase im Cerebralsysteme" (2:308–343); "Die physische Grund der dämonischen Mystik" (3:335–495); "Atmosphären und Wirkungen im Zustande der Verzauberung" (5:296–505; cf. *Parsifal* Act II). He started reading this 31 May 1875. Although Cosima's entry for that day says he was not enjoying it, he continued with the work (CD 1 June: "the human being as image of the cross pleases both him and me;" CD 5 June: "R. told me about the mirage in Görres—if true, the reproduction of an event in the atmosphere is a very remarkable phenomenon!")

144. See CD 14 May 1878.

145. This Jena edition (Richtzenhayn) dates from 1563–68.

146. Published by Pertes, 1844.

147. Wackernagel, *Martin Luthers geistliche Lieder*.

148. Luther, *Passional Christi und Antichristi*, a work employed by Germans to counteract the claims of Papal Infallibility by Pope Pius IX at the First Vatican Council of 1869–70.

149. On Luther's relationship to Tauler, see Oberman, *Dawn of the Reformation*, 136–41. Luther does not relate himself to Eckhart (141) and there seems to be no direct connection between Eckhart and Luther "aber Eckharts Lehre von der Gerechtigkeit, seine christologisch bestimmte Theologie des Wortes, sein kreativer Umgang mit Sprache, die theozentrische Orientierung seines Denkens u.a. legen den Dialog mit Luthers Theologie nahe" (Kern, "Eckhart," 263).

150. CD 26 March 1875. See also the discussion of Gfrörer in chapter 9 below.

It was in the last ten years of his life that Wagner took a special interest in Luther.[151] Cosima's entry for 27 October 1873 tells how they started reading Meurer's life of Luther.[152] Wagner comments: "The absence of all ideality brings the soul blissful peace . . . and the way to this peace is through Jesus Christ."[153] The following days show an enthusiastic reading of Luther. For example, 5 November 1873: "In the evening Luther, to our great edification and enjoyment." On 7 November they read the address to the German nobility and on November 9 the march to Worms and on November 11 Luther at Worms. On November 19 they read Audin's life of Luther[154] but Wagner describes it as "Jesuitical." Then in Cosima's entries for 28 and 29 November 1881 we hear that Wagner was pleased with Bruno Bauer's article on Luther, written for the *Bayreuther Blätter*.[155] Wagner's interest in this great theologian (and "German nationalist")[156] is understandable and there are many links to Luther in his works.[157] Further Wagner was not just interested in his ideas. He had many associations with Luther's life,[158] one of the most

151. Westernhagen, *Werk*, 303.

152. Meurer, *Luther's Leben*.

153. *CD* 27 October 1873.

154. Audin, *Geschichte des Lebens, der Lehren und Schriften Dr. Martin Luther's*.

155. Bauer, "Pessimismus." However, Cosima writes that her husband was "vexed by the passage on Christianity, which, coming from this author, did not surprise me" (*CD* 29 November 1881). Note that in his Wahnfried library was Bauer, *Geschichte der Synoptiker*, a work that put forward a radical historical skepticism of the Gospels. On Bauer, see Schweitzer, *Leben-Jesu-Forschung*, 171–90; Mehlhausen, "Bauer"; Colin Brown, *Jesus*, 227–31.

156. At least Wagner so understood Luther. See Cosima's entry for 2 March 1873. She tells of how she and Wagner are deeply affected by the sacred songs of Luther: "He felt so terribly strongly for his German people, he could not bear to see how the Romans despised and exploited these poor Germans."

157. Apart from *Parsifal*, two works have obvious associations. First, *Tannhäuser und der Sängerkrieg auf Wartburg*, although having a "Catholic" ambience, is associated with Luther in that it was in the Wartburg that the imprisoned reformer "fought with the devil" and translated the New Testament into German. Secondly, *Meistersinger* has key associations with Luther through the figure of Hans Sachs; see, e.g., the chorus "Wach auf" in Act III, a poem the historical Hans Sachs wrote for the coming of the reformation to Nuremberg (Sachs, *Nachtigall*, 5). See also Wagner's sketches for "Luthers Hochzeit," a work of 1868 (a year after the completion of *Meistersinger*) intended to celebrate the 350th anniversary of the Reformation (*DTB* 304). It appears no music was composed but ten years later he considered writing a prose play "Luther's Wedding" (*CD* 5 July 1878).

158. After the death of his step-father, Ludwig Geyer, he lived for almost a year (October 1821 to September 1822) with Geyer's younger brother, Karl Geyer, who was a goldsmith in Eisleben (where Luther was born). He writes: "The quaint little town with the house where Luther lived and the manifold memorials to the time he spent there has often recurred to me in dreams, even to the present day; I have always wanted to

important being that he, like Luther, had a message to give the world that was so radical that he had to struggle with great opposition.[159]

In the final three years of his life (1880–83) Wagner wrote a series of essays, published in the *Bayreuther Blätter*, that are often referred to as the "regeneration writings." Some have dismissed them as poor and idiosyncratic in the worst possible sense and some ardent Wagnerians have been embarrassed by them. However, I will argue in the coming chapters that they contain some profound insights. One of the striking aspects of Wagner's "regeneration" writings is that he turns his back on certain aspects of Nietzsche's *Birth of Tragedy*. First of all he criticizes Nietzsche's aesthetic theories and the implications this has for his worldview. Secondly, and this is more relevant to our theme, he justifies his turn from Greek myth to Christianity, a process that culminated in *Parsifal*.[160]

Having traced Wagner's theological development, I focus on just two things. First, he was extremely well read, working through *complete* books.[161] Secondly, it is worth reflecting on what I think is his most important contribution not only to *Parsifal* but for theology in general: his understanding of God as centered on the person of Jesus Christ. His theological method right from the 1840s to his death was to start with Jesus of Nazareth and work out from there in concentric circles. This contrasts starkly with the debates carried out in the British media between the "new atheists" and defenders of the Christian faith where much of the debate seems to center around an abstract theism. Wagner emphasizes the importance of turning to the New Testament and reflecting on Christ's supreme sacrifice. Cosima notes in her entry for 26 September 1877: "We continue for a long time to talk about Christ, the Gospel account of the day before his death the sublimest thing ever produced by Man, incomparable, divine!"

---

visit it again" (*My Life* 7; *Mein Leben* 1:14). Indeed he did visit Eisleben again, including Luther's house; Cosima comments "sadness at its dilapidated state" (*CD* 27 April 1873).

159. In this connection, Forsyth, "Pessimism," 227, writes: "Wagner was a Luther of Art."

160. Hartwich, "Religion und Kunst," 311.

161. Taking just one work, anyone working through Gfrörer's three volume *Geschichte des Urchristentums* would come out knowing rather a lot about the New Testament and its environment! Note that he also had some Greek (he would need it for Gfrörer), even trying a little Greek conversation with the Dannreuthers (Spencer, *Wagner Remembered*, 256). Among the Greek works in his Wahnfried library is Passow, Rost, and Palm, *Handwörterbuch der griechischen Sprache*; he also had the New Testament in Greek (Jager and Tischendorf, *Novum Testamentum*) and a bi-lingual Bible (Hebrew and German for the Old Testament; Greek and German for the New).

3

Background to *Parsifal* II

Wagner's Development of the Drama

Introduction

In discussing the development of Wagner's thought in the previous chapter there is one fundamental body of literature I did not cover: medieval German literature. Of these medieval works he read, the one that stands out for its theological profundity is Wolfram von Eschenbach's *Parzival*. It is a deeply Christian work addressing fundamental questions of God's faithfulness, Christ's incarnation and sacrifice, human weakness, and faith; further, it speaks of a whole spectrum of human life (rather like the Psalms of the Old Testament).

Wolfram holds certain clues to understanding *Parsifal*, especially regarding the grail, the spear, the blood of Christ, and the understanding of "paganism." Experiencing Wagner's stage work without a knowledge of Wolfram can still be a transforming experience but it is rather like reading the New Testament without a knowledge of the Old. Further, Wolfram not only gives the key to certain aspects of *Parsifal* but something of Wagner's theological intention can be discerned by comparing the two works. So just as biblical theology is enriched by studying the "tradition history" and the mutations in this history[1] and just as biblical theology is impov-

---

1. It is thereby possible to discern "revelation" through a study of the "mutations" in the tradition history (see, e.g., Gese, "Schriftverständnis"). I have much sympathy

erished if one deals exclusively with the "final form,"[2] so it is with *Parsifal*. I will therefore introduce Wolfram's work and then go on to consider what Wagner omitted, what he changed, and how he struggled to fashion his own drama.[3] In this study of tradition history, the Wagnerian scholar has a distinct advantage over the biblical scholar: whereas the latter is often engaged in inspired guesswork, the former has a large body of material to hand (theoretical writings, letters, and diaries) whereby one can often see exactly how Wagner treated his main source. I cannot promise to have excluded all guesswork and speculation but with a little research one can discern quite a lot about Wagner's "redactional" interests.

The Birth of *Parsifal*

In *My Life* Wagner relates that during his holiday in Marienbad[4] in 1845 he read Wolfram von Eschenbach's *Parzival*. He does not state that this was the *first* time he read the work.[5] Rather he simply says that "I had therefore chosen my summer reading with care,"[6] taking with him the versions of Simrock (1842)[7] and "San-Marte" (Albert Schulz, 1836)[8] together with "the anonymous epic of Lohengrin with the great introduction by Görres."[9]

---

with this approach to the Old (and New) Testament (see Bell, *Irrevocable Call*, 314–20).

2. For example, I believe a study of the book of Genesis is impoverished if one simply studies the final form we have in the canon of Scripture. Again, see Gese, "Schriftverständnis."

3. Wagner, I am sure, was more indebted to Wolfram than he admits (compare his unwillingness to admit his indebtedness to composers such as Mendelssohn and Berlioz). See his criticism of a "lengthy linking" of Wolfram to his own poem, which he claims "has in fact no connection with it; when he read the epic, he first said to himself that nothing could be done with it, 'but a few things struck in my mind—the Good Friday, the wild appearance of Condrie. That is all it was'" (*CD* 20 June 1879).

4. He stayed there in the "Haus 'Zum Kleeblatt'" from 3 July to 9 August 1845. Marienbad was at the western end of what is now the Czech republic.

5. This is the assumption of Beckett, *Parsifal*, 1: "Wagner first read Wolfram von Eschenbach's *Parzival* in the summer of 1845."

6. *My Life* 302; *Mein Leben* 1:315: "Sorgsam hatte ich mir die Lektüre mitgenommen."

7. This was in his Dresden library but later was missing (Westernhagen, *Dresdener Bibliothek*, 20).

8. We know that this was in his Dresden library (Westernhagen, *Dresdener Bibliothek*, 110). He also possessed a second volume of San-Marte (1841) that included *Willehalm*, Albrecht's *Young Titurel*, together with a discussion of Wolfram's life and work and the grail; he also had Lachmann's edition of the Middle High German (1833), the sixth edition of 1926 becoming the standard scholarly edition.

9. Görres, *Lohengrin*. The "Introduction" was in fact ninety-four pages long.

There are in fact indications that he knew something of Wolfram before 1845. In 1840 he had met in Paris Gottfried Engelbert Anders and through him the Prussian philologist Samuel Lehrs,[10] who showed him "the annual proceedings of the Königsberg German Society," which introduced him to the Tannhäuser and Lohengrin legends[11] that had links to Wolfram. Therefore Wagner may well have known of Wolfram's work before 1845.[12]

But whatever the time of first reading, it was in 1845 that Wagner first read Wolfram in *detail*[13] and it is worth setting this crucial reading in context. His ground breaking *Der fliegende Holländer* had been performed two years earlier in 1843 and *Tannhäuser*, which had been recently completed, was to be performed in October 1845. His next operatic work was to be *Lohengrin*. The eponymous hero of this work was the son of Parzival. One possible option for Wagner would have been to compose two operas, *Lohengrin* and "Parzival," both reflecting a medieval Christian world. *Lohengrin*, set in the tenth century, did precisely that and was completed three years later in 1848; but what was to become his drama "Parsifal" had to wait thirty-seven years before completion in 1882.[14]

Wolfram von Eschenbach's *Parzival*

Since Wagner's main source was Wolfram's *Parzival*,[15] I outline certain aspects of the work and some of the story,[16] focusing on the most relevant

10. He describes the relationship with Lehrs as "one of the most beautiful friendships of my life" (*My Life* 171; *Mein Leben* 1:181).

11. See *My Life* 212–13; *Mein Leben* 1:223–24.

12. Cf. Kinderman, "Introduction," 5–6.

13. Ibid., 5.

14. Wagner was prompted later to change the name from "Parzival" to "Parsifal" through his reading of Görres, *Lohengrin*, VI, who derives the name (wrongly) from "Parsi" or "Parseh Fal" meaning "der reine oder arme Dumme" (the pure or poor fool). Wagner did not adopt the spelling "Parsifal" until March 1877 (*CD* 14 March 1877: "he will be called Parsifal" and compare *CD* 3 March and earlier entries where the spelling is "Parzival"). On the supposed etymology, see his letter to Judith Gautier, 22 November 1877 (*SL* 877): "'Parsi fal' means: 'parsi'—think of the fire-loving Parsees—'pure'; 'fal' means 'mad' in a higher sense, in others words a man without erudition, but one of genius. . . . You will see . . . why this naïve man bore an Arabian name!" Wagner did recognize that this etymology was not fully convincing but in an undated letter to Judith, he notes: "What do I care about the real meaning of Arabic words, and I fancy that there will not be an excessive number of Orientalists among my future audiences!" (Barth, Mack, and Voss, *Wagner*, 240).

15. Other sources will be discussed in chapter 10 below.

16. References will be made to Hatto's translation (*WolPH*) and to the segment and

sections, and attempting to portray some of the atmosphere and theology of the work. *Parzival* was composed around 1200 AD and comprises sixteen books, divided into 827 segments,[17] each segment having thirty-lines, that is fifteen rhymed couplets yielding a total of 24,810 lines. The work is deeply theological, the main ideas being set out in the much-discussed prologue (*WolPH* 15–16; 1.1–4.30). The very opening couplet sets out Wolfram's main idea: "Ist zwîvel herzen nâchgebûr, daz muoz der sêle werden sûr," translated by Hatto as "If vacillation dwells with the heart the soul will rue it" (*WolPH* 15), by San-Marte as "Verderben wird der Seele kund, Wohnt Zweifel in des Herzens Grund," and by Simrock as "Wem Zweifel an dem Herzen nagt, Dem ist der Seele Ruh' versagt." This "Zweifel" (doubt) in San-Marte and Simrock, translations that Wagner used, was to be central for Wagner's *Lohengrin*,[18] not only regarding Elsa's doubt concerning Lohengrin but also what Lohengrin says about his father (prose sketch of 3 August 1845): "Now know therefore, my father is called Parzival; through the highest knights' virtue and through fighting earthly doubt, which despairs of the divine, he became worthy to be called to be king of the Grail."[19] However, Wolfram's "zwîvel" is more likely to mean "double-mindedness" rather than "doubt,"[20] and this sets the agenda for the whole story. The two protagonists are Parzival who is "double-minded" and Gawan who is constant, "perfectly *staete* in every situation."[21] The whole work is governed by biblical thought, especially the letter of James[22] and Jewish Wisdom Literature, and one could say that the theological emphasis is very much that of "free will" and self-improvement rather than predestination and grace.[23]

line of the Middle High German. Wagner's principal source, as we have seen, was that of the Magdeburg Gymnasium teacher Albert Schulz (for the extent of his writing on Wolfram, see Pretzel and Bachofer, *Bibliographie*) who produced a fairly free translation of the Middle High German and occasionally attention will be drawn to those instances where San-Marte deviates from the MHG.

17. Apart from books 2–4, each starts with a new segment.

18. On the themes of faith and doubt in *Lohengrin*, see Kienzle, *Religion und Philosophie*, 103–19.

19. "Nun wisset denn, mein Vater heißet Parzival; durch höchste Rittertugend u. durch Bekämpfung des irdischen Zweifel's, der am göttlichen verzagt, ward er würdig zum König des Gral's berufen zu werden" (von Soden, *Lohengrin*, 156, quoted in Kienzle, *Religion und Philosophie*, 105).

20. The meaning of "zwîvel" is one of the most contested issues in *Parzival* scholarship.

21. Duckworth, *Parzival*, 312.

22. This was recognized by a work Wagner read, San-Marte, *Ueber das Religiöse in den Werken Wolframs von Eschenbach*, 175–76, who refers to Jas 1:6–8.

23. Duckworth, *Parzival*, 283–86.

Books 1 and 2 preface the material he took over from Chrétien de Troyes. Book 1 tells of Gahmuret of Anjou, who marries the infidel Queen of Zazamanc, Belacane, who gives birth to Feirefiz "to carry the Infidel strand of the story." Book 2 tells of Gahmuret and his second wife, Herzeloyde, who gives birth to Parzival, the "exemplar of deeper Christian chivalry."[24] As Parzival explains later in book 9, his father "impelled by knightly ardour, lost his life in a joust";[25] this was especially tragic since he died overseas and before the birth of Parzival. The circumstances of his death and their effect on Herzeloyde are important for Wagner's drama; but the events of book 1, the "infidel strand," are not directly taken up by Wagner, although they may have influenced Wagner's development of Kundry and his attitude to "paganism" as we shall see.

From book 3 Wolfram builds upon Chrétien.[26] Book 3 relates how Herzeloyde brings up Parzival, teaching him of God, and light and darkness (i.e., good, and evil, *WolPH* 71–72). One day on a hunt Parzival meets three knights (later joined by another) who tell him of King Arthur (*WolPH* 72–74). Parzival explains to his mother that he wishes to become a knight. To protect him from the fate of her husband she gives him an inferior horse and dresses him in fool's clothes so if he is found he will be beaten and sent back to her (*WolPH* 75). He sets off for Arthur's court with a final kiss from his mother. When he leaves she falls to the ground and dies of sorrow (*WolPH* 75–76). As we will see, the circumstances of Herzeloyde's death become central for the psychological drama of Act II of Wagner's stage work.

On his journey Parzival meets Sigune, his cousin (*WolPH* 80), who tells him how Orilus had slain his uncle (Galoes) and Prince Schionatulander, her knight-servitor and beloved (*WolPH* 81). Parzival promises to avenge these killings (*WolPH* 82). He journeys on, wishing to come to the court of King Arthur, and on his way encounters Ither of Gaheviez, known as the "red knight" (*WolPH* 83–84). He then arrives at the court of King Arthur, where it is clear that he has never learned the customs of courtly society (*WolPH* 85). He explains he wishes to become a knight but has no armor but would like to have that of the "red knight," whom he learns is an enemy of Arthur (*WolPH* 86). He then goes out to kill Ither (*WolPH* 80) and puts on his red armor (*WolPH* 90). This impulsive behavior is clearly

---

24. Hatto's comments in *WolPH* 426.

25. *WolPH* 242, cf. 62.

26. Hatto surmises that Wolfram understood Chrétien's episodes in an incomplete cruciform structure that he then develops into his own (*WolPH* 425–26). Such a structure may be a simplification though. So Hatto speaks of "the vital Parzival sequence" of books 3, 5, 9, 13, 15, and 16, taken from the vertical central column of the cross (427). However, book 6 is also crucial for his story (see below).

reflected in Wagner's stage work (the killing of the swan; seizing Kundry by the throat; fighting with the loved ones of the flower maidens). However, in Wolfram he later comes to regret killing Ither,[27] his sense of guilt being a slow gradual process (Wagner's portrayal of his sense of sin is, as we shall see, much more immediate).

He then comes to another castle and meets its lord, Gurnemanz de Graharz (*WolPH* 91) and tells him "My mother asked me to seek advice of a man whose locks were grey" (*WolPH* 92). Parzival's wounds are tended to by two young women (*WolPH* 93–94). Gurnemanz names him "The Red Knight" and asks why he is always talking about his mother (*WolPH* 95). He offers various advice including the importance of compassion[28] and not to ask many questions (*WolPH* 96), something central for Wolfram's drama but which Wagner considered "preposterous and totally meaningless."[29]

In book 4 Parzival comes to the city of Belrepeire where he frees Queen Condwiramurs by defeating King Clamide (*WolPH* 100–116) but sparing his life (*WolPH* 115). Clamide is told to go to King Arthur to ask for pardon (a pardon he is granted, *WolPH* 116–19). Parzival and Condwiramurs are to marry but he asks leave to see how his mother fares and to seek adventure (*WolPH* 119).

Book 5 is central for understanding how Wagner develops his *Parsifal*. Here we learn that Parzival on his further travels comes to a lake where he meets an "Angler." He asks where he can find shelter for the night and the Angler tells him of the nearby "lone mansion" (*WolPH* 120) and that if he finds it he shall take care of him that evening (*WolPH* 121). Parzival is welcomed at the castle by a page and explains "The Angler sent me here." He is entertained richly by the knights (*WolPH* 121–22) who tell him the Angler is here. "Go and join him—he esteems you a noble guest" (*WolPH* 122).[30] They mount the stairs to a hall (*WolPH* 122). There are great fires[31] and the "lord of the castle"[32] is seated "on a sling-bed over against the middle of the

27. *WolPH* 91: "Later, on reaching years of discretion, Parzival wished he had not done it." However, his sense of wrongdoing is stronger in his confession made to Trevrizent in book 9: "I slew Ither of Cucumerlant with my sinful hand" (*WolPH* 242).

28. The term used is "erbarmen" rather than "mitleiden" (170.25; 171.25).

29. *SL* 459; *SB* 11:107.

30. Although the "Angler" is to be identified with Anfortas, Parzival does not quite make this identification here and neither does the reader.

31. *WolPH* 123: "Here at Wildenberg none ever saw such great fires at any time." The location "Wildenberg" translates into "Munsalvaesche" ("Wild Mountain"), although Salvaesche can mean "salvation" as well as "savage."

32. The text implies that he is the "Angler" although only later in book 6 is this made explicit. See Cundrie's reference to the "Sorrowful Angler" (*WolPH* 164).

fireplace" (*WolPH* 123). "[H]e was more dead than alive." He invites Parzival to be seated close beside him. Because of his ailment, "he maintained great fires and wore clothes of ample cut." Then we are told: "A great company of grave knights were sitting where they were presented with a sad spectacle. A page ran in at the door, bearing—this rite was to evoke grief—a Lance from whose keen steel blood issued and then ran down the shaft to his hand and all but reached his sleeve" (*WolPH* 123).[33] There is "weeping and wailing throughout that spacious hall" (*WolPH* 123–24). He carries it around all four walls and then runs out again "whereupon the pain was assuaged."[34] Then two "noble maidens" enter, as do a duchess and "her companion," beautifully dressed and carrying lights (large candles) and four more enter carrying a "precious stone" (*WolPH* 124).[35] Then the princess Repanse de Schoye enters carrying the "gral." As carer of the gral she was "required to be of perfect chastity and to have renounced all things false" (*WolPH* 125). She sets the gral before his lordship. The meal is then explained: "whatever one stretched out one's hand for in the presence of the Gral, it was waiting, one found it all ready and to hand," whether it be food (*WolPH* 126) or wine (*WolPH* 127). "The noble company partook of the Gral's hospitality" and "Parzival well observed the magnificence and wonder of it all, yet, true to the dictates of good breeding, he refrained from asking any question" (*WolPH* 127). He remembers that Gurnemanz had advised him against asking questions. He is then offered a sword, which was meant "to prompt him to ask a Question" (*WolPH* 127). As the gral is carried out, Parzival notices a "most handsome old man" on a sling bed whose hair "was more silvery even than hoar-frost" (*WolPH* 128). It is not revealed who this is, but later we learn from Trevrizent in book 9 that this is Titurel, Parzival's great grandfather (*WolPH* 254–55). Parzival is then taken to his bed by "modest young ladies" (*WolPH* 129).

After distressing dreams he wakes in the morning to discover that he is alone in the castle (*WolPH* 130). He puts on his armor and is about to leave the castle gate (he notices the tracks of many horses) when he is rebuked by a page for not asking the question (*WolPH* 131). He travels, following the tracks left, but as the tracks fade he encounters a maiden (Sigune) lamenting

33. The idea of the bleeding lance becomes central for the closing scene of *Parsifal* (*WagPS* 234–35), discussed in chapter 6 below.

34. Note that nothing is said here of the lance being placed in the wound (cf. Cicora, "Medievalism and Metaphysics," 35) but such a procedure is described in book 9 (*WolPH* 249), the venom on the spear-head drawing the frost from his body.

35. On the significance of the number four (especially regarding the grail castle) see McConnell, "Symbols," 211–13. Wagner likewise has four (squires) carrying the covered shrine of the grail (*WagPS* 142–43).

with a dead knight in her arms. She tells him that the castle he has just visited is Munsalvaesche whose realm is Terre de Salvaesche. She explains that Titurel bequested it to his son, King Frimutel (*WolPH* 132–33). Two of his sons are Trevrizent and Anfortas.[36] She tells him he is Parzival (cf. Kundry's revelation in Act II) and that he encountered her before (*WolPH* 133). She rebukes him for not asking the question that would have healed Anfortas (*WolPH* 135). Book 5 ends with Parzival engaging with Orilus but sparing his life (*WolPH* 139–46).

Book 6 begins by telling of how King Arthur leaves his castle to seek the "Red Knight" (i.e., Parzival) to whom he was indebted and whom he wishes to invite to the Round Table (*WolPH* 147). The scene then changes to Parzival who is lodging in the forest in heavy snow. One of Arthur's falcons attacks a goose and "[f]rom its wound three red tears of blood fell upon the snow."[37] This reminds Parzival of the complexion of Condwiramurs and he becomes lost in thought "till he fell into a trance" (*WolPH* 148).[38] Parzival meets with King Arthur and is welcomed and praised by all at his court (*WolPH* 161–62). But a maiden appears, mounted on a mule, "whose manners were quite crazy" (*WolPH* 163). She was talented and "spoke all languages—Latin, Arabic and French." She had studied dialectic and geometry and had mastered astronomy. Her name is Cundrie "the sorceress." She is strikingly dressed. A long black plait "about as soft as boar's bristles" hangs down over her hat and dangles on her mule and her features are likened to those of the dog, bear, and lion (*WolPH* 163–64),[39] something Wagner was to adopt for his "Sphinx-like" Kundry.[40] Not surprisingly Wolfram can conclude: "Seldom (or never?) were lances broken for her love" (*WolPH* 164).

She tells King Arthur that "the Round Table has been maimed by the presence at it of Lord Parzival" (*WolPH* 164). She then asks Parzival: "how it came about that when the Sorrowful Angler was sitting there, joyless and despondent, you failed to free him from his sighs!"[41] He had received the

36. Therefore, whereas Amfortas is the son of Titurel in *Parsifal*, in Wolfram he is the grandson.

37. Lévi-Strauss, "Chrétien," 228, suggests Wagner "turns [the episode] into the wounded swan" (*WagPS* 126–31).

38. Compare how Parsifal also "falls into a complete trance" after the kiss in Act II (*WagPS* 194–95).

39. Note also the description of Chrétien: "Her eyes were two holes, as small as those of a rat; her nose was like that of a monkey or a cat; her lips were like those of an ass or an ox; her teeth resembled in colour the yolk of an egg; she had a beard like a goat" (Loomis, *Grail*, 39).

40. See chapter 5 below.

41. Here (*WolPH* 164–65) it becomes explicit that Anfortas is to be identified with the "Angler."

sword, saw the gral, the silver knives, and the bloody lance. She tells him that "your Question would have brought you more than Tabronit, city of fabled wealth in heathendom"; this his brother Feirefiz had won. She speaks of his mother's constancy and praises his father (*WolPH* 165). But the son "has strayed . . . from the path of fame" (*WolPH* 166). The narrator tells how Cundrie "has mortified the Waleis [i.e., Parzival]" (*WolPH* 166). He now realizes that he will never be happy until he has seen the gral and goes in search of it (*WolPH* 171); but at the same time he renounces God, thinking that if he were all-powerful, he would not have brought such shame on him (*WolPH* 172).

The emphasis at the end of book 6 passes to Gawan and books 7, 8, and 10–13 tell of his knightly exploits and progress in love (stories based on Chrétien) and this partly serves to express the extended period during which Parzival searches for the grail and is isolated from society.[42] Gawan also functions to express the standard by which Parzival is judged, although when it comes to chastity Parzival is on a higher plane.[43] But in the middle of this Gawan block is book 9, fundamental for Parzival's spiritual journey. Here he encounters two figures that Wagner was to add to his "Gurnemanz" of Act III: Kahenis,[44] an "old knight" (*WolPH* 228–31), and Trevrizent (231–55). The "old knight" (*WolPH* 228) wearing an coarse grey cloak (*WolPH* 229) rebukes him for bearing arms on Good Friday (*WolPH* 229). This leads Parzival for the first time "to ponder Who had brought the world into being," and he adds a Christological focus ["if this is His Helpful Day, then let Him help" (*WolPH* 231)]. His horse then heads for Fontane la Salvaesche where he meets "the austere Trevrizent" (*WolPH* 231) who also rebukes him for bearing arms "at Holy-tide" (*WolPH* 233). Parzival responds: "guide me now: I am a sinner" (*WolPH* 233). He explains that "[o]nly now . . . do I realize how long I have been wandering with no sense of direction. . . . I am deeply resentful of God, since He stands godfather to my troubles" (*WolPH* 235). Trevrizent explains that God "never wearied of giving His steadfast aid against the soul's being plunged into Hell" and "his sublime nature took on human shape for our sakes" (*WolPH* 236). He explains the "fall," "incarnation," and "atonement" (*WolPH* 236–38).

Parzival tells him "My deepest distress is for the Gral" (*WolPH* 239) to which Trevrizent explains "no man can win the Gral other than the one

---

42. Jones, "Gawan," 40.

43. This is made clear in book 8 (Duckworth, *Parzival*, 316). See also the end of book 10 (*WolPH* 279).

44. His name is later revealed by Trevrizent (457.11; *WolPH* 234 gives the name as "Gabenis").

who is acknowledged in Heaven as destined for it."[45] Further, those living at Munsalvaesche are "formidable fighting men . . . continually riding out on sorties in quest of adventure." These Templars

> live from a Stone whose essence is most pure. It is called "Lapsit exillis." By virtue of this Stone the Phoenix is burned to ashes, in which he is reborn.—Thus does the Phoenix moult its feathers! Which done, it shines dazzling bright and lovely as before! Further: however ill a mortal may be, from the day on which he sees the Stone he cannot die for that week, nor does he lose his colour. . . . Such power does the Stone confer on mortal men that their flesh and bones are soon made young again. This Stone is called "The Gral."[46]

He adds:

> Today a Message alights upon the Gral governing its highest virtue, for today is Good Friday, when one can infallibly see a Dove wing its way down from Heaven. It brings a small white Wafer to the Stone and leaves it there. The Dove, all dazzling white, then flies up to Heaven again. Every Good Friday, as I say, the Dove brings it to the Stone, from which the Stone receives all that is good on earth of food and drink, of paradisal excellence.[47]

The Stone has a mediatorial function in that it "has to give them the flesh of all the wild things that live below the aether" (*WolPH* 240).

Parzival tells Trevrizent that chivalric life is his one desire and that he wishes to join the company of the gral (*WolPH* 240–41). Trevrizent tells him of Anfortas. "The agony with which he was punished for his pride should move you and wretched me to never ending pity!"[48] He says that his pursuit of love beyond wedlock "brought harm to the world through him" (*WolPH* 241). So we have the idea that he brings the whole world down through his sin. However, the knights of the gral have *not* been so affected (and could suggest that Wagner himself had a positive view of the knights in his drama):[49] "In its service knights and squires must guard against licentiousness. . . . A noble Brotherhood . . . have warded off men from every land,

---

45. Compare Gurnemanz's words to Parsifal (*WagPS* 140–41).

46. *WolPH* 239; 469.1–28.

47. *WolPH* 240; 469.29—470.14.

48. *WolPH* 241; 472.23–24: "daz sol iuch und mich armen / immer mêr erbarmen." Note that the word "Mitleid" is not used here, "erbarmen" being Wolfram's preferred term.

49. See chapter 10 below.

with the result that the Gral has been revealed only to those who have been summoned to Munsalvaesche to join the Gral company" (*WolPH* 241).

Parzival reveals his identity to Trevrizent and confesses his crime of slaying Ither. Trevrizent realizing that Parzival is his nephew, rebukes him for this crime and warns him that if it is unatoned he will face God's judgement since Ither and Parzival were of one blood (*WolPH* 242). Parzival was the cause of much distress not only for slaying Ither but also because Herzeloyde "died of anguish for you!" (*WolPH* 243).

Trevrizent then explains that when his own father Frimutel lost his life, his eldest son Anfortas was summoned to the gral as King and Lord Protector. But when he came of age, when "the first bristles begin to show," love assailed him. But he sought someone other than the gral commanded (*WolPH* 243–44). The woman is not mentioned here[50] but later in book 12 we discover it was Orgeluse (*WolPH* 309). Then came the punishment when, in a joust, he was wounded in the scrotum (*WolPH* 244). The "pagan" (i.e., Muslim) inflicting the wound[51] corresponds partly to Wagner's Klingsor. He was a "heathen born of Ethnise, where the Tigris flows out of Paradise. This pagan was convinced that his valor would earn him the Gral. . . . He sought chivalric encounters in distant countries, crossing seas and land with no other thought than to win the Gral" (*WolPH* 244). After being wounded Anfortas returned with the lance head in his body.[52] This was then removed by a physician. Anfortas was carried into the presence of the Gral but "it came as a second affliction to him that he might not die" (*WolPH* 244–45).

They called to the aid of Gehon, Phison, Tigris, and Euphrates (the rivers coming out of Paradise), used the blood of the pelican (*WolPH* 245) and various herbs but nothing could heal him. But it was written on the gral that if someone were to ask the question, then Anfortas would be healed "but he shall be King no more" (*WolPH* 246). Later Trevrizent tells him that when frost had made Anfortas' wound even more painful, the lance was placed in his wound,[53] the venom on the spear head being hot. Anfortas is taken to a lake called Brumbane for healing by the breeze (*WolPH* 249) and a rumor spread that he was a fisherman (*WolPH* 250). Parzival says that he saw him at the lake assuming he was fishing. As in book 6 it is again clear that Anfortas is the Angler, i.e., the "fisher king," so central to the grail legends and subsequent developments. Many of the details of Trevrizent's address

50. *WolPH* 244: "as to who she was, let it rest." Cf. Gurnemanz's not naming Amfortas' seductress: "a woman of fearsome beauty" (*WagPS* 120–21).

51. He is not named but we are told "[h]is name was engraved on his lance" (*WolPH* 244).

52. Contrast Wagner's version where the lance is kept by Klingsor.

53. This, we saw above, is not actually related in the narrative of book 5.

are taken up and modified by Wagner, the details of which will be discussed below, but one point should be now highlighted. Wapnewski rightly points out that both Parzival of Wolfram and Parsifal of Wagner are emotionally compassionate ("emotional mitleidig") on first meeting the grail king (book 5; Act I); however he needs his own *passio* for authentic *compassio*.[54] He finds the clue in a couplet in *Parzival* book 9 where Trevrizent tells of the lance being placed into Amfortas' wound so as to take away the frost and the reaction of those around him: "dô machte ir jâmers triuwe / des toufes lêre al niuwe" (493.13-14). Hatto translates: "The sincere outpouring of their grief renewed the doctrine of the Baptism!"[55] Wapnewski translates more freely: "Da erfuhren sie in ihrem Mitleid den Sinn des Christenthums auf neue, unmittelbare Weise." He believes that this hints at what Wagner was working at, namely the passion of Christ as the core of Christian belief manifest in the suffering of Amfortas.[56] And Parsifal's *passio* becomes true *compassio* after he has passed through his journey of suffering.

As already mentioned, books 10-13 largely concern Gawan but two figures feature who are important for Wagner. First, there is the seductress Orgeluse. We learn that Anfortas was in love with her, that Parzival resisted her charms,[57] and that Gawan won her heart. The second figure is the sorcerer Clinschor who has the art of necromancy and can "bind men and women with his spells" (*WolPH* 309, book 12), including knights (*WolPH* 319, book 13). He has power over a whole land, which is "one great marvel, and its magic holds night and day!"(*WolPH* 277); to some extent he also has power over Orgeluse (*WolPH* 309-10). He was castrated for sleeping with Iblis, the king of Sicily's wife (*WolPH* 329). Wagner's Klingsor is modeled on this figure. Like Clinschor he has his own kingdom and is a sorcerer. But there are significant differences: the power he exercises over the seductress in his service, Kundry, can be overwhelming, and he castrated himself in an effort to join the knights of the grail.

Parzival reappears in book 14 where he is brought into combat with a knight whom he later learns is Gawan (they cease fighting once they realize who their opponent is [*WolPH* 344]). A similar pattern occurs in book 15 where Parzival and Feirefiz are in combat, not knowing that they are half-brothers. But as soon as they learn of their blood relationship (they have never met before), they cease fighting and are reconciled (*WolPH* 372-73).

54. Wapnewski, *Der traurige Gott*, 254.

55. *WolPH* 250.

56. Wapnewski, *Der traurige Gott*, 255: "der Passionsgedanke als Kern des christlichen Glaubens, sichtbar gemacht vor der Leidensstatt des gemarteten Herrn."

57. *WolPH* 310. He resisted her because he was already married to Condwiramurs who was even more beautiful than Orgeluse.

The final part of book 16 telescopes much. We hear that Trevrizent encourages the ailing king; they are waiting for Parzival to come and put the question. They continue to carry him to the gral "whether he liked it or not" (*WolPH* 391) where he has to open his eyes and "was made to live against his will and not die" (*WolPH* 392). Parzvial arrives with his half-brother. Asking where the gral is, Parzival genuflects in that direction "praying that the affliction of this man of sorrows be taken from him." Then he puts the crucial question "Dear Uncle, what ails you?"[58] Amfortas is healed and Parzival becomes king (*WolPH* 395) after which Trevrizent reflects on God's mysterious purposes.[59] Parzival is reunited with his wife, Condwiramurs, and sees his two sons, Kardeiz and Loherangrin (*WolPH* 397).[60] Kardeiz is crowned to rule territories (*WolPH* 398); the queen and Loherangrin ride to Munsalvaesche (*WolPH* 399) but on their journey they find Sigune dead on her knees in prayer. They place her in the tomb of Schionatulander who is untouched by decay.

In the castle the gral is brought in. "With ceremony they received from the Gral meats both wild and tame: for this man mead, for another wine . . ." (*WolPH* 402). Feirefiz wonders how empty cups become full, for he cannot see the gral. Titurel is present but now bedridden (*WolPH* 404). Feirefiz falls in love with Repanse de Schoye; Parzival tells him that he can seek her love provided he renounces his "gods" and fights "the Adversary of God on high." Miraculously, the font tilts toward the gral and fills with water. Parzival explains the Trinity and incarnation and Feirefiz, perhaps more interested in Repanse de Schoye than God, is baptized and "afterwards the Gral was unveiled to his vision" (*WolPH* 405–6). This baptism of a "pagan" has most likely influenced Kundry's baptism in *Parsifal* Act III.

After this "Writing was seen on the Gral to the effect that any Templar whom God should bestow on a distant people for their lord must forbid them to ask his name or lineage. . . . When such a question is put to him the people there cannot keep him any longer" (*WolPH* 406).[61] Towards the end of book 16 the story is told of how Loherangrin knew a woman's love in Brabant and became the Prince there. But she put the forbidden question and he had to leave (*WolPH* 410). Finally he mentions his sources, "Master

---

58. *WolPH* 395; Book 16; 795.29: "oeheim, waz wirret dir?"

59. See Groos, *Grail*, 220–41, on the problem of Trevrizent's "retraction" and especially 234–37 for allusions to Rom 11:33–36.

60. They have not been previously mentioned.

61. The rationale (which is not entirely clear) is that because Anfortas suffered for so long the gral community is averse to asking questions themselves.

Chrestien of Troyes" (the only mention) and "Kyot" (*WolPH* 410), his supposed source, which is generally accepted as "an elaborate literary hoax."[62]

Wagner's Development of Wolfram's *Parzival*

Wolfram's work has been almost universally claimed as the greatest of the German medieval romances. The work is rich in its atmosphere of chivalry and adventure, and in theology. But although Wagner on occasions felt able to praise Wolfram,[63] he was far from satisfied with the work (see below) and, as with sources for his other stage works, felt he had to rework radically the material, focusing on key scenes. Anyone adapting *Parzival* for the stage would have to remove material, but it is striking how far Wagner goes. For example, of the active characters of Wolfram—who together with their named relations, dead or alive, come to 181[64]—Wagner has just Parzival, Anfortas, Klingsor, Kundry, and Gurnemanz (although some of these are combinations of Wolfram's characters).[65] "Gawan" is mentioned just once in passing in Wagner's stage work[66] and the figure of King Arthur is completely removed. Further, there is nothing in Wagner of the adventures in love (apart from Parzival's *misadventures* in Act II). Comparing Wagner to Wolfram, one could come to the conclusion that "[i]n its hostility to the senses and to women, *Parsifal* is a profoundly inhuman spectacle" that glorifies "a barren masculine world";[67] however, it may be not irrelevant that

62. Stevens, "Narrative Sources," 110 (cf. Hatto in *WolPH* 429). Kyot is introduced in book 8 (*WolPH* 213) and again in book 9 (*WolPH* 232; 453–55).

63. A decade after he voiced his criticisms to Mathilde, Wagner was able to say that Wolfram was a "great artist who attained great mastery" (*CD* 13 July 1869), although, a further four year further on, he said he was not as great as the writer of the *Niblungenlied* (*CD* 3 July 1873). See also *What is German?* (partly written in 1865 and finally published in *Bayreuther Blätter* February 1878) where he praises the German re-workings of *Parzival* and *Tristan* (*PW* 4:160; *GSD* 10:45; *JA* 10:93).

64. See the "Glossary of Personal Names" given by Hatto in *WolPH* 439–47. The number 181 does not include names given in catalogues or those belonging to the sphere of general medieval knowledge (e.g., Aristotle).

65. Gurnemanz is a combinations Wolfram's Gurnemanz, Kahenis, and Trevrizent; Klingsor combines Wolfram's Clinschor and the unnamed "pagan" who inflicts the wound on Anfortas (*WolPH* 244); on Kundry see below.

66. In Act I Amfortas calls on "Gawain!" and the second knight tells him that Gawain did not stay since he went out searching for new healing herbs (*WagPS* 112–13). Cf. *WolPH* 262: "Gawan espied a herb whose root he declared good for wounds." Orgeluse notes that he is "adept in both medicine and chivalry."

67. Wapnewski, "Literary Works," 91.

Wagner was partly inspired to compose the work by the love of two women: Mathilde Wesendonck and Judith Gautier.

Wagner took from Wolfram two crucial scenes. The first, one that Beckett surmises was "the primary spark which fired Wagner's dramatic imagination," was the scene in book 5 where Parzival encounters Anfortas in the castle of the gral (*WolPH* 123). Here we have the "dramatic contrast between an old man laden with knowledge and grief and the careless, ignorant young man who is to be his heir."[68] This was to form the basis for Act I of *Parsifal*. The second crucial scene (book 9) is Parzival's encounter with Kahenis who, like Trevrizent, rebukes him for carrying arms on Good Friday: "If you believe in His Incarnation and His Passion for us this Day which we are now observing, this armour ill beseems you. Today is Good Friday, in which the whole world can rejoice and at the same time mourn in anguish."[69] In addition to these two scenes, he took over various other scenes including the final healing of Anfortas of book 16 and the baptism of Feirefiz. But he was unhappy with Wolfram's main ideas: Parzival's "despair in God is stupid and unmotivated and his conversion is even more unsatisfactory." Further, the "question" is "*so* utterly preposterous and totally meaningless."[70] If the question was to be removed, Wagner needed an alternative way of relating Parzival to Anfortas. As he struggled with his plot he realized that he could relate them by having Parzival undergo the same experience as Anfortas, and the answer came in his radical development of Kundry. I now consider the various stages through which Wagner fashioned his drama.

As we saw, Wagner read Parzival in 1845 in Marienbad. The next we know of his thinking on Parzival is a notebook of 1854, but here he is not working on the drama itself but introducing the character Parzival into the third act of a preliminary sketch for *Tristan*, an idea that was eventually dropped.[71] A passage in *My Life* (October 1854, Zürich) mentions this bringing together of the characters of Tristan and Parzival and, more significantly, Tristan and Amfortas.[72] After writing of the Schopenhauerian

68. Beckett, *Parsifal*, 5.

69. *WolPH* 229. In fact the opening wording and some of the ideas here are used by Wagner in a letter to Ludwig of 14 April 1865, discussed in chapter 7 below (*SL* 641–42).

70. *SL* 459; *SB* 11:107.

71. See *DEAP* 12: "*Tristan* auf dem Krankenlager im Schloßgarten. . . . ein Pilger sei zu bewirten gewesen. . . . Knappe erzählt vom Pilger.—Parzival.—Tiefer Eindruck. Liebe als Qualen—Meine Mutter starb, als sie mich gebar; nun ich lebe, sterbe ich daran, geboren worden zu sein:—warum das?—'Refrain Parzivals—vom Hirten wiederholt'—Die ganze Welt nichts wie ungestilltes Sehnen! Wie soll es denn je sich stillen?—Parzivals Refrain[?]"

72. Note that "Anfortas" and "Amfortas" "coexist in the manuscript tradition of

inspiration for *Tristan und Isolde* he says this: "I wove into the last act an episode I later did not use: this was a visit by Parzival, wandering in search of the Grail, to Tristan's sickbed. I identified Tristan, wasting away but unable to die of his wound, with the Amfortas of the Grail romance."[73]

He was only to return to thinking through the drama itself in 1857. In *My Life* we read that after reading Wolfram in 1845 he had given no further thought to Parsifal until "Good Friday" of 1857[74] when he wrote the first sketch for the drama:

> [O]n Good Friday I awoke to find the sun shining brightly into this house for the first time: the garden was blooming, and the birds singing, and at last I could sit out on the parapeted terrace of the little dwelling and enjoy the longed-for tranquillity that seemed so fraught with promise. Filled with this sentiment, I suddenly said to myself that this was Good Friday and recalled how meaningful this had seemed to me in Wolfram's *Parzival*. Ever since that stay in Marienbad, where I had conceived *Die Meistersinger* and *Lohengrin*, I had not taken another look at that poem; now its ideality came to me in overwhelming form, and from the idea of Good Friday I quickly sketched out an entire drama in three acts.[75]

This sketch is no longer extant but, according to Chamberlain, it gives the nucleus of the drama we know, including some important scenes

---

Wolfram's *Parzivâl*." Wagner later settled for the form "Amfortas" and shifted the stress from the first to the second syllable (*SL* 457 n. 1).

73. *My Life* 51; *Mein Leben* 2:524: "Im letzten Akte flocht ich hierbei eine jedoch später nicht ausgeführte Episode ein: nämlich einen Besuch des nach dem *Gral* umherirrenden *Parzival* an *Tristans* Siechbette. Dieser an der empfangenen Wunde siechende und nicht sterben könnende *Tristan* identifizierte sich in mir nämlich mit dem *Amfortas* im Gral-Roman."

74. Note, however, that he had related Amfortas to Tristan in 1854 as we have just seen.

75. *My Life* 547; *Mein Leben* 2:561 (*DEAP* 12–13). *DEAP* 13, notes that the details Wagner gives in *My Life* are inconsistent and the experiences of April 1857 that he describes are unlikely to have been on Good Friday. In 1857 Good Friday fell on 10 April whereas he did not move into the Asyl until eighteen days later (Köhler, *Titans*, 599). Wagner himself later said that it was not literally "Good Friday." See Cosima's entry for 22 April 1879: "R. today recalled the impression which inspired his 'good Friday Music'; he laughs, saying he had thought to himself, 'In fact it is all as far-fetched as my love affairs, for it was not a Good Friday at all—just a pleasant mood in Nature which made me think, 'This is how a Good Friday ought to be.'" This Good Friday experience in fact arose during his infatuation with Mathilde Wesendonck and one could speculate on the link between "Good Friday" and his longing for Mathilde.

together with fragments of musical motifs.[76] That may be so but Kinderman rightly points out that "[t]o judge from the extant sources . . . it seems certain that some crucial aspects of the drama still remained undeveloped."[77]

The following year, 1858, showed further developments in his thinking on *Parsifal*, often associated with his love for Mathilde Wesendonck.[78] In the Spring or Summer he wrote a musical fragment for Mathilde: "Wo find ich dich, du heil'ger Gral, dich sucht voll Sehnsucht mein Herze" ("Where do I find you, you holy grail, my heart full of desire seeks you").[79] This fragment ends in rising sixths characteristic of the Dresden Amen and grail theme. Then in the "Diary since the Time of my Flight from the Asyl (Tagebuch seit meiner Flucht aus dem Asyl) 17 August 1858" there is an entry for 1 October 1858 that includes a discussion about "compassion" (he speaks of "Mitleiden" rather than "Mitleid.")[80]

But the next crucial stage comes from the end of that year, described in a letter to Mathilde Wesendonck of December 1858 (around 20th): "Parzival has preoccupied me very much: in particular, there is a curious creature, a strangely world-demonic woman (the messenger of the grail) who strikes me with increasing vitality and fascination."[81] It is important to bear in mind that Wagner had not yet identified her with the "Kundry" of Act II. In view of Wagner's fascination with this "curious creature" it may seem strange that she is not mentioned in the next discussion of Parzival, an extended letter (again to Mathilde Wesendonck) of 29–30 May 1859. But this omission may be because he was working on *Tristan* Act III (this was completed on 6 August 1859) and related this Act to the figure of Anfortas. *Tristan* Act III concerns "the deepest and most unprecedented suffering and yearning" and Wagner feels that "no one has ever taken the matter so seriously before." This idea of suffering, he explains, has turned him against Parzival for "this would again be a fundamentally evil task."[82] Anfortas is

76. Chamberlain, "Notes sur Parsifal," 222: "Cette esquisse est le vrai noyau du drama que nous possédons aujourd'hui; non seulement elle contenait des scènes importantes de celui-ci, mais outre des fragments de motifs musicaux."

77. Kinderman, "Introduction," 12.

78. In this year his passion for Mathilde reached a peak with the "morning confession" (see the English translation in *My Life* 778–80) but things became so intolerable for his wife Minna that they left the Asyl (next door to the Wesendonck's villa) on 17 August. But see also Newman, *Life II*, 512: "in the deepest sense it was *Tristan* rather than Minna and Mathilde, that drove him from the Asyl."

79. *DEAP* 13; Golther, *Mathilde Wesendonk*, 26.

80. *DEAP* 13–14; Golther, *Mathilde Wesendonk*, 52–53.

81. *SL* 434; *SB* 10:211.

82. *SL* 457; *SB* 11:104.

"the centre of attention and principal subject." He has a spear wound and perhaps another "in his heart" and longs to die. He hopes that a glimpse of the grail will close his wound but it gives him one thing only: "its very sight increases his torments by conferring immortality upon them."[83] Wagner confesses: "It suddenly became dreadfully clear to me: it is my third-act Tristan inconceivably intensified."[84]

He also explains in this letter that the grail is not, as in Wolfram, a stone that fell from the sky (see above); it is the chalice of the last supper and the vessel in which Joseph of Arimathea caught the blood of Christ as he was on the cross.

> The Grail, according to my *own* interpretation, is the goblet used at the Last Supper in which Joseph of Arimathea caught the Saviour's blood on the Cross. What terrible significance the connection between Anfortas and this miraculous chalice now acquires; *he*, infected by the same wound as was dealt him by a rival's spear in a passionate love intrigue,—his only solace lies in the benediction of the blood that once flowed from the Saviour's own, similar, spear-wound as He languished upon the Cross, world-renouncing, world-redeeming and world-suffering! Blood for blood, wound for wound—but what a gulf between the blood of the one and that of the other, between the one wound and the other.[85]

Here we perceive the drama of "Parzival" as Act III of *Tristan* "inconceivably intensified." A little later in this letter Wagner discusses the genesis of the grail myth, bemoaning the fact that all the Christian legends have "a foreign, pagan origin." He states that the early Christians learned that "the Moors in the Caaba at Mecca (deriving from the pre-Muhammadan religion) venerated a miraculous stone . . . that had fallen from heaven. However, the legends of its miraculous power were soon interpreted by the Christians after their *own* fashion, by their associating the sacred object with Christian myth."[86] This was made much easier by the legend of Joseph

---

83. *SL* 457. Wagner moves from the singular dative object to the plural ("aber der Gral giebt ihm immer nur das Eine wieder, eben dass er *nicht* sterben kann; gerade sein Anblick vermehrt aber nur seine Qualen, indem er ihnen noch Unsterblichkeit giebt" (*SB* 11:104).

84. *SL* 457; "Mir wurde es plötzlich schrecklich klar: es ist mein Tristan des dritten Aktes mit einer undenklichen Steigerung" (*SB* 11:104). See chapter 7 below for further discussion of this.

85. *SL* 457; *SB* 11:104–5.

86. *SL* 459; *SB* 11:106. Note that earlier in the letter (458) he speaks of "leafing through your book." This was a copy of Wolfram Mathilde Wesendonck sent him (see

of Arimathea fleeing to Southern France with the chalice of the Last Supper. "Only now did sense and reason enter into it, and I feel a very real admiration and sense of rapture at this splendid feature of Christian mythogenesis, which invented the most profound symbol that could ever have been invented as the content of the physical-spiritual kernel of any religion." He then continues: "Who could not shudder with a sense of the most touching and sublime emotion to hear that this same goblet, from which the Saviour drank a last farewell to His disciples and in which the Redeemer's indestructible blood was caught and preserved, still exists, and that he who is pure in heart is destined to behold it and worship it himself."[87]

To those who are disquieted by such language (in that it could remind one of medieval "relics") one could perhaps say that this is simply incarnational theology and this may suggest that regarding Christ's divinity, Wagner had a sense of "incarnation" and not just an idea of a sinless Christ.[88] Wagner then scolds Wolfram for senselessly misinterpreting the grail. Further he "hadn't the first idea of what he was doing" for Parzival's "despair in God is stupid and unmotivated and his conversion is even more unsatisfactory." The "question" is "*so* utterly preposterous and totally meaningless."[89] Wagner then puts his finger on the problem with the drama: Parzival is "indispensably necessary as the redeemer whom Anfortas longs for" but if the latter is "to be placed in his true and appropriate light, he will become of such immense tragic interest that it will be almost impossible to introduce a second focus of attention, and yet this focus of attention must centre upon Parzival if the latter is not simply to enter at the end as a deus ex machina

---

his letter of 23 May 1859, *SB* 11:99). Secondary literature (e.g., Mertens, "Wagners Gral," 99) and editions of his letters (*SB* 11:482 n. 99, and *SL* 458 n. 2), give this edition as the second improved edition of San-Marte (Leipzig 1858) and refer back to Golther, *Mathilde Wesendonk*, 140 n. 1. I assume Golther made a false inference since this edition is not in the Wahnfried library. The book could be San-Marte's two-volume *first* edition, which is in the Wahnfried library and which he previously possessed but left in Dresden (San-Marte, *Leben und Dichten*). Another possibility is that it could be Eschenbach, *Parzival und Titurel*. His Dresden library contained Simrock in the two-volume second edition (see above) but this third edition was in one volume (Wagner refers to "Ihr Buch" (singular "your book"). But Wagner is almost certainly referring to San-Marte's work (and I think it must be the first edition), the second volume including a lengthy excursus on the legends of the holy grail (357–454). What he writes to Mathilde Wesendonck about the "Moors of Caaba," etc., corresponds exactly to San-Marte, *Leben und Dichten*, 2:366–67.

87. *SL* 459; *SB* 11:106–7.

88. Contrast Kienzle, "A Christian Music Drama?" 109–10. See chapter 11 below for further discussion.

89. *SL* 459; *SB* 11:107. On this question, see above.

who leaves us completely cold."[90] How to bring Parzival into the foreground seems to be the nub of his problem. In this letter Wagner almost seems to have given up on his *Parsifal* drama. He sees that he has "to compress everything into *three* climactic situations of violent intensity" for "*my* art consists in working and representing things in *this* way." He continues: "And—am I to undertake such a task? God forbid! Today I take my leave of this insane project; Geibel can write about it and Liszt can compose it!—When my old friend Brünnhilde leaps into the funeral pyre, I shall plunge in after her, and hope to die a Christian! So be it! Amen!"[91]

As well as giving some crucial insights into Parzival the letter makes it clear that Wagner was still struggling with his own version of the drama. The solution came a year later, as evidenced by a letter of early August 1860: "Did I not tell you once before that the fabulously wild messenger of the grail is to be one and the same person as the enchantress of the second act. Since this dawned on me, almost everything else about the subject has become clear to me."[92] Wagner then gives a description of her: "This strangely horrifying creature who, slave-like, serves the Knights of the Grail with untiring eagerness, who carries out the most unheard-of tasks, and who lies in a corner waiting only until such time as she is given some unusual and arduous task to perform—and who at times disappears completely, no one knows how or where?"[93] But although she is "untiring in serving the Holy Grail with dog-like devotion" she has "a secret contempt for its knights." He continues: "her eye seems always to be seeking the right one,—and she has already deceived herself once—but did not find him. But not even she herself knows what she is searching for: it is purely instinctive."[94]

So this figure of Kundry becomes the crucial link between Amfortas and Parzival that Wagner was searching for. The only woman in Wolfram who makes any link at all between the two is the seductress Orgeluse but only in the sense that Amfortas is in love with her when he should have followed the gral's leading and Parzival manages to resist her charms (but largely because he was already married). But Wagner makes the link so much stronger and more psychologically and dramatically compelling.

90. *SL* 459–60; *SB* 11:107.

91. *SL* 460 (*SB* 11:107–8; Golther, *Mathilde Wesendonk*, 148). Emmanuel Geibel was the author of a tragedy *Brunhild* (1857) and composed poems of which Wagner had a low opinion. He speaks of Geibel's "bunglings" ("Stümpereien"; *CT* 24 August 1872); Wagner used a cognate ("bungler"; "Stümper") for his own composing talents (*SL* 455; *SB* 11:69)!

92. *SL* 500 (Golther, *Mathilde Wesendonk*, 243).

93. *SL* 500 (Golther, *Mathilde Wesendonk*, 243).

94. *SL* 500 (Golther, *Mathilde Wesendonk*, 243–44).

Kundry, "certainly the strangest and perhaps the most profound of all Wagner's characters,"[95] can therefore be seen as a combination of various characters from Wolfram. First, there is "Cundrie la sorcière," a grail messenger; second, Orgeluse, a seductress held (to some extent) in the power of the sorcerer Clinschor (*WolPH* 309–10);[96] thirdly, Parsifal's cousin Sigune, "a melancholy maiden and penitent."[97] These serve as models for Kundry in each of the three acts of Wagner's *Parsifal*.[98] There is also an aspect of Trevrizent, the bringer of news (Kunde), who tells Parzival of the death of his mother on being abandoned by her son (*WolPH* 243); and there is an element of Feirefiz, the "pagan," who is baptized at the end of Wolfram's epic. In addition to characters from Wolfram, there are key additional elements to Kundry outside of Wolfram's poem. One of them may be the figure of Savitri[99] from Wagner's unfinished drama *Die Sieger*;[100] another is the figure of the penitent Mary Magdalene; allusions to her are unmistakable in Act III.[101]

Once Kundry's key role was determined, the next stage was to write his second prose sketch. This second sketch is the first *extant* prose sketch we have and was composed in August 1865 and contains the essential plot we find in the final version.[102] This was written in response to King Ludwig's request within the space of just a few days, 27–30 August, and was sent to him on 31 August.[103]

95. Beckett, *Parsifal*, 9.

96. This seductress is responsible for the fall of Anfortas (but Wolfram only relates this later in his poem; see Beckett, *Parsifal*, 10).

97. Kinderman, "Introduction," 13.

98. Ibid.

99. He mentions Savitri in the context of Parzival and Lohengrin in his letter to Mathilde Wesendonck of August 1860 (*SL* 499, cited in chapter 2 above).

100. *PW* 8:385–86; *DTB* 303. In an earlier incarnation Savitri rejected a Brahmin's son but now loves the chaste Ananda. However, she renounces him and enters the Buddha's community.

101. See the anointing scene where Kundry "draws from her bosom a golden phial and pours part of its contents over Parsifal's feet, which she then dries with her hastily unbound hair" (*WagPS* 222–23). Cf. *Jesus of Nazareth* (*PW* 8:293): "Mary [Magdalene] takes a costly Phial from her bosom . . . pours its contents on his head, washes his feet, dries and anoints them, amid sobs and tears."

102. See *BB* 46–61; *DEAP* 68–77.

103. See his letter to Ludwig of 29 August 1865: "Since you wish it so, I am engaged for the first time in setting down in writing my plan for 'Parzival'" (*SL* 663). This wording would seem to suggest that this was indeed the "first prose draft"; but the wording may simply indicate that it was the first detailed sketch.

The overwhelming concern of Wagner over the next years was the completion and production of the *Ring* (which also involved the building of the Festspielhaus in Bayreuth). Once Wagner had completed the *Ring* and had undertaken the mammoth task of overseeing the first performances in 1876, he was able to devote himself fully to *Parsifal* with the second prose sketch[104] appearing in February 1877.[105] The poem was completed a little later in April 1877[106] and this was to form, with a few variations, the final libretto.[107]

The music was composed in two drafts between September 1877 and April 1879[108] and the final score was completed on 13 January 1882.[109] The relatively slow pace at which he worked on the final score was probably due to this poor health and the time he took in writing essays. But one wonders whether he took his time since he knew this would be final work. On hearing that the king had decided not to attend any of the performances of *Parsifal* he wrote: "it is the last thing I shall write. The tremendous feeling of weariness which leaves me today with only the strength to pen these few lines tells me where I stand with my powers. *Nothing* more can be expected of me." He ends: "From one who gladly and fervently longs to die *soon*."[110] A series of sixteen performances were given in Bayreuth from 26 July to 29 August 1882[111] under the direction of the great Jewish conductor Hermann Levi (together with Franz Fischer);[112] and Wagner was to die "soon," for just six months later (13 February 1883) as he was working at his desk in the Palazzo Vendramin on the Grand Canal in Venice, he took his final breath.

104. Or third prose sketch if one includes that of 1857.

105. *DEAP* 77–87.

106. *DEAP* 90–134.

107. The variations can be seen in *DEAP* 90–134: "Die Dichtung vom Jahr 1877 und die Varianten der gestochenen Partitur vom Jahr 1883."

108. The first draft, the "Kompositionsskizze," was written mainly in pencil and generally has three staves (one for voices, two for the orchestra). The second draft, the "Orchesterskizze," was then made immediately afterwards mainly in ink; again he would usually use three staves with comments on the orchestration. Wagner would go back and forth between these drafts, working on one act at a time (see Kinderman, "Genesis," 134).

109. In the autograph score the date of 25 December 1881 is given to coincide with Cosima's birthday (cf. Wagner's explanation in *CD* 14 January 1882); she was actually born at midnight of 24 December (see Hilmes, *Herrin des Hügels*, 20) and celebrated her birthday on 25 December.

110. *SL* 923; *KB* 3:244.

111. The first two performances were given for "die Mitglieder des Patronat-Vereins" (26, 28 July) and then there were fourteen public performances.

112. See chapter 9 below for further discussion of Wagner's employment of Levi.

4

The Dramatic Outline of *Parsifal*

Introduction

In this chapter I outline the drama of *Parsifal*. As we saw in the previous chapter, in comparison to Wolfram's epic little happens on stage. Many would agree that the essence of the drama is in the "internal" development of the characters; to this I would also add the spiritual dimension in that the presence of Christ as mediated by the grail and the spear is a fundamental part of the drama.

In giving this dramatic outline I will focus on the libretto and stage direction with an occasional reference to the music. Doing justice to explicating the drama of *Parsifal* would require a full length "commentary," which, in the present work, I cannot offer.[1]

Setting of Parsifal

The action for Parsifal takes place in two kingdoms on the same mountain range. First there is the land of the grail (Acts I and III) situated in "landscape in the style of the northern mountains of Gothic Spain" (*WagPS* 106–7). Secondly there is Klingsor's magic castle, situated "on the southern

---

1. Despite the vast literature on Wagner, there is a lack of detailed "commentaries" on the stage works. Perhaps in years to come commentaries comparable in detail to those written on New Testament books will appear.

slope of the same mountain range, facing Moorish Spain" (*WagPS* 156–57). This opposition is highly significant in that it opposes a Christian realm of the grail to that of "paganism."[2]

The story behind *Parsifal* starts with Titurel, the "pious hero" ("der fromme Held"; *WagPS* 122–23). He was entrusted with the grail used at the Last Supper and the spear that pierced Christ's side and he built a sanctuary for these holy relics. He also gathered a company of pure (celibate) knights to serve the grail and to minister in acts of charity; it is also suggested that they also engaged in mission outside of their community.[3] Klingsor wished to join the company and in a desperate attempt to quell his sexual urge castrated himself. He was not allowed to enter the company and thence became an enemy of it.

The key person who links these two kingdoms is Kundry. She laughed at Christ as he hung on the cross and was condemned to eternal wandering; only Klingsor knows of her full history and she came under his power. He built a magic garden where beautiful women were to seduce any who would enter.

When Titurel became old, his son Amfortas took on his role as king of the knights of the grail. He decided to set out with the holy spear to destroy the kingdom of Klingsor. But on arriving in Klingsor's realm Amfortas was seduced by Kundry; intoxicated with passion, the spear fell from his hand. Klingsor, waiting in ambush, seized it and inflicted a wound in Amfortas' side. With the help of Gurnemanz, his companion, Amfortas managed to return to the realm of the grail but had this wound that refused to heal. Added to this is his sense of guilt, which is made unbearable when the grail is revealed. But in a vision he is told that his suffering will come to an end through a perfect fool, who will come to understanding through "Mitleid" ("compassion"): "Enlightened through compassion, the perfect fool" ("Durch Mitleid wissend, der reine Tor").

Act One

An aspect of Wagner's genius is that the drama begins not as the curtain rises at the beginning of Act I but with the first sounds that arise from the "mystic abyss."[4] The slow "love feast" (or "Communion") theme is played in

2. On the nature of this "paganism" see chapter 10 below.

3. See *WagPS* 210–11, where in Act III Gurnemanz tells Kundry: "We send out no more on missions" ("Auf Botschaft sendet sich's nicht mehr").

4. *PW* 5:335; *GSD* 9:338.

unison on strings and woodwind forming a musical arch,[5] beginning in Ab major and moving to C minor. Most of the prelude is in Ab major, which, as noted in chapter 1 above, has a particular association for Wagner.[6] The theological significance of the prelude will be discussed in chapter 10 below and I now pass on to the point when the curtain is raised.

The scene is a shady forest in the precincts of the castle of the grail, Monsalvat, a path to the left rising to the castle and towards the rear there is a "deep-set forest lake." It is daybreak[7] and Gurnemanz and two squires are sleeping under a tree. Trombones from the unseen castle sound a solemn call; Gurnemanz awakes and rouses the squires for prayer. After a moment of silent prayer two knights enter and Gurnemanz asks how Amfortas is today; the second knight tells that after taking the healing herb of the knight Gawain, the pain returned "even more searingly" and that Amfortas asks that they prepare a bath. Gurnemanz says that only one person can help Amfortas but when asked who that is, he evades the question and tells them to see to the bath. Suddenly Kundry comes flying in on her horse.[8] The stage direction tells that she is in wild garb, "her black hair is loose and dishevelled, her complexion deep and ruddy-brown, here eyes dark and piercing, sometimes flashing wildly, more often lifeless and staring" (*WagPS* 110–11). She hands Gurnemanz a phial of balsam that she has brought from Arabia and then throws herself on the ground in exhaustion. As the sick king is brought in by a train of knights and squires, Gurnemanz says how it grieves his heart to see "the liege lord of the most victorious race in the pride and flower of his manhood fall a slave to his sickness!" Amfortas hopes that after "a night of wild distress" the waters of the holy lake will refresh him and ease his anguish. He calls for Gawain but is told that he left a healing herb and went out on a new search. Amfortas responds angrily because he has flaunted the grail's command in leaving the grail's domain without per-

---

5. The combination is the first player on each of the desks of first and second violins, 'cellos, first clarinet and bassoon, with the cor anglais added towards the top of the "arch."

6. Meyer, *Gralsgeschichte*, 381, quoting Beckh, *Tonart*, contrasts this opening in Ab to that of the A major to the Prelude to *Lohengrin* Act I: "Das Lohengrin-A-dur der Weltenhöhen deutet entsprechend auf den heiligen Gral in Weltenhöhen, den fernen unerreichbaren . . . Hingegen im 'Parsifal' werden wir vom Beginn an unmittelbar in das Grals-heiligtum selbst versetzt, dringen ins Innere dieses Heiligtums." Note that Beethoven's Opus 110 Piano Sonata, also in Ab major, was considered by Wagner to "number among the mysteries" (*CD* 21 December 1879).

7. "Daybreak" is highly significant in many of the stage works of Wagner (e.g., *Götterdämmerung* Act II Scene 2).

8. She appears almost as a "Walküre" figure (cf. "Gundryggia," *WagPS* 156–57). Cf. *CD* 14 March 1977.

mission. He fears that he will fall into Klingsor's snares (*WagPS* 112–13). Amfortas says that he awaits the appointed one who is "enlightened through compassion"—the "pure fool"—and that he feels he knows him already and would like to call him "death" (*WagPS* 114–15).

Inviting him to be practical, Gurnemanz suggests he tries the phial, which he explains was brought from Arabia by Kundry. Amfortas thanks her and says he will try the balsam. In an outburst Kundry rejects his thanks and bitterly asks how it can possibly help and tells him to go to his bath (*WagPS* 114–15).

As Amfortas leaves for his bath (he is accompanied by the first and second squires)[9] the third squire taunts Kundry: "Hey, you there! Why do you lie there like a wild beast?" She retorts: "Are the beasts not holy here?" sung to the grail theme. The fourth squire wonders whether her balsam will lead to Amfortas' ruin. Gurnemanz rebukes them "Did she ever harm you?" (*WagPS* 116–17), and there follows an extended section, "Gurnemanz's narration."[10] The five stories told are (1) Kundry; (2) Amfortas and the loss of the spear; (3) Titurel and the grail; (4) Klingsor; (5) Amfortas' prophetic vision.[11] Abbate comments: "The stories do not simply pass chronologically from furthest to most recent past; rather they generate a temporal circle that will constantly and inevitably turn back to a single event. This event is Klingsor's wounding of Amfortas, a moment laden with mystic significance."[12]

The first part of the first section functions as a "Lied" and begins and ends in E minor (I.396–420). Gurnemanz explains that when the brothers were fighting in far off lands they did not know how to send tidings or even where; but Kundry "rushes and flies there and back, bearing the message faithfully and successfully" (*WagPS* 116–17). However, the mood changes both in music and text as the third squire claims she hates them and the fourth says she is a heathen, a sorceress (*WagPS* 116–19). Gurnemanz now shifts to "uneasier speculation about her past."[13] He concedes that she may be under a curse and wonders if she is here reincarnated, expiating for some sin from an earlier life (sung to the "Liebesmahl" theme) and now making atonement by her service to the knightly order (*WagPS* 116–19).[14]

9. The stage direction is not clear ("Squires come and go") but their return is marked a little later (*WagPS* 116–17, 120–21).

10. There is some dispute as to where this "narration" begins but Abbate, "Words and Music," 54, rightly argues that the musical structure suggests it begins here.

11. One of the characteristics of Wagner's dramas is that often the "action" consists of extensive recollections (e.g., Wotan in *Die Walküre* Act II; Isolde in *Tristan* Act I).

12. Abbate, "Words and Music," 54.

13. Ibid., 55.

14. Note the variation of the prophecy motif (*FTG* theme 54).

The third squire wonders whether her guilt has brought distress to the knights. The stage direction "recollecting" ("sich besinnend"; I.458) indicates that Gurnemanz now sinks deeper into contemplation of Kundry's past.[15] Gurnemanz recalls that when she was away for a long time misfortune did befall them. One would expect Gurnemanz to recall the event with the spear; in fact "he comes dangerously close to a memory of the Spear but evades it."[16] This evasion may well be expressed by the spear motif played in the 'cellos and double basses but in reverse order.[17] Gurnemanz explains that he knew her for a long time but Titurel knew her for even longer (and now for the first time in the Act the magic/Kundry motif is "spun out, developing into a continuous accompaniment for Gurnemanz' words").[18] He tells the squires that while Titurel was building the castle he found her asleep in the undergrowth in the wood "numb, lifeless, as if dead." Gurnemanz says that he found her shortly after "we suffered that misfortune which that evil doer (i.e., Klingsor) beyond the mountains brought upon us so shamefully." The Kundry narrative then "culminates in his angry demand":[19] "Ho, you! Listen and say: whereabouts were you roaming when our master lost the Spear? Why did you not help us then?" (*WagPS* 118–21), but he says that not realizing that Kundry was the seductress in Klingsor's service.

Kundry quietly utters that she never helps. The third squire asks why she is not sent after the missing spear if she is so loyal. Gurnemanz explains that this is "forbidden to all." With deep emotion he says that he saw this wondrous spear "wielded with unhallowed hand!" (*WagPS* 120–21).

We now enter the second part of the narrative, which concerns Amfortas and the loss of the spear.[20] Gurnemanz recollects how Amfortas, on trying to vanquish the sorcerer, was enticed away by "a woman of fearsome beauty" ("ein furchtbar schönes Weib"; but he does not identify her as Kundry). In her arms "he lay intoxicated" and let the spear fall. There was a deathly cry; Gurnemanz tells of how he rushed in and saw Klingsor laughing, having stolen the spear. He fought to cover the king's flight "but

---

15. Abbate, "Words and Music," 55.

16. Ibid.

17. In I.465–67 they play Cb Bb Ab Gb, which if reversed renders the spear motif (*FTG* theme 1 h). This is probably not accidental; sometimes Wagner even builds new themes by reversing themes (see, e.g., Scruton, *Death-Devoted Heart*, 200).

18. Abbate, "Words and Music," 55. For the magic/Kundry motif, see *FTG* theme 4.

19. Ibid.

20. Ibid. Abbate thinks that the Db–Eb–Db sung by Gurnemanz to "He! Du! Hör" ("Ho, you! Listen") "is a germinal musical cell from which the main motif for the next story will spring" (*FTG* theme 1e, in particular 1cd), the narrative of the spear (although 1cd involves a minor rather than a major second).

a wound burned in his side; this wound it is which will never heal" (*WagPS* 120–21).

As the first and second squires return from the lake, the third asks Gurnemanz if he knew Klingsor, but again he evades a question, and asks how the king is. The first two squires say he has been refreshed by the bath and the balsam has eased his pain; but Gurnemanz reflects: "This wound it is which will never heal!" The third squire presses Gurnemanz: "tell us plainly: you knew Klingsor—how could that be?" (*WagPS* 122–23). One would expect the next third part of the narration to concern Klingsor but again Gurnemanz answers evasively with the story about Titurel and the grail. He explains that Titurel, the "pious hero," knew Klingsor well. For when "savage foes' craft and might threatened the realm of the true faith," angels of the Savior came down "in holy, solemn night"[21] with two wonderful gifts. First, there was given "the sacred vessel, the precious holy Cup from which He drank at the Love Feast (beim letzten Liebesmahl), in which too His divine blood flowed from the Cross."[22] Second, he was given "that same spear which shed [his blood]." Titurel built a sanctuary for these "holy relics."[23] He tells the squires (the four are now gathered around him) that they were called into its service "by paths denied to sinners"; it is given "only to the pure" ("nur dem Reinen") "to whom the Grail's mighty power grants the strength to work divine salvation" (*WagPS* 122–25) and this is underlined by "one of the strongest cadences so far heard in Act One,"[24] an orchestral crescendo using the grail motive and ending on an F# major triad (I.620–22).[25]

The F# is then sustained by a timpani roll over which Gurnemanz tells of how the service of the grail was denied to Klingsor (*WagPS* 124–25), so introducing the fourth part of his narration. He lived secluded in the valley in "a rich heathen land"[26] (i.e., Moorish Spain).[27] "Powerless to stifle the

---

21. Note the introduction of the "angel" motif (*FTG* theme 14).

22. Contrast Robert de Boron who implies the blood was caught *after* Jesus had been taken down from the cross (see chapter 10 below).

23. The term "relics" can have a rather negative connotations. In speaking of "what remains" (Latin *reliquiae*) Wagner employs the unusual term "Heiltum": "Dem Heiltum baute er das Heiligtum" ("for the saving objects he built a holy place"). See chapter 5 below for further discussion.

24. Abbate, "Words and Music," 56.

25. Note the associations of F# major with "transcendence." See the discussion of Kundry's baptism in chapter 5 below.

26. The key moves momentarily into B minor (I.627–29), the dark key of Klingsor (see chapter 1 above).

27. Klingsor's characteristic theme is here introduced (*FTG* theme 7).

sin within him, on himself he laid dastardly hands which he then turned towards the Grail." The guardian (Titurel) drove him out. Klingsor's "deed of shameful sacrifice" gave him knowledge of "evil magic." He transformed the desert into a magic garden in which "bloomed women of infernal beauty." He waits to lure the knights of the grail "to sinful joys and hell's damnation"; and many have indeed been ruined. Amfortas went out to subdue "this plague of sorcery." Gurnemanz tells them that they know what happened to him (*WagPS* 124–25). The only hope now is found in a holy vision given to Amfortas (this forms the brief fifth section of the narration) when he was in fervent prayer before the "looted sanctuary": "Enlightened through compassion, the innocent fool; wait for him, the appointed one," sung to the prophecy motif. The four squires begin to repeat these key words in their chorale but are rudely interrupted (*WagPS* 126–27).

The stage direction tells that "[f]rom the lake are heard shouts and cries from the knights and squires." A wild swan flying over the lake that "[t]he king hailed as a happy omen" is shot by an arrow and "falls lifeless to the ground exhausted" (*WagPS* 128–29). Parsifal (not named) is led in and accused of killing the swan, which he readily admits to. "Indeed! Whatever flies I can hit in flight!" He is sternly rebuked by Gurnemanz. "Unprecedented act! You could murder (Du konnest morden), here in the holy forest, where tranquil peace surrounded you?" To the next phrase Wagner significantly uses a variation of the "faith" theme: "Did not the woodland beasts tamely come near and innocently greet you as friends?" He asks what harm the "faithful swan" did to him. He points to the "blood still congealing, the wings drooping lifeless, the snowy plumage stained dark, the eyes glazed— do you see his look?"[28] Parsifal, having followed Gurnemanz's words "with growing emotion" breaks his bow and hurls his arrows away. Asked how he could commit this crime, Parsifal answers "I didn't know." To a series of questions Parsifal likewise answers I don't know: "Where are you from?" "Who is your father?" "Who sent you this way?" When asked his name he says he had many but knows none of them now (*WagPS* 132–33). After Gurnemanz sends the squires to see to the king's bath, Parsifal explains that the only thing he does know is that his mother was called Herzeleide and he lived with her in the woods and wild moors. To Gurnemanz's question "Who gave you the bow?" he explains that he made it himself to scare away the eagles. Gurnemanz says that Parsifal seems "eagle-like and nobly born" and asks why his mother did not let him learn to use better weapons.

---

28. *WagPS* 130–31. The "snowy plumage stained dark" could have been partly inspired by the episode of Parzival seeing the drops of blood of the wounded goose falling on the snow (see chapter 3 above, and *WolPH* 148).

At this point Wagner gives a stage direction bringing Kundry's situation up to date: during Gurnemanz's recital of Amfortas' fate, she has been "violently writhing in furious agitation." But he adds that now "still lying in the undergrowth, eyes Parsifal keenly."[29] She interjects: "His mother bore him fatherless, for Gamuret was slain in battle! To preserve her son from a similar untimely hero's death, she brought him up in the desert to the folly, a stranger to arms—the fool!" (*WagPS* 134–35). Parsifal retorts that he wanted to be like the "glittering array of men mounted on fine creatures." He ran after them and used his bow to defend himself against wild beasts and giants. Kundry adds: "Robbers and giants knew his strength: they learnt to fear the fierce boy" (*WagPS* 136–37). Surprised, Parsifal asks: "Who fears me?" Kundry replies "The wicked!" Parsifal asks: "They who threatened me, were they wicked?"[30] Gurnemanz laughs (he sees Parsifal is naive). Parsifal then asks "Who is good?" The significance of these words is found in the slowly rising A Bb Db, which points to the holy grail,[31] an instances where a leitmotif gives a clue to the meaning of the words.

Gurnemanz then suggests that his mother whom he deserted now grieves for him. But Kundry says: "She grieves no more: his mother is dead." Alarmed, Parsifal asks who says this. Kundry replies: "As I rode by I saw her dying: she bade me greet you, fool." Parsifal "springs furiously at Kundry and seizes her by the throat" (*WagPS* 136–37). Gurnemanz restrains him and again rebukes him: "What has the woman done to you? She spoke the truth; for Kundry never lies, though she has seen much." Parsifal is "seized with violent trembling" and utters "I am fainting!" Kundry "at once hastens to a spring in the wood and now brings water in a horn, sprinkles Parsifal with it and then gives it to him to drink." Gurnemanz commends her: "Well done, according to the Grail's mercy: they vanquish evil who requite it with good."[32] But Kundry confesses: "I never do good; I long only for rest, only rest in my weariness." She turns away and creeps towards a thicket in the wood. "To sleep! O that no one would wake me!" "No! Not sleep! Horror

29. In a letter to Mathilde Wesendonck of early August 1860 there is a detailed description of Kundry's inner state after Parsifal's arrival: "strange are the things that must go on inside her. . . . The woman suffers unspeakable restlessness and excitement. . . . What is going on inside her? Is she appalled at the thought of renewed flight, does she long to be freed from it? . . . [S]he gazes with a strangely inquisitive look (sphinx-like) at Parzival" (*SL* 500; Golther, *Mathilde Wesendonk*, 244).

30. Note the use of the B minor triad (I.992), associated with Klingsor.

31. This is given its own leitmotif "Wer ist gut?" (*FTG* theme 60). These intervals correspond to the first three notes of a variation of the grail theme (theme 25). But the ambiguity of the theme can be seen in that it forms a part of the magic/Kundry motive (*FTG* theme 4).

32. Cf. Rom 12:21. Note the use of the variation on the grail motif (*FTG* theme 26).

seizes me!"[33] Her final words before she disappears behind the bushes are: "In vain to resist. The time has come."[34] "Sleep—sleep—I must" (*WagPS* 138–39).

The mood changes with a section starting in A major as "the sun stands high." Gurnemanz tells Parsifal: "The king is returning from the bath; the sun stands high; now let me lead you to our hallowed feast for if you are pure, the Grail will give you drink and food."[35] We have here the first indication that the grail can provide food and drink for those who are pure, an idea taken from Wolfram and other grail traditions. We now have the move to the land of the grail. The stage direction shows how Gurnemanz is now tender towards Parsifal: "He has gently taken Parsifal's arm round his own neck and put his own arm around the boy's body." Parsifal asks: "Who is the Grail?" Gurnemanz explains that it cannot be expressed in words, "but if you yourself are called to its service that knowledge will not remain withheld."[36] Gurnemanz tells him that "I know you aright; no earthly path leads to it, and none could tread it whom the Grail itself had not guided." It could be said that we are now entering a new phenomenal realm.[37] Parsifal says "I scarcely tread, yet seem already to have come far" to which Gurnemanz replies: "You see, my son, time here becomes space" (*WagPS* 140–41).

These words[38] are reflected in the stage direction that the two "appear to walk"; the woods disappear and now the way leads upwards through walls of rock.[39] During the scene change the "transformation music"[40] "moves in painful dissonance" and "the great bells of Monsalvat are heard pealing . . . from afar"[41] and Gurnemanz and Parsifal enter the castle of the

33. The stage directions uses language one could use for an animal: "She falls into a violent trembling, then lets her arms and legs drop wearily and totters away."

34. Klingsor uses the exact same words of this second sentence at the beginning of Act II: "Die Zeit ist da" (*WagPS* 156–57).

35. I have modified *WagPS* 141, which translates "wird . . . dich tränken und speisen" with "will be meat and drink to you." However, for Wagner the grail only offers a vegetarian diet of bread and wine (although his 1865 sketch is ambiguous in that it speaks of the grail "supplying the community with food and drink" [*BB* 47]).

36. This reflects Trevrizent's words in book 9 of Wolfram's *Parzival*: "no man can win the Gral other than one who is acknowledged in Heaven as destined for it" (*WolPH* 239).

37. See chapter 11 below.

38. See the discussion in chapter 5 below.

39. *WagPS* 140–41; cf. how in Wolfram, Parzival mounts stairs into the hall of the gral (*WolPH* 122).

40. For analyses of the transformation music see, e.g., Lorenz, *Parsifal*, 71–76; Kinderman, "Genesis," 158–75.

41. Forsyth, "Wagner's 'Parsifal,'" 279.

grail. Gurnemanz tells Parsifal: "Now observe well, and let me observe, if you are a fool and innocent, what knowledge may be divulged to you." The knights of the grail enter singing: "At this latest Love Feast, prepared day after day, as on the last occasion may it refresh us today." Two processions of squires enter and others carry in Amfortas and the four squires bring in the covered shrine of the grail (*WagPS* 142–43).[42] Youths sing halfway up the dome of the castle: "As once His blood flowed with countless pains for the sinful worlds[43]—now with joyful heart let my blood be shed for the great Redeemer. His body, that he gave us strength to purge our sin, lives in us through His death." To the gentle faith theme the boys then sing from the very top of the dome "as if the Holy Ghost descended, like a dove, unseen, to fill the house where they are sitting":[44] "The faith endures, the dove, the Saviour's loving messenger, hovers. Drink the wine poured out for you and take the bread of life!" (*WagPS* 144–45).

After a complete silence, the voice of Titurel is heard "from a vaulted niche behind Amfortas' couch, as if from a tomb." He asks if Amfortas is now ready to perform his office (which is keeping him alive). "Shall I today look on the Grail and live? Must I die without my Saviour's guidance?" Amfortas says he cannot do it because of the torture the grail induces in him and asks his father to do it: he can live and let Amfortas die. Titurel tells him that he "within the grave" lives "by the Saviour's grace"; but he is too feeble to serve and orders Amfortas to uncover the grail, which may serve to expiate his sin. Amfortas says it must remain uncovered (*WagPS* 144–45).[45] There then follows a crucial monologue that will be analyzed in detail in chapter 5. Briefly put, Amfortas tells of the guilt he experiences which is made even more intense by looking on the grail. He cries out for mercy and asks that his life be taken away (*WagPS* 146–49).

The king's extended outburst of despair is softly answered by the boys and youths ("Knaben und Jünglinge") singing unseen from the dome: "Enlightened through compassion, the innocent fool; wait for him, the appointed one." The knights add that he should "wait confidently" and "serve the Office today!" Titurel again commands "Uncover the Grail!" but now accompanied by the woodwind playing pianissimo the rising sixths of the grail motif. Amfortas raises himself and acolytes remove the cover from the

42. Note the importance of the number four for Wolfram (see chapter 3 above).

43. I have amended the English singular (*WagPS* 43) to the plural (cf. *WagPS* 142: "Den sündigen Welten.")

44. Forsyth, "Wagner's 'Parsifal,'" 280.

45. It is significant that Kundry's motif (*FTG* theme 36) plays at "No! Leave it uncovered!"

golden shrine and take from it an "antique crystal chalice" from which they also remove a covering.

Voices from high then sing: "Take this my body, take my blood, in token of our love!" Amfortas bows before the chalice and an increasing darkness falls upon the hall. When it is completely dark, boys then sing: "Take this my blood, take my body, in remembrance of me!" (*WagPS* 148–49). Then a dazzling ray of light falls from above on the crystal cup, which now grows in a brilliant crimson, indicating that the blood of Christ is now miraculously appearing. Amfortas raises the grail and "waves it gently to every side, blessing the bread and wine with it." Titurel exclaims: "O heavenly rapture! How brightly our Lord greets us today!"[46]

Amfortas sets the grail down, its glow fades and the darkness lifts. The acolytes replace the chalice in the shrine and cover it. The four squires then distribute the two flagons of wine and the baskets of bread, these elements having been provided miraculously by the grail.

The following chorus in three sections speaks of a series of "transubstantiations" (using the verb "wandeln"), which will be discussed in detail in chapter 5 below. Amfortas takes no part in the Communion. His wound begins again to bleed and is he taken out on his litter; the knights embrace one another and slowly leave. The stage direction summarizes Parsifal's reactions in this grail scene: "Parsifal, on hearing Amfortas' previous loud cry of agony, had made a violent movement towards his heart, which he clutched convulsively for a long time; now again he stands motionless, as if petrified."[47] Gurnemanz "shakes him by the arm" and asks: "Do you know what you have seen?"[48] Shaking his head slightly, Parsifal "presses his heart convulsively," indicating that he has a vague sense of "compassion" at this point,[49] something that will intensify beyond recognition in Act II. Gurnemanz calls him a fool and tells him to go away and "leave the swans in peace." He pushes Parsifal out but then a voice "from high up" sings "Enlightened through compassion, the innocent fool" ("Durch Mitleid wissend, der reine Tor"). Voices from the mid-height and summit add "Blessed in faith!" ("Selig im Glauben!" *WagPS* 154–55).

---

46. This section will be studied in more detail in chapter 5 below.

47. "Parsifal hatte bei dem vorangehenden stärksten Klagerufe des Amfortas eine heftige Bewegung nach dem Herzen gemacht, welches er krampfhaft eine Zeitlang gefaßt hielt; jetzt steht er noch wie erstarrt, regungslos da" (*WagPS* 152–55).

48. *WagPS* 154–55. Kienzle, "A Christian Music Drama?" 123, points to the abbreviated version of the "Heilandsklage," which then follows.

49. Deathridge, "Strange Love," 162.

Act Two

As Act II begins it is as though we are transported to the realm of hell, graphically painted with Klingsor's dark key of B minor. In his magic castle Klingsor has implements of witchcraft and necromancy and he sits before a metal mirror. His first words "The time has come" ("Die Zeit ist da") recall those of Kundry in Act I as she makes her exit. He tells of how his magic castle "lures the fool" and that "in deathly sleep the woman is held fast by the curse," a curse that, he claims, he has "the power to loosen." He calls up Kundry as "nameless one," "primeval witch," "rose of hell," "Herodias," and "Gundryggia" (*WagPS* 156–57). She screams and then groans. Klingsor wonders why she has been with the knights since, he claims, they treat her "like a beast" and she has achieved the goal of capturing "that chaste guardian of the Grail" (*WagPS* 158–59). Also does she not fare better with Klingsor? She makes a series of broken utterances and says that she served the knights, to which Klingsor suggests that she does this to make good the wrongs she has maliciously done to them. Klingsor tells Kundry that today they have to deal with "the most dangerous" who is "shielded by his foolishness" (*WagPS* 160–61). Kundry refuses but Klingsor says that he can force her because only with him does she have no power. Laughing, she inquires if he is chaste. This provokes his fury: "Why do you ask that, accursed witch?" (*WagPS* 162–63);[50] he then broods over his self-castration. But he gloats that Titurel's race has been ruined and looks forward to guarding the grail. Asked how she liked Amfortas, Kundry says that he was weak as all the knights are. They all fall victim to her curse. But she longs for release from "endless sleep." Klingsor says that the one who spurns her sets her free and says she should try it with the boy who is approaching (*WagPS* 162–63).

She first refuses but Klingsor relates how the boy is handsome and how the guards, trying to "defend their beautiful witches," have been wounded by the boy (e.g., he has disarmed the hero Ferris, another he has struck in the arm and another in the thigh; *WagPS* 164–65): "Each takes home a wound" (*WagPS* 166–67). During this Kundry breaks into "wild hysterical laughter, which turns to a convulsive cry of woe" and then disappears. Klingsor sees that Parsifal in "childish amazement" "gazes at the deserted garden." He sees Kundry "already at work" and says that whatever prophecies were made about him, he will fall into Klingsor's power once he is "deprived of purity" and will remains his slave (*WagPS* 166–67).

He sinks with the whole tower and the magic garden rises and fills the whole stage. We see "tropical vegetation" and "luxuriant display of flowers"

---

50. See chapter 7 below.

and Parsifal gazes down in astonishment. Beautiful maidens rush in: "Here was the uproar" they say and demand vengeance on Parsifal for wounding their lovers. They see their "foe" high up on the rampart, holding Ferris' sword with the blood of another on it (*WagPS* 166–71). Parsifal jumps down into the garden and asked why he smote their lovers he responds, "Lovely children, how could I not smite them? They barred my way to you, my fair ones" (*WagPS* 172–73). Realizing that he will not harm them, their mood changes into gaity and merry laughter and, adorning themselves with flowers, they compete for Parsifal's love (*WagPS* 172–85). Parsifal, frustrated by their quarreling over him, is about to escape when he hears Kundry's voice: "Parsifal! Stay!" (*WagPS* 184–85). Standing still[51] Parsifal realizes that "once in a dream my mother called me that." Kundry, now metamorphized, invites him to stay since "bliss and surpassing delight await you." She tells the flower maidens to leave him alone, go home, and tend their wounded heros. They do not want to go but nevertheless say farewell to the "fair boy, you—fool!" (*WagPS* 186–87).

Parsifal wonders whether he has dreamt all this. He sees Kundry appear "through an opening in the banks of flowers, a young woman of great beauty . . . on a couch of flowers, wearing a light, fantastic, veil-like robe of Arabian style." She tells him that she named him "foolish innocent" ("tör'ger Reiner"), "Fal Parsi," "innocent fool" ("reinen Tor"), "Parsifal." This name was given to him by his dying father Gamuret when Parsifal was still in his mother's womb. Kundry tells him that she has waited here to tell him and asks: "what drew you here, if not the wish to know?" He says that he never saw nor dreamt of what he now sees and which fills him with dread. He asks if she "blooms in this bank of flowers?" She tells him that her home is far away where she has seen much. She saw the child on its mother's breast.[52] His mother was full of sorrow for his father's love and death and to prevent the same happening to her son she tried to shelter him "from weapons and men's strife and fury" and from gaining knowledge. She tells of his mother's great distress when he "roamed late and far" and she wonders whether he feared her kisses when she found him and her arms clasped him tight. But one day he left and she waited day and night. "Grief consumed her pain and she craved death's release: her sorrow broke her heart, and Herzeleide died" (*WagPS* 188–91).

Parsifal "sinks overcome with distress at Kundry's feet." "Mother! sweet dear mother! Your son, your son had to murder you!" Kundry tells him to "assuage that distress . . . in the solace which love offers you." Parsifal

---

51. Notes of Kniese (*DEAP* 198).

52. This next section is discussed in more detail in chapter 7 below.

asks how could he forget his mother and then adds: "Ah, what else have I forgotten?"[53] Kundry instructs him that he needs to confess and understand and to learn "to know the love that enfolded Gamuret when Herzeleide's passion engulfed him in fire!" She who once gave him life and being sends as a last greeting of a mother's blessing, "the first kiss of love" (*WagPS* 192–93).

She gives him a long kiss on the lips. But Parsifal "suddenly starts up with a gesture of the utmost terror" and presses his hands hard against his heart. "Amfortas! The wound! The wound! It burns within my heart. . . . I saw the wound bleeding: now it bleeds in me!" But then he realizes that the pain is not really the physical wound but the "torment of love" and "sinful desire" (*WagPS* 194–95).

Parsifal falls into a complete trance telling that his "dull gaze is fixed on the sacred vessel; the holy blood flows: the bliss of redemption . . . trembles within every soul around." Only in his heart will the pangs not be stilled. "The Saviour's lament I hear there," a lament from his (the savior's) profaned sanctuary: "Redeem me, rescue me from hands defiled by sin!" Flinging himself in despair on his knees he cries out: "Redeemer! Saviour! Lord of grace! How can I, a sinner, purge my guilt?" (*WagPS* 194–97).

Since Kundry has "lost him as her victim"[54] she realizes he can set her free (cf. *WagPS* 162–63) and her "astonishment has changed to passionate admiration." "Honoured hero! Throw off this spell! Look up and greet your fair one's coming." Parsifal then realizes exactly how her lips kissed away Amfortas' salvation. "Yes! This voice! This was how she called him . . . the lips . . . they quivered for him, thus she bent her neck." Kundry bending over him with caressing movements is then cast away: "Corrupter! get away from me! Forever, forever away from me!" (*WagPS* 196–97).

Kundry calls him "Cruel one" ("Grausamer"). If he feels others sorrows he should feel hers also. "If you are a redeemer, what maliciously stops you from uniting with me for my salvation?" She seems to assume that Parsifal is the redeemer and that he is Christ in new form (possibly reincarnated): "Through eternities I have waited for you, the Saviour so late in coming, whom once I dared revile." She speaks of the curse that afflicts her, asleep and awake, in death and life, that torments her endlessly through this existence ("endlos durch das Dasein quält"). She tells of how she laughed at Christ as he was on the cross and "his gaze fell upon" her.[55] Now she seeks him from world to world to meet him once again. (She appears to be identifying Christ with Parsifal in this passage.) She cannot weep but

53. See the discussion in chapter 7 below.
54. Forsyth, "Wagner's 'Parsifal,'" 293.
55. See chapter 5 below for a more detailed analysis.

only "shout, rage, storm and rave in an ever-renewed night of madness from which, though repentant," she scarcely wakes. She asks to weep upon the breast of the one she longed for yet despised and rejected (i.e., Christ). She asks to be united to Parsifal for one hour only and, though God[56] and the world disown her, through Parsifal she can be cleansed of sin and redeemed (*WagPS* 198–201).

Parsifal tells her that they would both be damned if he yielded to her embrace and that he can be the instrument of salvation if she will turn aside from her desires. "The solace to end your sorrows comes not from the source from which they flow: salvation shall never be bestowed on you until that source is sealed to you." Parsifal here seems to be saying that she must shun a so-called salvation that comes from sexual union with him. Rather, she should turn to "another salvation," which is that of the "brotherhood pining in dire distress, scourging and mortifying their flesh."[57] He then adds: "But who can know aright and clear the only true source of salvation?" He also speaks of the "blackness of earthly error, that while feverishly pursuing supreme salvation yet thirsts for the fount of perdition" (*WagPS* 200–201).

Kundry "in wild ecstasy" asks him, "Was it my kiss which made you all-seeing?" She suggests that he should "redeem the world" if that be his destiny and "make yourself a god for an hour" and let her be damned forever. Parsifal says he offers her redemption, which Kundry then assumes can only come through sexual union. Parsifal says that love and redemption shall be hers if she will show him the way to Amfortas. Kundry "breaking out in fury" tells him: "Never shall you find him!" He who "fell by his own Spear" can perish. Parsifal asks who wounded him and Kundry explains that it was "he—he—who once punished my laughter" but whose curse also gives her strength. She threatens to call the spear against Parsifal if he grants Amfortas mercy. Then "beseechingly" she asks for "pity" (Mitleid") that she be his for one hour. He responds "Away unholy woman." Kundry "starting up in a wild fury" calls on Klingsor to "bar his path" and she curses any path that leads away from her. She gives Parsifal into Klingsor's power. Klingsor appears on the rampart brandishing the lance at Parsifal. "Halt! I have the right weapon to fell you! The fool shall fall to me through his master's Spear!" He hurls the spear, which "remains poised above Parsifal's head." Parsifal seizes the spear. He makes the sign of the cross with it and Klingsor's whole domain collapses, the garden withering to a desert. Only

---

56. It is not clear which "God" Kundry is referring to here. It could be the redeemer Christ.

57. On the idea of a celibate knighthood see *WolPH* 251.

Kundry remains and Parsifal tells her that she knows where she will find him. Parsifal then hurries away with the spear (*WagPS* 204–7).

Act Three

The prelude to Act III expresses the long, painful, and lonely struggle of Parsifal. The curtain rises on a scene again in the precincts of the grail, a "pleasant spring landscape." Many years have passed and Gurnemanz is now an old man. He hears groaning and finds Kundry asleep in the thorn bushes.[58] He wakes her (as though out of hibernation) explaining that "Winter has fled, and Spring is here!" (*WagPS* 208–9). As she opens her eyes she screams. She is now in the "coarse robe of a penitent" similar to the one in Act I "but her face is paler and the wildness has vanished from her looks and behaviour." Gurnemanz seems offended that she has no word for him. Kundry then utters these words (her only words in this act): "To serve . . . To serve" ("Dienen . . . Dienen"). Gurnemanz explains that there is now little for her to do. The knights engage in no more missions and they just have to eat herbs and roots,[59] something they have learnt from beasts in the forest. She goes into a hermit's hut and he notices that she moves differently from before (previously she moved like an animal) and wonders whether "the holy day" (Good Friday) has brought about his change. He thinks that he has awoken her on this day for her salvation (*WagPS* 210–11).

Returning from the hut and carrying a water pitcher, Kundry goes to the spring and sees a figure approaching from the distance and points him out to Gurnemanz. He asks: "Who is there approaching the holy spring, in sombre apparel of war?" Parsifal enters wearing black armor "with closed helmet and lowered spear." Gurnemanz asks if he has lost his way; Parsifal shakes his head. "Do you offer me no greeting?" asks Gurnemanz. Parsifal bows his head. Gurnemanz tells him: "Here you are in a hallowed place: no man comes here armed" (*WagPS* 212–13). He asks him if he knows which "holy day" it is. Again Parsifal shakes his head. Gurnemanz tells him that it is "the supremely holy Good Friday." He tells him to lay down his weapons and not to offend the Lord who "bereft of all arms, offered His holy blood to

---

58. This may be the very spot where she went to sleep in Act I.

59. Cf. Wolfram's *Parzival* where, towards the end of book 9, we read that Parzival stayed with Trevrizent (who corresponds to Gurnemanz) for a fortnight: "herbs and roots of necessity were their best fare." Then we read something that anticipates Wagner's Act III: "his host took away his sins and nevertheless counselled him as a knight" (*WolPH* 254).

redeem the sinful world (der sündige Welt)."[60] Parsifal then thrusts his spear
into the ground, lays down his shield and sword, opens his helmet and lays it
down. Gurnemanz then realizes that this figure is the one "who once killed
the swan" and recognizes the holy spear. "O most holy day that I should
awaken to now!" exclaims Gurnemanz (*WagPS* 214–15). Parsifal recognizes
Gurnemanz even though "grief and care" have bowed him so low. Parsifal
explains that he has come "through error and the path of suffering" and
that he seeks to bring salvation to "him whose deep lamenting" he "heard
in foolish wonder." He explains that an evil curse drove him "in trackless
wandering" and he faced "numberless dangers, battles, and conflicts" that
forced him from his path. But he dared not wield the holy spear in conflict (*WagPS* 216–17). He has brought it home "unprofaned." Gurnemanz
rejoices: "O mercy! Bounteous grace! O wonder! Holy, highest wonder!" He
tells Parsifal that if there was a curse driving him from his rightful path, that
its power is broken; for he is in the domain of the grail and the brotherhood,
desperate for healing, awaits him. Amfortas longs only for death. The grail
has remained "enclosed within the shrine" since Amfortas hopes to hasten
his end and "he cannot die while he beholds it." Divine bread is denied and
common food cannot sustain them (*WagPS* 218–19). The "dispirited and
leaderless knighthood wander about, pale and woeful." Even Gurnemanz
awaits death and Titurel, who no longer sees the grail, is dead (*WagPS*
220–21).

Parsifal "springing up in intense grief" believes it is he "who caused
all this woe!" "What transgression, what burden of guilt must my foolish
head have borne from all eternity, since no atonement, no repentance can
free me of my blindness." Parsifal is about to faint; Kundry brings a bowl
of water and is about to sprinkle Parsifal with water but Gurnemanz gently
repulses her. Gurnemanz says that the "holy spring itself shall refresh and
bathe our pilgrim." He suspects that Parsifal will today "fulfil a lofty task"
and "perform the holy Office" (*WagPS* 220–21).

Parsifal asks if he will be led to Amfortas and Gurnemanz tells him that
he will and that "the solemn death rites of my dear lord summon me within,"
which will "sanctify the noble father slain by his son's guilt."[61] Kundry bathes
Parsifal's feet and Gurnemanz sprinkles his head: "May this purity bless you,
pure one! Thus may the load of all guilt be washed away!" Kundry "draws
from her bosom a golden phial and pours part of its contents over Parsifal's
feet, which she then dries with her hastily unbound hair" (*WagPS* 222–23).
Gurnemanz anoints his head to greet him as king. "Pure of heart! Pitying

---

60. Note the use of the singular "Welt" (cf. *WagPS* 142–43).

61. The "death rites" hence refer to Titurel's sanctification.

sufferer, enlightened healer! As you have endured the sufferings of the redeemed, lift the last burden from his head!"[62]

The stage direction explains "Unperceived, Parsifal scoops up water
from the spring" and announces "My first office I thus perform." With the
water he sprinkles Kundry's head and the flute plays the faith motif in F#/
Gb major:[63] "Receive this baptism, and believe in the Redeemer!" The faith
theme then moves to the muted first violins and Kundry "appears to weep
bitterly" (*WagPS* 224–25).[64]

As the music moves into B major[65] Parsifal "gazes in gentle rapture
on wood and meadow, which are now glowing in the morning light." He
observes "[h]ow fair seem the meadows today," to which Gurnemanz says
"This is . . . the magic of Good Friday (Karfreitagszauber)" (*WagPS* 224–25).
Parsifal believes this to be a "day of utmost pain." But Gurnemanz explains
that it is not so. The "tears of repentant sinners . . . besprinkle field and
meadow. . . . Now all creation rejoices at the Saviour's sign of love" (*WagPS*
226–27).[66]

Kundry "looks up at Parsifal with tearful eyes" and he says that those
who mocked him (the flower maidens) he now sees withering and that
they perhaps long for redemption. Kundry's tears are a "dew of blessing"
that makes the meadow smile (*WagPS* 226–27). He kisses her on the fore-
head and a peel of bells is heard in the distance. Gurnemanz announces:
"Midday: the hour has come. My lord, permit your servant to guide you!"
(*WagPS* 228–29).

The scene changes to the hall of the grail. Two processions of knights
enter. In the first Amfortas is carried on a litter, preceded with the covered
shrine with the grail. They ask the second procession whom they carry in
sorrow. It is Titurel they carry; the "conquering weight of years" has laid him
low since he could no longer look upon the grail (*WagPS* 228–29). The one
they carry, Amfortas, the "sinful guardian" of the grail, is to blame. He is to
serve the office for the last time. The coffin is opened and "all utter a sudden
cry of woe" (*WagPS* 230–31). Amfortas confesses that he who longed to
die has brought death upon his father. Since his father now "behold[s] the
Redeemer's very self" he asks his father to call on the Redeemer, to grant

---

62. *WagPS* 224–25. These words are addressed to the redeemer, not Parsifal (see the
discussion in chapter 6 below).

63. The significance of this key will be discussed in chapter 5 below.

64. This scene is discussed in more detail in chapter 5 below.

65. This key has a certain "spiritual" quality in that it is the key of the so-called
"Liebestod" (love-death) of *Tristan* but more appropriately termed Isolde's
"Verklärung" (transfiguration), discussed in chapter 7.

66. This important section will be discussed in chapters 7 and 10 below.

his son repose (*WagPS* 230–33). The knights press upon him to uncover the grail as his father exhorts. Amfortas refuses; he opens his garment and asks the knights to plunge their swords into him. "Slay the sinner with his agony, then once more the Grail shall shine clear on you!" (*WagPS* 232–33).

Parsifal, Gurnemanz, and Kundry appear. Parsifal touches Amfortas' wound with the point of the spear: "But one weapon serves: only the Spear that smote you can heal your wound."[67] Amfortas' face lights up "in holy ecstasy." Parsifal announces that he will now perform his task and tells the knights that he brings back the holy spear; he then uncovers the grail (*WagPS* 234–35). The grail start to glow[68] and the boys, youths, and knights sing the final couplet: "Miracle of supreme salvation! The Redeemer redeemed (Erlösung dem Erlöser)!" As the boys alone sing the high Ab from the highest in the dome,[69] a beam of light shines from above and a white dove descends and hovers over Parsifal's head. Kundry "slowly sinks lifeless to the ground" and Amfortas and Gurnemanz kneel in homage to Parsifal who "waves the Grail in blessing over the worshipping brotherhood of knights" (*WagPS* 236–37).

67. As I noted in chapter 3 above, the essential idea is that the spear bleeds with Christ's blood (see further chapter 6 below).

68. At this point (III.1098–99) a modulation is realized by transforming the grail theme (see the analysis of Lewin, "Tonal Spaces," 345–47, in terms of "Riemann space" and "Stufen space.")

69. III.1120–22; see the close of Paul Verlaine's poem *Parsifal*: "Et, ô ces voix d'enfants chantant dans la coupole!"

5

Encounter with "Christ" in *Parsifal*

Introduction

In this chapter I consider how two of the main characters, Amfortas and Kundry, encounter Christ at specific points in the drama[1] and how the knights of the grail relate to him. In doing so I will be providing a transition between the discussions of the narratives in chapters 3 and 4 and the systematic reflection on theological themes in *Parsifal* (e.g., Christology, atonement, predestination, doctrine of God) in chapters 6 to 10.

Chapter 6 will focus on issues of the "person" and "work" of Christ but for now I want to highlight two essential points about Christ in *Parsifal*. The first is that "Christ" or "Jesus" is never named as such in the work. Rather Wagner employs the terms "Erlöser" (redeemer), "Heiland" (savior), "He on the cross" or simply "Him."[2] However, there can be no doubt that Wagner's redeemer is Christ:[3] the overriding emphasis is that the "redeemer" is the

---

1. A study of Parsifal's encounter with Christ will be reserved for chapter 7 below.

2. Hence I put Christ in quotation marks in the title of this chapter.

3. Contrast Syer, "Grail Scene," 190 n. 9: "Although allusions abound, and Wagner referred to Christ in discussing the work, he clearly did not want to limit the identity of the Redeemer to a singular individual in a conventional religious context." In fact throughout the *Parsifal Companion* (from which this quotation comes) the phrase "the undisclosed redeemer" is used (e.g., Kienzle, "A Christian Music Drama?" 111). Beckett, "Review of A Companion to Wagner's Parsifal," 454, rightly comments: "To pretend even for the sake of argument that the Grail of the opera does not symbolize

one who suffers and dies for humankind on the cross on Good Friday and whose presence is mediated through the Communion of bread and wine! Further, the title "redeemer" is clearly central to Wagner's view of Jesus.[4]

The second point I highlight is how Christ is made present for his followers. This may appear to be a special problem for *Parsifal* since there is no explicit resurrection and hence one cannot say, as in the New Testament, that the risen Christ is *with* his believers (Matt 28:20) or *lives in* the believers (Rom 8:10; Col 1:27). It has sometimes been suggested that in *Parsifal* the only things Christ leaves to mediate his presence on earth are two "relics," the grail and the spear.[5] Wagner actually uses the term "Heiltum" (literally, "saving object")[6] through which the redeemer's presence is mediated: Christ's blood appears miraculously in the grail and the spear can even "bleed" with Christ's blood. We are therefore going beyond the usual concept of "relic," even beyond most of those that supposedly have miraculous powers.[7] But there are two additional ways in which Christ's continued presence is manifest. First, those who belong to the redeemer participate in his being and the redeemer also lives in them (cf. John 15:4), an idea I discuss below. Secondly, the redeemer lives on in the community through the Holy Spirit (the same idea is found in the sketches for *Jesus of Nazareth*).[8] It can be no accident that at the end of the first great chorus in Act I the boys ("Knaben") sing "The faith endures, the dove, the Saviour's loving messenger, hovers" ("Der Glaube lebt; die Taube schwebt, des Heilands holder Bote")[9] to a motif that is usually termed "faith" but could just as easily be called "dove."[10] Further, once Parsifal has achieved his goal at

---

the presence of Christ in the chalice of the Last Supper, or that the crucified redeemer of Good Friday is not the Christ of ordinary Christian belief, is no more than politically correct defiance of common sense."

4. E.g., almost at the beginning of the sketches for *Jesus of Nazareth* Judas tells Barabbas that Jesus "calls himself the Redeemer" (PW 8:285; *DTB* 241: "er selbst nenne sich den erlöser"). On this title, see chapters 7 and 10 below.

5. This is suggested by Kienzle, "A Christian Music Drama?" 111. On the complex traditions of the "grail" see chapters 3 and 10.

6. *WagPS* 122–23.

7. Küng, "Theology for Our Time," 321, points to the twelfth-century traditions of bringing views of the mass and grail traditions together with miracles associated with the host and blood of Christ. It is at this extreme end of the "relic" spectrum that one must place the grail and spear of *Parsifal*.

8. See *PW* 8:297 (*DTB* 246): "Peter feels himself inspired with the Holy Spirit: in high enthusiasm he proclaims the fulfilment of Jesus' promise: his words give strength and inspiration to all."

9. *WagPS* 144–45.

10. *FTG* theme 11.

the end of the work, the Holy Spirit in the form of a dove descends from on high. The significance of this dove has often been neglected such that in many productions it is simply omitted.[11] But its rôle is quite fundamental since it suggests how Christ is going to be present with the community of knights once the curtain comes down.

I turn to consider how two main characters, Amfortas and Kundry, encounter Christ, and then finally consider how the knights of the grail are related to their savior. The focus will be on the issue of participation; discussion of the role of the Holy Spirit will be discussed in a later chapter.

Amfortas

To some extent Amfortas is a representative of Christ and is identified mystically with him despite his "fall." This identification is partly seen by the fact that Amfortas is wounded with the very spear that was thrust into Christ's side and partly because Amfortas has a wound in his side, a wound that hence corresponds to that of Christ.[12] However, his participation in Christ is not one such that he can be redeemed, as can be discerned in his monologue in Act I. Here he declares that *in his view* it is only through repentance that he can reach the redeemer:[13]

11. Wieland Wagner intended such an omission in his "dechristianized" 1951 Bayreuth production, but Hans Knappertsbusch said he would refuse to conduct if the dove were not included. Wieland did then allow the descent of the dove but only to such a height that the conductor was the only one to see it. Cf. Nike Wagner, *Wagners*, 142.

12. See Amfortas' words, "the wound, like His, struck by a blow from that same Spear which pierced the Saviour" (quoted in context below). According to Wolfram, the spear is thrust into Amfortas' scrotum. As Trevrizent explains to Parzival: "Jousting, he was wounded by a poisoned lance so seriously that he never recovered, your dear uncle—through the scrotum (heidruose)" (*WolPH* 244; 479.12). Simrock has "Schambein" ("pubic bone"). However, San-Marte left "heidruose" untranslated (presumably to avoid offense): "Jedoch verwundet ward auch er / Durch seines Gegners giftigen Speer" (Mertens, "Wagners Gral," 105). Wagner most likely located the wound in Amfortas' side in order to parallel the wound inflicted on Christ. It is unlikely that he changed it simply because of any nineteenth-century sensibilities.

13. *WagPS* 146–47 (note that much of this rhymes, indicated by emphasis).

O punishment, unparalleled punishment	O Strafe, Strafe *ohnegleichen*
of—ah!—the wronged Lord of mercy!	des—ach!—gekränkten *Gnadenreichen*!
For him, for His holy greeting,	Nach ihm, nach seinem <u>Weihegruße</u>,
must I ardently yearn;	muß sehnlich mich's *verlangen*;
by the repentance of my inmost soul	aus tiefster Seele <u>Heilesbuße</u>
must I reach Him.	zu ihm muß ich *gelangen*.

But although here he thinks repentance will help him it is significant that Amfortas is *not* brought near to the redeemer through repentance,[14] and in fact he comes to see it just a few lines later (*WagPS* 146–49): "and now from my wound . . . spills forth the fevered blood of sin, ever renewed from the fount of longing that—ah! no repentance of mine can ever still!"[15] Repentance can bring no healing (physical and spiritual) to Amfortas; it is only through the application of the spear that Parsifal recovers (and from which Christ's blood flows) that he is healed and redeemed (at the end of Act III). Likewise Kundry is not helped by repentance.[16] The limitation of such repentance will have important implications for the understanding of "grace" in *Parsifal*.[17]

In between these two passage quoted above, we have a crucial section where, through the remarkable combination of text and music, Amfortas expresses his agony:[18]

---

14. Note, however, that in Act III Gurnemanz also says that Amfortas is "repentant of his sin" (*WagPS* 218–19).

15. This is further discussed in chapter 6 below.

16. See below.

17. See chapter 8 below.

18. *WagPS* 146–47 (modified; again I have indicated the rhyming pattern by emphasis).

The hour draws near:	Die Stunde naht:
a ray of light descends upon the holy vessel:	ein Lichtstrahl senkt sich auf das heilige Werk:
the covering falls.	die Hülle fällt.
The divine contents of the sacred chalice	Des Weihgefäßes göttlicher *Gehalt*
glow with radiant glory;	erglüht mit leuchtender *Gewalt*;
thrilled by the agony of ecstasy,	durchzückt von seligsten Genusses Schmerz,
I feel the fount of divine blood	des heiligsten Blutes *Quell*
pour into my heart:	fühl' ich sich gießen in mein Herz:
the ebb of my own sinful blood	des eig'nen sündigen Blutes *Gewell'*
in mad tumult	in wahnsinniger *Flucht*
must surge back into me,	muß mir zurück dann fließen,
to gush in wild terror	in die Welt der Sünden*sucht*
into the world of sinful passion:	mit wilder Scheu sich ergießen:
it breaks open the door anew	von neuem sprengt es das *Tor*,
and now rushes out	daraus es nun strömt her*vor*,
here, through the wound, like His,	hier, durch die Wunde, der seinen *gleich*,
struck by a blow from that same Spear	geschlagen von desselben Speeres *Streich*,
which pierced the Redeemer,	der dort dem Erlöser die Wunde stach,
from whose wound the Holy One wept tears of blood for man's disgrace	aus der mit blutgen *Tränen* der Göttliche weint' ob der Menschheit Schmach
in the heavenly yearning of pity.	in Mitleid's heiligem *Sehnen*.

In chapter 3 above I noted that Wagner wrote in his letter to Mathilde Wesendonck that the suffering figure of Amfortas is the "third-act Tristan inconceivably intensified" ("Tristan des dritten Aktes mit einer undenklichen Steigerung").[19] I will return to this in chapter 7 below, but for now I note that the suffering of Tristan in Act III is "inconceivably intensified" in the figure of Amfortas not through his physical or psychological suffering but in his spiritual agony, an agony that he shares with the suffering Christ who "wept tears of blood."[20] He has a conviction of sin that is simply absent

19. *SL* 457; *SB* 11:104.

20. On this line, cf. Luke 22:44: "In his anguish he prayed more earnestly, and his sweat became like great drops of blood falling down on the ground." Luke 22:43–44 is omitted in important ancient manuscripts but is in Luther's Bible.

in *Tristan* Act III. But despite the differences between the suffering of Tristan and Amfortas it is striking that Tristan's desperation reaches a climax when he curses the draught and blames himself for brewing it (*WagTS* 142):

Accursed be that fearful draught	Den ich *gebraut,*
that I brewed,	der mir <u>geflossen,</u>
that flowed into me,	den wonneschlürfend
that I quaffed	je ich <u>genossen</u>—
with endless delight,	verflucht sei, furchtbarer Trank!
and accursed be he who brewed	Verflucht, wer dich *gebraut!*
it!	

The stage direction adds: "He sinks back unconscious" ("Er sinkt ohnmächtig zurück"). Both Tristan and Amfortas suffer because of a "cup." Tristan's words, "Accursed be that fearful draught that I brewed, that flowed into me," can be compared with those of Amfortas: "I feel the fount of divine blood in mad tumult must surge back into me." Tristan's cup of suffering is one that leads to an erotic passion that cannot be quenched and can only be fulfilled in death; Amfortas' cup of suffering is the cup that Christ had to drink. In Gethsemane Jesus, aware of his coming agonising death, prayed: "Abba, Father, for you all things are possible; remove this cup from me; yet, not what I want, but what you want" (Mark 14:36).[21] And here we find the idea of Christ's identification with humanity, something that artists, composers, and playwrights have tried to express in their works.[22]

As we saw above Amfortas' identification with Christ is focused on the wound they both share. But in itself it is not a redemptive identification, which we will see elsewhere in *Parsifal*.[23] Nevertheless there is also a note of consolation for Amfortas. As Wagner writes to Mathilde Wesendonck: "*he* [Amfortas], infected by the same wound as was dealt him by a rival's spear in a passionate love intrigue,—his only solace lies in the benediction of the blood that once flowed from the Saviour's own, similar, spear wound as He

---

21. The "cup of suffering" (and "cup of judgement") has a rich Old Testament background. See also Mark 10:38.

22. One of the most remarkable artworks to express this identification is the crucifixion by Matthias Grünewald (1470–1528) in his Isenheim Altarpiece, a triple-transforming polyptych (Hayum, *Isenheim Altarpiece*, plate 7). The remarkable central painted panels of the "closed state" show a suffering Christ who fully identifies with human pain (it was displayed on the high altar in the chapel of the Antonite house, a hospital dedicated to those afflicted with "Saint Anthony's Fire"). On Wagner's exalted view of religious painting, especially of the crucifixion, see chapter 11 below.

23. See below on Kundry and the knights of the grail.

languished upon the Cross."[24] It is only at the very end of the drama that he experiences a saving identification with Christ as the redeemer's blood is infused into his veins by the holy spear.[25]

Kundry

Wagner formed his Kundry out of various characters from Wolfram: Cundrie la sorcière, Orgeluse, Sigune, and even an element of Trevrizent.[26] Another way of approaching her psychological and ontological constitution is to consider the names Klingsor gives here at the beginning of Act II: "nameless one, primaeval witch, rose of hell! You were Herodias, and what else? Gundryggia there, Kundry here" ("Namenlose, Urteufelin! Höllenrose! Herodias warst du, und was noch? Gundryggia dort, Kundry hier") (*WagPS* 156–57). She is not directly related in the libretto to the "wandering Jew" Ahasuerus;[27] but Wagner did make the connection in his prose sketch of 1865 by describing her as an "eternal Jew"[28] and in the final stagework depicts her as someone who is "endlessly [afflicted] through this existence" ("endlos durch das Dasein quält") (*WagPS* 198–99).

The figure of the wandering Jew was not always entirely negative. For example Matt 16:28 and John 21:20–23 were used to found the legend.[29] That the figure is not entirely negative in Wagner's own mind is seen in the

---

24. *SL* 457; *SB* 11:105 (letter of 30 May 1859).

25. See chapter 6 below.

26. In addition there are elements of Mary Magdalene and Savitri (see chapter 3 above).

27. This legend first appeared in its definitive form in a pamphlet of 1602, "Kurtze Beschreibung und Erzählung von einem Juden mit Namen Ahasverus" (Jacobs, "Wandering Jew," 462). Ahasuerus was a Jerusalem shoemaker who, on taunting Jesus on the way to the crucifixion, was told by Jesus: "go on forever till I return." He is therefore a doomed sinner without the hope of the rest of death until Christ returns.

28. *BB* 54: "Kundry is living a never-ending life of constantly alternating re-births as the result of an ancient curse which, in a manner reminiscent of the Wandering Jew, condemns here, in new shapes, to bring to men the suffering of seduction." *DEAP* 72: "Kundry lebt ein unermeßliches Leben unter stets wechselnden Wiedergeburten, in Folge einer uralten Verwünschung, die sie, ähnlich dem 'ewigen Juden', dazu verdammt, in neuen Gestalten das Leiden der Liebesverführung über die Männer zu bringen."

29. Matt 16:28: "Truly I tell you, there are some standing here who will not taste death before they see the Son of Man coming in his kingdom." The use of this in the pamphlet of 1602 goes beyond its use in Matthew's Gospel. John 21:20–23 concerns the rumor that the beloved disciple would live until Jesus returns.

person of the Flying Dutchman[30] who is eventually redeemed[31] and the fact that Wagner himself identified with this figure.[32] However, there were negative portrayals of the wandering Jew. Eugène Sue in his influential *Juif errant* (1844) had Herodias accompanying Ahasuerus "restlessly throughout history until, like Wagner's Kundry, she finds redemption."[33] We do not know whether Wagner knew this work.[34] But he was most likely directly influenced by Heinrich Heine's *Atta Troll* who combined the figures of Herodias and Salome[35] and Wagner's Kundry is probably a reincarnation of both.[36] However, the parallel cannot be pushed too far since Kundry is sometimes represented as a "pagan":[37] the Fourth Squire says "She's a heathen, a sorceress" ("Eine Heidin ist's, ein Zauberweib") (*WagPS* 118–19).[38] Although the term "pagan" is popularly used for a non-Christian, it is strictly used for a non-Jew, something Wagner would know from his Luther Bible (e.g., Rom 3:29). Further, in Wolfram the terms "heathen" and "infidel" are used of Muslims.[39]

Klingsor's negative naming of Kundry functions rather as a "speech act"[40] and a "negative baptism."[41] He takes on the role of "accuser" (cf. Job; Zech 3). However, the way Wagner constitutes Kundry is much more complex. First of all, she is part human and part animal, and he was no doubt influenced here by Wolfram's portrayal of Cundrie: "[H]er nose was like a dog's, and to the length of several spans a pair of tusks jutted from her jaws."

30. Borchmeyer, "*Der fliegende Holländer* und seine Metamorphosen."

31. See also the illustrations of Gustave Doré in Schreckenberg, *Jews in Christian Art*, 295, of the redeemed wandering Jew.

32. *SB* 11:137.

33. Borchmeyer, "Recapitulation," 12.

34. It is in neither his Dresden nor Wahnfried library. We do know, however, that he admired Sue's book *Joan of Arc*. See *CD* 24 June 1872 and 24 October 1873.

35. Borchmeyer, "Recapitulation," 12. See also Prawer, *Heine*, 67–68.

36. Borchmeyer, "Recapitulation," 12.

37. Borchmeyer, "Kundrys Lachen," 449.

38. Note also that she represents unredeemed nature, something related to her "animal" characteristics discussed below. See Borchmeyer, "Kundrys Lachen," 449: "Kundry verkörpert die heidnische, die noch unerlöste Natur."

39. See, e.g., Hatto in *WolPH* 21, who equates "heathendom" with Morocco and Persia. The "infidel order" gets its "papal law from Baghdad" (20). See chapter 10 below.

40. See the discussion in Bell, *Deliver Us from Evil* (following the index entry to "speech acts/events," 439).

41. The issue of the "power" of words is controversial. E.g., there is disagreement as to whether Adam's naming the animals in Gen 2:19 is "an exercise of sovereignty" (von Rad, *Genesis*, 83); contrast Westermann, *Genesis 1–11*, 228: "The meaning is not . . . that man acquires power over the animals by naming them."

Her ears "resembled a bear's" and her face was "rugged." Her nails "looked like a lion's claws" (*WolPH* 163–64). We see Wagner writing of Kundry's animal characteristics in his letter to Mathilde Wesendonck of August 1860. He writes of Kundry's "serving the Holy Grail with dog-like devotion." She does not know what she is searching for; "it is purely instinctive." "[S]trange are the things that must go on inside her"; "she clings to him [Parzival]"; she "suffers unspeakable restlessness and excitement." And then he makes it clear: "Cowering in a corner, she witnesses Anfortas' agonized scene: she gazes with a strangely inquisitive look (sphinx-like) at Parzival."[42] This sphinx-like character, half-animal, half-human, is found in the final libretto of Act I. First Squire: "Has she flown through the air?" Second Squire: "Now she's crawling on the ground." First Squire: "And her mane is sweeping the moss" (*WagPS* 111). Then a little later the squires taunt her. Third Squire: "Hey, you there! Why do you lie there like a wild beast?" (*WagPS* 117). Further, elements of the libretto suggest that she "hibernates"[43] and that her "wanderings" are related to the seasons.[44] In addition to this sphinx-like nature Wagner characterizes her as both bad and good. She mocked the crucified Christ, seduces chaste knights, but at the same time she serves the holy grail with "dog-like devotion" (could this dog-loving composer offer higher praise?). Wagner's view of Kundry reflects St. Paul's nuanced assessment of human plight in Rom 7:7–25: although in desperate need of redemption (Rom 7:24), the human being is *both* a good creation of God (7:22) *and* a slave to sin (7:14b).[45] Further, Paul's point is not so much that this contradiction is *within* the human person but rather that the human being *is* the contradiction.[46] Sometimes Wagner's portrayal of Kundry approaches Paul's profound understanding of the human condition.

I now turn to our specific question: how does Kundry encounter Christ? One of her fundamental characteristics is that she flies through time. This is implied by Klingsor's call at the beginning of Act II and it is also clear in Gurnemanz's narration in Act I. And since she flies through time she was the one character of the stage work to encounter the earthly Jesus.

42. *SL* 500; Golther, *Mathilde Wesendonk*, 244.

43. See the stage direction at the beginning of Act III where Gurnemanz finds Kundry asleep in "a densely overgrown thorn thicket" and drags her out "quite stiff and lifeless" (*WagPS* 208–9).

44. Borchmeyer, "Kundrys Lachen," 449: "Kundry hält ja regelmäßig einen förmlichen Winterschlaf."

45. In Wagner's New Testament Rom 7:4–5, 7–25 was marked with a single vertical line in the margin; Rom 7:6 was marked with double vertical lines (quoted in the Jesus of Nazareth sketches, *PW* 8:332; *DTB* 263).

46. See Bell, "Reading Romans," 49–51, and the literature cited there.

Her mocking of Christ is partly based on the legends of the "eternal Jew." In most of the traditions this Jew is unkind (to a greater or lesser extent) as Jesus is *on the way to the cross*.[47] Those conversant with the legend can therefore tend to interpret this scene as Kundry laughing at Christ on the via dolorosa.[48] However, in *Parsifal* Kundry laughs at Christ *as he hung on the cross*,[49] something Wagner makes clear by the music as we shall see.

According to the notes made by Porges, as Kundry recalls the encounter, she falls into a trance as in a dream.[50] "I saw Him—Him—and laughed (mocked) . . . His gaze fell upon me!" ("Ich sah ihn—ihn—und lachte . . . da traf mich sein Blick"). These utterances are related to the music in an intricate way. In II.1175 the timpani play "very quiet, but heavy" ("sehr leise, aber schwer"). This rhythm is used elsewhere by Wagner to express death, indeed a violent death, of the heros Siegmund and Siegfried (see *Walküre and Götterdämmerung*).[51] This rhythm is found again in 1177, 1179–80, 1189–90, and clearly alludes to the violent death of Christ.[52] Then in 1176 the bass clarinet plays a motif that is related to suffering. This short motif

47. For depictions in art of the "wandering Jew" see Schreckenberg, *Jews in Christian Art*, 291–96. So in an image of the thirteenth-century English Benedictine Matthew Paris, Cartaphilus (a precursor of Ahasuerus) hits Jesus on the way to the cross and tells him to go more quickly (291). In a late eighteenth-century French woodcut we see the eternal Jew as a cobbler who did not let Jesus rest at his house on the way to Calvary (292). Then the cycle of illustrations by Gustave Doré for the poem by Pierre Dupont (1856) again shows the eternal Jew as a Jerusalem cobbler (294). But there is also an image of him passing the crucified Christ (295). These illustrations "made a deep impression in its time" (294). Wagner met Doré in Paris in 1861. *CD* 19 October 1878 tells of how Doré's "retreat of the 10,000" (based on Xenophon's *Anabasis*) "gives him great pleasure" and that "he remembers Doré with pleasure." *CD* 25 July 1879 tells that "R. much admires" Doré's illustrations (although he did not like those for Cervantes *Don Quixote*; see the entry for 16 June 1869). Cosima possessed a copy of Doré's illustrated Bible (*CD* 24 April and 5 September 1870).

48. See Borchmeyer, "Kundrys Lachen," 447: "Wie der ewige Jude Ahasver nach der bekanntesten Version der mittelalterlichen Legende dem *kreuztragenden* Jesus verwehrte, sich auf seinem *Leidensweg* aufzuruhen und ihn mit einem Schlag zu Eile anspornte, so hat Kundry Jesus auf dem *Kreuzweg* verlacht" (my emphasis).

49. For example Holloway, "Music and Imagery," 42, rightly speaks of "the laughter at Christ on His cross."

50. *DEAP* 206: "Hier wird sie ganz entrückt, wie im Traum."

51. We also hear something similar in Act I just after Titurel calls on Amfortas: "Amfortas, my son, are you in your place?" ("Mein Sohn Amfortas, bist du am Amt?"; *WagPS* 144–45). See I.1248–49, 1253, 1257.

52. See *CD* 3 October 1881: "[Richard] goes to his desk and asks my father whether he has ever used the kettledrum below F. My father says no, since it does not sound right, but R. says he will use it all the same, and he whispers in my ear the passage for which he needs it: '*ich sah ihn—ihn*.'" However, Wagner only writes below F in II.1189–90 (going down to E).

Example 1: Kundry's Recollection of Her Encounter with Christ

occurs repeatedly earlier in the Act when Kundry relates to Parsifal how his mother died (896–901, 907–8) (it is also used in Parsifal's response, 923–25; 933–35; 947–53). She died of a broken heart and hence her name

"Herzeleide" ("heart's sorrow"). Perhaps this music is pointing to this *feeling* of "heart's sorrow"? The motif is a "turn" and a similar turn occurs in the "savior's lament" ("Heilandsklage").[53]

Then in bars 2.1177–82 we have muted 'cellos, third clarinet, and cor anglais playing the first half of the "love feast" or "Communion" motif. This motif occurs right at the beginning of *Parsifal* and forms an arch. It can be analyzed into smaller components and the part at the very top of the arch (c) is associated with suffering.

Example 2: Love Feast Theme

In this passage in Act II two changes are made to this theme. First, Wagner gives the minor key version. Secondly, and this is highly significant, when we get to the suffering element of the motif it somehow gets stuck on this and repeats it three times in measures 1179–81: it is unable to progress much further and complete the whole motif.[54] Then in 1181–82 there is a triplet-like motif on flutes, oboes, and clarinets in thirds and sixths. A related rhythm is found earlier when Kundry tells of the death of Parsifal's mother (II.915ff) but in unison.[55] The violins then play a Kundry motif (1182–83), often associated with her seductive qualities (note the highly chromatic nature of this motif). In m. 1183 we have the "laughing motif," rising demi-semi quavers on the flutes and piccolo, which Kundry completes with virtually a two octave downward leap "lach-te" ("laughed.")[56] In mm. 1184–85 we have the suffering (Wehelaut) motif (clarinets and second violins moving to 'cellos and violas, playing descending thirds). In measures

53. On Wagner's use of the "turn" see chapter 7 below.

54. Compare mm. 100–101 towards the end of the Prelude to Act I. Note also the undulating figure in the "Good Friday music" (III.687–88). See also the music when Kundry kisses Parsifal in Act II and its relation to the Prelude to Act I of *Tristan* (discussed in chapter 7 below).

55. It may be significant that the rising grail theme is made of sixths (in the second half of the second measure). The grail is clearly associated with the blood of Christ.

56. This laughing motif occurs first at II.225–26, accompanying Klingsor's "accursed witch" ("Verfluchtes Weib!"). But there the leap downwards is just a minor seventh (*FTG* theme 34d, gives the first part of this laughing motif but the falling interval of the minor seventh is not given). Here at II.1183 Wagner adds a further octave to the descent.

1185–88 the 'cellos play the "Heilandsklage" theme I discussed above. This includes a semi-tone interval from A# to B (m. 1188) that accompanies Kundry's words "sein Blick," "his look." This semi-tone interval is used in *Tristan* to signify the "Blick" of desire or yearning. It is striking that Wagner uses exactly the same notes found in *Tristan*, A# to B. Christ looks into Kundry's eyes and thereby looks into her very soul. It has been said that one of the clearest expressions of the soul is the eyes through which "one can read the soul and know whether it contains something good or evil."[57]

Then in m. 1192 there is something that is hardly perceptible: a four note chord on the three trombones and bass tuba in the form of the so-called "Tristan chord" F B D# G#. Although this chord was used by earlier composers,[58] it took on a "rootless" and highly significant quality for Wagner and came to be called the "Tristan chord" because of its use in *Tristan und Isolde* (it is the very first chord of the Prelude to Act I, m. 3); it is followed by the "look motif" (A#–B) discussed above.

Example 3: Prelude to Act I of *Tristan und Isolde*

Tristan und Isolde concerns an erotic love so intense and so overwhelming that it can only be consummated in death. The Tristan chord here in m. 1192 appears almost imperceptibly (it is marked pp, pianissimo) and he uses exactly the same notes as in *Tristan*: F B D# G#.[59] Millington suggests that the use of the chord "brings the religious and the sexual into close proximity."[60] This is rather ambiguous and perhaps deliberately so: there is

57. Pedersen, *Israel I–II*, 175. In a different context Hegel wrote: "if we ask in which particular organ the whole soul appears as soul, we will at once name the eye; for in the eye the soul is concentrated and the soul does not merely see through it but is seen in it" (Hegel, *Aesthetics: Lectures on Fine Art*, 1:153, quoted by Scruton, *Death-Devoted Heart*, 213 n. 5). On the "look" see Sartre, *Being*, 393–98; Merleau-Ponty, *Perception*.

58. See Danuser, "Tristanakkord," 840–41. See, e.g., Beethoven's Piano Sonata No. 18 in Eb Major, op. 31 no. 3, first movement, measures 36, 38.

59. As in the case of the "sein Blick" A#–B, there is in theory a one in twelve chance of having these particular pitches.

60. Millington, *Wagner*, 263. He adds: "Redemption also has its erotic aspect."

indeed a danger in trying to tie Wagner down by labelling "leitmotifs"[61] or, in this case, a single chord. But nevertheless I think one can be more precise in this instance. I think it unlikely that the chord points to Kundry's sexual attraction to the suffering Christ;[62] more likely is that it points to Christ's love for Kundry (and this raises the interesting theological question as to whether *eros* and *agape* can be so easily separated).[63] Related to this is that the chord presents a *desire* for union between Christ and Kundry, something that Christ initiates (note the emphasis on "*sein* Blick")[64] but which Kundry cannot "receive."[65] (This interpretation finds some support in the production of Otto Schenk from the Metropolitan Opera, Kundry being played by Waltraud Meier.) Another significant aspect of the use of the chord is the use of the three trombones and bass tuba, the instrumentation of a "trombone choir" ("Posaunenchor"), popular in German church music.[66] Wagner is suggesting a "sacred erotic love."[67]

61. Wagner never used the term "leitmotif"; rather he spoke of "melodic moments of feeling." Nevertheless there are instances in which he did "label" motifs. Cooke, "Musical Language," 227, asserts: "He never intended his music to convey the conceptual idea of the drama." This, however, is not always true as Deathridge, "Reviews," 84, establishes.

62. Compare Salome's sexual obsession with Jokanaan in Strauss' *Salome*.

63. See the discussion in chapter 7 below.

64. Kundry's words "da traf mich sein Blick" have an interesting parallel in Luke 22:61, where Jesus "turned and looked at Peter" after he had denied him three times (this is only in Luke). Wagner adopts this Lucan version of Peter's denial in his sketches for *Jesus of Nazareth*, Act V: "Jesus calls 'Peter' ('Simon')—he looks round, is horrified at sight of Jesus, covers his face, and plunges down the steps and out" (*PW* 8:294); "Jesus ruft: 'Petrus' ('Simon')—der blickt sich um, erschrickt bei Jesus' anblick, verhüllt sein gesicht und stürzt über die treppe hinab fort" (*DTB* 245).

65. I use the verb "receive" rather than "accept" to suggest that she has no free decision here. On this issue see chapter 8 below.

66. Ahrens, "Posaunenchor," 1752, points out that the Posaunenchor originated in the Herrnhüter congregation. Joh. A. Hiller in 1768 reports that the then cantor of the Leipzig Thomas Church, Joh. Fr. Doles, used a "choir of trombones" to strengthen the choir of singers and to join the episodes of singing. It also looks as though descant trombones were also in use in Leipzig at the time that Wagner was there growing up.

67. Another possibility is that the Tristan chord points simply to some "mystical" aspect. Note its use in a negative sense in I.468 (use of the "magic motif"; *FTG* theme 4). Lorenz, *Parsifal*, 29–45, writes of the "mystic chord" ("Der mystische Akkord"), the diminished chord with an added minor seventh (C Eb Gb Bb) from which one can derive the Tristan chord (placing the Eb an octave higher). Such a chord is common in *Parsifal*; by "inversion" Lorenz arrives at four "Klangstellungen" and the rough uses of each are: 1. Klangstellung (i.e., root position) around 600 times; 2. Klangstellung (first inversion) over 250 times; 3. Klangstellung (second inversion) around 150 times; 4. Klangstellung (third inversion) around eighty times (31). So common is the chord that he thinks it significant when it is not used, and in such cases he thinks it points to "Klarheit und Helle" (clarity and brightness).

After this remarkable passage, Kundry expresses her wish to encounter the savior: "Now I seek Him from world to world to meet Him once again" ("Nun such' ich ihn von Welt zu Welt ihm wieder zu begegnen").[68] But she is powerless; even repentance cannot help her.[69] Yet although she cannot be in "union" with Christ, she can, perhaps, be in "union" with Parsifal. She expresses this wish just before this passage: "If you are a redeemer, what maliciously stops you from uniting with me for my salvation?" ("Bist du Erlöser, was bannt dich, Böser, nicht mir auch zum Heil dich zu einen?") (II.1135–42). She also repeats it afterwards: "let me weep upon his [Christ's] breast, for one hour only be united to you and though God and the world disown me, through you I can be cleansed of sin and redeemed" ("laß' mich an seinem Busen weinen, nur eine Stunde mich dir vereinen, und, ob mich Gott und Welt verstößt, in dir entsündigt sein und erlöst!") (II.1259–66).[70] She sets up Parsifal as a substitute for Christ.

The redemption of Kundry and her union with Christ does come but not until Act III when she is baptized by Parsifal. From III.570–607 Wagner uses the key signature of B major, the last four bars of which correspond to Parsifal's announcement "My first office I thus perform" (*WagPS* 224–25); he also uses this key signature for the first part of the Good Friday Music (III.628–64). Between these two sections we have Kundry's baptism (III.608–27) for which Wagner uses the key signature of Ab major, the home key of the whole work. As this section begins the flute plays the faith/dove theme in Gb major (six flats, here using flat accidentals). But the enharmonic key of F# major (six sharps) is also suggested by the surrounding key of B major. Wagner rarely does things by accident, and one wonders whether this F#/Gb ambiguity is pointing to some sort of "transcendence."[71]

68. One may compare Wagner's words in *Religion and Art* that to hope for redemption is to seek union with him (*PW* 6:214; *GSD* 10:213; *JA* 10:119), discussed in chapter 8 below.

69. "I cannot weep, can only shout, rage, storm, rave in an ever-renewed night of madness from which, though repentant, I scarcely wake" ("ich . . . kann nicht weinen, nur Schreien, wüten, toben, rasen in stets erneueter Wahsinns Nacht, aus der ich büßend kaum erwacht") (*WagPS* 198–99).

70. *WagPS* 198–99.

71. One could compare his use of enharmonics in *Das Liebesmahl der Apostel*. In bars 265 and 268 there is a rising theme like the holy grail theme (but without the sixths) of *Parsifal* set to the words "heiligen Geist" ("Holy Spirit") and in m. 274 we have a chord on the words "Geist," the first minim written as an F# major chord (F# A# C# F# A#) and tied to a crotchet written as a Gb major chord (Gb Bb Db Gb Bb). He may have written it this way to help singers get used to the flat key (mm. 241–92 have the Bb major key signature). But whatever the case, can it be fortuitous that it is precisely when he puts music to "send' uns Unmündigen deinen heiligen Geist" ("send us children your Holy Spirit"; note that Luther translates *nēpios* as "unmündig" [Matt 11:25; 21:16;

The faith theme in the "transcendent" key of F#/Gb major then moves into Ab on the muted first violins (III.615–20) as Kundry "bows her head to the ground and appears to weep bitterly" (*WagPS* 224–25). Then as she is baptized there is the "annihilating sound" of death. Cosima in her entry for 3 February 1879 writes: "[Richard] plays for me . . . the baptism of Kundry with the annihilating sound of the kettledrum: 'Obliteration of the whole being, of all earthly desire,' says R." Wagner said "the entry of the kettledrum in G . . . is the finest thing I have ever done." It so happens that in the final score the G is played by not by the timpani but by muted 'cellos and double basses.[72] But the main point to note is that the rhythm outlined is that of the first half of the grail motif.[73] Wagner clearly wants to show how Kundry's baptism is related to death (denial of the will-to-life) and the hints of the grail theme may allude to the blood of Christ that "appears" in it. Added to this is the "Heilandsklage" theme in mm. 624–25.[74]

Gal 4:1, 3]) that he employs F#/Gb major (cf. the "dove" theme in *Parsifal* III.608–15)?

72. Cosima's entry of 3 February 1879 was written just after Wagner had completed the second draft; Wagner may have changed his mind in the final orchestration because of technical issues (it would be difficult for the timpani to tune to the low G here—at the previous entry it is tuned to F sharp (III.601) and at the subsequent entry to F [III.705–6]). I am grateful to John Deathridge for a personal communication on this issue (23 October 2009).

73. Deathridge, "Strange Love," 173.

74. Note the crucial (and subtle) juxtaposition of the "Heilandsklage" and the grail theme in the "Transformation Music" (I.1111, 1113).

Example 4: Kundry's Baptism

Kundry's baptism is therefore her "death." Such a view is often related to the Schopenhauerian "denial of the will," a view that Wagner obviously had in mind in view of Cosima's entry. But there is another element that has influenced both Schopenhauer and Wagner, and that is the New Testament idea that baptism involves a death with Christ, expressed by Paul in Rom 6:3: "Do you not know that all of us who have been baptized into Christ Jesus were baptized into his death." Further, this baptism involves a union with Christ, implied already in verse 3 ("baptized into Christ Jesus") but also made explicit in verse 5a: "For if we have been united with him in a death like his . . ." Paul goes on in verse 5b to speak of being united with Christ "in a resurrection like his." Since Wagner appears to bracket out the resurrection, all his emphasis on union with Christ is on his death in which believers participate.

Some confirmation that Wagner is relating Kundry's baptism to union with Christ is found in III.620 where we find a chord that is almost the "Tristan chord" (F B D# G#): F C D#(Eb) G#(Ab). The precise Tristan chord is given later in Act III in the Good Friday Music (III.705) as Gurnemanz is just about to sing "Ihn selbst am Kreuze kann sie nicht erschauen" ("He Himself on the cross can she [nature] not see"). This chord is played on the timpani and double basses (giving F B) and on the flutes, oboes, etc. (giving D# G#); and, as in Kundry's baptism, the timpani and double basses also outline the grail theme but in an even briefer form.

Example 5: Gurnemanz's Witness to Christ Crucified

Kundry's union with Christ therefore occurs at her baptism but it can be said to be finally consummated at her death right at the end of the drama. This is a difficult issue and one to which I will return.

Knights of the Grail

Although no final "redemption" is achieved until the very end of the work, the knights of the grail nevertheless belong to Christ and have union with him.[75] One way this union is achieved is through the Eucharist. In Act I the blood of Christ appears in the grail miraculously. After "Take this My blood, take My Body, in remembrance of Me!" ("Nehmet hin mein Blut, nehmet hin meinen Leib, auf daß ihr mein gedenkt!"), there is this stage direction: "Here a dazzling ray of light falls from above on the crystal cup, which now glows in a brilliant crimson, shedding a soft light on everything" ("Hier dringt ein blendender Lichtstrahl von oben auf die Kristallschale herab; diese erglüht sodann immer stärker in leuchtender Purpurfarbe, alles sanft bestrahlend").[76] After the blood thus "appears" in the grail, the stage direction runs as follows: "Amfortas, transfigured, raises the Grail aloft and waves it gently round to every side, blessing the bread and wine with it. All are on their knees" ("Amfortas, mit verklärter Miene, erhebt den 'Gral' hoch und schwenkt ihm sanft nach allen Seiten, worauf er damit Brot und Wein segnet. Alles ist auf den Knien").[77] This ritual which Amfortas performs is the consecration of the elements whereby bread and wine are transubstantiated into Christ's body and blood.[78] It is significant that just a little earlier the stage becomes dark and may allude to the "night" of Tristan (i.e., the noumenal realm).[79] But then, after Titurel's "O heavenly rapture! How

75. This therefore puts a question mark against those productions that portray the knights in an extremely negative light.

76. *WagPS* 150–51; I.1469–70. Cf. Amfortas' words, quoted above: "The divine contents of the sacred chalice glow with radiant glory" ("Des Weihgefäßes göttlicher Gehalt erglüht mit leuchtender Gewalt" (*WagPS* 146–47; I.1348–51).

77. *WagPS* 150–51; I.1472–75.

78. Essentially the same view is put forward in the notes made on the first Bayreuth productions with slightly different wording: "Amfortas . . . erhebt nun den Gral und schwenkt denselben langsam nach beiden Seiten der Halle, gerade so, wie der Priester mit der Monstranze das Volk segnet. In dem Momente, als Amfortas den Gral erfaßt, ergreifen die Knappen zu beiden Seiten die Weinkrüge und Brotgefäße und halten sie zum Segen hoch empor" (*DEAP* 146). Wagner had attended Communion with greater regularity when composing *Parsifal* (see, e.g., the report of his final meeting with Nietzsche in Sorrento, discussed in chapter 10 below), although how regular one cannot say. Also although a convinced Protestant, in 1865 after the birth of his first daughter Isolde, Wagner held a series of discussions with the Catholic priest Petrus Hamp; among the issues discussed was the doctrine of transubstantiation and the eucharistic rite. See Hamp, *Geisteswerkstatt Richard Wagners*, 14 (cited in *DEAP* 20). Note also that Wagner's Wahnfried library contained a rich collection of the mystery plays of Pedro Calderón de la Barca (in Spanish and German translation together with commentaries).

79. The stage direction at I.1445–46 is: "While Amfortas bows devoutly in silent prayer before the chalice, an increasingly dark twilight extends over the hall"

brightly Our Lord greets us today!" ("O heilige Wonne! Wie hell grüßt uns heute der Herr!"),[80] there is a reverse "transubstantiation" whereby Christ's body and blood now turn into bread and wine (and at this point the light of day re-appears, recalling the "day" of Tristan, i.e., the phenomenal world!)[81]

I follow these "transubstantiations" now through the libretto. First we have the "boys" ("Knaben") singing from on high (*WagPS* 150–51):

Wine and <u>bread</u> from the Last Supper	*Wein* und <u>Brot</u> des letzten Mahles
the Lord of the Grail once turned,	wandelt' einst der Herr des Grales
through the power of pity and love,	durch des Mitleids Liebesmacht
into the *blood* which He shed,	in das *Blut*, das er vergoß,
into the <u>body</u> which He broke.	in den <u>Leib</u>, den dar er bracht'.

The turning of the wine and bread of the Last Supper "through the power of pity and love" ("durch des Mitleids Liebesmacht") into the blood that he shed and the body that he broke may signify that Jesus then went on to offer himself as a sacrifice. Alternatively, there could be an allusion to the Roman Catholic view of "transubstantiation."

In the second stage, the youths (Jünglinge) sing (from half way up the dome) of a reverse transubstantiation (I.1510–44; *WagPS* 150–51), the blood and body turning into wine and bread:

Blood and <u>body</u> of that holy gift,	*Blut* und <u>Leib</u> der heil'gen Gabe
the loving spirit of blessed consolation,	wandelt heut' zu eurer Labe
now turn for your refreshment	sel'ger Tröstung Liebesgeist
into the *wine* poured out for you,	in den *Wein*, der euch nun floß,
into the <u>bread</u> that feeds you today.	in das <u>Brot</u>, das heut' ihr speist'.

Then thirdly there is yet another transformation as two groups of knights sing, one of "turning" the bread into bodily strength and the other of turning the wine into "fiery blood of life."

("Während Amfortas andachtvoll im stummen Gebet zu dem Kelche sich neigt, verbreitet sich eine immer dichtere Dämmerung über die Halle") (*WagPS* 148–49). Then at I.1456–57: "Beginning of complete darkness" ("Eintritt der vollsten Dunkelheit"; not included in Salter's libretto). Note also that both passages are written in Ab major, the key is associated with the night of Act II of *Tristan*.

80. *WagPS* 150–51.

81. See the stage direction at I.1485–87 (*WagPS* 150–51): "Hier tritt die frühere Tageshelle wieder ein" ("Daylight returns").

Knights (first half)

Take of the <u>bread</u>,	Nehmet vom <u>Brot</u>,
turn it confidently	wandelt es kühn
into <u>bodily</u> strength and power;	in <u>Leibes</u> Kraft und Stärke;
true until death,	treu bis zum Tod;
steadfast in effort,	fest jedem Müh'n,
to work the Saviour's will!	zu wirken de Heilands Werke!

Knights (second half)

Take of the *wine*,	Nehmet vom *Wein*,
turn it anew	wandelt ihn neu
into the fiery *blood* of life.	zu Lebens feurigem *Blute*.
Rejoicing in the unity	Froh im Verein,
of brotherly faith,	brudergetreu
let us fight with holy courage.	zu kämfen mit seligem Mute!

It has been argued by some that Wagner held solely to this reverse transubstantiation[82] and by others that he held solely to the orthodox view.[83] I suspect Wagner's views on "transubstantiation" are not entirely consistent and the above threefold passage suggests that he actually held to both views: first a transubstantiation of wine and bread into the savior's sacrificed blood and body (either in the Eucharist or on Calvary or both); secondly, a reverse transubstantiation of blood and body into wine and bread that feeds the knights;[84] thirdly, a "transubstantiation" whereby bread is transformed

82. See Cicora, "Medievalism and Metaphysics," 51, who argues that Wagner's aim was "a this-worldly religiosity."

83. Beckett, "Review of *A Companion to Wagner's Parsifal*," 454, considers that in the "reverse transubstantiation" passage Wagner was "musing with (typically) more emotion than reasoning, let alone theology, on the Grail, the eucharist, and the passion of Christ, but in an entirely orthodox spirit." But is this "musing" really in such an "orthodox spirit"?

84. Cosima's entry for 26 September 1877 tells of how her husband played the Prelude to Act I and "speaks . . . about this feature, in the mystery of the Grail, of blood turning into wine, which permits us to turn our gaze refreshed back to earth, whereas the conversion of wine into blood draws us away from the earth." This is viewed as one of Wagner's positive theological steps forward by Küng, "Theology for Our Time," 329–30. He comments: "In the last century when the Eucharist was celebrated privately only for reasons of subjective piety, without any consequences for the social existence of the individual, one got unnecessarily incensed at such statements. In our [twentieth] century, when in view of millions of starving people 'in foreign lands' the Church has made 'Bread for the world' its slogan, one has become aware again that a eucharistic 'Communion' commits one to the *Communio* (the community) with mankind; one recognizes

into bodily strength and wine transformed into fiery blood of life. This final transformation is, as we shall see in chapter 6 below, crucial for Wagner's controversial view of "regeneration."

One reason the "uncovering of the Grail" is so crucial (and this was something Amfortas was trying to frustrate) is that it was a means for the knights to participate in Christ through this triple transformation of the elements just discussed. But even without this uncovering one can still speak of Christ living in members of the community, knights, youths, and boys, but living in them through his death![85] This bring me to consider the highly "mythical" nature of participation in Christ. As Parsifal and Gurnemanz come into the castle of the grail they are entering a world where time (and space) are transformed (Gurnemanz sings: "You see, my son, time here becomes space" ("Du siehst, mein Sohn, zum Raum wird hier die Zeit").[86] The mythical nature of the reality we are dealing with is encapsulated by the words sung by the youths ("Jünglinge") shortly after the "Transformation Music" (*WagPS* 142–45):

---

unmistakably again that the Eucharist may not be withdrawn from the world but that the memory of His suffering must lead to practical compassion, to a change in the inhuman circumstances on our earth: 'the work of the Savior'" (329). "Bread for the World" ("Brot für die Welt") is a major charity in Germany run by the Protestant churches.

85. The idea of Jesus living in his disciples through his death (durch sein Tod) is anticipated in his sketches for *Jesus of Nazareth*: "Ye understand me not, for still am I without you: therefore I give to you my flesh and blood to eat and drink, that I may dwell within you" (*PW* 8:299). "Ihr verstehet mich nicht, denn noch bin ich ausserhalb eurer: drum geb' ich euch mein fleisch und blut, Dass ihr es esset u. trinket, damit ich euch innwohnen möge." These words "stehen im Original am linken Blattrand, unter der Überschrift, quer" (*DTB* 249).

86. Lévi-Strauss, "Chrétien," 219, considered these words to be "probably the most profound definition that anyone has ever offered for myth" (contrast Newman, *Study of Wagner*, 356, who describe the words as "a piece of metaphysical crudity not only fatuous in itself, but doubly absurd as the accompaniment to a mere trick of scene-shifting"). The comments of Lévi-Strauss are to be taken seriously. The movement of Parsifal and Gurnemanz from the forest to the castle of the grail (during which we hear the "transformation music" ["Verwandlungsmusik"]) can be compared to the disciples of Jesus ascending the "high mountain" in the Gospel account of the transfiguration (Mark 9:2; see Bell, "Transfiguration," 165–66). Although Wagner has no "mountain" corresponding to the Mount of Transfiguration, the stage direction points to an "ascent" (I.1157–58; *WagPS* 140–41): "The way leading upwards through the walls of rock, the scene has entirely changed. Gurnemanz and Parsifal now enter the mightly hall of the castle of the Grail" ("Durch aufsteigende gemauerte Gänge führend, hat die Szene sich vollständig verwandelt. Gurnemanz und Parsifal treten jetzt in den mächtigen Saal der Gralsburg ein"). Cosima's entry inverts the "time" and "space": "Today I have set a philosophical precept to music: 'Hence space becomes time' (Hier wird der Raum zur Zeit)" (*CD* 21 December 1877).

As once His blood flowed	Den sündigen Welten,
with countless pains	mit tausend Schmerzen,
for the sinful worlds—	wie einst sein Blut geflossen—
now with joyful heart	dem Erlösungshelden
let my blood be shed	sei nun mit freudigem Herzen
for the great Redeemer.	mein Blut vergossen.
His body, that He gave to purge our sin,	Der Leib, den er zur Sühn' uns bot,
lives in us through His death.	er lebt in uns durch seinen Tod.

The mythical nature of this reality is first seen in that Wagner is suggesting a union with Christ by using a chord closely related to the Tristan chord precisely on the word "blood."[87] There can be no doubt that this chord is again associated with Christ's sacrificial death and with the idea of union with him. Here Wagner shares very much the world of the book of Leviticus and the letters of St. Paul. The sin-offering "atones" by the Israelite identifying with the sacrificial animal, the key element being the blood. See Lev 17:11: "The soul of the flesh is in the blood. I [God] give it to you on/for the altar to atone for your souls; for the blood atones through the soul."[88] This idea is developed by St. Paul in that the Christian identifies with Christ, the sacrificial victim, the "sin offering" (Rom 8:3), and thereby comes to participate in his death. Wagner likewise believes that those who belong to the redeemer participate in his being.

The mythical nature of the reality of Christ is also suggested by the youths singing that his blood flowed for "sinful worlds"[89] reflecting the idea that there are many "worlds" through which characters such as Kundry have "flown." It is also instructive to compare Wagner's view of the relationship of the knights to the redeemer to what we find in St. Paul and the letter to the Hebrews. Wagner shares Paul's idea of participation in Christ, something absent in Hebrews; but Wagner does share something with Hebrews that is absent in Paul's understand of the believer's relationship to Christ, and this is what can be termed "identical repetition." Hübner gives three examples of "identical repetition." The first concerns natural phenomena: "[E]s ist immer wieder dieselbe Nacht, die den Morgen und den Tag gebiert" ("It is time and again the very same night which gives birth to the morning and the

---

87. I.1208. Rather than having F B D# G# we have everything a semi-tone higher F# C E (A) and with the A placed an octave lower to give the "mystic chord" F# A C E (I.1208).

88. On this translation, see Bell, *Deliver Us from Evil*, 194–95.

89. *WagPS* 143 translates with the singular: "for the sinful world."

day").[90] The second example concerns the psyche of human being whereby the acts of gods can subsequently affect human beings such that they become a child of Aphrodite, Zeus, etc.[91] Such "identical repetition" is found in Paul's Adam myth in that the first human being affects the behavior of all after him such that Adam's sin is projected in human beings and the sin of human beings is projected in Adam's.[92] The third type of identical repetition is where a god stamps a group of people (a tribe, city, etc.) with rules of behavior, and having disclosed this to them it is then identically repeated in that group. This third type of identical repetition (and to some extent the second also) is found in Heb 2:5–13; 10:19–22; 12:1–2; 13:12–13. Christ is the "pioneer of salvation" (2.10), the "pioneer and perfecter of faith" who himself is "perfected" (2:10; 5:9; 7:28). For the author of Hebrews Christ's life, death, and exaltation was a "Schlüsselszene"[93] that gives rise to a pattern of identical repetition. In some sense Jesus is the "redeemed redeemer" (cf. "The redeemer redeemed!").[94]

Many of Wagner's ideas of Jesus in *Parsifal* and elsewhere find a resonance in this very Jewish letter. Not only do we find the same pattern of "identical repetition" but also Wagner's *Parsifal* reflects the stress found in Hebrews on the sinlessness of Christ (Heb 4:15) and the opposition between the Old Covenant and the New (Heb 8:1—10:39).[95]

Wagner therefore brings together Paul's participation ("he lives in us through his death") and the "identical repetition" of Hebrews: Christ shed his blood for "sinful worlds"; now those who belong to him are to shed their blood "for the hero of redemption" ("dem Erlösungshelden"). But, unlike Paul, participation in Christ is solely in his death and, unlike Hebrews, there is no following the redeemer to some future glory. One of the most important sources for his thinking on this is Schopenhauer, who writes: "suffering

90. Kurt Hübner, *Wahrheit*, 135. The precise nature of identical repetition has been helpfully developed by Fischer, "Glaube und Mythos," in terms of "theoretical" and "practical" knowing. I have developed these ideas of "identical repetition" in Bell, "Myth of Adam," and Bell, *Deliver Us from Evil* (see the index of subjects and names).

91. Kurt Hübner, *Wahrheit*, 135–36.

92. Note, however, that Paul does not use this pattern when it comes to the believer's relationship to Christ. See Bell, "Myth of Adam," 23–36.

93. See Sellin, "Mythologeme," 211.

94. This formula raises the question of possible influence from Gnosticism. Although Hebrews does have some parallels (in 2:10–18) I argued that there was probably no "influence" as such (Bell, *Deliver Us from Evil*, 307–15). Further, both Hebrews (and Wagner) have views that are decidedly anti-gnostic (i.e., stressing Jesus' full humanity, suffering, and death). On Wagner and Gnosticism, see chapter 6 below.

95. In his New Testament Wagner marked Heb 2:13–14; 5:12–14; 8:13; 9:22–26; 10:1, 4; 11:1; 12:24 (see also his use of the letter in his *Jesus of Nazareth*).

is the process of purification by which alone man is in most cases sanctified, in other words, led back from the path of error of the will-to-live. Accordingly, the salutary nature of the cross and of suffering is so often discussed in Christian devotional books, and in general the cross, an instrument of suffering not of doing, is very appropriately the symbol of the Christian religion."[96] He then continues: "In fact, even the preacher, Jewish indeed but very philosophical, rightly says: 'Sorrow is better than laughter: for by the sadness of the countenance the heart is made better' (Eccles. vii, 3)."[97] In *Parsifal* Wagner relates the cross to the denial of the will and through this comes salvation and this denial of the will can only come about by union with Christ.[98] However, despite all this apparent stress on death and denial of the will, there is another aspect to salvation in *Parsifal*, something that will be explored in chapters 7 and 8 below.

96. *WWR* 2:636; *ASSW* 2:816.

97. *WWR* 2:636; *ASSW* 2:816.

98. It is possible that Wagner's view of union with Christ was influenced to some extent by Plato's *Symposium*, a work he held is high regard. See *CD* 6–9 April 1870; 4 June 1871; 5 April 1882.

6

Theological Reflections I
Christology and Atonement

Introduction

HAVING LOOKED AT HOW Amfortas, Kundry, and the knights of the grail have encountered Christ in the drama of *Parsifal*, I now begin to reflect more systematically on the theology of *Parsifal* taking into account some of Wagner's other music dramas together with letters, diaries, and theoretical writings. It is appropriate that I begin with what traditionally has been called the "person and work of Christ," for this is the very center of Wagner's theological concern.

Person of Christ

One of the issues raised at the end of the previous chapter was the "mythical" nature of Christ in *Parsifal*. This needs to be further analyzed and related to the question of the "Christ" Wagner actually "believed in" and whether there was a distinction between the two. It may help to clarify the issues if we consider the figure of "Wotan." Clearly Wotan of the *Ring* has a different ontological status to the Wotan that Wagner himself would relate to in everyday life. He could graphically portray the complex figure of Wotan in the *Ring* but in normal discourse he would not speak of someone "going to

Valhalla."[1] Is it then the case that Christ also had these differing ontological statuses for Wagner?

In order to tease out what sort of Christ Wagner presents in *Parsifal* (and how it relates to his own faith) it is necessary to highlight that any speech about Christ being "sent" into the world and dying as a sacrifice for sin is mythical to some extent; and this includes the New Testament witness to Christ. In speaking of a "mythical Christ" we will always have to specify a point along a spectrum.[2] At the close of the previous chapter we saw that the Christ of *Parsifal* is not clearly rooted in "history,"[3] this being suggests by the many "worlds" through which characters such as Kundry have "flown." She is the only one in the drama who encounters the "earthly" Christ but does so as someone who flies through time as a primeval witch, rose of hell, Herodias, and Gundryggia.[4]

Such is the mythical Christ of *Parsifal*. But what of Wagner's own view? It *could* be argued that in the second stage in his theological development—which I identified in chapter 2, the early period of his exile, 1849–54—Wagner assumed a mythical Christ.[5] At the end of *Art and Revolution* (1849) he writes this:

> Thus would *Jesus* have shown us that we all alike are men and brothers; while *Apollo* would have stamped this mighty bond of brotherhood with the seal of strength and beauty, and led mankind from doubt of its own worth to consciousness of its highest godlike might. Let us therefore erect the altar of the future, in Life as in the living Art, to the two sublimest teachers

1. Contrast the words of Hitler at Hindenburg's funeral: "Departed General go now to Valhalla" (Scholder, *Third Reich II*, 210).

2. Placing the idea of "Christ" along this spectrum is something which Kurt Hübner, *Wahrheit*, 399, fails to do: he speaks simply of a "historical" or "mythical" Christ.

3. I use quotation marks because, as will become clear, Wagner's idealism excludes a naïve view of history as events independent of the subject.

4. Note also the "for the sinful worlds" ("Den sündigen Welten") sung by the youths after the transformation music (*WagPS* 142–43).

5. In fact, this view could already be there in late summer 1848 when he composed *The Wibelungen*. As Kühnel, "Prose Writings," 578, puts it, "[t]here was a correspondence . . . between history and mythology: the Hohenstaufen ruler Frederick I (Barbarossa) and Siegfried, the hero of the Nibelungenlied, were the heirs and last representatives of the primordial kingdom—Barbarossa in history, Siegfried in mythology." In this work Wagner relates the "native Stem-god" ("[j]ener . . . heimische Stammgott") with Christ, the Son of God, "father (at least spiritual) of *all* men" (*PW* 7:287; *GSD* 2:144–45). Note also the identification of Christ and Siegfried in that they are both a "son of God" (*PW* 7:289). Five years earlier in 1843, Wagner composed his *Das Liebesmahl der Apostel*; there is a clear similarity between the melody used in m. 232 "in the name of Jesus of Nazareth" ("im Namen Jesu von Nazareth") and the Siegfried theme that first occurs in *Die Walküre* Act III (Kirsch, "Biblische Scene," 168).

of mankind:—*Jesus, who suffered for all men; and Apollo, who raised them to their joyous dignity.*[6]

Here Apollo and Jesus are set alongside each other as "teachers"[7] and this juxtaposition could be taken to imply a fully mythical view of Christ. However, there are a number of problems with this logic. First, it should be noted that theologians are perfectly able to speak of Adam and Christ in parallel, the former being fully mythical, the latter being only partially mythical (cf. Rom 5:12–21).[8] Secondly, we know that Wagner was studying serious works of historical scholarship concerning Jesus all of which had no doubt that Jesus was a historical figure[9] and he stresses on a number of occasions the "historically intelligible figure of Jesus of Nazareth."[10] Thirdly, his comments on the profound significance of Jesus' death suggest that he was thinking of a historical person. See, for example, Cosima's entry for 28 October 1873: "Talked with R. about Buddhism and Christianity. Perception of the world much greater in Buddhism, which, however, has no monument like the Gospels, in which divinity is conveyed to our consciousness in a truly historic form." Wagner is therefore thoroughly anti-gnostic since it is essential for him that Jesus did actually suffer.[11] We find this anti-gnostic

---

6. *PW* 1:65; *JA* 5:309. *GSD* 3:41: "So würde uns denn *Jesus* gezeigt haben, daß wir Menschen alle gleich und Brüder sind; *Apollon* aber würde diesem großen Bruderbunde das Siegel der Stärke und Schönheit aufgedrückt, er würde den Menschen vom Zweifel an seinem Werthe zum Bewußtsein seiner höchsten göttlichen Macht geführt haben. So laßt uns denn den Altar der Zukunft, im Leben wie in der lebendigen Kunst, den zwei erhabensten Lehrern der Menschheit errichten:—*Jesus, der für die Menschheit litt, und Apollon, der sie zu ihrer freudenvollen Würde erhob!*"

7. Relating Christ to Apollo is fitting since he is the son of Zeus and the key figure in wisdom and oracles. On the role of Apollo in Christian art, see Kemp, "Götter," 175; on his fundamental role in oracles, see Rosenberger, *Griechische Orakel*. Apollo was to become crucial in Nietsche's *Birth of Tragedy*.

8. It is therefore mistaken to argue for a "historical Adam" on the basis that Paul speaks of a "historical Christ." Even though Paul may well have had the view that Adam really did "exist," he existed not in *ordinary* history but rather in *primeval* history. I suggest that the theological interpreter is free to develop an Adam–Christ "parallel"/"anti-parallel," the former being "non-historical" and the latter being "historical."

9. He was reading Strauß in the 1840s. Perhaps we can add Lessing's works on the "historical Jesus" since he had Lessing's works in his Dresden library (Lachmann, *Gotthold Ephraim Lessing's sämtliche Schriften*). In his Wahnfried library he had a reprint of this work (published 1853–57). We have noted in chapter 2 that Wagner also studied works by Renan and Gfrörer in his later period.

10. *SL* 898 (letter to Hans von Wolzogen, 17 January 1880).

11. One may be tempted to assign gnostic thought to Wagner on the basis of the final line of *Parsifal* "The Redeemer redeemed" (see chapters 5 and 7). Ideas of a "redeemed redeemer" could have come to Wagner through reading of Manichaeism (e.g., Görres, *Mystik*, 5:17–18) but ideas that Jesus was not truly human, that he did not suffer

view expressed in Gurnemanz's narration in Act I where emphasis is placed on Christ's suffering and death by speaking of the two central symbols of the drama, the grail and the spear, both fundamental to Christ's flowing blood: "the sacred vessel, the precious holy Cup from which He drank at the Love Feast, in which too His divine blood flowed from the Cross, and with it that same spear which shed it."[12] Further, his comments on how Christ is superior to that of Buddha can hardly have any weight if he held the view that Christ was not a historical figure who suffered: "Christ wishes to suffer, suffers, and redeems us."[13] Fourthly, and this is related to the previous point, Wagner rejected a docetic Christology, which contrasts starkly with Schopenhauer's view that Christ had a "phantom body" ("Scheinleib").[14] For Schopenhauer, Christ simply represented one of those "universals" and so he was not committed to the historical existence of Christ. As Breckridge expresses Schopenhauer's view, "[w]hereas our bodies are a phenomenon of the will, [Christ's] body was not."[15] Wagner's view is completely different. For him the death of Christ, the giving of his body and shedding of his blood, was a supreme sacrifice for sins.

In view of this one has to say that for Wagner himself Christ was *not* simply a mythical figure like Wotan.[16] He was clearly a "historical figure."[17] But Wagner did not have a naïve view of "history" as "facts" independent of the "subject"; he recognized, particularly in his later writings, that we make "representations" of the past that are subject dependent.[18] Further, as soon as discourse about Christ being a sacrifice is introduced, we are entering a mythological dimension of Jesus' personhood. But this mythical aspect of Christ is for Wagner an aspect of his most fundamental reality. Wagner does not interpret Christ, as Schopenhauer does, "always in the universal, as the

---

on the cross, are so thoroughly alien that it must be seriously questioned whether his thought was related to "gnosticism."

12. *WagPS* 122–23: "daraus er trank beim letzten Liebesmahle, das Weihgefäß, die heilig edle Schale, darein am Kreuz sein göttlich Blut auch floß, dazu den Lanzenspeer, der dies vergoß." Note that the spear also "bleeds" when it is applied to Amfortas' wound at the end of Act III.

13. *CD* 28 October 1873.

14. *WWR* 1:405; *ASSW* 1:550.

15. Breckenridge, "Compassion and Knowledge," 55.

16. I think the same can be said for his discussion of Christ in *The Wibelungen*. Wagner does identify Wotan with the "God of the Christians" and relates the "Stem-god" to Christ. But Christ is clearly in a quite different category.

17. On the historical figure of Jesus see also his letter to Hans von Wolzogen of 17 January 1880 quoted below.

18. See Wagner's striking discussion of the virginal conception discussed in chapter 8 below.

symbol or personification of the denial of the will-to-live."[19] Christ is *not* to
be included among those "mythical symbols" of which Wagner writes in the
famous first sentence of *Religion and Art*.[20] Indeed Wagner actually denies
that Christ is a "Symbol" of the divine; rather he is an image, a real replica
("Bild, wirkliches Abbild") of the divine.[21] If symbols, like metaphors, merely *depict* reality, one could argue that the distinction between "Symbol" and
"Abbild" corresponds to the distinction made in *Religion and Art* between
"das bedeutet" ("that signifies") and "das ist" ("that is.")[22] It is also highly
significant that Wagner uses the same word "Abbild" as Schopenhauer does
for music being "a copy" ("Abbild") of the will itself.[23]

It appears, then, that there is no great discrepancy between the Christ
of Wagner's own faith and the Christ figure presented in *Parsifal*.[24] This then
brings us to the central christological question regarding Wagner's understanding of Jesus: in what way did he understand Christ to be divine? A
number of scholars tend towards a "low" Christology in that Jesus' divinity
is seen simply in terms of his "sinlessness." So according to Kienzle, Wagner
did not conceive of his divinity "in the sense that Christ is descended from
the highest deity who has created the world, but rather felt that Christ was
solely human—but He was the perfect human being. Therein rested His
divinity."[25] She believes that Wagner would therefore agree with Gfrörer:

19. *WWR* 1:405; *ASSW* 1:550.

20. *PW* 6:213; *GSD* 10:211; *JA* 10:117. Kurt Hübner, "Meditationen," 134, does not
appreciate that Wagner's view of Jesus includes "history" as well as "myth." He argues
that since for Wagner "die Wahrheit des Christentums alleine in der Kunst liegt, so sind
dessen Heilsereignisse nicht als eine historische Wirklichkeit zu verstehen." Further
he argues that the salvation events concern "'mythische Symbole' von 'sinnbildlichem
Wert'" and therein lie their "'verborgene tiefe Wahrheit'" (see *GSD* 10:211). "Kreuzi-
gung, Jungfraugeburt usw. sind also für Wagner gar keine historischen Vorgänge,
sondern mythische Urbilder, in denen die Lösung der religiösen Grunderfahrung erfaßt wird" (Kurt Hübner, "Meditationen," 134–35).

21. *PW* 6:217; *GSD* 10:215; *JA* 10:121.

22. *PW* 6:224; *GSD* 10:222; *JA* 10:129. Wagner is alluding to the Zwinglian versus
the Lutheran (and Catholic) view of the Eucharist. I will discuss this important section
of *Religion and Art* in subsequent chapters.

23. *WWR* 1:257; *ASSW* 1:359. See the discussion in chapter 11 below.

24. One could draw a rough parallel between the understanding of Christ in the
"Johannine school" and that presented in the Gospel of John (i.e., there is no great
discrepancy between the two). Note that the Gospel is legitimated by the "Paraclete,"
the "Spirit of truth," thereby giving the evangelist "his unprecedented freedom towards
historical 'facts' and the authority to remodel tradition radically" (Hengel, *Johannine
Question*, 102). Wagner likewise exercised the same freedom in his various portrayals
of Jesus.

25. Kienzle, "A Christian Music Drama?" 109.

"I understand God's son as not the metaphysical essence that traditional dogmatism teaches us lies far away from human experience, but rather I use this term to describe the ethical and spiritual perfection through which Christ distinguished Himself from other human beings."[26] Likewise Mösch rejects any idea of what one can call "incarnation" in Wagner's Christology. In a section entitled "Without God and Grace" ("Ohne Gott und Gnade") he argues that although Wagner in his later years cannot be simply described as an "atheist," his Christology is decidedly "low." He points to Cosima's entry for 20 September 1879 ("R. says, 'I do not believe in God, but in [the divine] (godliness), which is revealed in a Jesus *without sin*'").[27] He also argues for a low Christology on the basis of Cosima's entry for 15 June 1872 where we read that "Christ was a divinely appointed mortal." However, this is a quotation of Pastor Sydom who "was attacked by the whole consistorial council." It is true that Wagner clearly has some sympathy with Sydom but his own point is the problem with the Jewish conception of God. "'The old Jewish God always ruins the whole thing,' R. observes."[28] It is also worth quoting a little further, for Wagner adds: "no one will abandon the old God, but for that very reason they are denying Christ."[29]

One could make the case that Wagner does not have an incarnational Christology in the sense that he certainly avoids speaking of Christ being "descended" from a creator God; further, it is the case that *Lohengrin* points to the problems of "incarnation" and indeed the whole opera could be seen as an illustration that incarnation cannot work.[30] Further, a low Christol-

---

26. Quoted and translated by Kienzle, "A Christian Music Drama?" 109–10. Gfrörer, *Geschichte III*, 3: "Ich verstehe unter Gottes Sohn nicht das metaphysiche, menschlicher Erfahrung ferne liegende Wesen der hergebrachten Dogmatik, sondern ich bezeichne damit die sittliche und geistige Vollkommenheit, durch welche sich Christus von anderen Menschen unterscheidet." Note that Gfrörer believed that John's high Christology comes from a logos theology of the "alexandrinisch-jüdische Theosophie" (335). This then accounts for texts such as John 1:1, 27; 8:58; 17:5, etc.

27. This is discussed in chapter 10 below.

28. *CD* 15 June 1872.

29. *CD* 15 June 1872.

30. In a letter to Hermann Franck (30 May 1846) Wagner writes this about *Lohengrin*: "The symbolic meaning of the tale I can best sum up as follows: contact between a metaphysical phenomenon and human nature, and the impossibility that such contact will last. The moral would be: the good Lord (I mean the Christian God) would do better to spare us His revelations since He is not permitted to annul the laws of nature: nature—in this case human nature—is bound to take her revenge and destroy the revelation" (*SL* 129–30; *SB* 2:511–12). According to Mertens, "Wagners Gral," 97, the fact that incarnation does not work out (hence no "redemption") means that according to *Lohengrin* the myth of the grail is not Christian. However, there are nevertheless clear Christian elements as expressed in Lohengrin's "narration" in Act III.

ogy can be found in his sketches for *Jesus of Nazareth*.[31] However, there are indication that he did not stay with this low Christology. We have seen in chapter 3 above that Wagner does have an "incarnational theology" when he writes to Mathilde Wesendonck (letter of 30 May 1859) about the grail, an "incarnation" that is reflected again in his idea of Christ being an "Abbild" of the divine.[32] There are then five further points that question a low Christology. First, it is striking that in *Religion and Art* Wagner speaks of Jesus as "Son of God" born of a virgin,[33] indeed born of "that sublimely virginal Mother of God" ("jene erhabene jungfräuliche Gottesmutter").[34] Secondly, in *Parsifal* itself most references to God are actually to Christ.[35] Thirdly, in *Parsifal* Christ is referred to as the "redeemer" and sometimes as the "savior." The striking thing about these two terms, "savior" and "redeemer," from a biblical perspective is that although they can be used of human beings, they can only truly be applied to God himself[36] and Wagner may well have been aware of this. His use of these terms for Jesus (and the sense in which they are used)[37] would seem to point to a high Christology. One can further add that Christ's sinlessness alone is simply not sufficient to qualify him as "redeemer" and "savior," especially since Wagner, like St. Paul and Luther, has such a strong view of sin and a correspondingly strong view of grace.[38] Wagner lived in the world of Luther (this was especially so in his

31. *PW* 8:301: "Jesus knows and practices God's-love through his teaching of it: in the consciousness of Cause and Effect he accordingly is God and Son of God; but every man is capable of like knowledge and like practice,—and if he attain thereto, he is like unto God and Jesus" (*DTB* 249: "Jesus weiss es, und die gottesliebe übt er durch seine lehre von ihr: im bewusstsein der ursache und der wirkung ist er somit gott und gottes sohn: aber jeder mensch ist fähig zu gleichem wissen und gleicher ausübung,—und gelangt er dazu, so ist er gleich Jesus und gott.")

32. Cf. Heb: 1:3 where Christ is an "Ebenbild" of God, this being in the context of a high Christology of Hebrews 1 (and not simply in relation to Gen 1:27).

33. He writes of the relationship of the "Gottes-Knaben" to the "jungfräulichen Mutter" (*GSD* 10:222; *JA* 10:129), a text I will return to in subsequent chapters.

34. *PW* 6:223; *GSD* 10:222; *JA* 10:129.

35. See chapter 9 below for a discussion of the relevant passages.

36. This is discussed in more detail in chapter 7 below.

37. So although Elsa can address Lohengrin as "mein Erlöser" (*JA* 2:162) he is not redeemer in the sense that Jesus is and in fact is himself in need of "redemption."

38. In the New Testament those writers who have the most pessimistic anthropology tend to have the highest Christology and strongest understanding of grace (see especially Paul and John). At the other end of the spectrum stands the letter of James which has a relatively optimistic (and Jewish) anthropology and a lower Christology and a weaker concept of grace. It is perhaps significant that although James was an important element in Wolfram (Wapnewski, *Parzival*, 28–45) there is nothing of this in Wagner's *Parsifal*.

last ten years), read his Bible translation and his writings, and thoroughly immersed himself in this world of God and grace.[39] The fourth argument for a higher Christology is that Wagner does speak of "Christ's transcendence." So Cosima's entry for 8 August 1974 tells of how her husband "talks about longing one day to find in music something that expresses Christ's transcendence, something in which creative impulse, an emotion which speaks to the emotions, can be seen."

In order to be a little more precise about Wagner's Christology, I turn again to Mösch who concludes that for Wagner Jesus is to be seen as an "Integrations figure" ("Integrationsfigur"), as a "form of the divine in anthropomorphic mode" ("Gestalt des Göttlichen in anthropomorphistischer Weise").[40] The context of this last quotation taken from *Religion and Art*[41] is that Wagner speaks of the "miracle of divinity of the herald of salvation" ("Wunder der Göttlichkeit des Heils-Verkünders") and, in Ellis' translation, "[t]he very shape of the Divine had presented itself in anthropomorphic guise" ("Hiermit war dann die Gestalt des Göttlichen in anthropomorphischer Weise von selbst gegeben"). What was this "anthropomorphic guise"? "[I]t was the body of the quintessence of all pitying Love (mitleidvollen Liebe), stretched out upon the cross of pain and suffering."[42] This crucified Christ was not a symbol but a "Bild, wirkliches Abbild"; he was an "image, a real replica."[43] But a replica of what? The context suggests he is a replica of the divine. This view then of "anthropomorphism" does not necessarily lead to a low Christology. Indeed there is a long theological tradition of speaking of God in such an "anthropomorphic guise."[44]

How then is Wagner's view of Christ related to the question of God? One way of answering this is to say he had a "Christo-monism." This term was applied in a negative way by Paul Althaus in response to the views of Karl Heim and especially Karl Barth. Althaus was concerned that Heim and Barth were concentrating divinity in the person of Christ.[45] But Althaus'

---

39. Contrast the subheading "Ohne Gott und Gnade" in Mösch, *Weihe, Werkstatt, Wirklichkeit*, 29.

40. Mösch, *Weihe, Werkstatt, Wirklichkeit*, 32

41. *GSD* 10:215; *JA* 10:121.

42. *PW* 6:217; *GSD* 10:215; *JA* 10:121.

43. *PW* 6:217; *GSD* 10:215; *JA* 10:121.

44. See Jüngel, "Anthropomorphismus." His conclusion emphasizes the *humanity* of God ("*Menschlichkeit* Gottes"). My contention is that this is precisely what Wagner is emphasizing in *Religion and Art* and elsewhere throughout his work.

45. Althaus, *Die christliche Wahrheit*, 56: "Aber beherrscht wurde die theologische Lage der letzten Jahrzehnte und guteteils bis heute durch den engen christomonistischen Offenbarungsgedanken. Die beiden einflußreichen Theologen, Karl Heim und

own view was highly problematic: he held to an idea of "Ur-Offenbarung,"[46] a view which is very much at odds with Wagner's understanding of God. Wagner saw God primarily in Jesus Christ and this was driven by two things: first, Jesus' supreme sacrifice; secondly, a desire to get rid of the Jewish "creator God."[47] These issues will be discussed later, but for now I note Wagner's "reduction" of God to the person of Jesus in a letter to Constantin Frantz. After reading Frantz's *Federalism*, Wagner offered him some critical remarks in a letter (14 July 1879).[48] He wrote that "there is no religion that can guide us along the right path, since—in my own estimation—this must first be revealed to us, and Jesus Christ must first be recognized and imitated by us." He then berates the Catholic Church and he sets the "Church" against "Christ."[49] He criticizes Frantz for "thinking of the Christian religion only in the popular guise of God the Creator and His first revelation to the Jews."[50] He then emphasizes: "If the common people were made to forget about God in the 'burning bush' and shown instead only the 'sacred head sore wounded' they would understand what Christianity is all about, and perhaps this 'head' will one day rise up, as the true creator of religion, out of the chaos towards which we are all inexorably hastening."[51]

Therefore in both *Parsifal* and in his writings Wagner is defining God in terms of the suffering redeemer Jesus Christ. But there is a remaining problem. Does not the drama suggest that Parsifal himself is seen as the "redeemer"? Anyone watching Act III may well get the impression that Parsifal is a type of Christ, especially when Kundry as a "Mary Magdalene"

Karl Barth, wie weit sonst auch verschieden und gegensätzlich, gingen hier in der gleichen Richtung."

46. See Althaus, *Die christliche Wahrheit*, 37–60; Althaus, "Ur-Offenbarung." Note that Althaus together with Werner Elert opposed the Barmen Declaration (formulated by Barth and others) and offered their response in the Ansbacher Ratschlag ("Ansbach Advice") which was printed by "Evangelium im Dritten Reich" (Scholder, *Third Reich II*, 164).

47. See chapter 9 below.

48. But note that Wagner admired Frantz's "A Happy Evening" (see *CD* 14 September 1878).

49. *SL* 894.

50. *SL* 894.

51. *SL* 895. The editors relate the quotation to the hymn by Paul Gerhardt (1607–76), "O Haupt voll Blut und Wunden." This hymn, based on words of Arnulf von Löwen (1250) "Salve caput cruentatum," and the melody of Hans Leo Haßler (1601), is a well known Easter Hymn (see *Evangelisches Gesangbuch: Für Gottesdienst, Gebet, Glaube, Leben* [Stuttgart: Gesangbuchverlag, 1996], 202–4; *Hymns Ancient and Modern* [London: William Clowes, 1916], 140–41 [known as Passion Chorale]). This hymn would no doubt be especially important for Wagner since the melody (but not the text) is used by Bach in his *St Matthew Passion*.

figure washes his feet and then anoints them and dries them with her hair.[52] Wagner actually rejected the view that Parsifal was a Christ figure: he tells Cosima that "W[olzogen] goes too far in calling Parsifal a reflection of the Redeemer: 'I didn't have the Redeemer in mind when I wrote it.'"[53] Such a denial then coheres with Beckett's understanding of some crucial lines of Gurnemanz in Act III (*WagPS* 224–25):

Pure of heart!	Du Reiner!
Pitying sufferer,	Mitleidsvoll Duldener,
enlightened healer!	heiltatvoll Wissender!
As you have endured the suffer-	Wie des Erlösten Leiden du
ings of the redeemed,	gelitten,
lift the last burden from	die letzte Last entnimm nun sei-
his head!	nem Haupt!

These words, argues Beckett, are addressed to Christ, not to Parsifal.[54] This makes sense in that there is a change of subject ("As *you* [Christ] have endured . . . lift the last burden from *his* [Parsifal's] head").[55] However, a few lines earlier, Gurnemanz nevertheless calls Parsifal the "pure one" ("Rein-er") (*WagPS* 222–23):

52. See the stage directions (*WagPS* 222–23): "Kundry bathes Parsifal's feet with humble zeal. . . . Kundry draws from her bosom a golden phial and pours part of its contents over Parsifal's feet, which she then dries with her hastily unbound hair." ("Kundry badet Parsifal mit demutsvollem Eifer die Füße. . . . Kundry [zieht] ein goldenes Fläschen aus ihren Busen und gießt seinen Inhalt auf Parsifals Füße aus; jetzt trocknet sie diese mit ihren schnell aufgelösten Haaren.") Cf. Luke 7:36–50, although here it is not specified that this woman is Mary Magdalene. She is simply a "sinner" who comes in, bathes Jesus' feet with her tears, dries them with her hair and then anoints with the anointment (v. 38). After this pericope Mary Magdalene, "from whom seven demons had gone out" (8:2), is mentioned as a follower of Jesus but she is not identified with this sinner of Luke 7:36–50. It was only in much later tradition that the identification was made. Further she was equated with the "Mary" who anoints Jesus' feet in John 12:1–8 (but in the text this was Mary the sister of Martha).

53. *CT* 20 October 1878: "[Wolzogen] zu weit ging, indem er Parsifal ein Ab-bild des Heilandes nennt. 'Ich habe an den Heiland dabei gar nicht gedacht.'" I have slightly modified the English translation of *CD*. Wagner was responding to Wolzogen, "Bühnenweihfestspiel," 301, where he calls Parsifal "ein menschlich-mystisches Abbild unseres *Heilandes*."

54. Beckett, *Parsifal*, 53.

55. The other alternative is that "As *you* have endured" refers to Parsifal and "lift the last burden from *his* head" refers to Christ, or to Amfortas. But this is impossible since just before this Gurnemanz addresses Parsifal so: "thus I do bless *your* head, to greet you as king" ("so segne ich dein Haupt, als König dich zu grüßen") (*WagPS* 224–25).

May this purity bless you,	Gesegnet sei, du Reiner, durch
pure one!	das Reine!
Thus may the load	So weiche jeder Schuld
of all guilt be washed away!	Bekümmernis von dir!

Beckett sums up this paradox by writing that "[Parsifal] is both innocent and guilty, both the bearer of redemption and himself in need of redemption."[56] These words raise the issue of the relationship between Christ and the church;[57] but the point I wish to stress now is that in a primary sense Parsifal *cannot* be the redeemer since he himself is in need of redemption.[58] It is highly significant that it is only on the lips of Kundry, the deceiver, that he is called a redeemer. She functions as such a deceiver in Act II when she is under the spell of Klingsor.[59] She asks Parsifal (*WagPS* 198–99):

If you are a redeemer,	Bist du *Erlöser*,
what maliciously stops you	was bannt dich, *Böser*,
from uniting with me for my	nicht mir auch zum Heil dich zu
salvation?	einen?
Through eternities I have waited	Seit Ewigkeiten harre ich
for you,	deiner,
the saviour so late in coming,	des Heilands, ach! So spät!
whom once I dared revile.	Den einst ich kühn geschmäht.

With the words "the saviour so late in coming" ("des Heilands, ach! So spät!") Kundry replaces Christ with Parsifal.[60] However, Wagner himself

56. Beckett, *Parsifal*, 52. The same can be said of Brünnhilde at the end of *Götterdämmerung*.

57. Parsifal could be seen as an embodiment of the redeemer's original act of salvation. See Kurt Hübner, "Meditationen," 141: "Der gekreuzigte Erlöser im *Parsifal* ist keine historische Figur wie in der Bibel. Das Heilsereignis wird in diesem Werk vielmehr wie eine Arché, ein Ursprungsereignis aufgefaßt, das stellvertretend in immer neuen Variaten—siehe den reinen Toren, den Parsifal—beständig wiederkehrt." See also Kurt Hübner, "Christentum," 283–84. But I think Hübner has made the error of making Wagner's redeemer purely mythical. For further discussion on Wagner's understanding of the church, see chapter 10 below.

58. As he sings in Act II: "Redeemer! Saviour! Lord of grace! How can I, a sinner, purge my guilt? ("Erlöser! Heiland! Herr der Huld! Wie büß' ich, Sünder, solche Schuld?") (*WagPS* 196–97).

59. Note that her character is completely different in Act I. Here "her sense of truthfulness is so marked that she blurts out to Parsifal the news of his mother's death in the most careless, matter-of-fact way possible" (Irvine, *'Parsifal' and Wagner's Christianity*, 40).

60. According to the notes made by Porges on II.1150ff, Kundry here falls into an illusion and exchanges the redeemer for Parsifal ("Kundry verfällt hier in die Illusion,

was clear that Parsifal was not the redeemer. This is confirmed by the change from the sketch of 1877 to the final poem; in the sketch Parsifal sings "Ich will dich lieben und erlösen" ("I will love you and redeem you")[61] but this is changed to "Lieb und Erlösung soll dir werden" ("Love and redemption will come to you") in the final version.[62]

To conclude this section on Christology, one can says that Jesus Christ was the very center of Wagner's spiritual life and although he was often critical of the established church, he wanted to do everything to preserve Christ "in His total purity." In a letter to Hans von Wolzogen of 17 January 1881, he writes,

> although we are merciless in abandoning the Church and the priesthood and, indeed, the whole historical phenomenon of Christianity, our friends must always know that we do so for the sake of that same Christ whom—because of His utter incomparability and recognizability—we wish to preserve in His total purity, so that—like all the other sublime products of man's artistic and scientific spirit—we can take Him with us into those terrible times which may very well follow the necessary destruction of all that at present exists.[63]

Work of Christ

One of Wagner's clearest summaries of the atonement is in his 1879 open letter *Against Vivisection*: "The monstrous guilt of all this life a divine and sinless being took upon himself, and expiated with his agony and death. Through this atonement (Sühnungstod) all that breathes and lives should know itself redeemed, so soon as it was grasped as pattern and example to be followed."[64] Here we can discern five points about the atonement. First, it presupposes our "monstrous guilt." Secondly, the sinless and divine Christ took upon himself the world's guilt. Thirdly, expiation was by his suffering and death. Fourthly, every living being (and this includes animals) should know itself redeemed. Fifthly, Christ's example of suffering should

---

daß sie Parsifal mit dem Heiland verwechselt") (*DEAP* 206).

61. *DEAP* 84. This is also found in the first extant sketch of 1865 (*BB* 58).

62. See Borchmeyer, "Kundrys Lachen," 446 (*WagPS* 202–3).

63. *SL* 898–99. The words "like all the *other* sublime products of man's artistic and scientific spirit" I take not to mean that Christ is simply a human "product." See *PW* 6:217 (*GSD* 10:215; *JA* 10:121) where Wagner writes that Christ is an image of the divine (discussed above and in chapter 11 below).

64. *PW* 6:203; *GSD* 10:202.

be followed. Wagner adds that this is a free-willed suffering experienced by saints and martyrs "to bathe them in the fount of compassion (Quelle des Mitleidens) till every worldly dream (jedes Weltwahnes) was washed away."[65] It is noteworthy that the idea of an "angry God" being appeased finds no place.

There are many such instances where Wagner writes or speaks about Christ's sacrifice. One aspect of his sacrifice that was to become increasingly important for Wagner was the blood of Christ. He took this from the New Testament and it is rather ironic for Wagner, who puts much of the blame for negative views of animals at the door of the Old Testament,[66] that St. Paul's understanding of the sacrifice of Christ was a development of the levitical sacrifices, especially of the sin-offering.[67] Paul is not entirely clear about the "mechanism" by which the sacrifice of Christ works, but the idea of "blood" is central and related to "blood" is the "soul," the entity through which the Christian is united to Christ.[68] Many of these themes we find in Paul occur also in *Parsifal*: sacrifice, participation, blood, and "regeneration." This list may appear perfectly respectable in a Christian theological context, but the last two issues, "blood" and "regeneration," which Wagner discusses in his later writings, have caused some consternation because Wagner relates them to "race." Some claim that such views in the later writings have nothing or little to do with *Parsifal* and are an aberration. Others believe they are important for understanding the stage work but believe them to reflect a "pernicious racist ideology."[69] My own approach is to engage in a critical reading of these writings and see if there is anything to be gleaned from them, especially in relation to *Parsifal*.[70]

65. *PW* 6:203 (modified); *GSD* 10:202. Ellis in a footnote points to the parallel in Parsifal Act II: "O blackness of earthly error, that while feverishly pursuing supreme salvation yet thirsts for the fount of perdition!" ("O, Weltenwahns Umnachten: in höchsten Heiles heißer Sucht nach der Verdammnis Quell zu schmachten!") (*WagPS* 200–201).

66. See *PW* 6:203; *GSD* 10:203.

67. See, e.g., Bell, "Sacrifice and Christology."

68. See the discussion at the end of chapter 5 above, and the fuller treatment in Bell, *Deliver Us from Evil*, 189–291. Note that I understand the "soul" not as a cognitive entity but rather as a supra-temporal, supra-spatial entity of which the body is its manifestation.

69. Millington, *Wagner Compendium*, 308, clearly has these writings in view when he writes: "it can scarcely be argued that [*Parsifal*] is untainted by the pernicious racist ideology of the composer's latter years."

70. Kühnel, "Prose Writings," 614, writes that these writings lack "a clear line of thought" and "proceed largely by association of ideas and feature numerous repetitions and a verbosity which is tiresome in parts." Nevertheless, he does think that they shine an important light on *Parsifal*.

These writings come in the form of an initial essay, *Religion and Art*,[71] which then has three supplements: *What Use Is This Knowledge?*;[72] *Know Thyself*;[73] *Heroism and Christianity*.[74] In all these works Wagner discusses among others things "degeneration" and "regeneration." One of the reasons many think these writings are not worthy of Wagner is because he engages with Arthur Gobineau who wrote on the inequality of races, although such engagement is found explicitly only in *Heroism and Christianity*. He knew Gobineau personally and read his works with some care.[75] Often he responds positively, as can be seen from Cosima's diaries and in *Heroism and Christianity*.[76] However, at crucial points Wagner disagrees with Gobineau and it is, I believe, precisely at such points that light can be thrown on *Parsifal*.[77]

Wagner first discusses the question of "degeneration" ("Entartung") (together with "depravity" ("Verderbtheit"]) and the relation to "blood" ("Blut") in his essay *Die Wibelungen* composed in the summer of 1848 and completed later. Some find that his later "racist ideology" can be traced back to this work and even that it anticipated some of Gobineau's work.[78] However, Gobineau worked independently of Wagner and we will see that

71. "Religion und Kunst" was published in *Bayreuther Blätter*, October 1880, 269–300.

72. "'Was nützt diese Erkenntnis?' Ein Nachtrag zu 'Religion und Kunst,'" published in *Bayreuther Blätter*, December 1880, 333–41. Ellis translates this rather oddly as "What Boots This Knowledge?"

73. "Ausführungen zu 'Religion und Kunst.' 'Erkenne dich selbst,'" published in *Bayreuther Blätter*, February-March 1881, 33–41.

74. "Ausführungen zu 'Religion und Kunst.' Heldentum und Christentum," published in *Bayreuther Blätter*, September 1881, 249–58. Ellis translates this as "Hero-Dom and Christianity." What was to be a concluding supplement, *On the Womanly in the Human* (PW 8:396–98; JA 10:172–74), was never completed; in fact it was as he was writing this essay that he died.

75. Wagner had four of his works in his Wahnfried library. The significant one though is Gobineau, *Essai sur l'inégalité*. He may have first encountered his work through Pott, *Rassen* (which is in Wagner's Wahnfried library) which was a critique of Gobineau's work. But he may have read this after first meeting Gobineau in Rome in 1876. Wagner then read all four volumes of the *Essai* in 1879 and then invited Gobineau to Wahnfried.

76. Wagner speaks of "[t]he author of the great work before us" (PW 6:280) or of Gobineau's "fine acumen" (277).

77. In this section I focus on *Heroism and Christianity*, since only here is Gobineau explicitly discussed. In future chapters I will consider the finest of these essays, *Religion and Art*, and others which deal with the questions such as Christology, faith, and antisemitism.

78. Deathridge, "Strange Love," 164–65. Note also that Wagner's essay *Judaism in Music* (1850) is also considered by many, but not all, to be "racist." I will discuss this essay in chapter 9 below.

the differences in their approaches are more significant than the similarities. According to Gobineau, the biological and cultural degeneration of races occurs through their "mixing." To some extent Wagner accepts this[79] but he adds two crucial dimensions to the discussion. First, he adopts a Darwinian perspective on the origin of the human species;[80] secondly, he adds a strong religious dimension to his anthropology, appealing to Schopenhauer's metaphysics of the "will," and criticizes Gobineau for failing to see the universal cultural structures as in religion and art.[81] Thus Wagner expresses the regenerative role of art: "the less recognizable the races, the lower humanity has sunk: all the more strongly and clearly must art assert itself."[82] In addition to these two crucial elements, Darwinism and religion, he adds the issue of "diet."[83]

Wagner writes that "whilst yellow races have viewed themselves as sprung from monkeys, the white traced back their origin to gods."[84] However, he then goes on to *reject* this[85] since "a review of all the races makes it impossible to deny the oneness of the human *species*,"[86] a clear allusion to Darwin.[87] What is it then that distinguishes the white race?[88] "With fine acumen Gobineau discovers it, not in an exceptional development of moral qualities, but in a larger store of the temperamental attributes from which

79. "[W]e may fitly take world-history as the consequence of these white men mixing with the black and yellow, and bringing them in so far into history as that mixture altered them and made them less unlike the white. Incomparably fewer in individual numbers than the lower races, the ruin of the white races may be referred to their having been obliged to mix with them; whereby, as remarked already, they suffered more from the loss of their purity than the others could gain by the ennobling of their blood" (*PW* 6:276; *GSD* 10:276).

80. Cf. Westernhagen, *Werk*, 285.

81. Hartwich, "Religion und Kunst," 314.

82. *CD* 29 May 1881.

83. He sees degeneration in terms of meat eating and regeneration in terms of vegetarianism. I am not sure how seriously to take this in view of Wagner's own practice regarding a vegetarian diet (see chapter 1 above).

84. *PW* 6:276; *GSD* 10:276.

85. Gutman, *Wagner*, 422, does not seem to recognize Wagner's position when he writes that he "described the Aryans, the great Teutonic world leaders, as sprung from the very gods, in contrast to the coloured man, to whom he conceded the rather lowly Darwinian descent from the monkey." Strictly speaking Darwinian theory was proposing that human beings and "monkeys" had a common ancestor.

86. *PW* 6:276–77; *GSD* 10:276–77.

87. Note, however, that he could have gained this idea of unity of humans from Kant's "Von den verschiedenen Rassen der Menschen" (see below).

88. Wagner clearly believes in the superiority of the white races (*PW* 6:277; *GSD* 10:277).

these morals flow."[89] So in the exceptional development of morals Wagner approves of Gobineau's determination of the "basic characteristics" ("Grundeigenthümlichkeiten") of white races. But he then departs from Gobineau by adopting Schopenhauer's view of the will and intellect. In relation to these "basic characteristics" he continues: "These we should have to look for in that keener and withal more delicate sensibility of Will which shews itself in a complex organism, united with the requisite intensity of Intellect."[90] In this positive case then, "in answer to the cravings of the will, the intellect shall rise to that clear-sightedness which casts its own light back upon the will, and, taming it, becomes a moral prompting."[91] In contrast to this one can have the state where the intellect is overpowered by the craving will: this is the "lower nature."[92] He argues that "it is just the strength of consciousness of Suffering, that can raise the intellect of higher natures to knowledge of the meaning of the world."[93] He adds: "Those natures in which the completion of this loftly process is evidenced by a corresponding deed, we call Heroic."[94]

The plainest type of heroism is found in Heracles who frees the world by his labors, and Wagner finds a parallel in Siegfried. Both were conscious of divine descent and are likened to Aryans.[95] However, a new type of hero is now required in view of the degeneration of the races. He agrees with Gobineau, "the talented and energetic author," that the races have fallen, but goes beyond him in looking for a new hero: "we now must seek the Hero where he turns against the ruin of his race, the downfall of its code of honour, and girds his erring will to horror: the hero wonderously become divine—the *Saint*."[96]

89. *PW* 6:277. *GSD* 10:277: "Mit schöner Sicherheit erkennt ihn Gobineau nicht in einer ausnahmsweisen Entwicklung ihrer moralischen Eigenschaften selbst, sondern in einem größeren Vorrathe der Grundeigenthümlichkeiten, welchen jene entfließen."

90. *PW* 6:277. *GSD* 10:277: "Diese hätten wir in der heftigen, und dabei zarteren, Empfindlichkeit des Willens, welcher sich in einer reichen Organisation kundgiebt, verbunden mit dem hierfür nöthigen schärferen Intellekte, zu suchen."

91. *PW* 6:277. *GSD* 10:277: "wobei es dann darauf ankommt, ob der Intellekt durch die Antriebe des bedürfnißvollen Willens sich bis zu der Hellsichtigkeit steigert, die sein eigenes Licht auf den Willen zurückwirft und, in diesem Falle, durch Bändigung desselben zum moralischen Antriebe wird."

92. *PW* 6:277; *GSD* 10:277.

93. *PW* 6:277; *GSD* 10:277.

94. *PW* 6:277. *GSD* 10:277: "Wir nennen die Naturen, in welchen dieser erhabene Prozeß durch eine ihm entsprechende Tat als Kundgebung an uns sich vollzieht, Helden-Naturen." Note the phrase "erhabene Prozeß," perhaps better translated as "sublime process," echoing Schopenhauer's view of the "sublime."

95. *PW* 6:277-78; *GSD* 10:277-78.

96. *PW* 6:279; *GSD* 10:279: "Für unsere Absicht ist es nämlich nun wichtig, den

His argument then takes a Schopenhauerian turn, speaking of "the vow of total world-renunciation."[97] Such a vow issues from heroic motives and is not to be seen as a "cowardly self-surrender" ("feige Selbstaufgebungen").[98] The saint overtakes the hero in his "endurance of suffering, his self-offering for others";[99] "almost more unshakable than the hero's pride is the saint's humility, and his truthfulness becomes the martyr's joy."[100]

There then follows a rather strange section on "blood" and "race"; although some of the details appear rather bizarre, his point about the blood of Christ does throw some light on *Parsifal*. Appealing to Gobineau, he argues that the semitic character influenced "Hellenism" and "Romanism"; it is even preserved in the "Latin" race, the property (Eigenthum) of this race being the Roman Catholic Church. Although this church had canonized saints, there are no longer any "genuine Saints," "Hero-martyrs of the Truth"; "the blood of Christendom itself is curdled." He adds: "And what a blood? None other than the blood of the Redeemer's self, which erewhile poured its hallowing stream into the veins of his true heroes."[101] This may find an echo in two passages in *Parsifal*. First, in Act I Amfortas despairs of "the fevered blood of sin" (*WagPS* 146–49):

Helden wiederum da aufzusuchen, wo er gegen die Verderbniß seines Stammes, seiner Sitte, seiner Ehre, mit Entsetzen sich aufrafft, um, durch eine wunderbare Umkehr seines misleiteten Willens, sich im *Heiligen* als göttlichen Helden wieder zu finden."

97. *PW* 6:279 (*GSD* 10:279): "It was a weighty feature of the Christian Church, that none but sound and healthy persons were admitted to the vow of total world-renunciation; any bodily defect, not to say mutilation, unfitted them." In the note, Ellis rightly points to Klingsor's self-mutilation of which Gurnemanz narrates in Act I (*WagPS* 124–25).

98. Ellis in *PW* 6:279 n., thinks Wagner is alluding to aphorism 38 of Nietzsche's *Morgenröte* (published in July 1881): "The same drive evolves into the painful feeling of *cowardice* under the impress of the reproach [that] custom has imposed upon this drive: or into the pleasant feeling of *humility* if it happens that a custom such as the Christian has taken it to its heart and called it *good*" (Nietzsche, *Daybreak*, 26 [modified]). Ellis is no doubt correct to detect such an allusion to Nietzsche's work even though the precise expression "feige Selbstaufgebungen" is not there. See *KSA* 3:45 (1.38): "Der selbe Trieb entwickelt sich zum peinlichen Gefühl der *Feigheit*, unter dem Eindruck des Tadels, den die Sitte auf diesen Trieb gelegt hat: oder zum angenehmen Gefühl der *Demuth*, falls eine Sitte, wie die christliche, ihn sich an's Herz gelegt und *gut* geheissen hat."

99. *PW* 6:279; *GSD* 10:279–80.

100. *PW* 6:279–80; *GSD* 10:280.

101. *PW* 6:280. *GSD* 10:280: "Und welches Blut wäre dieses? Kein anderes als das Blut des Erlösers selbst, wie es einst in die Adern seiner Helden sich heiligend ergossen hatte."

and now from my wound, in holiest Office,	und aus der nun mir, an heiligster *Stelle*,
the custodian of the most divine treasure	dem Pfleger göttlichster <u>Güter</u>,
and guardian of its redeeming balm	des Erlösungsbalsams <u>Hüter</u>,
spills forth the fevered blood of sin,	das heiße Sündenblut ent*quillt*,
ever renewed from the fount of longing	ewig erneu't aus des Sehnens *Quelle*,
that—ah! no repentance of mine can ever still!	das, ach! keine Büßung je mir *stillt*!

One has to proceed carefully here since this essay, *Heroism and Christianity*, was written four years after the completion of the libretto.[102] But this problem with Amfortas' "blood" does chime in with what Wagner writes in the essay.[103] Then at the end of the drama we have an anticipation of those words from *Heroism and Christianity*: "And what a blood? None other than the blood of the Redeemer's self, which erewhile poured its hallowing stream into the veins of his true heroes."[104] Holding the spear aloft, Parsifal proclaims (*WagPS* 234–35):

That this could heal your wound	Der deine Wunde durfte *schließen*,
I see pouring with holy blood	ihm seh' ich heil'ges Blut *entfließen*
yearning for that kindred fount	in Sehnsucht nach dem verwandten <u>Quelle</u>,
which flows and wells within the Grail.	der dort fließt in des Grales <u>Welle</u>.

The idea here is that, as in Wolfram's *Parzival* book 5, blood flows from the spear; but for Wagner this blood is that of the savior (i.e., the same blood that appears in the grail). At the words "for the kindred fount" ("nach dem

102. The poem was completed 19 April 1877 and the essay was published in the *Bayreuther Blätter* in September 1881.

103. Gutman, *Wagner*, 427, however, elaborates in such a way as to go well beyond the libretto: "Amfortas contrasts the divine blood of Christ in the Grail with his own sinful blood, corrupted by sexual contact with Kundry, a racial inferior, this criminal miscegenation epitomizing the Aryan dilemma. . . . The evil blood spilling from the wound is fed by a craving to repeat the transgression."

104. *PW* 6:280. *GSD* 10: 280: "Und welches Blut wäre dieses? Kein anderes als das Blut des Erlösers selbst, wie es einst in die Adern seiner Helden sich heiligend ergossen hatte."

verwandten Quelle") Wagner uses the "savior's lament" ("Heilandsklage") leitmotif.

Returning to *Heroism and Christianity* Wagner writes things that seriously relativize any claim that Wagner's religion was "racist": "The blood of the Saviour, the issue from his head, his wounds upon the cross,—who impiously would ask its race, if white or other? Divine we call it, and its source might dimly be approached in what we termed the human species' bond of union, its aptitude for Conscious Suffering."[105] Then arguing within a Darwinian framework, he appears to put limits on Darwinian evolution: "thenceforth she [Nature] brings no new, no higher species to light, for in it she herself attains her unique freedom, the annulling of the internecine warfare of the Will."[106] He continues:

> The hidden background of this Will, inscrutable in Time and Space, is nowhere manifest to us but in that abrogation; and there it shews itself divine, the Willing of Redemption (Wollen der Erlösung). Thus, if we found the faculty of conscious suffering peculiarly developed in the so-called white race, in the Saviour's blood we now must recognise the quintessence of free-willed suffering itself (des bewußt wollenden Leidens selbst), that godlike Pity (göttliches Mitleiden) which streams through all the human species, its fount and origin.[107]

Wagner regards the "blood in the Redeemer's veins" as a "divine sublimate of the species itself" such that it can save humankind. From this speculation "hovering between Physics and Metaphysics" Wagner is able to derive "a second and the weightiest distinction of his work, namely the simplicity of [Jesus'] teaching, which consisted almost solely in Example."[108] The focus of his "example" is his self-giving sacrificial death. The gist of Wagner's argument (it is not always clear!) is that the self-sacrifice of Christ is not just a heroic act of a single person but rather something that overcomes the world. Wagner stresses the work of the redeemer and the simplicity of his teaching,

---

105. *PW* 6:280. *GSD* 10:280–81: "Das Blut des Heilandes, von seinem Haupte, aus seinen Wunden am Kreuze fließend,—wer wollte frevelnd fragen, ob es der weißen, oder welcher Race sonst angehörte? Wenn wir es göttlich nennen, so dürfte seinem Quelle ahnungsvoll einzig in Dem, was wir als die Einheit der menschlichen Gattung ausmachend bezeichneten, zu nahen sein, nämlich in der Fähigkeit zu bewußtem Leiden."

106. *PW* 6:280; *GSD* 10:281. Current thinking on evolution corresponds to Wagner's conclusion that the human species will not further evolve.

107. *PW* 6:280–81; *GSD* 10:281. Note that Ellis has translated "Mitleiden" as "Pity"; "fellow-suffering" would be a more accurate translation.

108. *PW* 6:282; *GSD* 10:282–83.

which is rooted in the example he set in dying for humankind. "The blood
of suffering Mankind, as sublimated in that wondrous birth, could never
flow in the interest of whosoever favoured a single race; no, it shed itself
on all the human family, for noblest cleansing of Man's blood from every
stain."[109]

In view of this, the Communion is therefore crucial for Wagner:

> Thus, not withstanding that we have seen the blood of noblest
> races vitiated by admixture, the partaking of the blood of Jesus,
> as symbolised in the only genuine sacrament of the Christian
> religion, might raise the very lowest races to the purity of gods.
> This would have been the antidote to the decline of races through
> commingling, and perhaps our earth-ball brought forth breath-
> ing life for no other purpose than that ministrance of healing.[110]

In view of this, it is perhaps worth reflecting here whether we find in
these "regeneration" writings a "pernicious racist ideology."[111] Wagner actually departs considerably from Gobineau and, as we have seen, appeals rather to Darwin.[112] Cosima's diaries show Wagner's interest in Darwin's *On the
Origin of Species* (1859) since 1872 and in the *Descent of Man* (1871) since
1877.[113] Darwin's view of the development of species is clearly opposed to
Gobineau's static view: whereas Gobineau accentuated the difference of the
races, Darwin stressed the "unity of the human race." This has influenced
Wagner's discussion of degeneration and regeneration who likewise stresses
the unity of the human race, and to this he adds a crucial theological dimension: in Jesus Christ one achieves the transformation of humankind from

---

109. *PW* 6:282–83. *GSD* 10:283: "Das in jener wundervollen Geburt sich sublimir-
ende Blut der ganzen leidenden menschlichen Gattung konnte nicht für das Interesse
einer noch so bevorzugten Race fließen; vielmehr spendet es sich dem ganzen
menschlichen Geschlechte zur edelsten Reinigung von allen Flecken seines Blutes."

110. *PW* 6:283. *GSD* 10:283: "Während wir somit das Blut edelster Racen durch
Vermischung sich verderben sehen, dürfte den niedrigen Racen der Genuß des Blutes
Jesu, wie er in dem einzigen ächten Sakramente der christlichen Religion symbolisch
vor sich geht, zu göttlichster Reinigung gedeihen. Dieses Antidot wäre demnach dem
Verfalle der Racen durch ihre Vermischung entgegen gestellt, und vielleicht brachte
dieser Erdball athmendes Leben nur hervor, um jener Heilsordnung zu dienen." As
Hartwich, "Religion und Kunst," 315, rightly points out, this has nothing whatsoever to
do with "nazistischem Blut und Boden-Kult."

111. Millington, *Wagner*, 308.

112. Hartwich, "Religion und Kunst," 316.

113. In his Wahnfried library he had *Origin* in French (1862) and German (1867).
He also had German translations of *Descent* (1871) and other works.

its natural state (with differentiation of races) to a true moral one where differentiation of races is overcome.[114]

Any "racism" Wagner shows has been changed and indeed mollified by his appeal to Darwin and to his Christian outlook. In fact Wagner criticizes "Brahminic religion" for being a "race-religion"[115] and contrasts the "sublime simplicity of the pure Christian religion" with the "Brahminic religion," which applies "its knowledge of the world to the ensurance of supremacy for one advantaged race."[116] It is therefore not surprising that Wagner often disagrees with Gobineau. This is not only found in *Heroism and Christianity* but also in several instances recorded in Cosima's diaries. Wagner met with Gobineau at Wahnfried 11–24 May 1881[117] and they travelled together to Berlin for Neumann's fourth *Ring* cycle;[118] on returning to Bayreuth on 31 May 1881, the Count then stayed until 7 June. Then a year later again, the Count stayed again at Wahnfried, 11 May–17 June 1882. Often the two agreed but there are also many instances of significant disagreement including issues of the Gospels' attitudes to the poor[119] and the composer being "downright explosive in favor of Christian theories in contrast to racial ones."[120] And the fundamental disagreement between the two is that Wagner believed the races could be regenerated, something Gobineau denied.[121]

To highlight the fundamental importance of Christ's sacrifice for Wagner, I consider two entries from Cosimas' diaries. Reflecting on Kant's discussion of "seeds" ("Keime")[122] he says (entry for 17 December 1881):

114. See *PW* 6:284: "To us Equality is only thinkable as based upon a universal moral concord, such as we can but deem true Christianity elect to bring about; and that only on the subsoil of a true, but no mere 'rational' Morality . . . can a true aesthetic Art bear fruit, the life and sufferings of all great seers and artists of the past proclaim aloud" (*GSD* 10:284–85).

115. *PW* 6:281; *GSD* 10:281.

116. *PW* 6:283; *GSD* 10:283.

117. *CD* 5 May 1881 explains that a letter was received from the Count to say he was at Wahnfried, but the Wagners were then in Berlin for Neumann's *Ring* and they returned to Bayreuth on 11 May.

118. *CD* 24 May 1881.

119. On 18 May 1881 "a quarrel develops between the Count and him about the Irish, whom Gob. declares to be incapable of working. R. becomes very angry, says he would not work under such conditions, either, and he castigates the English aristocracy. The Count goes so far in his ideas as to reproach the Gospels for interceding in behalf of the poor." As Gregor-Dellin, *Wagner*, 487, remarks, this was "not a sentiment calculated to appeal to an exrevolutionary who had written *Jesus of Nazareth* in 1848."

120. *CD* 3 June 1881.

121. See the further discussion in chapter 10 below.

122. See "Von den verschiedenen Rassen der Menschen" (Weischedel, *Schriften zur Anthropologie I*, 15–17).

"In Germany everything is in the process of dying out—for me a dismal realization, since I am addressing myself to the still-existent seeds. But one thing is certain: races are done for, and all that can now make an impact is—as I have ventured to express it—the blood of Christ."[123] This coheres with Wagner's view that "regeneration" of races can only take place through the blood of Christ. And in her entry for 23 April 1882 we read: "[Richard] reproaches Gob[ineau] for leaving out of account one thing which was given to mankind—a saviour, who suffered for them and allowed himself to be crucified." Although one should be aware that these theological views are related to Wagner's racial theories, they do highlight that for Wagner the sacrifice of Christ and the power of his "blood" for the renewal of humankind were fundamental.[124] For Wagner the regeneration of human kind can only come about by the blood of Christ. Some may consider this politically incorrect; but it is no more so than Paul's analysis of the human situation. For him, "all have sinned and fall short of the glory of God" (Rom 3:23); the only hope is justification through faith in Christ, "whom God publicly set forth as a mercy seat perceived through faith, by means of his blood . . ." (Rom 3:25).[125]

Wagner therefore believes that humanity can be renewed through the sacrifice of Christ, the blood being an essential element in this. In fact, one could speak not only of Christ's blood being infused but also that blood is the means by which human beings come to participate in Christ.[126]

In this discussion of the work of Christ I have focused on Christ's sacrifice. But there is an additional strand to consider: Jesus abolishing the law. I will discuss Wagner's attitude to the law of Moses in chapter 9 below, but for now I highlight Wagner's arresting idea that God is fettered by his own law and that the work of Christ is aimed at the freeing of God from his own law.[127] Such a view is found in the sketches for *Jesus of Nazareth*.[128] It is also found in the *Ring*, where Wotan is restricted by his "treatises"; in fact they have such a devastating effect that the only way he can resolve his plight is by sending a hero who works independent of him. Such heros, Siegmund and Siegfried, have to die. As a result of Siegfried's and Brünnhilde's sacri-

---

123. *CD* 17 December 1881.

124. Wagner is therefore far from the "elitism" of Gnosticism. Although gnostics were prepared to share their special gnosis with others, they were in certain respects "elitist." See Roukema, *Gnosis and Faith*, 168–70.

125. See Bell, "Sacrifice and Christology," 17–18.

126. See chapter 5 above.

127. Hartwich, "Jüdische Theosophie," 117: "Die Christologie Wagners zielt auf die Befreiung Gottes von seinem eigenen Gesetz."

128. See chapter 9 below.

fice, rest comes to Wotan.[129] But whereas all three, Siegmund, Siegfried, and Brünhilde, act independently of Wotan, according to the New Testament witnesses, Christ and God act together in the work of atonement.[130]

Was Jesus a Jew?

Finally, I consider an issue that is highly sensitive: did Wagner think Jesus was Jewish? Wagner was among the first "modern" thinkers to put forward the idea of a non-Jewish Jesus. In *Religion and Art* Wagner refers to the "historical fact" "that Jesus of Nazareth was born in a corner of their little land, Judaea."[131] He highlights Jesus' humble birth ("no birth place could be found for the Redeemer of the *Poor*")[132] and finds it "doubtful if Jesus himself was of Jewish extraction, since the dwellers in Galilee were despised by the Jews on express account of their impure origin."[133] This finds an echo in later scholarship on the question of Jesus' non-Jewish descent.[134] Wagner also believes that only when churches cease to exist will one discover the non-Jewish Jesus. Cosima records that her husband "gets heated about the assumption that Jesus was a Jew; it has not been proved, he says, and Jesus spoke Syriac-Chaldaean: 'Not until all churches have vanished will we find the Redeemer, from whom we are separated by Judaism.'"[135] In this connection, one comment of Wagner's is particularly instructive. He tells Cosima of a performance of "Nathan the Wise" "at which, when the line asserting that Christ was also a Jew was spoken, an Israelite in the audience cried 'Bravo.'"[136] This line in Lessing's play and the context (which speaks of the whole of Christianity being built upon Judaism) clearly irritated Wagner.[137]

129. See the end of *Götterdämmerung*: "Rest now, rest now, you god!" ("Ruhe! Ruhe, du Gott!," *WagRS* 349).

130. See Bell, "Sacrifice and Christology."

131. *PW* 6:232–33; *GSD* 10:232; *JA* 10:139.

132. *PW* 6:233; *GSD* 10:232; *JA* 10:139.

133. *PW* 6:233; *GSD* 10:232; *JA* 10:139. Renan, whom Wagner read, asserted that the population of Galilee was "very mixed" although he refrains from drawing any conclusions about "what blood flowed in the veins of him who has contributed most to efface distinctions of blood in humanity" (Renan, *Life*, 43).

134. Note that among the first to discuss this was the *Jewish* scholar Armand (Aaron) Kaminka, *Studien zur Geschichte Galiläas*, Berlin 1889, 64–65 (see Deines, "Jesus der Galiläer," 58–60).

135. *CD* 27 November 1878.

136. *CD* 18 December 1881.

137. See Act IV Scene 7 where the brother says to Nathan: "Und ist denn nicht das ganze Christentum / Aufs Judentum gebaut? Es hat mich oft / Geärgert, hat mir Tränen

Wagner therefore held to a non-Jewish Jesus. Some have gone further and suggested that Wagner not only held to a non-Jewish but also to an Aryan Jesus.[138] So Gutman writes: "In Christ's veins flowed a kind of superblood, which, though above individual race, was yet an archetypal manifestation of the Aryan species."[139] The problem with Gutman's assertion is that Wagner never said Jesus' blood was "an archetypal manifestation of the Aryan species." However, he does believe that Christ's blood is there to help every single race (including the Aryans!). Quoting again those words in *Heroism and Christianity*: "The blood of suffering Mankind, as sublimated in that wondrous birth, could never flow in the interest of howsoever favoured a single race; no, it shed itself on all the human family, for noblest cleansing of Man's blood from every stain."[140]

---

gnug gekostet, / Wenn Christen gar so sehr vergessen konnten, / Daß unser Herr ja selbst ein Jude war" (Göpfert, *Lessing Werke II*, 315).

138. Spencer and Millington in *SL* 805 affirm he did.

139. Gutman, *Wagner*, 425.

140. *PW* 6:282–83; *GSD* 10:283. These words are quoted in Bertram, *Seher von Bayreuth*, 328–29 (published in 1943!). He writes: "Das Mysterium des entdämonisierten, von göttlichem Willen geheiligten Blutes ist das Zentralgeschehen der Parsifal-Handlung" (327). Unfortunately he goes on (327–30) to liken Wagner's *Parsifal* theology to the views of blood and race of Alfred Rosenberg. Rosenberg actually thought *Parsifal* was "ideologically unacceptable" (Spotts, *Bayreuth*, 166). In fact, he had doubts about much of Wagner but was "converted" to *Götterdämmerung* when Hitler took him to Bayreuth in 1937 (Hamann, *Winifred Wagner*, 198, 274).

7

Theological Reflections II
Sin, Sex, and Suffering

Introduction

THE PREVIOUS CHAPTER HAS, among other things, highlighted the crucial place the "work of Christ" plays in the theology of *Parsifal*. In this chapter I want to reflect on the reasons why this work of Christ is so crucial for Wagner. The two fundamental problems facing humankind for Wagner were sin and suffering and he was convinced that Christ's own suffering and death atones for human sin and in some sense brings healing not only to humanity but also to the whole created order. These were not only his own personal views but also ideas expressed in *Parsifal*.

In order to gain some understanding of his views on sin and suffering it is also necessary to see the connection Wagner makes with "sex" or what one should more appropriately call "erotic love," something that in turn is related to "knowledge." One of the striking things is that all these issues— sin, sex, suffering, and knowledge—are also central for the mythology of Genesis 3, the "fall" of humankind.

The Fall

Wagner's strong sense of sin reflects the long tradition of Christian pessimistic anthropology that goes back to St. Paul. Wagner would come to know of such anthropology not only from reading the New Testament but also by his study of Luther, which intensified in the last ten years of his life, 1873–83.[1] His view of sin is reflected in a letter to Liszt of 7 October 1854 (shortly after he completed *Das Rheingold*): "let us treat the world only with contempt; for it deserves no better. . . . It is evil, *evil, fundamentally evil.* . . . It belongs to Alberich: no one else!! Away with it!"[2] The fundamental evil character of the world is in fact portrayed throughout the *Ring*. If one wanted a pessimistic view of humankind, here it is. Further, this sense of sin and helplessness is intensified in that even the "gods" do wicked things and suffer! Shortly after writing these words to Liszt, Wagner discovered Schopenhauer who obviously confirmed his pessimistic anthropology. Schopenhauer, like Wagner, had been influenced by Paul and Luther, and was also an admirer of St. Augustine.[3]

One can view Wagner's view of sin in the light of Genesis 1–3: a "good creation" (Gen 1:31a) is ruined by "sin" (Gen 3). Wagner's clearest expression of this is in *Das Rheingold* Scene 1 where he brilliantly "portrays" the creation of the world through those 136 measures based on an Eb major chord before the appearance of the Rhinemaidens. The creation does indeed seem to be "very good," the Rhine and its gold being reminiscent of the life-giving river Pishon that "flows around the whole land of Havilah, where there is gold; and the gold of that land is good" (Gen 2:11–12).[4] The Rhinemaidens entrusted with the gold enjoy their stewardship, although Flosshilde, even early in the scene, chides Woglinde and Wellgunde for guarding the "sleeping gold" badly.[5] Once the demonic figure of Alberich enters, the potential for catastrophe is there. He "lusts" after the Rhinemaidens[6] who in turn tease him. On being rejected he then "lusts" after the Rhinegold. His "fall" certainly has a sexual element and even his stealing of the Rhinegold uses vocabulary and phrases usually used for the rape of a woman.[7]

1. See chapter 2 above.

2. *SL* 319; *SB* 6:249.

3. I have found little reference to Augustine in Wagner's utterances. One of the few is in connection with a discussion the Wagners had with Herrmann Levi about Augustine in *CD* 20 January 1881: "We talk about Saint Augustine, whom friend Levi carries around with him into whom I glanced and who does not please me on account of the God Creator he is always praising."

4. Kurt Hübner, "Christentum," 276, points to this parallel. He also notes the rough correspondence between the world ash tree and tree of life (Gen 2:9).

5. *WagRS* 58.

6. Wellgunde exclaims "The lecherous rogue! ("Der lüsterne Kauz!") (*WagRS* 59).

7. *WagRS* 69: "He tears the gold from the rock with terrible force" ("Er reisst mit furchtbarer Gewalt das Gold aus dem Riffe").

There is no explanation as to how Alberich came to have this evil character just as there is no explanation in Genesis as to how the serpent fits into God's good creation. But Alberich brings about a "fall" that then has disastrous consequences for everyone. Further, there are two other elements in *Das Rheingold* that parallel Genesis 1–3. First, there is a command of "father" not to divulge the secrets of the power of the ring;[8] this parallels Gen 2:16–17 where God warns Adam not to eat the fruit of the tree of the knowledge of good and evil. Secondly, the "fall" both in *Das Rheingold* and Genesis concerns the danger of "knowledge," a crucial Wagnerian theme that I tackle below.

Wagner's mythology of the "fall" would appear to parallel that of Genesis 1–3. In Christian theology this view of "fall" was then developed by St. Paul who wrote of sin coming into the world.[9] But there is another aspect of Wagner's view of sin that questions this simple scheme of a "good creation" that is desecrated. According to this second view sin has always been there and creation has always been "fallen"; or another way of considering it is that the "fall" in something not related to "history." In a sense his ideas were already prepared by Genesis 1–11, which concerns *primeval* history.[10] But whereas in Genesis some sort of link is made between this and the "history" or "sagas" of Genesis 12–50,[11] Wagner's mythology of a "fall" is unrelated to "history." Somewhere in his myth making I suspect he was coping with Schopenhauer and Darwin, coming to the view that the world has always been in a fallen state and the world has always been a place of suffering and death. It was this view that caused so much consternation among some Christians in the late nineteenth century (and often still does). Theologians have attempted to hold together the ideas of an original good creation and that suffering (if not sin) has always been there. In *Parsifal* Wagner makes his own attempt using a mythical pattern of "identical repetition."[12] There is no mention in *Parsifal* of an Adam or of an original state of sinlessness and bliss. But by using the figures of Klingsor, Amfortas, and Kundry he

8. Flosshilde warns: "Father told us and bound us over to guard the bright hoard wisely that no false thief should filch it from the flood: be silent, then, you babbling brood!" (*WagRS* 67).

9. Rom 5:12: "Therefore, just as sin came into the world through one man, and death came through sin, and so death spread to all because all have sinned." Note also Rom 5:18 (doubly marked in Wagner's New Testament and quoted in the *Jesus of Nazareth* sketches [*PW* 8:338; *DTB* 266]).

10. Bell, *Deliver Us from Evil*, 46, 215.

11. Note the linking genealogies in Gen 5:1–32; 10:1–32; 11:10–32.

12. On "identical repetition," see chapter 5 above.

manages to express the "fall" of humankind and point to the fact that the world is not as it should be. It is to their "fall" that I now turn.

Sin, Sex, Suffering, and Knowledge

The striking things about all three figures (Klingsor, Amfortas, and Kundry) is that they all "fall" because of some sexual misadventure. Klingsor fell because he wanted to join the company of the knights of the grail but could not quell the inner sexual urge so he castrated himself. This is seen as a most terrible sin.[13] Kundry's fall is slightly more difficult to discern, but I think Wagner suggests a sexual element here also. It is true that the curse that comes upon her is a result of laughing at Christ on the cross (and in chapter 5 I rejected the view that she was sexually attracted to the crucified Jesus).[14] But the name "Herodias," given to her by Klingsor, suggests a perverted sexual attitude.[15] Her "fallen state" therefore pre-existed her encounter with Christ. Then when we consider Amfortas, his "fall" is most certainly linked to a sexual misadventure in that he was seduced by Kundry; this led to his wound that refuses to heal.

In each case then we have the connection between sin and sex; and to this one can add suffering. Klingsor suffers the most awful agony.[16] To Kundry's mocking question "Are you chaste?," Klingsor reacts furiously: "Why do you ask that, accursed witch?" He "sinks into gloomy brooding" (*WagPS* 162–63):

13. See Gurnemanz's narration: "I never knew of what sin he was guilty there, but he then wished to atone and indeed become sanctified. Powerless to stifle the sin within him, on himself he laid dastardly hands (Ohnmächtig, in sich selbst die Sünde zu ertöten, an sich legt' er die Frevlerhand) which he then turned toward the Grail . . ." (*WagPS* 124–25). See also the discussion in chapter 6 above.

14. As argued above, this could be inferred from the use of the Tristan chord but this is I believe a false inference.

15. Wagner probably brought together the figures of Herodias and Salome as argued in chapter 5 above.

16. Wagner, however, had little sympathy for him. Comparing Alberich to Klingsor, he told Cosima that "he once felt every sympathy for Alberich" who represents "the naïveté of the non-Christian world." But he likened Klingsor to the Jesuits: "he does not believe in goodness, and this is his strength but at the same time his downfall . . ." (*CD* 2 March 1878).

Dire distress!	Furchtbare Not!
The pain of untamed desire,	Ungebändigsten Sehnens Pein,
most horrible, hell-inspired	schrecklichster Triebe
impulse	Höllen*drang*,
which I had throttled to deathly	den ich zum Todesschweigen mir
silence—	*zwang*—
does it now laugh aloud and mock	lacht und höhnt er nun <u>laut</u>
through you, bride of the devil?	durch dich, des Teufels <u>Braut</u>?

Later in Act II Kundry tells Parsifal of the curse that afflicts her (*WagPS* 198–99):

If you knew the curse	Kenntest du den Fluch,
which afflicts me, asleep and	der mich durch Schlaf und
awake,	*Wachen*,
in death and life,	durch Tod und Leben,
pain and laughter,	Pein und *Lachen*,
newly steeled to new affliction,	zu neuem Leiden neu <u>gestählt</u>,
endlessly through this existence!	endlos durch das Dasein <u>quält</u>.

But Wagner reserves his most powerful portrayal of suffering for Amfortas in his monologues in Acts I and III. We have already quoted part of his Act I monologue in chapter 5 above. Here is part of his final despair in Act III (*WagPS* 232–33):

Already I feel the darkness of	Schon fühl' ich den Tod mich
death enshroud me,	umnachten
and must I yet again return	und noch einmal sollt' ich in's
to life?	Leben zurück?
Madmen!	Wahnsinnige!
Who would force me to live?	Wer will mich zwingen zu *leben*?
Could you but grant me death!	Könnt ihr doch Tod mir nur
	geben!

Here we have the full horror of suffering. We have seen already that in his letter to Mathilde Wesendonck of 30 May 1859 he tells her that "Parzival" is "my third-act Tristan inconceivably intensified."[17] Anyone experiencing *Tristan* Act III needs a fairly strong emotional constitution[18] and

17. *SL* 457; *SB* 11:104.

18. This is wonderfully expressed by Nietzsche, even if one does not agree with his analysis (Nietzsche, *Tragedy*, 100; *KSA* 1:135).

one wonders whether it is at all possible to intensify Tristan's suffering.[19] As he was composing this he wrote this to Mathilde Wesendonck (mid-April 1859): "Child! This Tristan is turning into something *terrible*! This final act!!! – – – – – – – I fear the opera will be banned—unless the whole thing is parodied in a bad performance—: only mediocre performances can save me!"[20] In fact, the tenor singing Tristan, Ludwig Schnorr von Carolsfeld, died just three weeks after the final performance in 1865 and at the age of twenty-nine. Wagner felt in some sense responsible for Schnorr's death.[21] Further, Dreyfus points out that,

> only three days [after his death] Wagner begins drafting a new prose narrative for *Parzifal* . . . in which the themes of a character being "driven to the abyss" by a form of love-sickness and a frenzied sympathy of one man for another's erotic torment play a crucial role. The draft . . . begins by naming Anfortas . . . who "lies stricken of a spear-wound received in some mysterious love adventure, which will not heal."[22]

How then can we compare the sufferings of Tristan and Amfortas? One thing they have in common is that they long to die but cannot. Concerning Amfortas Wagner wrote: "With the spear-wound and perhaps another wound, too,—in his heart—, the wretched man knows of no other longing in his terrible pain than the longing to die."[23] He demands a glimpse of the grail but this gives him one thing only: immortality.[24] His suffering

19. E.g., "Against the fearful torture of my agonies what balm could bring me relief?" (*WagTS* 141).

20. *SL* 452 (Golther, *Mathilde Wesendonk*, 123: "Kind! Dieser Tristan wird was *furchtbares*! Dieser letzte Akt!!! – – – – – – – Ich fürchte die Oper wird verboten—falls durch schlechte Aufführung nicht das Ganze parodirt wird –: nur mittelmässige Aufführungen können mich retten!").

21. Schnorr complained about an icy draught blowing across the stage as he lay sweating after his exertions. Millington, *Wagner*, 78, notes the extent to which Wagner was numbed by this event: it was three years before he could bring himself to pay tribute to Schnorr in his *Recollections of Ludwig Schnorr von Carolsfeld*. A rather different explanation for the appearance of the "Recollections" (and one that does not reflect well on Wagner) is given by Newman, *Life IV*, 30–47.

22. Dreyfus, *Erotic Impulse*, 31–32, quoting *BB* 46. This prose sketch was written in just three days (27, 28, 29 August 1865) with the "Reinschrift" for Ludwig completed 31 August (see *DEAP* 68–77).

23. *SL* 457; *SB* 11:104.

24. See Gurnemanz's words in Act III Scene 1: "The Grail has long lain enclosed within the shrine; thus its guardian, repentant of his sin, hopes to hasten his end, since he cannot die while he beholds it, and with his life to end his torment" ("Im Schrein verschlossen bleibt seit lang' der Gral: so hofft sein sündenreu'ger Hüter, da er nicht sterben kann, wann je er ihn erschaut, sein Ende zu erzwingen und mit dem Leben

goes even beyond that of Tristan in that he has an intense conviction of sin (which many in the West in the twenty-first century find hard to comprehend). Further, unlike Tristan, his sin has devastating consequences for others in that they cannot see the life-giving grail and therefore cannot experience Christ's presence among them.

In *Parsifal* we have then these three figures, Klingsor, Kundry and Amfortas, who endure the most terrible suffering, a suffering that has been brought on by sin that has a sexual dimension to it. But how are we to understand the figure of Parsifal? According to Wagner the etymology of his name is "perfect fool,"[25] which some have mistakenly understood as "*sinless fool.*" Further, the mistake has often been made of seeing him as a Christ-like figure. Wagner clearly denied that he was so and was critical of von Wolzogen for suggesting it.[26] But one can say that Parsifal is the human means by which Amfortas is delivered from his agony. Parsifal comes to "participate" in the sufferings of Amfortas. In Act I Parsifal appears to understand nothing of the significance of the grail (although he realizes that there is something about it which is of fundamental importance). We see a stark contrast between Amfortas, burdened with knowledge, and Parsifal, who knows "nothing."[27] Although Parsifal is this "perfect fool" he "grasps his heart" during the lament of Amfortas indicating some level of understanding, albeit unconscious; but nothing is made of this until Act II.

Parsifal's encounter with Kundry is the key central point of the drama, and I follow through the dialogue, starting with Kundry's "recollection" of Parsifal and his mother. Kundry tells Parsifal how many years ago she saw him on his mother's breast (*WagPS* 188–89). She tells of how Herzeleide lost her loving husband in battle and that she now wishes to save her son from the same fate. "She strove to hide and shelter you safe afar from weapons and men's strife and fury." And the thing that Herzeleide feared above all was that Parsifal should acquire knowledge: "She was all concern and foreboding lest you should ever acquire knowledge" (*WagPS* 190–91). She then starts to instill a sense of guilt. "Do you not still hear her cry of distress / when you roamed late and far?" But "[h]ow great was her joy and laughter when she sought and found you again." And Kundry wonders whether he feared his mother's kisses. But one day he did not return and this broke Herzeleide's heart, and she died.[28]

---

seine Qual zu enden") (*WagPS* 218–19).

25. See chapter 3 above.

26. See chapter 6 above.

27. This is striking in Wolfram (*WolPH* 123).

28. *WagPS* 190–91. This then forms an inclusio for this section. It begins: "I saw the

Parsifal "sinks overcome with distress at Kundry's feet" for being responsible for his mother's death: she died because he, despite her tender love and care for him, abandoned her to seek adventure. He cries out: "Your son, your son had to murder you! Fool! Blind, blundering fool, where did you wander, forgetting her, forgetting yourself too? Oh dearest, beloved mother! ("Dein Sohn, dein Sohn mußte dich morden! O Tor! Blöder, taumelnder Tor. Wo irrtest du hin, ihrer vergessend, deiner, deiner vergessend! Traute, teuerste Mutter!") (*WagPS* 190–93). Kundry responds that this sense of remorse is a good thing since he can now experience the solace that love offers, and she expresses this using complex rhymes:

If grief were still a stranger to you,	War dir fremd noch der *Schmerz*,
the sweetness of consolation	des Trostes <u>Süße</u>
would never comfort your heart:	labte nie auch dein *Herz*;
now assuage that distress,	das Wehe, das dich *reut*,
that woe for which you grieve,	die Not nun <u>büße</u>
in the solace which love offers you.	im Trost, den Liebe dir *beut*.

Parsifal does not pick up on this; instead he thinks of his mother. Then he alludes to his neglect of another responsibility: "Ah, what else have I forgotten? What have I ever remembered yet?" ("Ha! Was Alles vergaß ich wohl noch? Wess' war ich je noch eingedenk?)" (II:952–54; *WagPS* 192–93). The clue to these words is the found in the orchestra where we hear clearly the motif of the spear,[29] first played on the cor anglais (an instrument obviously related to suffering),[30] then on the horn and flute and then on the oboe and first violins. Not so noticeable is a fragment of the theme of the "Heilandsklage" ("savior's lament") on the violas (pp): this alludes to the suffering of Amfortas and of Christ, the redeemer.[31] The "turn" of the "Heilandsklage" fragment played here is actually a reversal of the original theme and it is highly significant that throughout much of this section we have

---

child on its mother's breast, its first childish sounds still laugh in my ear; though *sad* at heart, how *Herzeleide* also laughed" ("Ich sah das Kind an seiner Mutter Brust, sein erstes Lallen lacht mir noch im Ohr: das *Leid* im *Herzen*, wie lachte da auch *Herzeleide*"). Then it ends: "her *sorrow* broke her *heart*, and *Herzeleide* died" ("ihr brach das *Leid* das *Herz*, und *Herzeleide* starb"). Note also the word play on "Herzeleide."

29. The spear motif is taken from part of the love feast motif (segment d in the musical example 2 of chapter 5).

30. Wagner's famous use of this instrument to express pain is the beginning of *Tristan* Act III.

31. Kienzle, "A Christian Music Drama?" 123.

this recurring reversed "turn," which points to the suffering of Herzeleide, Amfortas, and Christ.[32]

Kundry is in control during this whole section and Parsifal simply reacts. Wagner expresses this sense of control musically in that Kundry has a stable though chromatic melody. By contrast Parsifal responds in incomplete motifs. Further Kundry sings in rhyme throughout this section; Parsifal does not (except that he repeats words: "Mutter"; "vergessend").[33] And one way this rhyme may work is that it springs surprises—two words that one does not usually associate are suddenly and unexpectedly brought together. This rhyming is especially strong in Kundry's "mother confessor" section:[34]

Confession	*Bekenntis*
will end guilt in remorse,	wird Schuld in Reue <u>enden,</u>
understanding	*Erkenntnis*
changes folly into sense.	in Sinn die Torheit <u>wenden.</u>

One could say that Kundry has been playing the "priest," instilling a sense of guilt but also offering the release of "confession." Now she starts playing the "sphinx" also in putting "riddles" to him. We saw her sphinx-like nature already in Act I where the stage direction indicates that Kundry cowers like a sphinx. Her sphinx-like nature continues here in Act II in that she puts riddles to Parsifal and Wagner clearly links this with the Oedipus myth.[35] Wagner first discussed the Oedipus myth in a section of *Opera and*

---

32. The shape of this reversed turn corresponds to that of Brünnhilde's theme in *Götterdämmerung*. Kienzle, "A Christian Music Drama?" 117, points out that Wagner's use of the turn here, "anything but a playful decoration," goes back to C. P. E. Bach (1714–88) who recommended its use "to intensify musical expression, especially in the imitation of speech in recitative passages of a free fantasy, passages that have the character of a lament involving a direct expression of feeling."

33. Note, however, that Parsifal does sing in rhyme when he is later in control (*WagPS* 200–201).

34. Note also the rhythmic pattern 3+7+3+7.

35. In Sophocles, one of the Wagner's "indispensables" (together with Homer, Aeschylus, the *Symposium*, *Don Quixote*, the whole of Shakespeare, and Goethe's *Faust*; CD 4 June 1871), Oedipus rebukes Tiresias for trying to throw out the very person who solved the riddle of the "versifying hound" (*Oedipus Tyrannus* 390–400). Wagner's Wahnfried library included the edition of Sophocles by Theodorus Bergk (Latin) and the translation into German by J. J. C. Donner. Apollodorus 3.5.8 tells of the famous riddle of the sphinx ("What is that which has one voice and yet becomes four-footed and two-footed and three footed") which Oedipus solves; the sphinx then commits suicide.

Drama,[36] possibly the earliest modern extended discussion of the Oedipus myth, and written when Freud (1856–1938) was not even born; in this discussion he includes the sphinx, whose riddles Oedipus solved.[37] Elements of the Oedipus myth are clearly central for *Siegfried* Act III;[38] they are also fundamental for *Parsifal* Act II. Wagner appears to be drawing on the female sphinx of Theban legend who puts riddles and tries to destroy, but who meets her match in Oedipus. Kundry's riddles are met by silence, but ultimately Parsifal does conquer as we shall see.

Kundry tells Parsifal to learn to know the love that enfolded Gamuret when Herzeleide's passion engulfed him in its fire! And the power of this passion is manifest in giving Parsifal his very life and being.

Learn to know the love	Die Liebe lerne *kennen*,
that enfolded Gamuret	die Gamuret <u>umschloß</u>,
when Herzeleide's passion	als Herzeleids *Entbrennen*
engulfed him in its fire!	ihn sengend <u>überfloß</u>!
She who once	Die Leib und *Leben*
gave you life and being,	einst dir *gegeben*,
to subdue death and folly	der Tod und Torheit weichen <u>muß</u>,
sends you	sie *beut'*
this day,	dir *heut'*,
as a last greeting of a mother's blessing,	als Muttersegens letzten <u>Gruß</u>,
the first <u>kiss</u> of love.	der Liebe ersten <u>Kuß</u>.

This then prepares us for the crucial turning point in the drama. The music that is played in the orchestra as Kundry kisses Parsifal deserves close attention. The 'cellos trace out the notes of the Tristan chord. In chapter 5 above I discussed how this chord is used in *Tristan* to represent the union of the lovers or more precisely their desire for union. It may be thought that here, in *Parsifal*, the chord simply reflects this erotic impulse. But Wagner is being highly ambiguous. This is because the chord is then played on the three trombones and bass tuba[39] and the chord is played with exactly

36. See *PW* 2:180–92; *GSD* 4:55–66; *JA* 7:178–90 (section 2.3).

37. *PW* 2:183; *GSD* 4:57; *JA* 7:181.

38. On discovering that the person in armor is "kein Mann" ("no man") he calls on his mother: "To save me, whom shall I call on to help me? Mother! Mother ! Remember me!" (*WagRS* 266). Later he identifies Brünnhilde with his mother as he asks: "So my mother did not die? Was the lovely women merely asleep?" (*WagRS* 268).

39. The order of notes though is F D# G# B.

the same instruments a little later in the Act when Kundry relates how she laughed at Christ on the cross and how his glance met her. I argued in chapter 5 above that the chord there is relating to Christ's love for Kundry, a self-giving love. And this chord is used again in the Good Friday music precisely at the point where Gurnemanz sings of Christ's sacrificial death.[40] And one of the highly significant aspects of the use of the chord in these two Act II passages is the instrumentation of a "trombone choir" ("Posaunenchor").[41] It is true that we are dealing with a wicked act of seduction;[42] but, if my analysis is correct, it is also much more than that. The other very interesting theological aspect of the music is that Wagner employs an undulating theme that corresponds to a fragment of the prelude to Act I of Tristan and is then later taken up in the Good Friday music of Act III.687–88.

Example 6: Kundry's Kiss

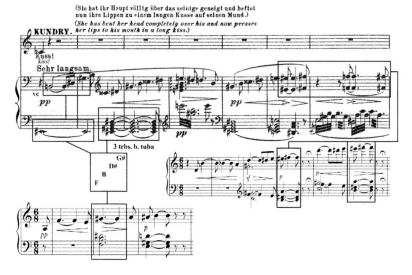

Now as Kundry kisses Parsifal he becomes fully aware of the nature of Amfortas' suffering; in fact he becomes fully identified with his

40. See chapter 5 above.

41. See chapter 5 above.

42. See CD 4 June 1878: "R. recalls the bars which accompany Kundry's kiss and in which the fatal motive of love's longing, creeping like poison through the blood, makes a shattering effect."

personhood.[43] As Wagner puts it: "Transferred wholly into the soul of Anfortas, he feels Anfortas' enormous suffering, . . . the unspeakable torment of yearning love."[44] Parsifal cries out (*WagPS* 194–95):[45]

Amfortas! The wound! The wound!	Amfortas! Die Wunde! Die Wunde!
It burns within my heart [Amfortas]	Sie brennt in meinem Herzen!

In a letter to King Ludwig (7 September 1865) Wagner wrote:

> The kiss which causes Anfortas to fall into sin awakens in Parzival a full awareness of that sin, not as his own sin but as that of the grievously afflicted Anfortas whose lamentation he had previously heard only dully, but the cause of which now dawns upon him in all its brightness, through his sharing the feeling of sin.[46]

Domingo suggests that "a totally different colour" in now required for Parsifal to reflect his new fundamental insight and maturity.[47] The text in Act II then continues[48] (*WagPS* 194–95):

O sorrow, sorrow!	O, Klage! Klage!
Fearful sorrow!	Furchtbare Klage!
From the depths of my heart it cries aloud.	Aus tiefstem Herzen schreit sie mir auf.
Oh! Oh!	Oh!—Oh!—
Most wretched! Most pitiable!	Elender! Jammervollster!
I saw the wound bleeding:	Die Wunde sah ich bluten:—
Now it bleeds in me!	nun blutet sie in mir!—
Here—here!	Hier—hier!

43. Porges notes: "[Parsifal] an die Seite greifend, wo Amfortas die Wunde hat, als wenn er selbst der Amfortas wäre" (*DEAP* 203).

44. *BB* 57, quoted in Dreyfus, *Erotic Impulse*, 32.

45. The words in square brackets refer to the leitmotif employed.

46. *SL* 664; *DEAP* 20.

47. Matheopoulos, *Domingo*, 213.

48. Note again that whereas Kundry has rhyming in her words, Parsifal does not.

But then Parsifal appears to contradict this: it is not the physical wound in the side[49] but the "flame" in his heart, the flame of sexual desire (*WagPS* 194–95):

No, no! It is not the wound.	Nein! Nein! Nicht die Wunde ist es.
Flow in streams, my blood, to it!	Fließe ihr Blut in Strömen dahin!
Here! Here in my heart is the flame!	Hier! Hier, im Herzen der Brand!
The longing, the terrible longing which seizes and grips all my senses!	Das Sehnen, das furchtbare Sehen, das alle Sinne mir faßt und zwingt!
O torment of love!	Oh!—Qual der Liebe!—
How everything trembles, quakes and quivers in sinful desire!	Wie alles schauert, bebt und zuckt in sündigem Verlangen!

This second section of Parsifal's monologue may suggest that the pain he feels is the torment of the sexual urge. But this is not quite the case and we get yet another "correction." We will see this in the text that follows, but it is also indicated in a remarkable comment Wagner made in the rehearsals. According to notes made by Heinrich Porges, Wagner said that with the words "Oh! Qual der Liebe" ("O torment of love") Parsifal comes to see the world as a place of sacrificial slaughter ("Now all at once Parsifal sees how the whole world is a sacrificial slaughter").[50] This sacrificial slaughter is related only partly to the suffering of Amfortas; I suggest that at the deepest level it refers to the sacrifice of Christ, who encompasses in his suffering the suffering of the whole world. Such an interpretation is confirmed by the following text where the stage direction says that Parsifal "falls into a complete trance":[51]

---

49. In the following (line 2) I have changed *WagPS* 195 "from it" to "to it" ("dahin"). The clue is in the 1865 sketch, which speaks of Amfortas' sinful blood rushing from his heart and "bursting the wound afresh" (*BB* 50).

50. "Jetzt sieht Parsifal auf einmal, wie die ganze Welt ein Schlachtopfer ist" (Wagner's "Probenbemerkungen" for 3.1037–38 ["Qual der Liebe"] [*DEAP* 203]).

51. *WagPS* 194–97. Note again that there is no rhyme here ("ich" and "mich" seem to be an accidental rhyme and are separated by two lines including a colon). Leitmotifs are named in square brackets. Domingo suggests that this passage is "one of the most sublime in *any* work" (Matheopoulos, *Domingo*, 213).

My dull gaze is fixed on the sacred vessel; [Grail]	Es starrt der Blick dumpf auf das Heilsgefäß;
the holy blood flows: [love feast]	Das heil'ge Blut erglüht:
the bliss of redemption, divinely mild,	Erlösungswonne, göttlich mild,
trembles within every soul around: [spear]	durchzittert weithin alle Seelen:
only here, in my heart, will the pangs not be stilled.	nur hier, im Herzen, will die Qual nicht weichen.
The saviour's lament I hear there, [saviour's lament]	Des Heilands Klage da vernehm' ich,
the lament, ah! the lamentation from His profaned sanctuary:	die Klage, ach! die Klage um das entweihte Heiligtum:
"Redeem Me, rescue Me [love feast]	"Erlöse, rette mich
from hands defiled by sin!"	aus schuldbefleckten Händen!"
Thus rang the divine lament in terrible clarity in my soul.	So rief die Gottesklage furchtbar laut mir in die Seele.
And I—fool, coward,	Und ich—der Tor, der Feige,
fled hither to wild childish deeds!	zu wilden Knabentaten floh ich hin!

The stage direction then indicates that Parsifal "flings himself in despair on his knees" ("stürzt verzweiflungsvoll auf die Knie") and he cries out (*WagPS* 196–97):

Redeemer! Saviour! Lord of grace! [spear]	Erlöser! Heiland! Herr der *Huld*!
How can I, a sinner, purge my guilt?	Wie büß' ich, Sünder, meine *Schuld*?

In this section we therefore see that Parsifal's pain in his "heart" moves down from a physical pain, down to a sexual yearning, and then ultimately to a spiritual agony.

I now want to draw out the central aspect of this remarkable passage: Parsifal comes to participate in the suffering of Christ. This is suggested by the libretto, Parsifal's words paralleling the lament of Amfortas in Act I who, as we saw in chapter 5 above, also participates in Christ.[52] And this communion with Christ's sufferings is underlined by the musical quotation of the

---

52. Some of the vocabulary is the same but more significant are the common ideas (e.g., the flow of blood).

"savior's lament" ("Heilandsklage"). This leitmotif was named by Hans von Wolzogen after Parsifal's words in II.1062–66: "The saviour's lament I hear there, the lament, ah! the lamentation from His profaned sanctuary" ("Des Heilands Klage da vernehm' ich, die Klage, ach! die Klage um das entweihte Heiligtum" (*WagPS* 194–95). This "lament," "Klage," refers fundamentally to the suffering of Christ in Gethsemane and on Golgotha. The very first occurrence of this "Heilandsklage" is towards the end of the Prelude to Act I, and in program notes for king Ludwig (for a private performance on 12 November 1880) Wagner writes: "There once more, from out of the awe of solitude, throbs forth the lament of loving compassion: the agony, the sacred cold sweat on the Mount of Olives, the divine suffering of Golgotha" ("Bangen, heiliger Angstschweiß des Ölberges, göttliches Schmerzens-Leiden des Golgatha").[53]

So what is the nature of the "savior's lament"? Parsifal quotes Christ's own lament: he asks to be redeemed from "hands defiled by sin." Some take the "defiled hands" to refer to Klingsor; but surely it refers to Amfortas.[54] He is the "sinful protector of the sanctuary."[55] Here is perhaps one clue to the final closing words of the stage work: "The Redeemer redeemed!" ("Erlösung dem Erlöser!").[56] The Redeemer is Christ,[57] an interpretation that is supported by the fact that the words are sung to the "love feast motif." One way in which redemption comes to Christ in the closing bars is that the grail, in which his blood appears, is no longer under the guardianship of the sinner Amfortas but under that of the "perfect fool," "Parsi-Fal."[58] Another sense in which Christ is "redeemed" is that he actually gains something himself from the redemption of the world.[59] In contrast to the figure of Lohengrin, whose "incarnation" and redeeming work fail, here the God-man succeeds

53. *PW* 8:389 (modified); *DEAP* 46 (*KB* 3:186–87).

54. See Borchmeyer, "Kundrys Lachen," 446.

55. Amfortas is referred to as the "sinful protector" ("der sündige Hüter") and "Guardian of the Grail" ("Du Hüter des Grals") in Act III (*WagPS* 230–31). The phrase "sinful protector of the sanctuary" ("sündige Hüter des Heiligtums") is used in Wagner's "programme" for the Prelude to Act I (*PW* 8:389 (modified); *DEAP* 46).

56. *WagPS* 236–37.

57. In theory the reference could also be to Parsifal or perhaps even, as Mertens, "Wagners Gral," 114, to Wagner himself.

58. On the (false) etymology, see chapter 3 above.

59. Note the sense in which Brünnhilde is both the redeemed and the redeemer at the end of *Götterdämmerung*; she is redeemed precisely in that in laying down her life she "gets something out it"!

in redeeming the world.[60] Although the ending of *Parsifal* has a "Christian" message, the precise nature of it is highly ambiguous.[61]

Returning to the lament, it must also be stressed that Christ's suffering does not just refer to the "hands defiled by sin." It must also refer to the suffering of Christ in Gesthemene and on Golgotha. Hence Wagner's comment made during the rehearsal that Parsifal comes to see the world as a place of sacrificial slaughter.

Now how are we to link the kiss of Kundry with the understanding that dawns on Parsifal? I suggest two explanations. The first is that Kundry corresponds to the serpent of Genesis 3. In a letter to Ludwig (7 September 1865) Wagner answers some of his questions: "'What is the significance of *Kundry's* kiss?'—That, my belovèd, is a terrible secret! You know, of course, the serpent of Paradise and its tempting promise: 'eritis sicut Deus, scientes bonum et malum.'"[62] The Latin quotation "you shall be as God, knowing good and evil" is a variation from the Vulgate of Gen 3:5: *eritis sicut dii scientes bonum et malum*.[63] I think Wagner's explanation is to be taken seriously; he is not offering a disingenuous explanation simply to please Ludwig. Relating Kundry to the serpent certainly opens up the dramatic structure of the work. We have already pointed to her "animal" characteristics (she is sphinx-like). Here in Act II Kundry, like the serpent of Genesis 3, tells lies, even claiming later in Act II that Parsifal is the "redeemer." Further, like the serpent she promises "knowledge" and as in Genesis 3 this coming to knowledge has a sexual connotation.

---

60. On Lohengrin's failure, see Mertens, "Wagners Gral," 97, who comments: "der Abgrund zwischen Diesseits und Transzendenz erweist sich als unüberbrückbar, die Menschwerdung Lohengrins misslingt, es gibt keine Erlösung." See also chapter 6 above.

61. The striking thing about "The Redeemer redeemed" is the similarity to the Gnostic "redeemed redeemer." On this see Rudolph, *Gnosis*, 121–22, 131. One of the clearest expressions is found in the "Hymn of Christ" in the *Acts of John* 95.4: "I will be saved, / And I will save" (Hennecke, *Apocrpha*, 2:228). These words are quoted by Augustine in Epistle 237 (*NPNF1* 1:587). Although there was some scholarship on Gnosticism that could have been available to Wagner, the idea of the "redeemed redeemer" was not developed until the early twentieth century by Richard Reitzenstein. But I have noted at various points how remarkably anti-gnostic Wagner's ideas were.

62. *SL* 664; *DEAP* 19–20: "'Welche Bedeutung es mit dem Kusse Kundry's hat?'— Das ist ein furchtbares Geheimnis, mein Geliebter! Die Schlange des Paradieses kennen Sie ja, und ihre lockende Verheißung: 'eritis sicut Deus, scientes bonum et malum.'"

63. The original Hebrew is *kē'lohîm* and can be rendered "as God" or "as gods" (see Skinner, *Genesis*, 75). As far as we know Wagner did not know Hebrew; but it is interesting to note that his Luther Bible in the Wahnfried library has the Old Testament in Hebrew and German (for details, see "Versions of the Bible used by Wagner" in the bibliography).

"Knowledge" in Wagner is often seen as a burden. Further, in his dramas he sometimes draws a striking contrast between a young care-free character and an experienced knowledge-laden character. So in *Meistersinger* we have Walther versus Hans Sachs; in the *Ring* Siegfried versus Wotan; and here in *Parsifal* we have the figure of Parsifal versus Amfortas. And in this passage we see Parsifal transformed from a perfect fool to a knowledge-laden character. And this comes about by a sexual encounter. So Kundry asks "Was it my kiss which made you all-seeing?"[64] or as Gutman nicely translates it "Did my kiss make you see the world so clearly?"[65] Yes it did. Genesis gives one explanation: there is a "fall," which has a sexual connection and is related to gaining a knowledge of good and evil.[66] And I now come to another explanation.

Although Wagner was critical of aspects of Schopenhauer, there is no doubt in my mind that Schopenhauer's distinction between the worlds of phenomena and noumena has colored his dramas *Tristan* and *Parsifal*. The depths of reality are not to be found in the phenomena, the appearance; the depths of reality are to be found in the noumena, in the thing-in-itself, the world-will; and in *Tristan* this noumenal world corresponds to the night. Schopenhauer argued that two of the best ways of approaching the noumenal realm are through the sexual encounter and through music. And it is surely no accident that after discovering Schopenhauer in 1854, Wagner was then to work on *Tristan*, a celebration of erotic love, and *Meistersinger*, a celebration of music itself.[67] The great difference, of course, is the agony of *Tristan* compared to the joy of *Meistersinger*, a contrast that to some extent can be explained through Schopenhauer's view of the "will": whereas sex represents the will in all its pain, music represents the will with no suffering.[68] Wagner, as we shall see later, actually came to the view that through music we *do* experience life as suffering,[69] but the point I emphasize here is that as Parsifal has his sexual awakening he comes to understand the depths of the created order, and in these depths he discovers the true agony of creation. He comes to see the Schopenhauerian "world-will" in all its horror.

This agony, as I argued above, refers primarily to Christ's suffering. But it also refers to the whole of creation, which one can say participates in this

64. "So war es mein Kuß, der welthellsichtig dich machte?" (*WagPS* 200–201).

65. Gutman, *Wagner*, 427.

66. See Barr, *Garden of Eden*, 57–73.

67. Cf. Magee, *Schopenhauer*, 386.

68. *WWR* 2:451 (*ASSW* 2:579): "music never cause[s] us actual suffering, but still remains pleasant even in its most painful chords." By contrast in "real life" "we ourselves are now the vibrating string that is stretched and plucked."

69. See chapter 11 below.

suffering of Christ. As Paul writes in Romans 8, the creation is "subjected to futility" (v. 20), is in "bondage to decay" (v. 21), and is "groaning in labor pains" (v. 22). Wagner's thinking here may well be influenced by Romans 8; but it may also be influenced by Darwin whose works we know he had read.

Parsifal's dialogue with Kundry in Act II shows that not only is Christ a sacrifice for sin; the whole creation also suffers with him. But this suffering is resolved. This is seen first in the Good Friday Music: "Now all creation rejoices at the Saviour's sign of love and dedicates to Him its prayer" ("Nun freut sich alle Kreatur auf des Erlösers holden Spur, will ihr Gebet ihm weihen").[70] Then at the very end of the drama the suffering of creation is resolved with the return of the spear to the knights of the grail, the healing of Amfortas, and the descent of the dove.

A Theology of Good Friday

In *Parsifal*, his crowning achievement, Wagner confronts the suffering of the world. He reflects on this at the of end of his article *The "Devotional Stage Festival" in Bayreuth in 1882*:

> Who can look, his lifetime long, with open eyes and unpent heart upon this world of robbery and murder organised and legalised by lying, deceit and hypocrisy, without being forced to flee from it at times in shuddering disgust? Whither turns his gaze? Too often to the pit of death. But him whose calling and his fate have fenced from that, to him the truest likeness of the world itself may well appear the herald of redemption sent us by its inmost soul. To be able to forget the actual world of fraud in this true-dream image (wahrtraumhafte[s] Abbild), will seem to him the guerdon of the sorrowful sincerity with which he recognised its wretchedness. Was he to help himself with lies and cheating, in the evaluation of that picture? [*To the artists*] You all, my friends, found that impossible; and it was the very truthfulness of the examplar which he offered you to work upon, that gave you too the blessed sense of world-escape (die Weihe der Weltentrückung); for you could but seek your own contentment in that higher truth alone. And that you found it, was proved me by the hallowed grief of our farewell, when after all those noble days the parting came. To us all it gave the surety of another joyful meeting.[71]

70. The suffering and the redemption of the whole of creation is a central theme in Rom 8:18–25.

71. *PW* 6:312; *GSD* 10:307–8. The article was published in *Bayreuther Blätter*

There was not to be another meeting on this earth. Wagner died just three and a half months later.

Although Wagner could see the agony of creation through the lens of Good Friday he could also see the renewal of creation through this supreme act. He understood the whole of *Parsifal* in the light of such a Good Friday. In a letter to Ludwig of 14 April 1865 Wagner writes: "A warm and sunny Good Friday, with its mood of sacred solemnity, once inspired me with the idea of writing 'Parzival.'"[72] And just a little earlier in the letter Wagner writes this (and if this is not profound theology I don't know what is):

> Today is Good Friday again!—O, blessèd day! Most deeply portentous day in the world! Day of redemption! God's suffer-ing!! Who can grasp the enormity of it? And yet, this same inef-fable mystery—is it not the most familiar of mankind's secrets? God, the Creator,—he must remain totally unintelligible to the world:—God, the loving teacher, is dearly belovèd, but not un-derstood:—but the God who suffers (Gott der Leidende),—His name is inscribed in our hearts in letters of fire; all the obstinacy of existence is washed away by our immense pain at seeing God suffering (Gott im Leiden zu sehen)! The teaching which we could not take in (Die Lehre, die wir nicht *begriffen*), it now takes hold of us (sie *ergreift* jetzt uns): God within us,—the world has been overcome (überwunden)! Who created it? An idle ques-tion! Who overcame it? God within our hearts,—God whom we comprehend in the deepest anguish of fellow-suffering (der im tiefsten Schmerz des Mitgefühles *begriffene* Gott)![73]

Lucy Beckett rightly notes that "[t]his is profoundly Christian in im-pulse and understanding." She also comments on the striking prose and the word play on "begreifen" (to take in) and "ergreifen" (to take hold of).[74] The "God within our hearts" is the suffering Christ. In the words of the "youths" ("Jünglinge"), he lives in us through his death.[75] So although Wagner had no resurrection, he nevertheless believed that Christ was present in our hearts in his suffering and death.

Wagner's contrast between the creator God and the God who suffers to some extent parallels Luther's *deus absconditus* and *deus revelatus*. For

November–December 1882.

72. *SL* 642. See also his account given in *My Life* 547 (*Mein Leben* 2:561), quoted in chapter 3 above.

73. *SL* 641–42, translation amended and emphasis added (Bauer, *Richard Wagner: Briefe*, 432–33; *KB* 1:82).

74. Beckett, *Parsifal*, 138.

75. *WagPS* 144–45.

Luther it is the latter with whom we are concerned. Likewise for Wagner, it is the God who suffers with whom we are concerned. He is the *deus revelatus*. On the other hand, the *deus absconditus*, the God who creates, is the one with whom we are not concerned.[76] For he concerns things that are above us. And "that which is above us does not concern us" *Quae supra nos, nihil ad nos*.[77]

Wagner in this passage from Act II brings together in a dense constellation the themes of sex, sin, and suffering, and for all his theological unorthodoxy I think he performs a crucial theological service in turning our eyes towards the God who suffers.

Love, Sex, and Redemption

So far one may get the impression that sex in *Parsifal* was thoroughly negative and that Wagner is following Schopenhauer in this respect. Schopenhauer thought the sexual impulse was the "kernel of the Will-to-live":

> The sex-relation in the world of mankind . . . is really the invisible central point of all action and conduct, and peeps up everywhere, in spite of all the veils thrown over it. . . . [T]he sexual impulse is the kernel of the Will-to-live, and consequently the concentration of all willing. . . . [Man] is concrete sexual impulse, for his origin is an act of copulation, and the desire of his desires is an act of copulation, and this impulse alone perpetuates and holds together the whole of his phenomenal appearance.[78]

Sexual desire is seen in entirely negative terms. "Indeed, [sexual desire] robs of all conscience those who were previously honorable and upright, and makes traitors of those who have hitherto been loyal and faithful. Accordingly, it appears on the whole as a malevolent demon, striving to pervert, to confuse, and to overthrow everything."[79] As we have seen in chapter 2 above, Wagner came to distance himself from Schopenhauer, coming to the view in *Tristan* that redemption is not *from* erotic love but *through* erotic love. I now set out how he came to change his view.

First of all, in a brief paragraph of his autobiography he speaks of his "being able to remedy some alarming weaknesses in one aspect of his

---

76. Cf. Saebo, "Yahweh as *Deus absconditus*."

77. Luther, *De servo arbitrio* (WA 18:605.20–21). On this see Jüngel, "Quae supra nos, nihil ad nos."

78. *WWR* 2:513–14; *ASSW* 2:656.

79. *WWR* 2:534; *ASSW* 2:682.

system,"[80] and he drafted a letter to Schopenhauer (December 1858) with the intention of explaining this modification.[81] Here he quotes a section of paragraph 44 ("The Metaphysics of Sexual Love") from *The World as Will and Representation* where the philosopher finds it "inexplicable" why two lovers should commit suicide when their love is "thwarted by external circumstances."[82] Wagner then explains that he depicts (presumably through *Tristan*) a way of salvation ("Heilsweg") through sexual love whereby one comes to a position of self-knowledge and self-renunciation of the will.[83] It is unlikely that this letter was even sent. The draft of the letter is brief and a fuller picture of his thinking is given in a letter to Mathilde Wesendonck (1 December 1858). He explains that he has been "slowly rereading" *The World as Will and Representation* and this inspired him "to expand and—in certain details—even to correct his system." The issue is "the path to salvation, which has not been recognized by any philosopher, and especially not by Sch., but which involves a total pacification of the will through love (vollkommenen Beruhigung des Willens durch die Liebe), and not through any abstract human love, but a love engendered on the basis of sexual love (der wirklich, aus dem Grunde der Geschlechtsliebe), i.e., the attraction between man and woman (der Neigung zwischen Mann und Weib keimenden Liebe)." He adds: "It is significant that in reaching this conclusion (as a philosopher, not as a poet, for as such I have my own material) I have been able to use the material of the concepts which Sch. himself provides."[84]

How then is this redemption through erotic love achieved? The answer does not seem immediately obvious, but I give Wagner's argument, the presentation of which he believes takes him "very deep and very far":[85]

> [I]t involves a more detailed explanation of the state in which we become capable of recognizing ideas, and of genius in general, which I no longer conceive of as a state in which the intellect is divorced from the will (Losgerissenheit des Intellectes vom Willen), but rather as an intensification of the individual intellect to the point where it becomes the organ of perception of the genus or species (eine Steigerung des Intellectes des

---

80. *My Life* 579; *Mein Leben* 2:593.

81. "Metaphysik der Geschlechtsliebe: Bruchstück eines Briefes an Arthur Schopenhauer"; "Metaphysics of sexual love: fragment of a letter to Arthur Schopenhauer" (*SB* 10:208).

82. *WWR* 2:532; *ASSW* 2:680.

83. *SB* 10:208

84. *SL* 432 (Golther, *Mathilde Wesendonk*, 79).

85. *SL* 432 (Golther, *Mathilde Wesendonk*, 79).

Individuums zum Erkenntnissorgan der Gattung), and thus of the will itself, which is the thing in itself; herein lies the only possible explanation for that marvellous and enthusiastic joy and ecstasy felt by any genius at the highest moments of perception, moments which Sch. seems scarcely to recognize, since he is able to find them only in a state of calm and in the silencing of the individual affects of the will (in der Ruhe und im Schweigen der individuellen Willens-Affecte). Entirely analogous to this view, however, I have succeeded in demonstrating beyond doubt that in love there lies the possibility of raising oneself above the individual impulse of the will to a point where total mastery over the latter is achieved, and the generic will (Gattungs-Wille) becomes fully conscious of itself, a consciousness which, at this level, is necessarily synonymous with total pacification (vollkommener Beruhigung).[86]

Wagner therefore seems to be saying that the person who loves with this intensity finds salvation, pacification of the "will."[87] But could it be that such erotic love not only redeems the one who loves but also the one who is loved? Erotic love at its most true involves a self-giving of oneself that can end in sacrifice.[88] If then on other occasions he sees such sacrificial deaths as redemptive, for example the death of Brünnhilde, is it illegitimate to make this connection? Could it then be said that Tristan's death redeems Isolde and Isolde's death redeems Tristan?

In order to answer the relationship of erotic love to redemption, I consider a range of Wagner's writings from the early 1850s through to the 1870s. The first is his letter to Röckel of 25/26 January 1854, which has illuminating comments on the sacrifice of Brünnhilde. He writes that "[n]ot even Siegfried alone (man alone) is the complete 'human being': he is merely the half, only with *Brünnhilde* does he become the redeemer; *one* man alone cannot do everything; many are needed, and a suffering,

86. *SL* 432 (Golther, *Mathilde Wesendonk*, 79–80).

87. I will consider in chapter 8 below whether Wagner really did believe in "pacification of the will."

88. A possible hint of this may be found in the fact that in 1877 Wagner sent Judith Gautier the text and music of the passage "Take my body and eat" "thereby suggesting a parallel between the mystery of the Eucharist—the transformation of matter into the most sacred substance—and the ardent physical surrender of sensual love" (Wapnewski, "Literary Works," 92). Note, however, that although Wagner's love towards Judith Gautier could be called "sacrificial" it actually caused his wife much heartache. Wagner had to stop his correspondence with Judith on 10 February 1878 and we read in Cosima's entry for 12 February: "The grief I was fearing has not passed me by; it has come upon me from outside. May God help me! . . . Oh, sorrow, my old companion, come back and dwell with me."

self-immolating woman finally becomes the true, conscious redeemer (die wahre wissende Erlöserin)."[89] One wonders then whether redemption through erotic love means a double sacrifice of man and woman, Siegfried and Brünnhilde, Tristan and Isolde. This necessity for the double sacrifice for redemption could fit in with Wagner's own view of androgyny. In the letter to Röckel of 25/26 January 1854 Wagner writes: "The highest satisfaction of individual egoism is to be found in its total abandonment, and this is something which human beings can achieve only through love: but the true human being is both man and woman, and only in the union of man and woman does the true human beings exist, and only through love, therefore, do man and woman become human."[90] The redeeming sacrifice therefore has to be by both man and woman, and this idea may cohere with the views of the Trinity of which Gfrörer writes and which Wagner read from 1874 onwards. This complex issue will be discussed in chapter 10 below, but for now it is worth emphasizing that for Wagner the most complete human being is Jesus Christ who bears the most perfect image of God, an image that men and women together must bear.[91]

For Wagner Jesus Christ was not only the most perfect and complete human being; his sacrifice was the supreme act of self-giving. This idea of self-sacrifice is tied up with the title "redeemer" ("Erlöser"), the most frequent name used for Jesus in *Parsifal.* Wagner would naturally learn of this through the Luther Bible together with church music and Lutheran hymns and liturgy. The term "Erlöser" is not actually used of Jesus in the New Testament,[92] the term *lutrōtēs* ("Erlöser" in the Luther Bible) being used only of Moses (Acts 7:35)[93] (whereas Wagner's other term for Jesus, "savior" ["Heiland," *sōtēr*], is used, especially in the later writings). In the Old Testament "redeemer" is always used of God[94] but there is the well-known exception, Job 19:25: "I know that my redeemer liveth" ("Ich weiß, daß mein Erlöser lebt").[95] Wagner quotes this at what could be considered the climax

89. *SL* 307; *SB* 6:68.

90. *SL* 303; *SB* 6:63.

91. See Gen 1:27. Perhaps this is what Wagner was trying to express when he said that "Christ must be entirely sexless, neither man nor woman" (*CD* 17 June 1880).

92. Note that modern versions of Luther's New Testament (e.g., 1970) use it in Rom 11:26 where it most likely refers to Jesus.

93. But the context (Moses delivering Israel from Egypt) is clearly not indicating any "divinity" of Moses.

94. See the uses of "Erlöser" in the Luther Bible: Pss 19:15; 78:35; Prov 23:11; Isa 41:14; 43:14; 44:6, 24; 47:4; 48:17; 49:7; 49:26; 54:5, 8; 59:20 (applied to Jesus in Rom 11:26; cf. 1 Thess 1:10); 60:16; 63:16; Dan 6:28.

95. The LXX does not use the term *lutrōtēs* but literally reads "For I know that he is

of *Religion and Art*[96] and he would know this text from the Luther Bible and its use in the misattributed Bach cantata 160[97] and possibly through Schütz's motet (SWV 393) and Handel's *Messiah*.[98] The reference there is clearly to Jesus Christ[99] and in the Old Testament text itself the reference is to a figure other than God.[100]

Although "Erlöser" is not used for Christ in the New Testament, the corresponding verb "erlösen" is used in relation to Christ's work of redemption.[101] Additional cases of "redemption" can be found in 1 Cor 6:20; 7:23; Rev 5:9; 14:3, 4, all of which use "erkauffen" ("to buy") and highlight Christ's costly redeeming death.

The term "redemption" is a transactional metaphor: one redeems someone by "paying the price." The idea of Jesus as redeemer became so powerful because the price he pays is that of his own life and this is one reason why the church came to use this title and why Wagner employed it to express Christ's self-giving love. But in *Parsifal* "Erlöser" is not used simply as a metaphor (which, by its nature, is exchangeable) but as an abbreviated myth (which is inexchangeable): the sinless Christ who miraculously came into the world laid down his life as a sacrifice for sin and lives in the community through his death. The costly nature of his love encompasses both "eros" and "agape" love, something suggested by the teaching on marriage in Eph 5:22–33. The author likens the husband's love for his wife to that of Christ's love for the church and his giving himself up for her. "Husbands, love your wives, just as Christ loved the church and gave himself up for her,

---

eternal who is about to deliver me."

96. *PW* 6:250; *JA* 10:160. *GSD* 10:251: "Ich weiß, daß mein Erlöser lebt!"

97. See the first tenor aria. Schweitzer, *Bach*, 2:138, assumes it is by Bach. Now it is attributed to Telemann (TWV 1:877) and dated 1725.

98. Although the score of Messiah was not in his Wahnfried library (*CD* 28 February 1879 confirms he did not have it) he did at least know the Overture. He did have other works in his library: *Cäcilien-Ode, Dettinger Te Deum, Belsazar, Israel in Ägypten, Judas Maccabäus, Alexanders Fest, Saul*, and *Samson*.

99. E.g., in the *Messiah* (soprano aria opening part III) the text continues with Job 19:25b–26 ("and that He shall stand at the latter day upon the earth. And tho' worms destroy this body, yet in my flesh shall I see God") and 1 Cor 15:20 ("For now is Christ risen from the dead, the first fruits of them that sleep"). The identification of the redeemer with Christ would obviously suit Wagner's "Christomonism," although the idea of resurrection would not so easily cohere with Wagner's effective denial of the resurrection.

100. See Clines, *Job 1–20*, 459. He argues that since the lawsuit is a dispute with God, it is unlikely that God himself would appear as his vindicator! The redeemer (*gōēl*) here is the "witness," "advocate," and "spokesman" of Job 16:18–21.

101. See Luke 24:21; Rom 7:24; 11:26; Gal 3:13; 4:5; 1 Thess 1:10; 2 Thess 3:2; 2 Tim 3:11; 4:17, 18; Titus 2:14; 1 Pet 1:18; Heb 2:15.

that he might sanctify her, having cleansed her by the washing of water with the word."[102] The section ends by speaking of the union of man and woman, the two becoming one flesh. The author adds these striking words: "This mystery is a profound one, and I am saying that it refers to Christ and the church."

In Ephesians the man is the redeemer figure. Wagner usually reverses this in having a woman redeemer. Although I think it unlikely that Wagner had sexual union with Mathilde Wesendonck, he experienced through her a saving and transforming love. And it was this love that was to inspire the composition of *Parsifal*. Earlier I quoted from Wagner's letter to Ludwig of 14 April 1865. After writing of "God whom we comprehend in the deepest anguish of fellow-suffering," he continues:

> I recalled the first sunny Good Friday of that first conception. A loving and tenderly devoted woman's heart had at that time taken me into its care and protection: the hope that I had cherished for years had now come to pass; I had been able to move into a little house of my own, with its own attractive garden, wonderfully situated with a splendid view over Lake Zurich and the Alps. I sit there—it was the first fine spring day!—on the verandah of my refuge, the bells were ringing,—the birds were singing, the first flowers gazed up at me; it was then, in the depths of my ecstacy, that Parzival was conceived.[103]

Wagner brings together a constellation of thoughts. After speaking of the "anguish of fellow-suffering," he goes on to explain that such suffering does lead through to redemption; and he associates the redemption of Good Friday with the love he experienced from a woman, Mathilde Wesendonck.

The power of love is important for *Parsifal*, and it is this self-giving love that the knights of the grail can also offer. Hans Küng likens the community of knights to the Qumran sectaries and described the charity of the

---

102. Many marriages of course do not live up to this. And it is significant that in his sketches for *Jesus of Nazareth* Wagner puts these words into Jesus' mouth: "The commandment saith: Thou shalt not commit adultery! But I say unto you: Ye shall not marry without love. A marriage without love is broken as soon as entered into, and whoso hath wooed without love, already hath broken the wedding. If ye follow my commandment, how can he ever break it, since it bids you do what your own heart and soul desire?—But where ye marry without love, ye bind yourselves at variance with God's law, and in your wedding ye sin against God; and this sin avengeth itself by your striving next against the law of man, in that he break the marriage-vow" (*PW* 8:303). Commenting on this, Žižek writes: "The true adultery is not to copulate outside of marriage, but to copulate in marriage without love" (Pound, *Žižek*, 152).

103. *SL* 642 ; *KB* 1:83. The reference is to moving into the Asyl of the Wesendonck's in 1857.

knights as "inhuman."[104] He thereby drives a wedge between the knights and Jesus of Nazareth, "the friend of sinners and publicans."[105] This, however, does not do justice to Wagner's portrayal of the knights in his stage work.

The redemption in *Parsifal* is achieved through "erotic love" in the sense of self-giving love, and it extends to the whole of the created order. The figure of Christ is so powerful because he is our inspiration and refuge in a world of suffering. Wagner wrote in *Religion and Art*:

> With the Redeemer in heart, let us recognise that not their actions, but their sufferings bring near to us the men of bygone days, and make them worth our memory; that our sympathy belongs not to the victor, but the vanquished hero. However great may be the peace of mind resulting from regeneration of the human race, yet in the Nature that surrounds us, the violence of ure-elements, the unchanged emanations of the Will beneath us and on either hand in sea or desert,—ay, even in the insect, in the worm we tread upon unheeding, shall we ever feel the awful tragedy of this World-being, and daily have to lift our eyes to the Redeemer on the cross as last and loftiest refuge.[106]

And so Gurnemanz sings this in the Good Friday Music (*WagPS* 226–27):

---

104. Küng, "Theology for Our Time," 319.

105. Ibid., 320, quoting Matt 11:19.

106. *PW* 6:246–47; *GSD* 10:247; *JA* 10:156–57.

No more can it see Him Himself on the Cross;	Ihn selbst am Kreuze kann sie nicht *erschauen*:
it looks up to man redeemed,	da blickt sie zum erlösten Menschen auf;
who feels freed from the burden of sin and terror,	der fühlt sich frei von Sündenlast und *Grauen*,
made clean and whole through God's loving sacrifice.	durch Gottes Liebesopfer rein und heil.
Now grasses and flowers in the meadow know	Das merkt nun Halm und Blume auf den *Auen*,
that today the foot of man will not tread them down,	daß heut' des Menschen Fuß sie nicht <u>zertritt</u>,
but that, as God with divine patience	doch wohl, wie Gott mit himmlischer *Geduld*
pitied him and suffered for him,	sich sein' erbarmt' und für ihn <u>litt</u>,
so man today in devout grace	der Mensch auch heut' in frommer *Huld*
will spare them with soft tread.	sie schont mit sanftem <u>Schritt</u>.

Excursus on *Eros* and *Agape*

The Swedish Lutheran theologian Anders Nygren made a clear separation between the divine "Agape-love" and human love, "egocentric Eros-love . . . which builds on the foundation of self-love."[107] Appealing to Luther's Heidelberg Disputation of 1518 (thesis 28)[108] he then goes on to argue: "Human love is acquisitive love, and so is created by the desirable nature of its object. God's love is itself creative—i.e., it makes something of that which is nothing."[109] Further, "[h]uman love is distinguished by the fact that in all things it seeks to own and prefers to receive rather than to impart its good."[110] I can see the point Luther makes in the Heidelberg Disputation but, as Nygren recognizes, he does not in fact speak in terms of agape and eros.[111]

---

107. Nygren, *Agape*, 722–23.

108. See *LW* 31:57–58.

109. Nygren, *Agape*, 725.

110. Ibid.

111. Ibid., 724. Wagner would be well aware of Luther's contrast between divine and human love in thesis 28, especially since it is discussed by Bruno Bauer, "Pessimismus," 289–90.

An alternative approach to that of Nygren is to be found in Novak, who argues that "true eros is ecstatically self-giving, so much so that the true lover allows himself or herself to be radically affected by his or her beloved."[112] Such erotic love is the love that God shows towards his people, and it is a love that cannot be neatly separated from agape-love. Wagner himself brings these two kinds of love together and I give two examples (and a third which *may* suggest the contrary).

First, *Tannhäuser* is regularly seen as dealing with two types of love: sacred and profane. Although a distinction can be made (just as one can be made between agape and eros),[113] Wagner brings them together. In his explanatory program for the overture to *Tannhäuser*, he understands the final rendition of the Pilgrim's Chorus as "the exultation of the Venusberg itself, redeemed from the curse of sinfulness, which we hear amid the holy hymn."[114] Further, in Act III of *Tannhäuser* we discover that Elisabeth's erotic love for Tannhäuser intensifies as she prays for him.[115]

My second example is taken from the first sketches Wagner made specifically for *Parsifal*: the flower maidens' scene in Act II. For the passage "Komm holder Knabe" we have the motif rising from the fifth to the octave with the harmony of sixths. This is precisely what we have at the end of the grail motif. This *may* suggest that the love of the flower maidens and the love expressed in the holy grail (in which the blood of Christ appears) is not as dissimilar as is usually assumed.[116]

These two examples suggest that the process of redemption could be seen as a bringing together of eros and agape. However, there are cases where Wagner views redemption as resulting in being freed from sexual desire, especially when such love is a "torment." In a sketch for Tristan he explains that Isolde in death is freed from "love as torment" ("die Liebe als Quall").[117] He related the transfigured Isolde to the assumption of the

---

112. Novak, *Musings*, 140 n 33.

113. Cf. Jüngel, *Geheimnis*, 436.

114. Quoted in Dreyfus, *Erotic Impulse*, 78 (cf. *PW* 3:231). *JA* 2:107: "Es ist der Jubel des aus dem Fluche der Unheiligkeit erlösten Venusberges selbst, den wir zu dem Gottesliede vernehmen."

115. See *GSD* 2:30 (*JA* 2:81): "Auf dem kleinen Bergvorsprunge rechts, vor dem Marienbilde, liegt Elisabeth in brünstigem Gebete dahingestreckt." Köhler, *Titans*, 173, finds it significant that Wagner uses "brünstig" ("on heat") rather than the usual "inbrünstig" ("fervent"). He suggests that Elizabeth becomes Venus. "Consumed with yearning desire, she waits for Tannhäuser to return, ostensibly for the sake of his 'salvation' but in fact for the sake of their joint love, which alone can bring him true healing." See also *On the Performing of Tannhäuser* (*PW* 3:183–84).

116. Cf. Voss, "Klage in der Wonne," 228.

117. Deathridge, "Postmortem on Isolde," 267 n. 28, refers to Prose sketches,

Virgin Mary, especially as represented in Titian's *Assunta dei Frari*. He first saw this in 1861, and after viewing it 1882 he commented (in the words of Cosima): "The glowing head of the Virgin Mary recalls to him his idea of the sexual urge: this unique and mighty force, now freed of all desire, the Will enraptured and redeemed."[118] However, although freed from sexual desire, could he not imply that Isolde and the virgin Mary, now transfigured, enjoy a redeemed erotic love?

Conclusions

Wagner's genius lay not only in his presentation of human and divine concerns through his combination of music and libretto but also in how he relates them to each other. In this chapter I have considered the themes of sin, sex, and suffering together with those of knowledge and redemption. Wagner has drawn from the mythology of Genesis 3 and the philosophy of Schopenhauer, but above all he has drawn from that deepest of all wells, the theology of the cross first developed in the New Testament writings. In Act II of *Parsifal* we have seen how Wagner brings together the kiss from a beautiful woman, understanding of the suffering of creation, and conviction of sin. Ultimately we are presented with the God who suffers, the *deus revelatus*, as the only redeemer. In Act III, immediately after Kundry's baptism, we are invited to participate in the renewal of creation, in the "magic" of Good Friday, and the nature of this "invitation" raises a constellation of issues, which will be addressed in the next chapter.

B II a 5 (*NA*), 53.

118. *CD* 25 April 1882.

8

Theological Reflections III

Predestination, Free Will, Conversion, and Denial of the Will

Introduction

IN THE PREVIOUS CHAPTER I discussed Wagner's strong view of sin and pessimistic anthropology. The correlate of this is a powerful view of grace and in this chapter I consider his thinking on predestination and free will together with his understanding of "conversion" and "denial of the will." These issues will be discussed in the context of "miracle," an important theme in the first part of *Religion and Art*.

Of all the miracles that are represented on stage in a performance of *Parsifal* there is one that can also occur off-stage, the miracle of conversion. It is perhaps a special kind of miracle and could be termed an "existential" miracle. In Wagner's stage work, one such conversion is that of Parsifal who, despite his moment of sudden insight in Act II, seems to undergo a slow process of transformation in his existential journey, much of this occurring between Acts II and III: "Through error and the path of suffering I came" (*WagPS* 216–17). The other conversion is that of Kundry. Although there is a slow transformation in her nature, again between Acts II and III, the fundamental point of her conversion occurs in that remarkable passage of her baptism just before the Good Friday Music (III.608–26).[1] Using the catego-

---

1. See the discussion of this in chapter 5 above.

ries of Luther, appropriate in view of Wagner's admiration for the reformer, one could say that Kundry's conversion in Act III is "by grace alone" (*sola gratia*: "receive this baptism"; "die Taufe nimm") and "by faith alone" (*sola fide*: "and believe in the Redeemer"; "und glaub' an den Erlöser");[2] but how is one to relate such "faith" to the activity of the "mind" and the "brain"? This may appear to be a very modern question but it is one Wagner addressed in his essay *Religion and Art* published in 1880, a work that can throw some light on *Parsifal*.[3]

In order to appreciate Wagner's argument in *Religion and Art* I consider the approach of Schopenhauer to conversion and grace, for it is upon this that Wagner builds.

Schopenhauer on Grace

In section 70 of the first volume of *The World as Will and Representation*,[4] Schopenhauer addresses the question of "salvation," something that is only possible through a denial of the will-to-life. Although the word "salvation" ("Heil"; "Seligkeit") is used sparingly in this section, volume 2 is rather more explicit in entitling section 49 "The Road to Salvation" ("Die Heilsordnung").[5] But whether or not the term "salvation" is used, the idea is unmistakably there.

Schopenhauer explains that earlier he "positively denied freedom as *liberum arbitrium indifferentiae*" and so presents this problem: how can "necessity" be reconciled to "denial of the will"? "We might perhaps regard the whole of our discussion (now concluded) of what I call the denial of the will as inconsistent with the previous explanation of necessity, that appertains just as much to motivation as to every other form of the principle of sufficient reason." But he explains: "Yet far from suppressing [free will of indifference] here, I call it to mind. In truth, real freedom, in other words, independence of the principle of sufficient reason, belongs to the will as thing-in-itself, not to its phenomenon, whose essential form is everywhere this principle of sufficient reason, the element of necessity."[6]

2. *WagPS* 224–25.

3. Although the poem was completed on 19 April 1877, he was to work on the music for a further five years, the full score being completed on 13 January 1882.

4. This section is towards the end of Book 4, "The World as Will: Second Aspect." It is in fact the penultimate section proper, section 71 being followed by a long appendix, "Criticism of the Kantian Philosophy."

5. *WWR* 2:634; *ASSW* 2:813. Note that the individual sections are given no titles in volume one.

6. *WWR* 1:402; *ASSW* 1:546.

He goes on to liken the suppression of the will to the "new birth" or "regeneration" as taught by the Christian church. He is skeptical about the "freedom of the will"[7] but if it is to be found anywhere, it is the "effect of grace" and the "new birth."[8] "It appears only when the will, after arriving at the knowledge of its own inner nature, obtains from this a *'quieter'* (*'Quietiv'*), and is thus removed from the effect of *motives* which lies in the province of a different kind of knowledge, whose objects are only phenomena."[9] Such "freedom" is possible only for human beings. "Therefore the hungry wolf buries its teeth in the flesh of the deer with the same necessity with which the stone falls to the ground, without the possibility of the knowledge that it is the mauled as well as the mauler. *Necessity* is the *kingdom of nature; freedom* is the *kingdom of grace.*"[10]

Schopenhauer writes that the "*self-suppression of the will* comes from knowledge, but all knowledge and insight as such are independent of free choice, that denial of willing, that entrance into freedom, is not to be forcibly arrived at by intention or design, but comes from the innermost relation of knowing and willing in man; hence it comes suddenly, as if flying in from without."[11] He points out that although the church speaks of grace, such grace needs to be *accepted;*[12] likewise "the effect of the quieter (die Wirkung des Quietivs) is ultimately an act of the freedom of the will."[13] The background to his thought here is "Quietismus,"[14] a movement that can be traced back to Miguel de Molinos (1628–96),[15] whose works Schopenhauer recommends to be read.[16] I think one has to say that on this issue of grace and free will that Schopenhauer is equivocating and, as I will argue, Wagner puts forward a stronger view of grace.

---

7. He devoted an essay to this theme. See *Ethics*, 33–120; *ASSW* 3:519–627.

8. *WWR* 1:404; *ASSW* 1:549.

9. *WWR* 1:404; *ASSW* 1:549.

10. *WWR* 1:404; *ASSW* 1:549.

11. *WWR* 1:404; *ASSW* 1:549.

12. He speaks of an "acceptance of grace" ("Aufnahme der Gnade") (*WWR* 1:404; *ASSW* 1:549). A more predestinarian formulation (one which may correspond more to St. Paul's view of grace) is "reception of grace." Note that the English "to accept" corresponds to "aufnehmen" and "to receive" to "erhalten."

13. *WWR* 1:404; *ASSW* 1:549.

14. See Frey, "Quietismus"; Meredith, "Quietismus."

15. Molinos was to have considerable influence on pietism, especially August Hermann Francke (1663–1727) and Gottfried Arnold (1666–1714), who translated his work into German (Idigoras, "Molinos").

16. *WWR* 2:614–15; *ASSW* 2:787.

For Schopenhauer, the one who symbolizes the *affirmation* of the will-to-live is Adam, not Adam as the individual but rather Adam as the "Idea of man in its unity."[17] The one who symbolizes the *denial* of the will is the "God become man." "As he is free from all sinfulness, in other words, from all willing of life, he cannot, like us, have resulted from the most decided affirmation of the will [i.e., sexual intercourse]; nor can he, like us, have a body that is through and through only concrete will, phenomenon of the will, but, born of a pure virgin, he has only a phantom body."[18] Schopenhauer is not interested in the "earthly Jesus"; nor the "mythical history in the Gospels." Rather what interests him is Jesus Christ in the "universal, as the symbol, or personification of the denial of the will-to-live."[19]

We have already seen how Wagner was both heavily influenced by Schopenhauer and also came to distance himself from him in a number of key respects.[20] This is also the case in respect to the constellation of issues now considered: "grace," "predestination," "free will," "conversion," and "denial of the will." In order to engage in a careful analysis I am going to consider first an important section of Wagner's essay *Religion and Art* that will throw *some* light on how Wagner understands conversion. I will then move on to what the drama of *Parsifal* tells us about these themes.

Wagner's Argument in *Religion und Kunst*, Paragraphs 2–4

In the second paragraph of *Religion and Art* Wagner explains that the "deepest basis of every true religion" is the "recognition of the frailty of this world" ("Erkenntnis der Hinfälligkeit der Welt") and the means of freeing ourselves from it. A "superhuman effort" ("übermenschliche Anstrengung") is required to disclose this special knowledge; the religious founder achieves this through the "invention" of mythic allegories[21] in order to lead to this

17. *WWR* 1:405; *ASSW* 1:549. Here Schopenhauer touches on his theory, explained earlier in his work, of the Platonic forms and how they can give us some access to the noumenal world.

18. *WWR* 1:405; *ASSW* 1:550 (on his view of the "phantom body" see chapter 6 above).

19. *WWR* 1:405; *ASSW* 1:550.

20. See chapters 2 and 7 above.

21. Although Wagner speaks of "invention" ("Erfindung") I would maintain that strictly speaking myth is *discovered* rather than *invented*. I would therefore rather speak of "Entdeckung der mythischen Allegorien." See Bell, *Deliver Us from Evil*, 23–65. The other issue Wagner's phrase raises is whether myth is "allegorical." I suspect that Wagner would in fact agree with Schelling's key point: "Die Mythologie ist nicht *allegorisch*,

knowledge through faith. The "sublime distinction" ("erhabene Eigentüm-lichkeit") of the Christian religion is that the "deepest truth" is disclosed to the "poor in spirit,"[22] whereas for the Brahmins it was for the "rich in spirit."[23] In the third paragraph he explains that Christianity is special because "[i]ts founder was not wise, but divine,"[24] his teaching being the "deed of free-willed suffering."[25] Wagner then argues: "To believe in him, means to emulate him; to hope for redemption, to strive for union with him."[26] Although the poor in spirit needed "no metaphysical explanation of the world"[27] since "its suffering lay open to their feeling," the "rich," i.e., the intellectuals of the church of the first three centuries, made everything unnecessarily complex.[28]

In the fourth paragraph he then asks how one is to "convert" in the sense of having a new understanding of the world. How is one to come to see the world and its "appearances" ("Erscheinungen") not as "the most absolute of realities" ("das Aller-Realste") but rather as "null" ("nichtig") and "optical delusion" ("augenscheinlich")? How can one come to see "the actual truth" ("das eigentliche Wahre") beyond this phenomenal world?[29] Such conversion can only occur by a miracle ("Wunder"). He defines miracle as "an incident that sets aside the laws of Nature"[30] or an "abrogation of the laws of nature" ("Aufhebung der Gesetze der Natur").[31] This is a fairly typical

---

sie ist *tautegorisch*" (Schelling, *Mythologie*, 195–96).

22. Cf. Matt 5:3: "Blessed are the poor in spirit, for theirs is the kingdom of God." Wagner quotes this in his sketch for *Jesus of Nazareth* (*PW* 8:328; *DTB* 261: "Selig sind, die das geistlich arm sind, denn das himmelreich ist ihr" (taken, with revised spelling, from Luther's 1545 translation). Cf. also Matt 11:25 (discussed below).

23. *PW* 6:214; *GSD* 10:212; *JA* 10:118.

24. See chapter 10 below for further discussion of this important point.

25. *PW* 6:214; *GSD* 10:213; *JA* 10:119.

26. *PW* 6:214 (modified translation); *GSD* 10:213; *JA* 10:119.

27. *PW* 6:214–15; *GSD* 10:213; *JA* 10:119.

28. *PW* 6:215; *GSD* 10:213; *JA* 10:119. Wagner seems to suggest that the church fathers made Christianity "artificial" ("künstlich"). On this see the very first sentence of *Religion and Art*: "One might say that where Religion becomes artificial, it is reserved for Art to save the spirit of religion . . . " ("Man könnte sagen, daß da, wo die Religion künstlich wird, der Kunst es vorbehalten sei, den Kern der Religion zu retten . . ."). Note also the third sentence: "But Religion has sunk into an artificial life, when she finds herself compelled to keep on adding to the edifice of her dogmatic symbols" (*PW* 6:213). "Die Religion lebt aber nur noch künstlich, wann sie zu immer weiterem Ausbau ihrer dogmatischen Symbole sich genötigt findet . . . " (*GSD* 10:211; *JA* 10:117).

29. *PW* 6:215; *GSD* 10:213; *JA* 10:119.

30. *PW* 6:215; *GSD* 10:214; *JA* 10:119–20: "Bezeichnen wir nun als Wunder einen Vorgang, durch welchen die Gesetze der Natur aufgehoben werden . . . "

31. *PW* 6:215; *GSD* 10:214; *JA* 10:120.

Enlightenment view.[32] Although Kant and Schopenhauer could give similar definitions,[33] Wagner then starts moving beyond their sphere of thought and I consider this in two stages. In the first stage he argues that since we ourselves impose laws of nature upon our experience, laws "founded on our own power of perception" ("in unserem eigenen Anschauungsvermögen begründet")[34]—something that is inextricably linked with our brain functions ("Gehirnfunktionen")—then belief in miracles "must be comprehensible to us as an almost necessary consequence of the reversal of the 'will to live,' in defiance of all Nature."[35] This discussion reflects a Schopenhauerian rather than a Kantian framework, and the language used here is mainly Schopenhauerian;[36] but his discussion is slowly beginning to move beyond Schopenhauer. In the second stage, Wagner has to deal with one of the great mysteries (or problems!) of a Schopenhauerian worldview: if our brain imposes causation on our experience (and if we are "determined" as Schopenhauer believes), how is it that we can come to the point of denying the will?[37] Or applying this to Wagner's argument, how is it that the faith in miracle (which Wagner relates to the conversion of the will-to-live) can come about? Wagner goes on to explain how this can occur, and his argument is somewhat different to Schopenhauer's.[38] He writes: "To the natural man, this reversal of the Will is certainly itself the greatest miracle, for *it contains an abrogation of the laws of Nature*; that which has effected it must consequently be far above Nature, and of superhuman power, since he finds that union with that which is the only thing to be longed for and aspired

32. Note that such a view differs somewhat from the biblical view. See Bell, *Deliver Us from Evil*, 111–14.

33. Kant, *Religion*, 100, speaks of God allowing "nature to deviate from such laws." Kant believes that faith in miracles is "dispensible" (98) and although there are "rational human beings" who are "not disposed to renounce belief in them," they "never allow this belief to intervene in practical matters" (99). Concerning Kant on miracles, see Colin Brown, *Miracles*, 103–7.

34. *PW* 6:215; *GSD* 10:214; *JA* 10:120.

35. *PW* 6:215; *JA* 10:120. *GSD* 10:214: ". . . so muß uns der Glaube an Wunder als ein fast nothwendiges Ergebnis der gegen alle Natur sich erklärenden Umkehr des Willens zum Leben begreiflich werden."

36. Schopenhauer tends to use "Gehirn" whereas Kant uses "Gemüt" and other "mind" terms. The term "will-to-live" is, of course, Schopenhauerian. Note, however, that "Anschauungsvermögen" is more in the world of Kant. I have found only one instance of this term in Schopenhauer and that is in the "Kritik der Kantischen Philosophie" (*ASSW* 1:606)!

37. This problem is discussed in Young, *Schopenhauer*, 192–94.

38. See *WWR* 1:402–3; *ASSW* 1:546–47, discussed above.

to."[39] The conversion of the will is the greatest miracle and, like all miracles, entails the suspension of the laws of nature. Such conversion can only come about by something beyond nature, by a "superhuman power."

The crucial question now is what is this "superhuman power" and how does it effect conversion? There are two possible explanations. The first is that this power is the kingdom of God and through this kingdom special knowledge is bestowed. Wagner speaks of "the union with that which is the only thing to be longed for and aspired to" ("die Vereinigung mit ihm als das einzig Ersehnte und zu Erstrebende gilt"). He explains: "It is this Other that *Jesus* told his poor of, as the 'Kingdom of God,' in opposition to the 'kingdom of the world;' He who called to Himself the weary and heavy-laden, the suffering and persecuted, the patient and weak, the friends of their enemies and lovers of all, was their 'Heavenly Father,' as whose 'Son' he himself was sent to these 'his Brothers.'"[40] Such special knowledge could be related to the "revelation" of which Wagner goes on to speak.[41] But there is a second possibility that has important implications for *Parsifal*: Wagner is implicitly equating the kingdom of God with Christ himself. Christ is the power that effects conversion. Equating the kingdom (God's kingly rule) with Christ is sometimes implicit in the New Testament texts and these paragraphs of *Religion and Art* suggest that this is something Wagner perceived. The "word of salvation" is related to the "Word made flesh," Jesus Christ himself. In support of this interpretation is that Wagner earlier speaks explicitly of union with Christ ("mit ihm Vereinigung suchen," paragraph 3)[42] and here (paragraph 4) he speaks of union with that which effects conversion ("die Vereinigung mit ihm").

39. *PW* 6:215 (modified and with added emphasis); *JA* 10:120. *GSD* 10:214: "Das größte Wunder ist für den natürlichen Menschen jedenfalls diese Umkehr des Willens, in welcher *die Aufhebung der Gesetze der Natur selbst enthalten ist*; das, was diese Umkehr bewirkt hat, muß nothwendig weit über die Natur erhaben und von übermenschlicher Gewalt sein, da die Vereinigung mit ihm als das einzig Ersehnte und zu Erstrebende gilt" (my emphasis).

40. *PW* 6:215-16 (modified); *JA* 10:120. *GSD* 10:214: "Dieses Andere nannte *Jesus* seinen Armen das 'Reich Gottes', im Gegensatz zu dem 'Reiche der Welt'; der die Mühseligen und Belasteten, Leidenden und Verfolgten, Duldsamen und Sanftmüthigen, Feindesfreundlichen und Allliebenden zu sich berief, war ihr 'himmlischer Vater', als dessen 'Sohn' er zu ihnen, 'seinen Brüdern', gesandt war." Note that Matt 11:28 (to which Wagner alludes) is preceded by a "binitarian" passage (Matt 11:25-27). Wagner is putting forward his own "binitarian understanding" that appears to "swallow up" the Father in the Son. See also the end of paragraph 6 (*PW* 6:217; *GSD* 10:216; *JA* 10:122), discussed in chapter 9 below.

41. *PW* 6:216; *GSD* 10:214; *JA* 10:120. Note that the kingdom of God can be related to the saving word and the righteousness of God. See Jüngel, *Paulus und Jesus*.

42. *PW* 6:214; *GSD* 10:213; *JA* 10:119.

Faith and Miracle

Three important conclusions follow from this analysis of paragraphs 2–4 of *Religion und Kunst* and its relationship to *Parsifal*. The first relates to Wagner's view of Christ's redeeming work. In Wagner's thinking, two elements of Christ's work seem to be operating. We could call these the redemptive act of Christ's death and the redemptive word that comes to us; it is what Eichholz calls the dual but integrated activity of God.[43] Both of these elements are to be found in *Parsifal*. One could say that a redemptive word comes to Kundry via Parsifal at a series of points in Act II after that crucial kiss. But it is only the "word" that comes to her in Act III that effects her conversion: "Receive this baptism, and believe in the Redeemer" ("Die Taufe nimm und glaub' an den Erlöser").[44] But the foundation of this redemptive word in *Parsifal* is the redemptive act that, unlike that of the New Testament witnesses, is not clearly located in space and time (this means that Wagner's understanding of Christ's atoning death is more mythical than that of the New Testament witnesses). It is a redemptive act in which Kundry comes to participate, her conversion ultimately coming down to a union with Christ.[45]

The second conclusion relates to the redemption just discussed, and that is the issue of "miracle." In certain respects Wagner is "baptizing" Schopenhauer's argument. Despite his general view of determinism, it seems that Schopenhauer has to suspend this in order to accommodate his idea of the "denial of the will."[46] This could be considered a major problem in his metaphysical scheme. To recall his argument, when human behavior runs according to the "principle of sufficient reason," when "motives" (a particular type of "cause") are at work, there can be no *liberum arbitrium indifferentiae*;[47] but in the case of the self-suppression of the will, we have

43. Eichholz, *Theologie*, 200: "nach 2. Kor 5 müssen das Christusgeschehen und das Zeugnis von diesem Geschehen als einheitliches, aber zweifältiges Handeln Gottes begriffen werden."

44. *WagPS* 224–25. Cf. Luther's view of baptism, whereby the saving word comes to the one baptized, *making* him a Christian (this was his view after 1522; see Althaus, *Luther*, 311–15).

45. See the musical expression of this discussed in chapter 5 above.

46. See Young, *Schopenhauer*, 193: "The turn to asceticism is (to borrow a term from Stephen Jay Gould) a 'skyhook' which occasionally descends from the noumenal into the phenomenal and disrupts the causal order of things. So Schopenhauer admits that the previous affirmation of universal causal determinism is now suspended to accommodate denial of the will." Young argues that entering the aesthetic state also involves skyhooks. I would say that one of Schopenhauer's problems is that he cannot explain what determines the subject-object correlation. Am I guilty of bringing in a God-of-the-gaps if I say that God determines the nature of the subject-object correlation?

47. *WWR* 1:402; *ASSW* 1:546.

"freedom of the will," the "effect of grace":[48] "it comes in suddenly, as if flying in from without."[49] He does introduce Christ into his argument but "always in the universal, as the symbol or personification of the denial of the will-to-live."[50] Wagner's baptizes this in that for him Christ is not a "Symbol" of the divine; rather he is an image, a real replica ("Bild, wirkliches Abbild") of the divine.[51] Further, for Wagner Christ neither belongs simply to the "Platonic Ideas" nor is he restricted to the noumenal realm.[52] Although there are occasions when Wagner denied the existence of "God," he clearly affirmed the "divine"[53] that transcends both the noumenal and phenomenal worlds. Relating Christ to Kundry's conversion, her faith is not a human work, but comes about by something "far above Nature, and of superhuman power."[54] Her transformation comes about, as we have seen, by means of a "saving word" and a "saving act" in which she comes to participate. Wagner's thought world in both *Religion and Art* and in *Parsifal* is going well beyond that of Schopenhauer.

The third conclusion regards something Wagner hints at but does not develop: it is what I call the loop of faith and miracle. On the one hand, Wagner writes that in conversion the human being comes to have "belief in miracles" ("Wunder-Glauben"; "Glaube an Wunder").[55] But, on the other hand, he suggests the human being also has a rôle in what one can obtusely call the "production of the miracle." Wagner seems to imply that since the usual causal nexus is "founded on our own power of perception, and bound inextricably with the functions of our brain," then in miracle a special sort of "causation" is imposed upon our experience.[56] The only miracle

48. *WWR* 1:404; *ASSW* 1:548.

49. *WWR* 1:404; *ASSW* 1:548.

50. *WWR* 1:405; *ASSW* 1:549.

51. *PW* 6:217; *GSD* 10:215; *JA* 10:121. This is further discussed in chapters 6 and 11.

52. Note, however, that in the Communion scene of *Parsifal* Act I the reality of Christ is perceived as the knights of the grail approach the "noumenal realm." Note the stage direction at I.1456: "Eintritt der vollsten Dunkelheit" (missing in *WagPS* 148–49) followed by "Nehmet hin mein Blut nehmet hin meinen Leib, auf daß ihr mein gedenkt!" (I.1459–64; Knaben "aus der Höhe").

53. See the discussion in chapter 10 below.

54. *PW* 6:215; *GSD* 10:214; *JA* 10:120.

55. *PW* 6:215; *GSD* 10:214; *JA* 10:119–20 (paragraph 4). Note that in paragraph 3 (*PW* 6:214–15; *GSD* 10:213; *JA* 10:119) he speaks of "faith in Jesus" ("Glaube an Jesus") and "faith in him" ("an ihn Glauben"). Such faith is in some sense related to "Glaube an Wunder" but Wagner does not make explicit what this relationship actually is.

56. Cf. Bultmann, "Wonder," 248, writing of the "primitive" idea of miracle writes: "Wonder was merely assigned to a causality different from that which produced the everyday events." For a discussion of this see Bell, *Deliver Us from Evil*, 328–30.

Wagner discusses is the miracle of conversion, "the greatest miracle"; "it contains an abrogation of the laws of Nature" ("die Aufhebung der Gesetze der Natur").[57] However, I maintain that his discussion can be extended to other miracles, miracles found in the New Testament.[58] Such miracles also contain (or entail) an "abrogation of the laws of nature." Through faith an alternative "causation" is imposed upon experience.

These words of Wagner's remind the theologian of the inextricable link made in the New Testament between faith and miracle. Wagner's discussion concerns what one could call the "existential miracle" of conversion; but could it not be applied to other miracles so as to establish an organic relationship between faith and miracle?[59] And could it be that Wagner himself took this route?

There are some indications that he did. One factor is that he admired Gfrörer, who was certainly open to the miraculous.[60] Gfrörer was scathing about figures such as Hegel who claimed they were impossible[61] and sharply criticized those who exclude the miraculous on the basis of some metaphysical presupposition.[62] Rather, argues Gfrörer, one should examine the texts in a historical method and then make a judgment. He points to various factors that suggest that the universe is not simply a collection of events under causation. First, one of the key factors is that the "most noble of human beings" accepted the "eternity of the human spirit" ("Ewigkeit

---

57. *PW* 6:215 (modified); *GSD* 10:215; *JA* 10:120.

58. Jesus does in fact perform a healing miracle in *Jesus of Nazareth*: the daughter of Levi, a publican, is "restored from serious illness." Jesus, however, points Levi to a greater miracle. Levi, falling at Jesus' feet, says: "'Lord, how have I deserved thy grace? My child liveth; thou hast wakened it from death!' *Jesus*: 'What lived, I have preserved to life: open thou thine heart, that *thee* I may awake from death!' *The Publican*: 'What shall I do, Lord, to please thee?' *Jesus*: 'Hear my word, and follow it'" (*PW* 8:286; *DTB* 242). Jesus is therefore concerned that the publican undergoes the "existential miracle" of obeying Jesus.

59. Cf Mark 11:23–24: "Truly I tell you, if you say to this mountain, 'Be taken up and thrown into the sea,' and if you do not doubt in your heart, but believe that what you say will come to pass, it will be done for you. So I tell you, whatever you ask for in prayer, believe that you have received it, and it will be yours."

60. According to *CD* 29 March and 5 April 1875, Wagner read the chapter on miracles (Gfrörer, *Geschichte III*, 265–341).

61. Gfrörer, *Geschichte III*, 268.

62. He opens his section on miracles ("Wunder") by attacking Voltaire ("Wunder seyen Dinge, die nie geschehen") and Hegel ("Wunder sind unmöglich") (Gfrörer, *Geschichte III*, 265–66). Over against them he places "the excellent minds of the ancient world" ("die ausgezeichnetsten Geister des Alterthums," 270) such as Thucydides, Polybius, Livy, Tacitus, Suetonius, who were open to the miraculous (268–74).

des menschlichen Geistes").[63] And did not Christ teach immortality?[64] If the soul survives death, does that not suggest another system of laws that lie hidden and does this not open a door to the miraculous?[65] Secondly, he points to things in history that suggest a supernatural element,[66] one of the most significant being the events narrated in the Gospel of John. He believes this gospel is based on eye-witness[67] and it is striking that he can support John over against the Synoptic Gospels.[68] As far as the miracles are concerned, he supports the historicity of the three healings, John 4:46–54 (healing of the boy in Capernaum), John 5:2–12 (healing of the paralytic) and John 9:1–12 (healing of the man born blind, although he admits that John may have elaborated his narrative).[69] In addition, he is open to the reports in the Synoptic Gospels that Jesus healed demoniacs.[70] However, he is skeptical about the turning of water into wine[71] and the resurrection of Lazarus.[72] The details of Gfrörer's arguments do not concern us, but the essential thing to bear in mind is that although he uses critical historical methods,[73] he is open to possibility of the miraculous.

There is evidence that Wagner shared such ideas. We know that Wagner rejected the growing materialism, a materialism to which Nietzsche was being increasingly attracted.[74] In fact the break between Nietzsche and

---

63. Gfrörer, *Geschichte III*, 275.

64. Ibid., 275–76: "Christus, der Sein Blut für die Menschheit hingab, hat die Unsterblichkeit gelehrt, oder auch besser, überall vorausgesezt, und Das genügt."

65. Ibid., 276.

66. He begins by giving the examples of the "Revolution" inaugurated by Jesus and which continues in the work of people like the "upright Englishman" ("rechtschaffener Engländer," presumably William Wilberforce) in abolishing slavery and the remarkable life of Joan of Arc (Gfrörer, *Geschichte III*, 278–87). Whether they truly point to the "miraculous" can be debated; he does admit that elements of the traditions of Joan belong to "ein Sagenkreis" (288).

67. See his earlier section on John's Gospel, Gfrörer, *Geschichte II.2*, 285–336.

68. So he supports John's view that Jesus died on 14th Nisan, not the 15th as the synoptics suggest (Gfrörer, *Geschichte II.2*, 202).

69. Gfrörer, *Geschichte III*, 290–99.

70. Ibid., 302–3. Such exorcisms are not reported in John.

71. Ibid., 310–11. This actually anticipates modern work on the miracles, which is more open to healing miracles than nature miracles.

72. Ibid., 312. He tells the story of Spinoza who said he would like to become a Christian if one could demonstrate the truth of this narrative, but found proof for it impossible.

73. Note elsewhere his defense of D. F. Strauß (ibid., 118–19).

74. On Nietzsche's growing attachment to materialism, see Nietzsche, *Daybreak*, x–xiii. On Nietzsche's turn to positivism, see Young, *Nietzsche*, 242–43.

Wagner can be partly understood in terms of his rejection of Kant/Schopen-hauer and his holding on to it. The first fruit of Nietzsche's new approach is seen in *Human All Too Human* and a particularly good summary of his history of philosophy is given in *Twilight of the Idols*, "How the 'True World' finally became a Fable." Referring to the Kantian-Schopenhauerian thing-in-itself, he writes: "The 'true world'—an idea that is of no further use, not even as an obligation,—now an obsolete, superfluous idea, *consequently* a refuted idea: let's get rid of it!"[75] As Young points out, Nietzsche was not proving naturalism; rather his turn to positivism was a decision.

Wagner as we know was appalled by *Human All Too Human* and by Nietzsche's turn to positivism. Wagner held on to the phenomenal/noume-nal distinction, and related to this he seemed to hold to an "open universe." Both he and Cosima were both interested in the paranormal and in the work of Georg Friedrich Daumer (1800–75).[76] His life can be divided into three periods: the first is marked by pietism and speculative philosophy influenced by Schelling; the second is as an opponent of Christianity; in the third stage he converted to Catholicism (1858) and became a forerun-ner of ultramontanism (the movement for centralizing power in the papal curia).[77] Although his Catholicism would not naturally attract Wagner (and especially not his proto-ultramontanism) he understood why he would want to convert.[78] Both Cosima and Richard were intrigued by his book on Kaspar Hauser.[79] Perhaps more significant is that Wagner possessed a copy of Daumer's book on miracles, which was opposing the rationalism of biblical critics like Strauß and Renan.[80] In view of Cosima's eye problem, which her doctor could not cure, they reflected on the healing properties of

75. Nietzsche, *Anti-Christ Etc*, 171.

76. On Daumer, see Heydorn, "Daumer"; Brecht, "Daumer."

77. On ultramontanism see *ODC* 1405.

78. *CD* 20 July 1873 records her husband saying "one might say at a certain time in Germany everyone of a passionate nature, everyone in need of a community and nauseated by Protestant orthodoxy, became Catholic."

79. Daumer, *Kaspar Hauser*. See *CD* 20, 21, 22, 24 July 1873. Incidentally, Dorguth compared the treatment of Schopenhauer's thought by professors of philosophy to that suffered by Caspar Hauser (Cartwright, *Schopenhauer*, 505). Hauser, a foundling, came to light in Nuremberg in 1828 when he was about sixteen years old. He claimed that he had been forced to spend most of his life in solitary confinement and his unknown origins led to many speculations (e.g., princely origins). He was cared for by Daumer himself. He was stabbed to death by an unknown person in Ansbach in 1833. Scho-penhauer refers to Hauser (and Dorguth's work on him) on a few occasions (*ASSW* 3:92–94, 303–4, 319; *ASSW* 4:144, 170).

80. Daumer, *Das Wunder*.

the "water at Lourdes," of which Daumer writes much.[81] But Cosima's entry for 18 February 1874 indicates the disappointment they felt in Daumer's book on miracles: although he is right in his attacks he is weak in positive matters.[82]

There are therefore indications that Wagner was open to miracles, and he returns to the theme in paragraph 7 of *Religion and Art*. This begins with a discussion of the "virgin conception" and at first it may appear that Wagner thought this miracle was "invented": "As though impelled by an artistic need (Wie von einem künstlerischen Bedürfnisse gedrängt) . . . Belief devised (verfiel der Glaube) the necessary miracle of the Saviour's birth by a *Mother* who, not herself a goddess, became divine through her virginal conception of a son without human contact, against the laws of Nature."[83] Further, he writes:

> In the history of Christianity we certainly meet repeated in-
> stances of miraculous powers conferred by pure virginity, where
> a metaphysical concurs very well with a physiologic explana-
> tion, in the sense of a *causa finalis* with a *causa efficiens*; but the
> mystery of motherhood without natural fecundation can only
> be traced to the greater miracle, the birth of the God himself:
> for in this the Denial-of-the-world is revealed by a life prefigu-
> ratively offered up for its redemption.[84]

Wagner is not entirely clear, but I do not think he is saying that the virginal conception was simply "invented" (as some New Testament schol-ars may suggest) and neither does he have a naïve view that the miracle occurred independent of the human mind. Relating this to his earlier dis-cussion of miracle, he seems to be saying that in miraculous events the hu-man mind imposes upon experience a special kind of causation ("impelled by an artistic need") such that Mary was able to conceive a child without intercourse with her husband. Such logic reflects the composer's idealism and if "the world is my representation"[85] Wagner is right not to exclude such miracles.

81. *CD* 21 February 1874.

82. She tells how her husband "spent the morning reading Daumer's new book at-tacking the Old Catholics, Strauss supporters, etc., defense of miracles. We thought we might find something profound in it, but find ineptitude; in his polemics against the others he is quite right, but in positive matters he is very superficial, even childish." She then adds: "On all these subjects Schopenhauer alone is profound and acute" (*CD* 18 February 1874).

83. *PW* 6:217–18; *GSD* 10:216; *JA* 10:122.

84. *PW* 6:218; *GSD* 10:216; *JA* 10:122.

85. *WWR* 1:3; *ASSW* 1:31.

He continues, and this brings us to the next topic, denial of the will: "As the Saviour himself was recognised as sinless, nay, incapable of sin (unfähig zu sündigen), it followed that in him the Will must have been completely broken ere ever he was born, so that he could no more suffer, but only feel for others' sufferings; and the root thereof was necessarily to be found in a birth, that issued, not from the Will-to-live, but from the Will-to-redeem."[86] It is interesting that Wagner here supports a particular view of Jesus' sinlessness: it was not possible for him to sin (*non posse peccare*), the alternative being that it was possible for him not to sin (*posse non peccare*).[87] But the issue I now focus on is the denial of the will.

Denial of the Will

Many have understood *Parsifal* to be concerned with the issue of the "denial of the will." First of all, a link can be made between Wagner's understanding of union with Christ and Schopenhauer's denial of the will, a point discussed in chapter 5 in relation to Kundry's baptism. Secondly, a case could be made that *Parsifal* is concerned with sexual abstinence. Thirdly, there were circumstances in Wagner's life whilst he was composing *Parsifal* that could explain the attraction of "denial of the will." He had been seriously ill[88] and he had been passionately in love with Judith Gautier but came to the realization that he had to give her up.[89] Fourthly, one could make a case that *Parsifal* is striking in its lack of "will."[90] This is perhaps one reason that

86. *PW* 6:218; *GSD* 10:216; *JA* 10:122–23.

87. On this distinction as far as the New Testament is concerned, see Fee, "Kenosis," 27–28. He relates *posse non peccare* to a Christology "from below" and *non posse peccare* to one "from above." On the debate in the patristic period, Beyschlag, *Das Christologische Dogma*, 8 n. 14, points to the distinction between Jesus' being "tatsächlich sündlos" and "zuständlich sündlos," the latter becoming increasingly important through the early Christian centuries.

88. This is clear from Cosima's diaries and from the late photographs (e.g., that of 1 May 1882 by Joseph Albert). Wagner's ill health is graphically brought out by Köhler, *Titans*, 559–60: Among his maladies were insomnia, depression, rheumatism, constipation, a hernia, stomach-catarrh, boils, eczema, erysipelas. But "[w]orst of all . . . were the heart spasms that 'rose up from his stomach' and left him wishing he were dead" (probably angina pectoris).

89. See chapter 3 above and the discussion below.

90. Magee, *Wagner and Philosophy*, 274, argues that Wagner's music "has an enormously powerful drive of assertiveness. . . . But in *Parsifal*, for the first time, this wilful assertiveness is largely absent."

although the work was not "banned" by the Nazis,[91] neither was it particularly popular.[92]

Without doubt there are some elements of Schopenhauer's "denial-of-Will" in *Parsifal*. However, there are a number of Christian aspects that go against Schopenhauer. One is the "bread of life" (*WagPS* 144–45) which gives strength to the knights of the grail (*WagPS* 150–53). Another is faith that "endures" ("Der Glaube lebt").[93] Chamberlain emphasized these anti-Schopenhauerian aspects a hundred years ago, pointing to *Art and Revolution* where Wagner speaks of the transformation of humankind through art from "Money-soul (Geldseele)" to the "star rays of the World-soul (Weltseele)."[94] Chamberlain applies this to faith in *Parsifal* and the triumphant ending of the work.[95] He stresses the aspect of "regeneration" in Wagner[96] and although this came to have some questionable interpretations after Wagner's death among the Bayreuth circle, this is nevertheless a key insight that is worth pondering and that coheres in many respects with a New Testament theology. Further the "drama" at the end of two allegedly

91. See Deathridge, "Strange Love," 173–74. He is critical of Spotts, *Bayreuth*, 192, who claims that "*Parsifal* was banned throughout Germany after 1939." Against this Deathridge points to the fact that between 1939 and the end of 1942 there were twenty-three performances of *Parsifal* in the Berlin Deutscher Oper alone (see Jefferson, *Schwarzkopf*, 230–36).

92. Hitler, though, had great admiration for the work. After the reoccupying of the Rhineland in March 1936 Hitler was passing through the "nocturnal Ruhr district" and "overcome by one of those moods of euphoria" he asked that the prelude to *Parsifal* be played. Listening to the record he is supposed to have said: "I have built up my religion out of *Parsifal*. Divine worship in solemn form . . . without pretenses of humility. . . . One can serve God only in the garb of the hero" (Fest, *Hitler*, 499, referring to Frank, *Im Angesicht des Galgens*, 213).

93. *WagPS* 144–45.

94. See *GSD* 3:30 (*JA* 5:298): "Aus dem entehrenden Sklavenjoche des allgemeinen Handwerkerthums mit seiner bleichen Geldseele wollen wir uns zum freien künstlerischen Menschenthume mit seiner strahlenden Weltseele aufschwingen." The translation of Ellis is especially awkward so I have modified it: "Out of the dishonoring yoke of slavery of common commerce with its pale money-soul we wish to rise up to free artistic humanity with its bright world-soul" (cf. *PW* 1:54).

95. Chamberlain, *Wagner*, 513: "in seinem allerletzten Werke, *Parsifal*, fand er nach einem Leben voller Enttäuschungen und Bitterkeiten die mächtig überzeugenden Töne für die Worte: 'Der Glaube lebt!' und der musikalische Schluss dieses Werkes führt uns eine Umbildung der tiefklagenden Weise vor, die Parsifal's genialer Blick als 'die Gottesklage' erkannt hatte—nunmehr zu einer erhabenen triumphierenden, von dem Glanz der Trompeten getragenen Bekräftigung des Glaubens an jene 'strahlende Weltseele' gestaltet."

96. Chamberlain, *Wagner*, 513: "Schopenhauer's Endpunkt ist die Verneinung des Willens zum Leben, der Wagner's die Bejahung der Möglichkeit einer Regeneration. Der Glaube ist eben die Seele der Kunst."

Schopenhauerian works, *Tristan* and *Parsifal*, speaks of something other than "denial of the will." Isolde's transfiguration, which Wagner later understood in the light of the assumption of the virgin Mary, is "life-affirming";[97] and the same can be said for the closing of *Parsifal*: "O supreme joy of this miracle. . . . Miracle of supreme salvation! The redeemer redeemed."[98] The whole positive thrust of *Parsifal* has been wonderfully captured by Verlaine's poem "Parsifal."[99]

Perhaps one could go to the point of saying that the essence of redemption for Wagner was not the denial of the will but the affirmation of the will. Such a position has been argued for by the very person who edited the standard edition of Schopenhauer's works, Arthur Hübscher.[100] This actually makes sense of *Tristan* and *Parsifal*, although in his draft letter to Schopenhauer and his letter to Mathilde Wesendonck (discussed in chapter 7 above) he claims he still holds to the "pacification" of the will. Perhaps he felt unwilling in these letters totally to disassociate himself from Schopenhauer's view of redemption.

Although there are references in Wagner's writings to Schopenhauer's denial of the will, Wagner, in opposition to the Frankfurt sage was a remarkably optimistic person, something many of his friends and fellow-workers comment on. It is also worth considering Wagner's personal life as he was composing *Parsifal*, which often reflects a life far from "denial of the will" despite his ill health. Although his libido could find little satisfaction in his marriage, his feelings towards Judith Gautier were powerful. "Judith" was always around him when he was composing *Parsifal*. So "[t]he rose-embroidered satin coverlet . . . allowed him to sense his lover's presence."[101] This cover, which he called "Judith," was for his "chaise-longue" and for "small pieces of furniture" (he requested six metres!): "All this for mornings well spent on 'Parsifal.'"[102] Also telling is his speech given at a banquet on the eve of the first performance of *Parsifal*. The chemist Friedrich Eckstein, who was present, tells that on Wagner's right hand there sat a very beautiful

---

97. Further, as we saw at the end of chapter 7, although she is free from sexual desire her will is "enraptured," perhaps indicating a redeemed erotic love.

98. *WagPS* 236–37.

99. This was published in the *Revue wagnérienne*, 8 January 1886.

100. Hübscher, *Denker*, 288–89: "Nicht in der Verneinung, sondern in einer Steigerung und Sublimierung des Willens sei das Heil zu suchen. Gerade in den starken, leidenschaftlichen Äußerungen des Willens liege der Keim zur Veredelung" (quoted in Seelig, "Leben," 106).

101. Köhler, *Titans*, 591.

102. See his letter to Judith Gautier of 22 November 1877 (*SL* 877). According to Köhler, *Titans*, 592, the cover was "spread over his piano."

woman with whom Wagner enthusiastically conversed: she was none other than Judith Gautier.[103] Opposite sat Cosima and Liszt.[104] Eckstein recalls the end of this speech: "Children, tomorrow it can finally start! Tomorrow all hell will be let loose! And so all of you who are involved in the performance must see to it that you have the devil in you, and you who are present as listeners must ensure that you welcome the devil into your hearts."[105] Perhaps Wagner had his mind on the flower maidens, creatures who were perhaps inspired by Judith's father, Théophile Gautier, to whom Baudelaire's *Fleurs du mal* was dedicated! But whatever he had in mind, the whole tenor of this speech seems a long way from "denial of the will."

103. Otto, *Wagner*, 610–11. Köhler, *Titans*, 590, notes that both Cosima's diary and Glasenapp's authorized biography failed to mention this.

104. Köhler, *Titans*, 591, relying on his imagination rather than any evidence, describes the speech that Wagner then gave: "Staring straight at Judith's sinful curves and at the two bigots seated opposite him, Wagner described as a black Mass a work that depicts Holy Communion . . ." The only thing that here corresponds to Eckstein's report is that Cosima and Liszt sat opposite. Eckstein also writes that Wagner singled out Liszt for special thanks, for his friendship and help, and without whom his whole artistic project would never have materialized (Otto, *Wagner*, 611).

105. Quoted in Köhler, *Titans*, 591 (German in Otto, *Wagner*, 611).

9

Theological Reflections IV
Parsifal, Judaism, and the Jewish People

Introduction

The final performance was magnificent. During the transformation music the master came into the pit, wriggled up to my desk, took the baton from my hand and conducted the performance to the end. I remained at his side because I was afraid that he might make a mistake, but my fears were quite groundless—he conducted with the assurance of one who had been nothing but a conductor all his life. At the end of the work the audience burst into applause that defies description. But the master did not show himself, but stayed with us musicians, making bad jokes, and when the noise in the audience showed no sign of abating after ten minutes, I shouted "Quiet! Quiet!" at the top of my voice. They heard it above, and really did quieten down, and then the master, still at the conductor's desk, began to talk, first to me and the orchestra, then the curtain was raised, the whole cast, chorus and technical personnel had assembled on the stage, and the master spoke with a warmth that reduced everyone to tears—it was an unforgettable moment.[1]

So wrote Hermann Levi on the final performance of Parsifal on 29 August 1882 to his father, Benedikt Samuel Levi, who was the chief Rabbi in Gießen.

---

1. Quoted and translated in Barth, Mack, and Voss, *Wagner*, 243–44.

The enormous affection he had for Wagner is evident.[2] Wagner comes across as someone of humanity, fun, and, of course, as a master musician. I quote this at the very beginning of this chapter simply to remind the reader that Wagner was held in high regard and affection by this great Jewish musician; and to Hermann Levi one can add names such as Samuel Lehrs, Karl Tausig, Joseph Rubinstein, Heinrich Porges, Angelo Neumann, and Lilli Lehmann. However, one needs to add that this good relationship with Jewish musicians and artists did not continue in Bayreuth after Wagner's death. This is seen, for example, in the cases of Levi himself[3] and Lilli Lehmann.[4]

The relationship of Wagner's *Parsifal* to Judaism and the Jewish people has been obliquely discussed in the previous chapters. Now, however, is the time to address this issue directly and theologically evaluate Wagner's position. One problem in dealing with this issue is that feelings naturally run high. Some engage in a head-on assault reaching conclusions that are often considered unfair.[5] Some seek to argue that Wagner was not really as anti-Jewish as one thinks and perhaps fail to face up to Wagner's antisemitism. My own approach is to try to give a balanced account of Wagner's attitude to Judaism and the Jewish people and consider its implications for *Parsifal*. I will also consider Wagner's views in the light of the New Testament, and this is where my approach will no doubt become controversial.

2. There is a cross in the Partitur Abschrift of Ernst Hausburg (Act III, upbeat to m. 835) with the marginal note (presumably written by Levi, this being the very score he used in 1882): "von hier ab dirigierte unser geliebter Meister am 29 August 1882 zum letzten male seinen Parsifal." There may be a play on the words of the knights of the grail "zum letzten Mal" after this transformation music of Act III (*WagPS* 230–31).

3. After repeated requests to be relieved of his duties, Hermann Levi eventually left Bayreuth in 1894 partly because of his bad relationship with Cosima. See the illuminating and frank letter to Cosima of 15 September 1890 together with Cosima's comments (Haas, *Levi*, 328, 382).

4. Wagner had a close relationship with Lilli Lehmann and she sang Woglinde, Helmwige, and the Woodbird for the first performance of the *Ring* in 1876 (and her sister Marie sang Wellgunde and Ortlinde). She was to sing in *Parsifal* but withdrew when she discovered that her former fiancé was employed in the scenery production. After Wagner's death she was to sing Isolde in the first Bayreuth production of *Tristan* (1886) but Cosima later withdrew the offer and suggested instead the smaller role of Brangäne, Isolde's servant. In view of her international profile as a Wagner singer this was seen as an act of humiliation. Writing to Cosima she commented that if Wagner had been alive she would be the first in his eyes, not the last ("Wenn Richard Wagner noch lebte . . . wäre 'ich nicht die Letzte, sondern die Erste in seinen Augen,'" Heer, Kesting, and Schmidt, *verstummte stimmen*, 238).

5. A good example of this is the lecture of Rose given in Bayreuth 1998 (published as Rose, "Wagner und Hitler"). W.-D. Hartwich begins his "Zusammenfassung der Diskussion" with the words: "Der Vortrag löste vehemente Kritik aus" (237).

Before proceeding I need to clarify the terms I use. The term "antisemitism" is not entirely fortunate and was first used by Wilhelm Marr in his pamphlet of 1862, *Der Judenspiegel*, and in 1879 he brought the term into political use by founding the "League of Antisemites" ("Antisemiten Liga"). Although my sources use the hyphenized form "anti-semitism" I shall write "antisemitism," partly because it is not the opposite of "semitism" and partly because the term "antisemite" is used for a hater of Jews and not a hater of "Semites" as such.[6] I use "antisemite" (and "antisemitism") for someone who hates or discriminates against Jewish *people*; I use the term "anti-Judaism" for a negative view of the Jewish *religion* (and here a hyphenized form makes sense). I believe it is possible to engage in "anti-Judaism" without engaging in "antisemitism." So those who engage in mission to Jewish people obviously think that the Jewish *religion* is wrong, defective, or at least incomplete, but, one hopes, have a love for the Jewish *people*.[7] This issue, we shall see, is relevant to Wagner's attitudes towards Jews and Judaism.

In the following discussion we will have to face the question of the relationship of Wagner's stage works to his theoretical writings, especially those writings where he attacks Judaism and even the Jewish *people*. One can be tempted to separate the theoretical writings from the stage works. Although Wagner's genius is found in his stage works,[8] his writings have to be seen as an integral part of his whole artistic project;[9] they illumine the stage works and underline the fact that Wagner knew exactly what he was doing. But as far as his writings on Jews and Judaism are concerned, some have been tempted to hive off the theoretical writings for apologetic reasons and this has been especially so in this age of increasing political correctness and, more seriously, since the holocaust.

One way of understanding Wagner's "antisemitism" is as a simple irrational hatred with little or no theoretical basis. His early attitudes could

6. Strictly speaking a "Semite" is a descendant of Shem and includes, e.g., Arabic people. See Bell, *Irrevocable Call*, 82 n. 220.

7. See Bell, *Irrevocable Call*, 402. Such a notable Leipzig "philosemite" and contemporary of Wagner was Franz Delitzsch (1813–90).

8. I have argued in previous chapters that his writings do contain some crucial insights (see also chapter 11 below) and I do not share Stravinsky's decidedly negative view of on his theoretical writings: "As I see them, the writings would be most useful simply as Exhibit A in a demonstration of the split between a man's genius and the accessory parts of his mind. Wagner had little talent for theoretical exposition" (quoted in Taylor, *Wagner*, 262).

9. It is interesting to note that king Ludwig initially got to know Wagner's world through his theoretical writings. As early as twelve years old (1857) he read *The Art-Work of the Future* and *Music of the Future*. Then in February 1861 he heard *Lohengrin* in the Munich Opera (Hilmes, *Herrin des Hügels*, 105).

be understood in these terms. His time in Paris was extremely difficult and he came to feel that the powerful Jewish composer Giacomo Meyerbeer (1791–1864) did little to help and even frustrated his ambitions.[10] Wagner also felt he had reason to be resentful towards Mendelssohn. In 1836 Wagner sent him the score of his Symphony in C; Mendelssohn not only failed to perform the work with the Leipzig Gewandhaus Orchestra but managed to lose it.[11] There were also bad experiences with other Jews that perhaps stoked his irrational fear.[12] It can also be said that his dislike of Jews was related to the issue of commerce and money![13]

All these factors may have been the catalyst for his antisemitism and anti-Judaism (and contributed to them). But Wagner's antisemitism actually had a deeper and indeed theological basis. I begin my discussion by considering Wagner's concept of God. This I suspect is one of the theological underpinnings of his antisemitism that deserves detailed consideration.

Wagner's Concept of God

Wagner had a dislike of the God of the Old Testament. He tells Cosima that the problem is "the old Jewish God."[14] Further he not only had problems with the Jewish concept of God but also with the "creator God."[15] In speaking of divinity he focused on Jesus and it is significant that he tends to refer

10. Meyerbeer, however, appears to have given Wagner much support; he was instrumental in ensuring that *Rienzi* was accepted for performance in Dresden and that *Der fliegende Holländer* was accepted in Berlin (Spencer, *Wagner Remembered*, 31; see also the letter there quoted, suggesting that Meyerbeer was indeed helping Wagner). However, in early January 1842 Wagner's attitude to Meyerbeer changed "almost overnight" (Köhler, *Titans*, 132) as seen in his letter of 5 January to Schumann where he describes Meyerbeer as an "intentionally sly deceiver" ("absichtlich schlauer Betrüger," *SB* 1:576). On this letter see the comment in *SB* 1:68–69.

11. The printed score of 1911 was prepared from the orchestral parts used for the performance of the work in Prague.

12. See, e.g., Schwabe, a Jewish businessman, who was a rival to Wagner's affections for Minna shortly before their marriage. There is also the figure of Maurice Schlesinger, a converted Jew and Meyerbeer's publisher, whom Wagner felt had exploited him in his Paris years (see Köhler, *Titans*, 90–91, 122–25).

13. See, e.g., *What is German?* (*PW* 4:158): "the Jews laid hand on those advantages, and upon the hindered and dwindling prosperity of the nation the Jewish banker feeds his enormous wealth." Although this is a late essay (written 1865 but not published until 1878 for the second number of the *Bayreuther Blätter*) his linking of Jews and money can be found in earlier writings (in fact as early as 1834; see *SB* 1:177–78, discussed below).

14. *CD* 11 June 1878.

15. See the discussion in chapter 7 above.

to Jesus of Nazareth, not Jesus Christ, perhaps because the latter has Old Testament messianic overtones.[16] Further, he wished to cleanse Jesus from Judaic and other elements. In a letter to Hans von Wolzogen of 17 January 1880 (the letter was in response to cutting out parts of Förster's essay for the *Bayreuther Blätter*) he writes of the "incomparably and sublimely simple and true redeemer who appears to us in the historically intelligible figure of Jesus of Nazareth, but who must be cleansed and redeemed of the distortation that has been caused by Alexandrine, Judaic and Roman despotism (von aller alexandrinisch-judaisch-römisch despotischen Veranstaltung)."[17]

Turning to *Parsifal*, it has been suggested that the final line, "The Redeemer redeemed," is to be understood in the light of Christianity being cleansed of Jewishness. In 1878 Wagner wrote an article in the first volume of *Bayreuther Blätter*, entitled *Public and Popularity*, where, among other things, he argues this: "That the God of our Saviour should have been identified with the tribal god of Israel, is one of the most terrible confusions in all world-history."[18] Cosima suggests that "Redemption to the Redeemer" is "the motto for this concluding article."[19] Wapnewski rightly points out that rather than confirming this interpretation, Wagner simply says the idea is "bold."[20] The two discussed the article the following day also, Wagner pointing to Schopenhauer's view of the "misfortune" that "Christianity was propped up on Judaism."[21] But there is no clear evidence that Cosima's interpretation was uppermost in his mind. The closing words are both central to the drama but they are also ambiguous and mysterious. The entry for 5 January 1882 (*Parsifal* was completed 13 January 1882) points to this centrality (and mystery): "He ... hints at, rather than expresses, the content of this work, 'redemption to the redeemer'—and we are silent after he has added, 'Good that we are alone.'"[22]

A clearer picture of Wagner's understanding of God in *Parsifal* can be gained by simply considering how he uses the word "God." It is used sparingly, in fact just seven times. The first is right at the beginning of the drama when Gurnemanz wakes the squires ("Knappen") (*WagPS* 106–7):

16. However, he is very happy to use the term "Christ" in *The Wibelungen* (*PW* 7:287, 289).

17. *SL* 898.

18. *PW* 6:77; *GSD* 10:86.

19. *CD* 25 July 1878.

20. Wapnewski, "Literary Works," 94.

21. *CD* 26 July 1878.

22. *CD* 5 January 1882 (translation modified).

Do you hear the call? Give thanks to God	Hört ihr den Ruf? Nun danket Gott,
that you are called to hear it!	daß ihr berufen, ihn zu hören!

The natural reference for the word "God" for someone familiar with the Lutheran tradition is to God the Father.[23] However, in the context of the whole stage work it is by no means clear this is the correct interpretation.

The next reference to "God" (this could be to either Christ or God the Father) is in Act II. Kundry tells Parsifal (*WagPS* 200–201):

though God and the world disown me,	ob mich Gott und Welt verstößt,
through you I can be cleansed of sin and redeemed!	in dir entsündigt sein und erlöst!

Then in Act III, where the knights bring in Titurel's coffin, there are three further uses of "God" (*WagPS* 228–29):

Second procession of Knights:	Zweiter Zug der Ritter:
"within the shrine of mourning	"Es birgt den Helden der Trauerschrein,
lies the hero with holy strength,	er birgt die heilige Kraft;
whom God Himself once took as His guardian:	der Gott einst selbst zur Plege sich gab:
we bear Titurel hither."	Titurel führen wir hier."
First procession of Knights:	Erster Zug der Ritter:
"Who brought him low that, in God's keeping,	"Wer hat ihn gefällt, der, in Gottes Hut,
once guarded God Himself?"	Gott selbst einst beschirmte?"

Again one may be tempted to see the reference to God the Father. But a good case can be made that the reference is to Christ, not to God the Father. Indeed the last reference is almost certainly to Christ: Titurel "guarded God" in the sense that he "guarded the grail" and it was in the grail that the blood of Christ miraculously appears.

The final use of "God" is in the "Good Friday Magic." Here the term (used twice) must refer to Christ, not to God (the Father). The relevant text was quoted in chapter 7 and the essential point is that Gurnemanz sings that the human being is "made clean and whole through God's loving sacrifice"

23. Note, for example, the hymn "Nun danket alle Gott" ("Now thank we all our God"). This hymn was in fact sung on the occasion of the "roof raising ceremony" for the Festspielhaus. See *CD* 2 August 1873.

and that "God with divine patience pitied him and suffered for him" (*WagPS* 226–27).

Therefore most if not all uses of "God" in the drama refer to Jesus, not to the "Father." In addition, the "Gottesklage" of which Parsifal sings in Act II refers to *Christ's* lament. This all seems to confirm the view put forward in chapter 6 above that Wagner holds to what one could call a Christo-monism.[24]

It appears then that only Christ is God for Wagner in *Parsifal*. Cosima's entry for 7 January 1880 records that her husband "regrets that G.[oethe] never managed to rid himself of the idea of God as a part of Nature concealed by Nature, whom one should not seek, although He is there; in consequence of this, one is obliged to look upon Christ, God's son, as a problematical being. 'It would be well worth the trouble to define what we mean by God, but who can do that?'"[25] The same sentiment is expressed in *What Use is This Knowledge?*: "Take Goethe, who held Christ for problematical, but the good God for wholly proven, albeit retaining the liberty to discover the latter in Nature after his own fashion; which led to all manner of physical assays and experiments, whose continued pursuit was bound, in turn, to lead the present reigning human intellect to the result that there's no God whatever, but only 'Force and Matter.'"[26] This error was corrected, according to Wagner, by Schopenhauer.[27]

Wagner also thinks that Schopenhauer has been misunderstood regarding the question of God and the following entry from Cosima's diary may suggest that he thought Schopenhauer was *not* an atheist. Saying that he deplored "the mistaken ideas about the dissemination of his philosophy," he comments: "These donkeys who do not believe in God and who think that such figures as Jesus of N[azareth] or a great creative genius move according to the ordinary processes of Nature! They cannot understand that what prevails here is a special urge, a noble need which in the end produces something good. But one must not think in this connection of the old Jewish God."[28] If one were to put a label on Schopenhauer I think it would have to be "agnostic," i.e., he would deny the *possibility* of knowing whether

24. Although *The Wibelungen* dates back to summer 1848 (and Wagner had changed his mind on many things since then), it is striking to note that he writes that "Christ, as Son of God, was father (at least the spiritual) of all men" (*PW* 7:287).

25. The work by Goethe is *The Conversations of Goethe and Chancellor Müller*.

26. *PW* 6:256; *GSD* 10:256.

27. *PW* 6:256; *GSD* 10:257.

28. *CD* 11 June 1878.

there was a God.[29] He rejected the arguments for the existence of God[30] which many theologians would reject also.[31] He also rejected Judaism and Islam, believing the latter to be worthless,[32] but valued Christianity, not in the sense that it is "monotheistic" but that it realized the vanity of a earthly happiness.[33]

Although Wagner brackets out the creator God in these later works, one wonders whether his views were different in the 1840s. It is interesting that in his programme (1846) for Beethoven's Ninth Symphony he does not appear to have any problems with Schiller's text, which concerns a creator God, the "loving Father."[34] However, in his *Introduction to the Year 1880* he expresses doubts about the God who dwells "above the starry tent" and emphasizes the "God within the human breast (Der Gott im Inneren der Menschenbrust), of whose transcendent being our great Mystics were so certain sure."[35] It is also instructive to consider his sketch for the Nibelungen-Myth made in Summer 1848. Here Brünnhilde, at the end of the drama, says: "One only shall rule, All-father thou in thy glory!"[36] But this did not make it into the final libretto of *Götterdämmerung*.[37] We do find in *Das Rheingold* (Scene

29. Magee, *Schopenhauer*, 287, speaks of Schopenhauer's "atheism." But this can only mean that he "did not believe in God" (53), not that he *denied* the existence of God. Magee's own exposition of Schopenhauer's position would suggest agnosticism: "Ignorance is ignorance, not a licence to believe what we like. All we know, at least to begin with, is that the possibility of there being aspects of reality which are outside the limits of human experience—and our being at some point connected with such aspects of reality—cannot be ruled out. We do not know whether this possibility is realized or not" (52).

30. *WWR* 1:510–14; *ASSW* 1:683–88.

31. The implication of his argument in *WWR* 2:7 (*ASSW* 2:16) is that "God" cannot be an "object" but only a "thing-in-itself."

32. See the excursus on religious pluralism in chapter 10 below.

33. *WWR* 2:444; *ASSW* 2:569.

34. Schiller's text, used by Beethoven, is: "Sure our Father dwells 'mid billions. To your knees, ye countless millions? Knowest thy Creator, world? Seek him where heav'n's tent is furled, Throned among his starry billions. . . . Seek him where the stars are strewn! Brothers, o'er the starry dome Surely dwells a loving Father!" ("Muss ein lieber Vater wohnen! Ihr stürzt nieder, Millionen? Ahnest du den Schöpfer, Welt? Such' ihn über Sternenzelt! Über Sternen muss er wohnen! . . . Such' ihn über'm Sternenzelt! Brüder, über'm Sternenzelt Muss ein lieber Vater wohnen!") Wagner comments: "uplifted in spirit, we turn from embracing the whole human race to the great Creator of Nature, whose beatific Being we consciously attest" (*PW* 7:254).

35. *PW* 6:34; *GSD* 10:30.

36. *PW* 7:311.

37. The original libretto for *Siegfrieds Tod* (completed 28 November 1848) did contain these words: "One alone shall rule: All-Father! Glorious god!" ("Nur Einer herrsche: Allvater! Herrlicher du!"; *WagRS* 361). However, they were deleted (probably

One) that the Rhinemaiden Flosshilde speaks of the "Father" who may possibly be a "creator God."[38] However, as a "Rheintöchter" ("Rhinedaughter")
she is most likely referring to the father "Rhein."

Although some exceptions can be found among his utterances, generally speaking Wagner disliked the Old Testament. Correspondingly he
disliked the "creator God" mainly because he was the "Jewish God." Also he
may have felt that it was this God who was responsible for the suffering in
the world. Wagner's strategy for grappling with the question of God can be
seen as twofold. The first is that he seems to "concentrate" God in the suffering person of Jesus of Nazareth (also keeping a role for the Holy Spirit).
The second is that he bracketed out the "creator God." So he was critical of
Strauß's *Life of Jesus* (although he found it better than he expected): "by God
they always mean the Jewish creator of the world, and do not admit that
here it is a manifestation of the divine principle."[39] In *Religion and Art* he
argued that tracing the God who suffered shame on the cross back to the
"Creator of heaven and earth" led to the "Atheism" of his day (something
Wagner clearly thought was a bad thing). A "wrathful God of Punishment"
was promising greater power than "the self-offering, all-loving Saviour of
the Poor." But this "Jehova in the fiery bush," this "reverend Father with the
snow white beard who looked down from out the clouds in blessing on his
Son" was doomed by Art; he "could say but little to the believing soul, however masterly the artist's hand." On the other hand, "the suffering god upon
the cross," "'the Head with wounds all bleeding' still fills us with ecstatic
throes, in the rudest reproduction."[40]

One possible way of understanding Wagner's "doctrine of God" is that
divinity must always be brought together with humanity. To have a deity
divorced from humanity is inadequate or even worthless. So the idea of the
God of Judaism or of the Koran is a worthless God. Wagner's thinking here
is clearly influenced by Luther.[41] The essential link between divinity and
humanity is seen throughout Wagner's works.[42] Wagner could be said to

before 18 December 1848) and far from ruling, the gods now "fade away in bliss before
man's deed" (362).

38. See *WagRS* 58–59: "Look to the gold! Father warned against such a foe," the foe
being Alberich.

39. *CD* 19 July 1878.

40. *PW* 6:217; *GSD* 10:215–16; *JA* 10:122.

41. See, e.g., *WA* 40.3:337,11: *Extra Iesum quaere deum est diabolus* ("To seek God
outside of Jesus Christ is the devil").

42. One of the striking examples is the person of Lohengrin. It is the case that he is
meant to *rescue* Elsa. As Cosima records in her entry for 1 March 1870, Wagner says:
"The Knight of the Grail is sublime and free because he acts, not in his own behalf, but

have a fairly extreme view of the "humanity of God." Further, Wagner found "God" a problem in the institutional manifestation of religion. In response to Cosima's comment "it was religion which introduced hypocrisy," Wagner said: "Say, rather, the -*isms*, Catholicism, Judaism, etc."[43] And one of the major problems in the manifestation of the Jewish religion was the law of Moses, to which I now turn.

The Law of Moses

Wagner's dislike of the God of the Old Testament finds a correlate in his dislike of the Mosaic law. In *What Use is This Knowledge?* (December 1880) Wagner quotes from Schiller's letter to Goethe: "If one would lay hand on the characteristic mark of Christianity, distinguishing it from all mono-theistic religions, it lies in nothing less than the *upheaval of Law*, of Kant's 'Impera-tive,' in whose place it sets free Inclination. In its own pure form it therefore is the presentation of a beautiful morality, or of the humanising of the Holy; and in this sense it is the only *aesthetic* religion."[44] Wagner then adds: "From this fair picture let us cast one glance upon the Ten Commandments of the Mosaic tables of the Law—which even Luther found needful to take as first instruction to a people both mentally and morally brutalised under rule of the Roman Church and Germanic fist-right—and we there shall discover no faintest trace of a truly Christian thought; taken strictly, they are mere *forbiddals*, to most of which the character of *commands* was first assigned by

---

for others. He desires nothing more for himself." However, Wagner made it clear in *A Communication to My Friends* that as far as *redemption* was concerned, this was some-thing Lohengrin himself needed. "Lohengrin sought the woman who should *trust* in him. . . . He sought the woman who would not call for explanations or defence, but who should *love* him with an unconditioned love. Therefore must he cloak his higher nature, for only in the non-revealing of this higher—or more correctly, heightened—essence, could there lie the surety that he was not adored because of it alone, or humbly wor-shipped as a Being past all understanding—whereas his longing was *not* for worship nor for adoration, but for the only thing sufficient to redeem him from his loneliness, to still his deep desire,—for *Love*, for *being loved*, for *being understood through Love*. With the highest powers of his senses, with his fullest fill of consciousness, he would fain become and be none other than a warmly-feeling, warmth-inspiring Man; in a word, a *Man* and not a God—i.e. no 'absolute' artist. Thus yearned he for Woman,—for the human heart. And thus did he step down from out his loneliness of sterile bliss, when he heard this woman's cry for succour, this heart-cry from humanity below. . . . [D]oubt and jealousy convince him that he has not been *understood*, but only *wor-shipped*, and force from him the avowal of his divinity, wherewith, undone, he returns into his loneliness" (*PW* 1:341).

43. *CD* 19 July 1878.
44. *PW* 6:258.

Luther's running commentary.""⁴⁵ Against the Ten Commandments he sets the Christian virtues of faith, hope, and love. However, Wagner argues that such theologic virtues "are commonly arranged in an order that appears to us not quite the right one for development of the Christian spirit; we should like to see 'Faith, Love, and Hope' transposed into 'Love, Faith, and Hope.'"⁴⁶ In his later commentary on the prelude to Act I of *Parsifal* these "virtues" appear precisely in this order.⁴⁷

Wagner's dislike of the law of Moses may have something to do with it being personally inconvenient for him⁴⁸ but his critique of the law probably goes back to Luther (even though he criticized Luther for his "running commentary").⁴⁹

Wagner's Antisemitism

Just as Wagner's theology can be seen to develop through the years (see chapter 2 above) so it is with his "antisemitism." One of the earliest traces of antisemitism is in a letter to his Leipzig friend Theodor Apel of 13 March 1934 written when he was just twenty-one years old.⁵⁰ However, this is vague and refers just to the Jewish attitude to money and is not very significant. Further, as a subscriber to "Jungen Deutschland," he supported the emancipation of Jews (together with that of women and slaves).⁵¹ It appears

45. *PW* 6:258; *GSD* 10:258 (cf. *BB* 202). Wagner presumably has in mind Luther's catechisms. See the "Kleiner Katechismus" where negative commands ("forbiddals") are given a corresponding positive formulation: "Das erst. Du sollt nicht ander Götter haben. Was ist das? Antwort. Wir sollen Gott über alle Ding fürchten, lieben und vertrauen" (*BSELK*, 507). The same pattern is found in the "Großer Katechismus" but at much greater length (*BSELK*, 560–72 for just the first commandment).

46. *PW* 6:259 (modified); *GSD* 10:259. Ellis' translation "corrects" Wagner's first mention of the triad to "Faith, Hope and Charity" to make it conform to 1 Cor 13:13. Also in the first triad he translates "Liebe" as "Charity" and in the second translates it as "Love."

47. *PW* 8:388–89; *DEAP* 45–46; *KB* 3:186–87.

48. Spencer and Millington in *SL* 161, point to the view in *Jesus of Nazareth* where "love is elevated to a position of paramount importance" and "when subjugated to the law or to the institution of marriage . . . the inevitable result is misery." They add that Wagner saw his affair with Jessie Laussot in this light. See his letter to Julie Ritter of 26/27 June 1850 (*SL* 200–207; *SB* 3:315–31). On this affair, see Cormack, "Laussot."

49. Luther, as opposed to Calvin, worked with a law/gospel dichotomy.

50. See *SB* 1:177–78 where he writes of "Weinrechnungen,—Schneiderrechnungen (denn unsereins hat ja hier gar keinen Kredit), das verfluchte Judengeschmeiß." Fischer, "Judentum," 41, finds it striking that Wagner does not complain about a particular Jew who holds back his money but has a generalized view of "the cursed Jewish vermin."

51. See the comments in *SB* 1:178 n. 1; 206 n. 3.

that his antisemitism really took hold as a result of his negative experiences with Meyerbeer and Mendelssohn during the Paris and Dresden years and as a result of his negative assessment of their art.[52] Interestingly, Katz argues that his negative image of these composers "was formed independently of their Jewish origin and was not at first connected with it."[53] The composition of his 1850 essay *Judaism in Music* therefore "marked the establishment of a quasi-factual foundation for his subjective judgment."[54] Therefore his antisemitism was "the result of a personal experience at a biographical turning point."[55] So for Katz, "Wagner was far from being bound to a system of thought or from aiming at one."[56]

The only thing that puts a question mark against this is that a "system of thought" was already well established in Europe, although there was no single type of antisemitism. First of all there was the long history of Christian antisemitism.[57] Secondly, there were writings against the Jews from figures of the Enlightenment,[58] German nationalist philosophers,[59] and romanticism.[60] In addition there were recent writings that Wagner in *Judaism in Music* reflects. One of these was Karl Marx's 1843 essay *On the Jewish Question*, although there is no evidence that Wagner knew this work.[61] Even if Wagner was not conversant with all this literature he would certainly be aware of such attitudes.

52. See above.

53. Katz, *Darker Side*, 31.

54. Ibid., 31–32.

55. Ibid., 131.

56. Ibid., 130.

57. Such antisemitism is found in all the main churches: Orthodox, Catholic, and Protestant. The literature on Christian antisemitism is vast and it is often difficult to find a balanced treatment. A very useful resource (with source material) is Rengstorf and von Kortzfleisch, *Kirche und Synagoge*.

58. See, e.g., Voltaire (Katz, *Prejudice*, 34–47) and Kant (Mack, *Jew*, 1–41).

59. Here the figure of Fichte stands out (see Bell, *Irrevocable Call*, 356–57).

60. Nietzsche argued that as an artist Wagner belonged to the Parisian "romantics" and "decadents" Delacroix, Berlioz, and Baudelaire; if he is right it could suggest Wagner's antisemitism grew in the atmosphere of Paris of the 1830s (and that his antisemitism belonged to the French rather than the Germans). See Borchmeyer, "Anti-Semitism," 178. On the French component, see below on Ernest Renan.

61. In fact, there is no evidence that Wagner knew any of his works. However, as suggested in chapter 2 above, he probably did hear of Marx's views via Bakunin. Kühnel, "Prose Writings," 597, finds a parallel between Wagner and Marx on their attitude to the Jews.

And so we turn to consider some aspects of his 1850 essay usually given in translation as *Judaism in Music*,[62] although a better translation may be *Jewry in Music*.[63] One writer who clearly influenced Wagner was the violinist Theodor Uhlig whom Wagner first met as a member of the Dresden Orchestra. He wrote a series of articles for the *Neue Zeitschrift für Musik* between 31 January and 23 July 1850.[64] Wagner read these articles closely[65] which "include virtually every significant element that Wagner was to repackage in 'Jewry in Music.'"[66] One of the central ideas of Wagner's essay is that Jews "take advantage of German music because it is already dead."[67] Conway suggests that the articles and letters written around the time of its publication reveal that Wagner "does not want the bourgeoisie . . . to listen to the music (as exemplified by that of Meyerbeer and Mendelssohn) that they happen to like." Rather he wants them "to commit to the social vision of music embodied in [Wagner's] post-*Lohengrin* concepts for opera as 'drama.'"[68] Wagner's article, according to Conway, "takes the form of an

62. This was originally published under the pseudonym K. Freigedank in the journal "Neue Zeitschrift für Musik" (issues for 3 and 6 September 1850). This journal was founded by Robert Schumann in 1834 but he passed over the editorship to Franz Brendel in 1844. The journal was concerned to look back to Bach, to criticize poor current music (see Schumann's 1837 critique of Meyerbeer's *Les Huguenots*) and to look expectantly to the future (Fischer, *Judentum in der Musik*, 18). Wagner's essay was republished as a pamphlet in 1869 by J. J. Weber, Leipzig, with a new preface (addressed to Marie Muchanoff, formerly Countess Nesselrode) and with minor changes to the text.

63. Conway, "Jews, Music and Wagner," 12, argues that "Judaism in Music" is a misnomer. "Judentum" in the nineteenth century did not mean the religious practices of the Jews but rather "the Jewish community" together with "petty haggling" and "cheating." I take Conway's point that Wagner's article did concern "Jewry" rather than "Judaism." However, I doubt that Wagner "knew little and cared less" about Jewish religious practices as Conway suggests. Note, incidentally, that in Gal 1:13–14 the term "Jüdenthum" in Luther's translation (rendering Ἰουδαϊσμός) *did* mean precisely Jewish religious practices.

64. They comprise two reviews of Meyerbeer's *Der Prophet*, a series of seven articles entitled "Zeitmässige Betrachtungen" ("Thoughts in Season") appearing between 23 April and 23 July, and a review of recent choral works by Mendelssohn and Meyerbeer (Conway, *Jewry in Music*, 259).

65. See *SB* 3:365.

66. Conway, *Jewry in Music*, 258. He therefore suggests that Uhlig was more than simply "the inspirer" of "Jewry in Music" as Rose, *Race and Revolution*, 90, suggests.

67. Conway, "Jews, Music and Wagner," 12.

68. Ibid., 13. Wagner witnesses to the great success of Meyerbeer's *Le Prophète* (he had just attended the forty-seventh performance of the work) in a letter to Uhlig of 24 February 1850 (*SL* 185; *SB* 3:240).

unconscious, indeed unwilling, confession—envy concealed as attack—of the tremendous achievements of musical Jews during Wagner's lifetime."[69]

Wagner's essay has, understandably, caused considerable offense, especially the ending which concerns the "going under" ("Untergang") of Jews, something that is highly significant for Wagner's understanding of the redemption of Jews and something frequently misunderstood. Since this conclusion concerns the ideological core of the essay, and since it may throw some light on *Parsifal*, I consider it in a little detail. Fundamental for understanding what Wagner means by the "Untergang" is the context. He writes of a Jew (Börne) who

> . . . came among us seeking for redemption: he found it not, and had to learn that only *with our redemption, too, into genuine Manhood*, would he ever find it. To become Man at once with us, however, means firstly for the Jew as much as ceasing to be Jew. And this had Börne done. Yet Börne, of all others, teaches us that this redemption can not be reached in ease and cold, indifferent complacence, but costs—as cost it must for us— sweat, anguish, want, and all the dregs of suffering and sorrow. Without once looking back, take ye your part in this regenerative work of deliverance through self-annulment; then are we one and un-dissevered! But bethink ye, that one only thing can redeem you from the burden of your curse: the redemption of Ahasuerus—*Going under!*[70]

The first point to appreciate is that Wagner speaks of the *redemption* of Jews and does so in connection to the redemption of non-Jews.[71] The two difficult things to ascertain is the nature of this connection and the meaning

---

69. Conway, "Jews, Music and Wagner," 13. Conway notes that at the beginning of the nineteenth century there were virtually no Jews active in "classical music." By the end of the century that had completely changed. Indeed the change can be seen already by 1850 when Wagner's article was published.

70. *PW* 3:100. Ellis' translation is based on the revised 1869 version. Fischer, *Judentum in der Musik*, 173, again using the 1869 version, reads: "Nehmt rücksichtlos an diesem durch Selbstvernichtung wiedergebärenden Erlösungswerke teil, so sind wir einig und ununterschieden! [1850: Nehmt rückhaltlos an diesem selbstvernichtenden, blutigen Kampfe Teil, so sind wir einig und untrennbar!] Aber bedenkt, daß nur Eines eure Erlösung von dem auf Euch lastenden Fluche sein kann: Die Erlösung Ahasvers,— der *Untergang!*"

71. St. Paul grappled with precisely the same problem in Rom 9–11 (Wagner had marked Rom 10:3–4; 11:16, 18 in his New Testament). Those concerned about Wagner's negative language about Jews could also consider St. Paul's.

of "going under" (Wagner does not make himself entirely clear[72]). I now put forward two possible ways in which to understand this connection.

The first one (and this may make Wagner's argument more palatable) is that the redemption that is costly and involves "self-annulment" ("Selbstvernichtung") is applicable to *both* Jew *and* non-Jew. So if the Jew engages in it then they are one with non-Jews. This may then further suggest that not only Jews but also non-Jews also must engage in the "going under" ("Untergang"). This redemptive "going under" could be understood as a radical baptism, being related to a "dying with Christ" (cf. Rom 6:3), precisely what Kundry undergoes in *Parsifal* Act III: "the baptism of Kundry with the *annihilating* sound of the kettledrum: '*Obliteration of the whole being* . . .'"[73] If my interpretation is correct, then for Wagner those Jews who submit to baptism cease to be Jews. But in what sense do non-Jews "go under." One possibility is that although most Germans were baptized, Wagner felt that there was so much nominal Christianity[74] that they needed to reappropriate their baptism in "sweat and anguish." Another aspect to this is to say that even non-Jews have some Jewishness in them that, through this radical baptism, is eliminated. Such a view, strange though it may appear, could cohere with Wagner's own feeling that he too is an Ahasuerus figure.[75] Nike Wagner has explored this idea with reference to the controversial book *Geschlecht und Charakter* (*Sex and Character*, 1903) of Otto Weininger, a Viennese Jew who converted to Protestantism.[76] Applying this to the "going

72. A point ably made by Fischer, "Judentum," 37–39.

73. *CD* 3 February 1879 (my emphasis). See the discussion in chapter 5 above.

74. See *PW* 1:350; *GSD* 4:304 (quoted in chapter 1 above).

75. See below for further discussion of this.

76. In this book, which could be seen as a counterpart to *Parsifal* (cf. Nike Wagner, *Wagners*, 124), he develops a theory (which with Freud remained undeveloped) that the psyche is made up of male and female, which for Weininger was an unhappy co-existence. The feminine as the "negative" therefore has to be exterminated (125). Likewise all personalities contain a mixture of Aryan and Jew and so the Aryan needs to conquer the Jewish aspect. The supreme example for Weininger was Jesus, who "first had to overcome the Jewishness in himself before discovering his own mission" (quoted in Nike Wagner, *Wagners*, 127). Despite the problems this approach may entail, Nike Wagner believes that it does illuminate something: the antisemite and the misogynist hate what is actually a part of themselves. Weininger then applied this to Wagner: "But even Wagner—the most thorough anti-Semite—cannot be acquitted of an admixture of Jewishness, even in his art." Weininger tests this assertion in relation to the responses his art receives: "There is no denying that Wagner's music produces the strongest impression both on the Jewish anti-Semite who cannot quite free himself from Jewry and on the anti-Semitic Indo-European who fears becoming addicted to him" (126). For Weininger, "achievements in the arts are not sublimations of drives, as in Freud, but the result of defensive reactions against hated parts of one's own ego" (126).

under" at the end of *Judaism in Music* would mean not only that the Jew ceases to be a Jew but a non-Jew blots out the Jewish aspect of their personhood. In case one may think all this belongs solely to a dark and eccentric strand of Viennese psycho-analysis one should consider the twentieth-century Lutheran interpretation of St. Paul. According to this view Paul not only attacks the Jews for their works-righteousness; he also attacks the "hidden Jew" within all of us.[77] Salvation then entails the conversion of the Jew, the *homo religiosus* par excellence, and the non-Jew who had this hidden Jew within him. What may distinguish Paul from Weininger, however, is that for Paul the fundamental problem lies not so much with the Jew per se but rather with Adam who incorporates both Jew and non-Jew.

One of the strengths of this first approach to this key paragraph in *Judaism in Music* is that it does explain Wagner's later attitude to Hermann Levi. If only Levi would come to faith in Christ, be baptized (and take Communion) all would be well. One could object and say that Mendelssohn had been baptized, yet for Wagner it seems this did not suffice[78] since he is one of the main targets in *Judaism in Music*.[79] However, Wagner may have been concerned about the motive for Christian baptism: was it a genuine step (note that Mendelssohn had been baptized as a child) and was it simply an attempt to "wash away the traces" of one's Jewish origin?[80] The other case to consider is Ludwig Börne whom Wagner has here specifically mentioned. He was baptized (as an adult) and changed his name from Juda Löw Baruch to (Karl) Ludwig Börne,[81] yet Wagner writes that although he ceased to be a Jew and was seeking redemption, he had not achieved it. But Wagner does not exclude the possibility of his redemption.[82] He implies that his problem was trying to achieve it "in ease and cold, indifferent complacence" rather than in "sweat, anguish, want, and all the dregs of suffering and sorrow." Perhaps Wagner chose Börne not only because his friend Röckel was one of his disciples[83] but also because it was a "hard case": he had the double disadvantage in Wagner's eyes of being a Jew and a journalist![84]

77. See, e.g., Günther Bornkamm, "Testament," 26.

78. Fischer, "Judentum," 38.

79. *PW* 3:93–96; Fischer, *Judentum in der Musik*, 163–67.

80. *PW* 3:87; Fischer, *Judentum in der Musik*, 152.

81. See *DBE2* 1:78.

82. This is the mistaken view of Gay, "Wagner," 260 (thereby agreeing with Rose).

83. Gregor-Dellin, *Wagner*, 209.

84. Kühnel, "Prose Writings," 613, writes of five J's "in which [Wagner] sees summed up all the negative features of his age": "Junker" (young Prussian aristocracy), "Juden" (Jews), and "Juristen" (lawyers), these three being mentioned in *What is German?* (*PW* 4:158), to which one can add "Jesuiten" (Jesuits) and "Journalisten" (Journalists). Cf. the

I now come to the second way in which to understand the connection between Jew and non-Jew in that final paragraph. According to this view although both Jew and non-Jew need a costly redemption, only the Jew needs to go through the process of "self-annulment" and the "going under." If they do so then Jew and non-Jew can be "one and un-dissevered." This "self-annulment" and "going under," which, according to this view, is applicable only to the Jew, is clearly *not* physical destruction. Again, the "going under" could refer to a radical baptism. It could, though, point to something else I need to explore. Kundry as an "eternal Jew" undergoes a "self-annulment" and "going under" at her baptism. But since she alone of all the characters in the drama has to undergo a "self-annulment" and "going under" in those final moments when she "slowly sinks lifeless to the ground in front of Parsifal, her eyes uplifted to him"[85] it could be argued that baptism does not suffice in her case. She needs to be baptized *and* she needs to go through a process of self-annulment at the end of the drama. Does this not then detract from the power of her baptism? I think not. New Testament theology redemption properly understood is not simply related to one single act whether that be baptism, coming to faith, acquittal at the final judgement, or resurrection to eternal life. Rather, each is one aspect of the whole redemptive process. If *Parsifal* is seen in the light of this, it means that Kundry's redemption is a unified event that brings together baptism, faith, and her final "sinking lifeless to the ground." Wagner understood this "sinking lifeless" to be a highly charged spiritual moment[86] and could be interpreted as the consummation of her union with Christ. Therefore her "going under" can be related to the whole process of her spiritual transformation.

Whichever of these two interpretations is adopted, it must be stressed that Wagner does see a possible redemption for Jews and it is significant that the philosopher and radical antisemite Eugen Dühring took particular exception to Wagner's view, suggesting that the composer had failed to redeem himself from the Jews.[87]

One question that remains is whether Wagner is "racist" in *Judaism in Music*. It is the case that Wagner does not use the term "Rasse/Race" here; he first uses the term in his writings written under the influence of Gobineau. Nevertheless Fischer maintains that we do find an early racist

---

four J's in *CD* 30 April 1878.

85. *WagPS* 236–37.

86. Cosima records on the day he completed the score: "He tells me that the A-minor chord (as Kundry falls to the ground) will make an impression on me; the terror of sanctity flows from it, and it will have to be very beautifully played, he says" (*CD* 13 January 1882).

87. See Borchmeyer, "Heine," 31, who refers to Dühring, *Judenfrage*.

view ("frührassistisch") in that he hypostasizes an unchanging Jewish essence ("ein unveränderbares jüdisches Wesen").[88] However, the only problem with this is that the close of the essay suggests that one cannot speak of such an unchanging essence.[89]

I now move on to Wagner's later antisemitism. On discovering Schopenhauer in 1854 Wagner's antisemitism was certainly reinforced; but it was also modified in that Wagner came to share the philosopher's view that Judaism was to be seen to represent an "unspiritual and heartless optimism." We see this view expressed already in a letter to Röckel of April 1855[90] and it is the light of this that one should consider the words to Wolzogen, quoted above (letter of 17 January 1880). Here Wagner expressed his wish to free the redeemer from anything "alexandrinisch-judaisch-römisch,"[91] i.e., to free him not only from Judaism ("judaisch") but also from Catholicism ("römisch") and from dogmatism ("alexandrinisch").[92]

His antisemitism was also fuelled by his reading Ernest Renan. In 1878–82 he read works by Renan in his series *History of the Origins of Christianity*.[93] From Cosima's diaries we discover that he started with his *Évangiles*,[94] then moved on to *The Apostles*,[95] and then *Saint Paul* with which he "is pleased."[96] He then read *The Antichrist*.[97] Then, against Cosima's recommendation, he read the *Life of Jesus* (1863)[98] and finally *Marc-*

88. Fischer, "Judentum," 38.

89. See also the points made by Bermbach in Fischer, "Judentum," 53: "Die den Juden hier zugeschriebenen Charakteristika seien keine natürlichen Merkmale, sondern historisch erworbene Verhaltensformen wie etwa bestimmte Sprechweisen, die auch wieder abgelegt werden könnten." But note some of Wagner's later views (*CD* 25 May 1878).

90. See *SB* 7:126–33, discussed in chapter 2 above. For the expression "unspiritual and heartless optimism" see *SB* 7:130: "Der eigentliche Kern des Judenthums ist aber jener geist- und herzlose Optimismus . . . "

91. *SL* 898.

92. Nietzsche referred to dogmatism as "sokratisch-alexandrinisch" (Nietzsche, *Tragedy*, 97; KSA 1:131).

93. The works in this series were *Vie de Jésus* (1863), *Les Apôtres* (1866), *St. Paul* (1869), *L'Anté-Christ* (1873), *Les Évangiles* (1877), *L'Église chrétienne* (1879), *Marc-Aurèle et la fin du monde antique* (1881).

94. *CD* 22, 23 April 1878.

95. *CD* 26, 29 April 1878.

96. *CD* 14 May 1878. She also says that "he reads to me with his splendid delivery the First Epistle to the Corinthians in Luther's translation."

97. He begins 18 May and ends 31 May 1878 (*CD* 18 May and 31 May 1878).

98. After Wagner's reading of *St. Paul* Cosima recommended the complete series to him "except for *The Life of Jesus*" since "his talent is insufficient for the Saviour"(*CD* 17 May 1878).

Aurèle.[99] Renan regarded the "Semites" as an inferior type of human beings, but for religious and cultural reasons rather than any biological reason. As far as *The Antichrist* is concerned, Wagner disagreed with Renan on the Jews. Whereas Renan criticized those Jews "who have remained Jewish," Wagner felt that Jews can never change.[100] Wagner was actually to go against this later in *Religion and Art* and *Heroism and Christianity* since he there argues that the Jews can be infused with the blood of Christ at the Communion.[101] As far as Renan's *Life* was concerned, a work which was to prove highly influential,[102] Cosima reports that it "does not displease him; among other things he feels that he has depicted the idea of God the Father very well."[103]

The antisemitism of Wagner's early and middle years was probably culturally and religiously based. But his antisemitism was to take on a racial aspect as can be seen from Cosima's entry for 7 April 1873.[104] Then in 1881 he read Gobineau's controversial work *Essai sur l'inégalité des races humaines* (1853–55),[105] which contributed to his view of the "races." However, Gobineau himself was not actually antisemitic; he actually praised the Jews as "a free, strong, and intelligent people"[106] and before the First World War some leading Zionists appealed to his arguments![107] As Borchmeyer points out, modern racial theories were initially far from being antisemitic.[108]

99. *CD* 21 November 1881; 16 January 1882.

100. See *CD* 25 May 1878, where Cosima relates that she read to her "the very spirited pages from Renan's *Antichrist* on the Jews; he is referring solely to the Jews who have remained Jewish and, says R., 'quite overlooks the main point that Jews can never really become anything else.'"

101. Therefore, perhaps the Communion for Wagner was not simply "vegetarian"! Cf. Beaufils and Evans, "Wagner," 604.

102. On Renan and his *Vie de Jésus* see Schweitzer, *Quest*, 180–92 (Schweitzer, *Leben-Jesu-Forschung*, 207–18); Neill, *Interpretation*, 193–94; Colin Brown, *Jesus in European Protestant Thought*, 233–38.

103. *CD* 10 June 1878.

104. See *CD* 7 April 1873. Cosima reports that the dean of Bayreuth suggests that intermarriage is the solution to the problems of the Jews. Her husband objects: "R. maintains that the Germans would then cease to exist, since the fair German blood is not strong enough to withstand this 'alkali.'" On "alkali," see Kant's view in Weischedel, *Schriften zur Anthropologie I*, 80: "Das flüchtige Alkali ist noch ein Stoff, den die Natur aus dem Blute wegschaffen muß."

105. His Wahnfried library contained Gobineau, *Essai sur l'inégalité* and Pott, *Rassen*.

106. Gobineau, *Inequality*, 59.

107. See the central European Zionists Elias Auerbach and Ignz Zollschau. See also Nicosia, *Palestine Question*, 18.

108. Borchmeyer, "Anti-Semitism," 179, who cites Mühlen, *Rassenideologien*, 126: "Not until the final decades of the nineteenth century did racial theories combine with

It is important to stress that his reading of Gobineau took place very late in the composition of *Parsifal*. And although Wagner was antisemitic, he would appear to agree with Gobineau that the Jewish people were "racially strong." He writes in *Know Thyself*: "The Jew ... is the most astounding instance of racial congruence ever offered by world-history."[109] But whereas Gobineau thought "racial strength" mattered, Wagner thought it did not: "if one looks at things without regard to time and space, one knows that what really matters is something different from racial strength—see the Gospels."[110]

One of the hardest statements of the mature Wagner on the Jews is at the end of *Know Thyself* and the fact that it appears to be a "premeditated" idea rather than an off-the-cuff remark makes it particularly distasteful.[111] The "solution" is that there should be no longer any Jews in Germany. It has been taken to imply that Wagner was supporting the antisemitic political movement that had its base in Berlin. "And the very stimulus of the present movement—conceivable among ourselves alone—might bring this great solution within reach of us Germans."[112] Köhler writes that "[i]n making this recommendation to the anti-Semitic movement, Wagner had crossed the Rubicon, for it went far beyond anything he had previously committed to paper." The ending was so serious because whereas *Judaism in Music* ended with the possibility of the redemption of the Jews, *Know Thyself* ended with the "great solution" that there will be in Germany "no longer—any Jews."[113]

---

what had earlier been religious or socio-cultural forms of anti-Jewish feeling, to produce a true racial anti-Semitism."

109. *PW* 6:271; *GSD* 10:271.

110. *CD* 14 February 1881.

111. Many antisemitic remarks in Cosima's diaries can to some extent be excused since they are uttered spontaneously. One remark that does leave much to be desired is this: "He makes a drastic joke to the effect that all Jews should be burned at a performance of *Nathan*" (*CD* 18 December 1881). Wagner is alluding to the theatre fire in Vienna (8 December 1881) just as the curtain was about to rise on Offenbach's *The Tales of Hoffmann*. According to *CD* 17 December 1881, "[t]he fact that 416 Israelites died in the fire does not increase R.'s concern over the disaster." He earlier made the comment that if people are buried in coal mines, he feels indignation; but not in the case where "this community die while watching an Offenbach operetta, an activity which contains no trace of moral superiority." As well as alluding to this tragedy, Wagner may be alluding to the fear that Nathan will be burned on an order from the Patriarch for bringing up a Christian girl (Rachel) as a Jew. One wonders whether this particularly struck Wagner since in Halevy's *La Juive*, a work he greatly admired, "Rachel," a Christian, was also brought up as a Jew.

112. *PW* 6:274; *GSD* 10:274.

113. *PW* 6:274; *GSD* 10:274.

Most will find Wagner's comments highly offensive. But there are some strange contradictions when one looks at the context of Wagner's writing. It is generally assumed that it is this work to which Wagner refers in a letter to Angelo Neumann of 23 February 1881: "I have absolutely no connection with the present 'anti-Semitic' movement: an article of mine which is shortly to appear in the Bayreuther Blätter will prove this so conclusively that it will be impossible for anyone of *intelligence* to associate me with that movement."[114] Since *Know Thyself* was published in February-March 1881 one would naturally think the reference was to this article.[115] But the problem is that in the letter Wagner appears to distance himself from the antisemitic movement whereas the article is clearly antisemitic. The background to this letter is that Neumann was to stage the *Ring* in Berlin, but its success was jeopardized because of Wagner's well-known antisemitism. Neumann explains: "A strong anti-Semitic party in Berlin had loudly proclaimed Wagner as their chief apostle; which moved George Davidsohn (a well-known political writer and friend of Wagner) to write, calling my attention to the risk we ran in our Berlin enterprises if the rumour spread that Wagner was a member of this society."[116] Neumann appealed to Cosima and hence the letter from Wagner to Neumann.

Was Wagner being disingenuous in his letter to Neumann? Was it, as Köhler puts it, "a tactical ploy"?[117] Can the letter to Neumann and *Know Thyself* be reconciled? I think not. It is the case that in the letter Wagner does not distance himself from *all* antisemitic movements but from one particular movement, the *present* movement in Germany, which had its base in Berlin. He writes: "I have absolutely no connection with the present 'anti-Semitic' movement" ("Der gegenwärtigen 'antisemitischen' Bewegung stehe ich vollständig fern"), i.e., the one that reached a high point in 1879–81, the key figures being Adolf Stoecker,[118] Wilhelm Marr,[119]

---

114. *SL* 906.

115. In a footnote Spencer and Millington suggest the reference is to *Know Thyself* (*SL* 906).

116. Neumann, *Recollections*, 132. Georg Davidsohn was in fact a Jewish journalist and editor of the *Börsenkurier*.

117. Köhler argues for it being a tactical ploy in view of Cosima's entry for 28 July 1878 (i.e., three years earlier!). The entry is not entirely clear: "At lunch our friend W. talks of a state of ferment against Israel. R. laughs; 'Is our *Bayreuther Blätter* responsible for that?'"

118. This Berlin Court preacher (Brakelmann, "Stoecker") gave his first speech against the Jews in autumn 1879.

119. Marr, *Sieg des Judenthums*, appeared in 1879.

Heinrich von Treitschke,[120] Eugen Dühring,[121] and Bernhard Förster.[122] But the problem remains that not only is *Know Thyself* antisemitic but also Wagner does not seem to distance himself clearly from precisely this Berlin antisemitic movement. He certainly criticizes various political parties (but he does not mention or allude to Stoecker's "Christlichen-sozialen Arbeit-erpartei" ["Christian-Social Workers Party"], founded in 1878). But when he speaks about the "present movement" he is either positive as in the final paragraph[123] or at most vaguely critical of the leaders: "However, an inner motive plainly lies at bottom of the present movement, little as it may be evinced by the behaviour of its leaders so far," this "motive" being "the re-awakening of an instinct lost to the German nation."[124] *Know Thyself* and the letter to Neumann therefore seem to be irreconcilable in this respect.

Another factor to bear in mind is that it was probably Cosima who made the ending more antisemitic.[125] But we are still left with the problem that Wagner accepted her suggestions and such changes were made before writing the letter to Neumann. Her entry for 10 February 1881 says that to-wards lunch Wagner read to her his "new article, 'Know Thyself'" and they discuss "[w]hether the Jews can ever be redeemed." Then there are some comments that either reflect the thoughts of Cosima or of both of them: "their nature condemns them to the world's reality. They have profaned Christianity, that is to say, adapted it to this world, and from our art, which can only be a refuge from prevailing conditions, they also expect world con-quest." Then for the evening she writes: "He maintains that I do not like his article, which sounds funny."[126] The next day she records: "Around lunch-time I find R. altering the ending of his article, to my regret,"[127] although one has to ask whether it really was regret! Her entry for that evening tells us: "he reads to me the revised ending of his article, which seems to me more

120. This Prussian historian published his first article on the Jewish question in autumn 1879.

121. Dühring, *Judenfrage*, appeared in 1881 (and, as we saw above, was critical of Wagner's hope for the redemption of the Jews).

122. He organized the petition against the Jews in 1880–81.

123. *PW* 6:274 (*GSD* 10:274): "And the very stimulus of the present movement—conceivable among ourselves alone—might bring this great solution within reach of us Germans."

124. *PW* 6:269; *GSD* 10:269.

125. Köhler, *Titans*, 573, argues "[i]t was Cosima who was to blame, for it was she who had ensured that Wagner himself had cast aside all shame. The insidious ending of 'Know Yourself' bears her imprint."

126. *CD* 10 February 1881.

127. *CD* 11 February 1881.

fitting than the first, and R. himself says that he always meant to write about us, not about the Jews. And yet I have to tell him what strange feelings it arouses in me when he alters anything at my instigation."[128] One problem in this evening entry is that in the article's final paragraph (and the penultimate paragraph) he *does* write "about the Jews" (see "this great solution"). But the general tenor of Cosima's entry is that the revised ending is more antisemitic. One change he may have made was to be more positive about the *present* antisemitic movement. But again there remains the problem that he and his wife were both concerned about the *Ring* performances in Berlin. Another possible change may have been to the penultimate paragraph, which speaks of there being no longer any Jews.

If the article he is referring to in the letter is *Know Thyself* another possibility is that after writing to Neumann Wagner made yet another change to the article but we have no record of this from Cosima's diary.[129] Another article Wagner may have in mind in his letter to Angelo Neumann is *Heroism and Christianity*,[130] the final supplement to *Religion and Art*. This was his final statement on the Jewish question and he sees hope for the Jewish people through "regeneration." The problem with this solution is that the article was not published until September 1881 and on 23 February 1881 he tells Neumann of an article "which is *shortly* to appear in the Bayreuther Blätter."[131]

The ending of *Know Thyself* presents puzzles. But I think it would be a mistake to take literally Wagner's words of the "great solution" that there will be in Germany "no longer—any Jews." Consider the following juxtaposition. In the evening of 11 February 1881 Cosima records that Rubinstein played "the Flower Maidens" and then Beethoven's 33 Variations "to our admiring delight."[132] Then when the couple are alone Wagner reads the revised ending of *Know Thyself* to Cosima. There is no way that Wagner would wish Rubinstein to be expelled from Germany. The same applies to another Jew close to Wagner's heart: we read that two months later that Levi was "affected by 'Know Thyself.'"[133] Levi must have known that what Wagner wrote about "Jews" did not apply to himself.[134]

128. *CD* 11 February 1881.

129. *CD* 1 March 1881 tells us that he "corrects proofs of 'Know Thyself.'"

130. This is suggested by Borchmeyer, "Anti-Semitism," 183, and again more recently in Borchmeyer, "Antisemitismus," 29.

131. *SL* 906 (my emphasis).

132. *CD* 11 February 1881.

133. *CD* 15 March 1881.

134. Wagner's comment in *CD* 11 October 1879 (quoted below) would also not apply to his circle of Jewish artists.

Wagner's antisemitism is complex and often difficult to fathom. It was also a "sophisticated" antisemitism. This may explain his ambivalence towards the "present movement" and why he refused to sign Bernhard Förster's 1880 petition demanding emergency laws against the Jews.[135] Cosima records that "he is annoyed by a renewed request to sign a petition against the Jews addressed to Prince Bismarck. He reads aloud the ridiculously servile phrases and the dubiously expressed concern: 'And I am supposed to sign that!' he exclaims."[136] What may at first appear a moral stance is somewhat relativized when one reads Cosima's entry for 11 October 1879: "I read a very good speech by the preacher Stoecker about the Jews. R. is in favour of expelling them entirely. We laugh to think that it really seems as if his article on the Jews marked the beginning of this struggle."[137] This may give some credence to words attributed to Hans von Bülow: "The master did indeed poke the fire, but he let others burn their fingers in it."[138]

Wagner's Relationships with Jewish Artists

We have already seen that Wagner's relationships with Jewish artists, especially Hermann Levi, demonstrate his complex attitude to the Jewish people. One reason Levi (and Fischer) were employed was because Wagner made an agreement with Ludwig II that *Parsifal* be performed with the orchestra, singers, and artistic personnel of the Munich Court Theatre. It is therefore suggested that Wagner was thus "compelled" to accept Levi.[139] However, it

135. Bernard Förster's "Petition in der Judenfrage, an Fürst Bismarck," published in the "Berliner Bewegung," objected to the wave of Jewish immigrants entering Germany from the East which was changing the fabric of German society.

136. *CD* 6 July 1880. Cosima's first reference to the invitation to sign the petition is *CD* 16 June 1880: "He does not sign it: he says (1) he has already done what he can; (2) he dislikes appealing to Bismarck . . . (3) nothing more can be done in the matter."

137. The speech is most likely the one given on 19 September 1879 in Berlin ("Unsere Forderungen auf das moderne Judentum"). It is unlikely that Wagner himself had much influence on Stoecker's antisemitism. A caricature appearing in the *Frankfurter Latern* shows Stoecker throwing balls of dung at a crowd, the dung being provided by a figure bowing towards the preacher and holding a garden fork of dung. This figure providing the "ammunition" can only be identified by the words "Wagner" written on one of his coat tails. This, however, is not the composer (contra Fischer, *Judentum in der Musik*, 123) but Adolph Wagner, an eminent economist at the University of Berlin, friend of Stoecker, vice-president of the antisemitic Christian Social Workers Party, and later president of Stoecker's Protestant Social Congress (Karlsson, "Stoecker," 223).

138. Jacob Katz, *Darker Side*, 114. Bülow himself actually signed the petition but later regretted it after discovering that Wagner had refused (Walker, *Hans von Bülow*, 18).

139. Cf. Millington, *Wagner*, 102, 108.

is by no means clear that he was so "compelled."[140] Furthermore we know that Wagner had great admiration for Levi and wrote a letter insisting that he conduct the work. The context for this is that Wagner received an anonymous letter[141] demanding that Levi should not conduct *Parsifal* because he was Jewish and, it was claimed, was having an affair with Cosima. Wagner showed Levi the letter, who packed his bags and left for Bamberg. Wagner then wrote to Levi (1 July 1881): "For God's sake come back at once. . . . You do not need to lose any of your faith, but merely to acquire the courage of your convictions! Perhaps some great change is about to take place in your life—but at all events—you are my Parsifal conductor!"[142] The words concerning "some great change" may reflect Wagner's wish that Levi become a Christian; we know that on other occasions Wagner did ask Levi to be baptized (see Cosima's entries for 19 January 1881 and 19 April 1881).

Cosima's diaries tell of Levi's return to Wahnfried:

> At 1 o'clock return of our poor friend Levi as a result of R.'s splendid reply to his letter. Very relaxed, indeed even very cheerful mood at lunch. R. calls for *Hebrew* wine! . . . When friend Levi tells us that he visited the cathedral in Bamberg, and shows evidence of a leaning toward Catholicism, R. talks about the ceremonies in our church and praises their simplicity and

140. Dreyfus, "Hermann Levi's Shame," 129, appeals to John Deathridge's point that "there is no document suggesting that the King threatened to withdraw the services of the orchestra if Wagner did not agree to allow Levi to conduct *Parsifal*." The only document that could suggest this is an introduction by Reinhold von Lichtenberg to Kniese, *Kampf*, in which he recounts a story told to him by Alexander Ritter. According to this story Wagner was told by the Munich Intendant that the orchestra would come to Bayreuth with Levi as conductor. Wagner replied saying that he wished to choose the conductor himself, but is then told that he has to take Levi. According to Ritter, "The Master, in the greatest agitation, stood silent at first for quite a while, then drummed his fingers on the window pane, then turned around and burst out: 'So, now I open my lovely festival house to the Jews!'" (quoted in Dreyfus, "Hermann Levi's Shame," 130). Dreyfus argues that this story is implausible on several grounds. First, this episode is not in Cosima's diaries (it is just the kind of story she would love to recount) and there is not even any indication that Ritter visited the Wagners before 1881. Secondly, in a letter to Ludwig of 19 September 1881 Wagner states that he accepts gratefully "the heads of this musical organisation . . . without asking whether this man is a Jew, this other a Christian" (quoted in Dreyfus, "Hermann Levi's Shame," 130; Newman, *Life IV*, 637). One must also bear in mind that Levi had dismissed the antisemitic Julius Kniese as chorus master and this story may be simply concocted to defame Levi and to suggest that Wagner was indeed forced to take on a Jewish conductor.

141. Spencer and Millington in *SL* 914 give the date 29 June 1881, but the account of Westernhagen, *Wagner*, 2:570–71, suggests 28 June 1881.

142. *SL* 914–15; *DEAP* 50.

feeling. He indicates to Levi that he has been thinking of having him baptized and of accompanying him to Holy Communion.[143]

Wagner clearly wanted Levi to convert to Protestantism! He had felt this for some time. Back in 1880 Cosima records that on receiving a letter from Levi, Wagner says: "I cannot allow him to conduct *Parsifal* unbaptized, but I shall baptize them both, and we shall all take Communion together."[144] This concern for Levi's baptism is found when Wagner first told Levi he was to conduct *Parsifal*. Cosima records that Wagner "announces to Herr Levi, to his astonishment, that he is to conduct *Parsifal*: 'Beforehand, we shall go through a ceremonial act with you, I hope I shall succeed in finding a formula which will make you feel completely one of us.'"[145]

There is a tradition that Levi did in fact convert but I have doubts about its reliability.[146] Rather he seems not to have broken away from his Jewish roots and this was partly due to the close relationship he enjoyed with his father. Katz considers that Levi "did not retain any positive religious ties to Judaism, but his attitude toward it was nevertheless not one of indifference."[147] But he was clearly prepared to look critically at Judaism and sympathetically at Christianity. It may surprise one to learn he became friends with Adolf Stoecker and Houston Stewart Chamberlain.[148] Further, in later life he took an interest in Schopenhauer and found comfort in his writings on suffering, death, and eternity.[149]

A number of writers have argued that Wagner treated Levi badly. Gutman, for example, paints an extremely bleak picture[150] but one that

143. *CD* 2 July 1881. Contrast the negative "spin" given by Adorno, *Search*, 8–9, who claims Wagner's behavior in this episode is "demonic."

144. *CD* 28 April 1880. The reference to "both" is to Levi and Henri de Rothschild. Wagner was concerned to hear that the latter had purchased the "Jamnitzer centrepiece" by the goldsmith Wenzel Jamnitzer.

145. *CD* 19 January 1881.

146. See Sohn, "Levi," 32; there is just one work in his bibliography, Porges, "Levi" and nothing there is mentioned of such a conversion.

147. Katz, *Darker Side*, 98.

148. Haas, *Levi*, 367.

149. Ibid., 368. Haas draws attention to texts he believes comforted Levi in his last days: "Therefore, if suffering has such a sanctifying force, this will belong in an even higher degree to death, which is more feared than any suffering" (*WWR* 2:636 [2.49]). Secondly he points to these words on music: "The inexpressible depth of all music, by virtue of which it floats past us as a paradise quite familiar and yet eternally remote, and is so easy to understand and yet so inexplicable, is due to the fact that it reproduces all the emotions of our innermost being, but entirely without reality and remote from its pain" (*WWR* 1:264 [1.52]).

150. Gutman, *Wagner*, 412–14. See also the works of Zelinsky, Gay, and Rose,

does not seem at all balanced. Wagner greatly admired Levi as a musician. Furthermore, he respected him as a Jew for holding to the biblical name (rather than "Löwe" or "Lewin" or "Lewy"),[151] a name he inherited from his father, Benedikt Samuel Levi. Wagner has been criticized for wishing that Levi convert to the Christian faith. But from a Christian perspective this is perfectly proper and indeed is to be commended:[152] Wagner was faithful to the New Testament witnesses in believing that Jewish people, indeed any people, can only be saved through faith in Christ and that it is the duty of Christians to share their faith with Jewish people, amongst others.[153]

To give a balanced picture of Wagner's attitude of accepting Levi as conductor, mention must be made of correspondence between him and Ludwig in October 1881, which puts Wagner in a not so glowing light. He wrote to the king to say that he accepts "gratefully the heads of this musical organisation [from Munich] . . . without asking whether this man is a Jew, this other a Christian." Ludwig responded (11 October 1881): "I am glad dear Friend, that in connection with the production of your great and holy work you make no distinction between Christian and Jew. There is nothing so nauseous, so unedifying, as disputes of this sort: at bottom all men are brothers, whatever their confessional differences."[154] This clearly incensed Wagner. He replied: "I can explain my exalted friend's favourable view of the Jews only in terms of the fact that these people never impinge upon his royal circle: for him they are simply a concept, whereas for us they are an empirical fact. If I have friendly and sympathetic dealings with many of these people, it is only because I consider the Jewish race the born enemy of pure humanity and all that is noble in man."[155] Despite these comments Wagner had great admiration for Levi and he proved to be a fine interpreter of Wagner's "crowning achievement"; and Levi continued to have great affection for the composer.

---

referred to in Dreyfus, "Hermann Levi's shame," 126 n. 1.

151. Gregor-Dellin, *Wagner*, 405.

152. Contrast the remarkably odd attitude of Harries, *After the Evil*, 131 (a former bishop of Oxford) who has no desire whatsoever for Jews to convert (see below).

153. If Gutman, *Wagner*, 425, asserts that "the Jews remained without hope of salvation in the Wagnerian cosmology," it is necessary to add some qualification. According to Wagner and the New Testament witnesses, Jews can only be saved through faith in Christ. But does this mean they are without hope?

154. Quoted in Newman, *Life IV*, 612.

155. *SL* 918 (letter of 22 November 1881). Perhaps Wagner had Ludwig in mind when he wrote this in *Know Thyself* about the Jewish people: "A wonderful, unparalleled phenomenon: the plastic daemon of man's downfall in triumphant surety; and German citizen of state to boot, with a Mosaic confession; the darling of *Liberal princes*, and warrant of our national unity!" (*PW* 6:271–72 [my emphasis]; *GSD* 10:272).

As a second example of a Jewish musician with whom Wagner worked, I consider very briefly Joseph Rubinstein (1847–84). Rubinstein was from a rich Russian Jewish family and wrote to Wagner after reading *Judaism in Music*. He said the alternatives for him were either to commit suicide or seek deliverance from his "Jewish deficiencies" by serving the one who had revealed them to him! He was a fine pianist being a pupil of Hellmesberger and Liszt and became "Wahnfried's supreme court pianist"[156] and indeed produced the first piano score for *Parsifal*.[157] Wagner's relationship with Rubinstein was not entirely straightforward; they sometimes engaged in heated debate about the Jews.[158] But Wagner (and Cosima) showed great personal kindness to this sensitive man who suffered a mental breakdown and tragically took his own life after Wagner's death (but not directly in response to this).[159]

Concluding on Wagner's relationship to Levi and Rubinstein, it is the case that he could be rather condescending to them. So he comments on how Rubinstein is "always preoccupied with himself" and on Levi's "gloominess" and that "the good Jew always suffers a melancholy lot in our midst."[160] And in the context of his dealings with Rubinstein and Levi, Wagner told Ludwig: "I have had to exercise the most extreme patience, and if it is a question of being humane towards the Jews, I for one can confidently lay claim to praise."[161] But Jewish musicians and artists were an integral part of Wagner's great project and despite the tensions there was enormous admiration and affection shown on both sides. This is an additional reason to understand fully the dismay of later generations of Jews who loved the work of Wagner yet were subjected to attempts to exclude them from the Wagnerian heritage.[162] And one should never forget that Wagner himself identified

156. So described in Wagner's letter to Ludwig, 16 March 1881 (*SL* 907).

157. The version usually now used is that of Karl Klindworth.

158. See Jacob Katz, *Darker Side*, 95–97. One rather strange combination of events is that on the morning of 18 December 1881 Wagner made his "drastic joke" about all Jews being burned at a performance of *Nathan the Wise* (see above) yet in the evening of the very same day he worked with Rubinstein (*CD* 18 December 1881).

159. It appears that the life as a concert pianist proved too much for Rubinstein. In fact, Wagner realized that this sensitive person would find such a life too demanding. Rubinstein's father expressed his wish that his son should pursue such a career. Wagner responded in a letter (22 January 1882) to his father. On taking his life in Lucerne on 22 September 1884 his father sent a moving letter to Wahnfried explaining what had happened (see Westernhagen, *Wagner*, 2:595–97). Rubinstein is buried in the Jewish cemetery in Bayreuth. To Cosima's credit, she made arrangements for his gravestone.

160. *CD* 20 January 1881.

161. *SL* 918 (letter of 22 November 1881).

162. See, e.g., Falk Solomon, the Rabbi of Bayreuth. Responding to Siegfried Wagner

with the plight of the "wandering Jew." Wagner expresses this in a letter to Mathilde Wesendonck (21 June 1859) that reflects those years of "wandering" 1858-64.[163] This theme also appears earlier in *A Communication to My Friends* (1851) in an extensive section where he discusses the Flying Dutchman as "wandering Jew" and his identification with such a figure, looking back especially to his unhappy years in Paris (1839-41).[164]

A Theological Critique of Wagner's Antisemitism

In the above discussion I have made a clear distinction between anti-Judaism and antisemitism. The former concerns a critique of the Jewish religion; the latter concerns a negative view of the Jewish people.

It is highly significant that in the letter to the Romans, as I interpret it, Paul is able to critique the Jewish religion as one of works-righteousness yet hold to the abiding election of the Jewish people.[165] If my understanding of Paul's view is followed, a Christian theologian can therefore affirm the continuing election of Israel and at the same time engage in a theological critique of Judaism. Further, it could be legitimate to criticize Judaism in certain respects that go beyond what the New Testament explicitly teaches,

---

he wrote: "We Jews, too, admire the work of Richard Wagner, and we find it painful when someone tries to destroy this admiration" (Hamann, *Winifred Wagner*, 95).

163. Golther, *Mathilde Wesendonk*, 151: "Ueber das Reiten könnte ich Ihnen noch viel schreiben. Ich muss mich hüten eine Passion für das Pferd aufkommen zu lassen, weil ich da wieder etwas kennen lernen könnte, was mir versagt bleiben muss. Und Vielem und manchem habe ich doch nun schon entsagt, und der Wanderung des ewigen Juden darf kein Pferd beigegeben sein."

164. So he relates the Dutchman to Odysseus and the Christian who, "without a home on earth, embodied this trait in the figure of the 'Wandering Jew'" (*PW* 1:307; *GSD* 4:265; *JA* 6:237-38). He then relates the longing of the Dutchman to his own longings for a "home." He speaks of his "utter homelessness in Paris" that roused his "yearning for the German home-land." But he continues: "yet this longing was not directed to any old familiar haunt that I must win my way *back* to, but onward to a country pictured in my dreams, an unknown and still-to-be-discovered haven, of which I knew this things alone: that I should certainly *never* find it here in Paris. It was the longing of my Flying Dutchman for '*das Weib*,'—not, as I have said before, for the wife who waited for Ulysses, but for the redeeming Woman, whose features had never presented themselves to me in any clear-marked outline, but who hovered before my vision as the element of Womanhood in its widest sense. This element here found expression in the idea: one's *Native Home*, i.e. the encirclement by a wide community of kindred and familiar souls; by a community, however, which as yet I knew not in the flesh, which I only learnt to yearn for after I had realised what is generally meant by 'home'" (*PW* 1:310; *GSD* 4:268; *JA* 6:240-41). On the whole issue of Wagner's relationship to the Dutchman, see Borchmeyer, "*Der fliegende Holländer* und seine Metamorphosen."

165. Bell, *Irrevocable Call*.

one example being the way animals are slaughtered. Although I think that both Wagner and Schopenhauer were unfair in attributing the negative treatment of animals in Germany entirely to Judaism,[166] both made prophetic utterances on the humane treatment of animals that are relevant to the debates today on the way animals are slaughtered[167] and on unnecessary vivisection.[168]

How does Wagner's critique match up to that of the New Testament witnesses? Arguably, one element common to Paul, John, and Hebrews, and one which Wagner shares, is the opposition to a law-based religion. These three New Testament witnesses seem to agree that the Old Testament law has been overtaken and certainly Paul, as I understand him, sees the danger of legalism in a religion of law.[169] Wagner is even more radical in that whereas Paul can at least believe that the law still has a function to condemn the sinner and has a role in ethics, although a very limited one,[170] Wagner sees virtually no role for it whatsoever. Further Wagner, as we have seen, has a negative view of the God of the Old Testament, which we find nowhere in the New Testament. Indeed he thinks Christianity needs to be purged of its Jewish heritage (although sometimes he appears to contradict this).[171]

Put briefly, my own view is that rather than being purged of its Jewish heritage Christian theology has to radically re-interpret this heritage including the Old Testament itself. Regarding the latter, many make the mistake of thinking that the Old Testament outlines what the Messiah should be like. But the Old Testament does not offer a "job description" that Jesus then is

166. In *Against Vivisection* (*PW* 6:199, 203; *GSD* 10:198, 202) Wagner specifically blames the teaching of the Pentateuch. Schopenhauer thinks that England has a more enlightened view on animal welfare since suggestions were made there that cruelty to animals should be punished by flogging (*PP* 2:372)!

167. The issue today is whether animals are stunned before slaughter. In Britain there are a significant proportion of cases in Jewish slaughter where animals are not pre-stunned. This debate is relevant not only to Jewish slaughter (*Shechitah*) but also to Islamic slaughter (*Halal*).

168. I accept that some experiments on animals may be justified in the name of medical research (contrast Wagner's wish for an unconditional ban in *Against Vivisection* [*PW* 6:210; *GSD* 10:209]); however, Schopenhauer's comments on the unnecessary use of animals in training medical students in nineteenth-century Göttingen are remarkably relevant for the current training of medical students in British universities (*PP* 2:373).

169. Note, however, that Paul's view is that one does not have to keep the law of Moses even though he can countenance the idea of Jewish Christians voluntarily keeping the law (Bell, *Jealousy*, 72–73).

170. On Paul's "third use of the law," i.e., the law as giving moral guidance to the Christian, see Rom 13:8–10.

171. See *CD* 27 January 1875 (quoted below).

supposed to fit. Rather the Old Testament is to be interpreted in the light of Jesus, not vice versa.[172] A good example of this is the suffering servant of Isaiah 52:13—53:12. According to the Old Testament text a human being can stand in our place to atone for sin. For Paul only God can stand in our place, i.e., Jesus Christ.[173]

One should also add that many aspects of New Testament theology only make sense in the light of the Old Testament. So Christ's sacrifice can only be understood in the light of the levitical sin-offering (Rom 3:25; 8:3; 2 Cor 5:14–21) and justification can only be understood in the light of what the Old Testament says about the condemnation of the sinner by the law, Christ bringing this condemnation to an end (Rom 10:4).

Some of Wagner's utterances suggest that he is very far indeed from seeing Jesus in the light of the Old Testament. This is particularly striking in a letter to Röckel of April 1855. He writes that in order to present the highest understanding in simple language one must turn to the Buddha's teaching on reincarnation in order to lead to a life full of sympathy for the whole created order.[174] Indeed he asserts that recent research has established that the original ideas of Christianity come from India and not from Judaism.[175] His interest in Indian religion is also reflected in a letter of the same time to Mathilde Wesendonck.[176] However, two things need to be borne in mind before any firm conclusions are drawn from these passages. First, Wagner's views were very much formed from reading Schopenhauer, and his main objection to Judaism here is that it represents an "unspiritual and heartless optimism" ("jener geist- und herzlose Optimismus").[177] Secondly, there are a number of indications that Wagner in fact moved away from an

172. Hofius, "Messias," 128–29.

173. Bell, "Sacrifice and Christology," 26–27.

174. *SB* 7:130: "Will man die höchste Erkenntnis in populäre Bilder bringen, so ist dieß nicht anders möglich, als in der reinen ursprünglichen Lehre des Buddha, und namentlich die Lehre von der Seelenwanderung zur Anleitung eines rein humanen, sympathievollen Lebens, namentlich auch mit Rücksicht auf die erkenntnißlose Thier- und Pflanzenwelt, gewiß die glücklichste Erfindung eines erhabenen, mittheilungsbedürftigen Geistes."

175. Note a possible negative allusion to Rom 11:17–24: "die ungeheure Schwierigkeit, ja Unmöglichkeit, diesen reinen, durchaus weltverachtenden und dem Willen zum Leben abgewandten Gedanken auf den fruchtlosen Stamm des Judenthums zu pfropfen, hat einzig alle die Widersprüche verursacht, die bis heute das Christenthum so traurig entstellt und fast unkenntlich gemacht haben" (*SB* 7:130). The allusion is to Rom 11:19: "Die Zweige sind ausgebrochen worden, damit ich eingepfropft würde." Paul uses the image of Israel as an olive tree into which Gentile Christians have been grafted.

176. *SB* 7:123 (letter of 20 April 1855).

177. *SB* 7:130.

attachment to Buddhism and came to see that aspects of Judaism, especially Jewish mysticism, did in fact illumine aspects of the Christian faith. That he abandoned the drama on *The Victors* (*Die Sieger*)[178] in favor of *Parsifal* is significant as is his interest in ancient Judaism through reading the works of Gfrörer.[179]

Perhaps the most important message Wagner can offer (and I realize that many will not share my view) is that Judaism has been superseded and that the way of salvation for Jewish people is through faith in Christ (hence Wagner's desire that Hermann Levi should come to faith and be baptized). Although his views on "regeneration" are spoiled by his pseudo-scientific views, he is correct in this respect: Jewish people, like any non-Christian, can be renewed through union with Christ. Wagner's desire for Jewish people to convert does not fit in with much current thinking and puts him at odds with those who think Jews should not be evangelized.[180] But I can fully support him on this issue and, more importantly, he has the New Testament on his side.

Positive Views on Jews and Judaism

Although many works on Wagner and the Jews simply fail to mention any of his positive views of Jews and Judaism, in some quarters the pendulum is starting to swing the other way where it is argued that Wagner was very much influenced by Jewish mysticism as he was composing *Parsifal*. I suspect the truth lies somewhere between the two extremes.

Perhaps Wagner's most positive views on Judaism are found in his admiration for Halévy. In 1842 he wrote articles praising *La Reine de Chypre*[181] and great though he thought this was, he esteemed his earlier work, *La Juive* (*The Jewess*), even higher.[182] He continued to admire *La Juive*. Cosima in her entry for 27 June 1882 writes: "At lunch he remarks on the beauties of *La*

178. The sketch fills only half a page (*DTB* 303).

179. See the discussion below on Gfrörer.

180. Since Wagner is attacked as a "systemic antisemite" by Harries, *After the Evil*, 15, a view that is simplistic, it may be worth reflecting on Harries' own views regarding the evangelization of Jewish people. He finds that he cannot pray that his Jewish friends be converted to Christianity (131) and if anyone is seeking to convert his advice is that they speak with their Rabbi (138)! On the issue of the church's mission to Israel (and a critique of Harries' views) see Bell, *Irrevocable Call*, 395–407.

181. See *PW* 7:205–22; 8:175–200.

182. See *PW* 7:221–22; 8:187–90 concerning *La Juive*. It is worth mentioning that this opera enjoyed great popularity until it was condemned to virtual oblivion by the Nazis. It has, however, undergone a recent revival.

Juive, the Passover celebrations, the final choruses, also the lively first act, and says it contains the best expression of the Jewish character." However, after seeing the work performed in Naples[183] Cosima records: "R. remarks how this work, originating in the school of Méhul and Cherubini, is full of life and refinement and is not at all Jewish, even in its treatment of its subject—it is just correctly observed."[184] But, as Hartwich correctly observes, his admiration for *La Juive* has nothing to do with worship in the synagogue but is rather appreciated as an expression of "Kunstreligion."[185]

What about Wagner's appreciation of Jewish mysticism? This is an involved subject that I intend to address in more detail elsewhere, but the essential claim to address is that Wagner's reading of the works of Gfrörer and in particular his discussion of the therapeutae by Philo of Alexandria in *On the Contemplative Life* (*De vita contemplativa*)[186] has influenced the grail scene in Act I of *Parsifal*. If this were true one could perhaps gain some comfort in attributing to Wagner philosemitism as an antidote to his antisemitism. I do not deny some general influence of Jewish mysticism in *Parsifal* but in my work I have found very little evidence that the mystical sect of the therapeutae has influenced the grail scenes.[187]

The key work to consider is Gfrörer's book on Philo.[188] This was in his Wahnfried library and we know Wagner started reading the introduction on 19 September 1879 and continued with the introduction the next day.[189] However, the next we hear of it is Wagner's lack of enthusiasm for the work, recorded on 15 October 1879: "R. comes to lunch with Gfrörer's *Philo* and

183. They arrived in Naples on 4 January 1880 and saw the opera in the San Carlo opera house on 17 January (*CD* 4 and 17 January 1880).

184. *CD* 17 January 1880. See also *CD* 17 January 1880: "Halévy, he says, was the first musical genre-painter, and he had more feeling than Cherubini: 'I liked him very much; he was a yearning, sensual character, but lazy.'"

185. Hartwich, "Jüdische Theosophie," 105: "Diese Sichtweise gleicht Wagners Kritik an der christlichen Kunst, die nur eine Dogmatik bebildet und den Kult ausschmückt. Und in der Tat weist die Passah-Szene in Halévys Oper keine Verbindung zur synagogalen Musik auf, sondern gestaltet das jüdische Ritual, das den Exodus aus Ägypten vergegenwärtigt, zum kultischen 'Mysterium' im Sinne des katholischen Meßopfers um. Daher konnte das Werk in der zeitgenössichen deutschen Kritik als Ausdruck der romantischen Kunstreligion wahrgenommen werden."

186. See Colson, *Philo IX*, 104–69 ("The Fourth Part Concerning the Virtues").

187. This is so argued by Hartwich, "Jüdische Theosophie," 109–11. Although I disagree with Hartwich on this I commend the work of this highly original scholar who died at the age of thirty-seven on 15 January 2006.

188. Gfrörer, *Kritische Geschichte*.

189. In the first edition of 1831 (the only edition I have been able to consult) the introduction is thirty-eight pages long, much of it contrasting Catholicism and Protestantism (which the Wagners appreciated, *CD* 20 September 1879).

says he does not intend to finish it." If one were to assume he at least finished the first major part of volume 1, an overestimate since apart from the introduction there are 534 pages of heavy reading, then he would encounter no proper discussion of the therapeutae.[190] Further, even if he did encounter such a discussion, it could hardly "influence" *Parsifal* since the final poem was completed over two years earlier (19 April 1877) and the two musical drafts (September 1877—16 April 1879, the "Kompositionsskizze"; 25 September 1877—26 April 1879; "Orchesterskizze") were also completed.

Now it is the case that he read Gfrörer's three-volume work on primitive Christianity starting back in December 1874, and parts do concern "Jewish mysticism." Wagner read on his own volume 3 (concerned with early Christianity) starting on 17 December and completed it 26 December, telling Cosima how much he has enjoyed it.[191] Then from 4 January to 1 February 1875 both read through volume 1, which does discuss ancient Judaism and other things: "his definition of how various nations visualize God";[192] "the definition of the Trinity made shortly before Christ's birth";[193] "the chapter . . . on angels and devils."[194] References to further reading can be found in Cosima's entries for January 9, 14, 15, 18, 25, 28, 29, 30. Cosima concludes in her entry for 2 February 1875: "R. very pleased with Gfrörer. He quotes to me Christ's answer to the question whether he was the Messiah: 'If I say the truth, why do ye not believe me?'—unutterably sad and sublime."[195] The entry which gives the strongest evidence of Wagner's admiration for Jewish mysticism is that for 25 January: "R. reads a lot of Gfrörer: the seven day silence before the seat of judgment in the books of the Jewish mystics makes a great impression on him."[196] Then there are these intriguing comments of Wagner noted in the entry for 27 January that suggests that

190. All I found was a passing reference to the therapeutae (I.1:458). Hartwich, "Jüdische Theosophie," 109–13, gives five references to Gfrörer's *Kritische Geschichte* but it is unlikely Wagner ever reached I.2:291, 299, 309, the references given by Hartwich to the therapeutae (unless Wagner were to skip to these later sections).

191. *CD* 17, 23, 26 December 1874.

192. *CD* 4 January 1875.

193. *CD* 6 January 1875; this must be volume 1, chapter 4: "Die jüdische Lehre von Gott. Die göttlichen Kräfte. Die Schechina, Memra. Der Sohn, der heilige Geist, die Mutter, der Vater. Jüdische Dreieinigkeit" (pp. 272–352). For a full quotation of Cosima's entry see chapter 10 below.

194. *CD* 8 January 1875. This must be volume I, chapter 5: "Die Lehre von den höheren Geistern, Engeln und Teufeln" (pp. 352–424).

195. The reference must be to John 8:46, which is in the middle of an "anti-Jewish" section of the gospel.

196. The closing section in volume 1, chapter 10 (pp. 285–92) concerns the final judgement.

Gfrörer has convinced Wagner that Christianity cannot be divorced from its Jewish roots:

> In the morning R. says to me: "I am becoming more and more convinced of the truth of Voltaire's saying that religion cannot be too absurd for the common people, and that Christianity cannot be separated from its Jewish roots. The Father in Heaven belongs to that idea, and a religion must remain naïve, childlike, and simple; the benevolent god who has arranged everything properly, even when we don't understand it, is for the common man the only consolation, the only inducement to resignation. Of course, once this faith is shattered, it can never be restored."

They start the second volume on 9 February 1875 and we find his treatment of John's Gospel discussed on 11 February.[197] Cosima mentions that they continue with him on 12 February. Then after the shock of hearing from Franz Overbeck that Gfrörer has been converted to Catholicism (26 March (Good Friday) and 27 March) for which they need some time to recover, we find them reading Gfrörer on miracles on 29 March[198] and 5 April.

Now the main problem in arguing that the rites of the therapeutae influenced the grail scene of Act I is that there is little in these three volumes about it. It is all in the two volume *Kritische Geschichte* where, in 1879, he made little progress. One could say that what he read in volume 1 of the *Geschichte* about Jewish mysticism appealed to Wagner and further enabled him to develop his mythology of the grail, and if this were true it would further demonstrate that Wagner's "antisemitism" was highly complex and nuanced. However, evidence that the grail scene has been influenced specifically by the rites of the therapeutae, whilst being *possible*, is *improbable*. The scene could just as well have been formed from church musical tradition, both Protestant and Catholic, together with Wagner's creative alterations. Further, in bringing together the "nourishing meal" and the "holy meal" in *Parsifal* Act I, a view found in the services of the therapeutae, Wagner could just as well have been influenced by figures such as Thomas à Kempis who also brought together these two aspects.[199]

In addition, there is a work that has many similarities with the grail scenes of *Parsifal*: *Das Liebesmahl der Apostel*. Although over those thirty-four years since the composition of *Das Liebesmahl* Wagner's composition

---

197. Cosima's entry is quoted and discussed in chapter 10 below. John's Gospel is discussed in Gfrörer, *Geschichte II.2*, 283–336.

198. This will be Gfrörer, *Geschichte III*, 265–341. See the discussion on *CD* 29 March 1875 in chapter 8 above.

199. See chapter 10 below.

and dramatic style had changed there are certain dramatic elements both works share. First, the grail scene staging, inspired by Wagner's visit to Siena Cathedral,²⁰⁰ is similar to the Frauenkirche in Dresden (where *Das Liebesmahl* was performed), both possessing a "dome."²⁰¹ Secondly, *Das Liebesmahl* is characterized by answering choirs.²⁰² Unlike the grail scene in *Parsifal* there are no female voices, but the male choir ("Chor der Jünger") is divided into three choirs at m. 73 and at 152 the choir of twelve apostles enters. Thirdly, as in *Parsifal* Wagner had a choir ("Stimmen aus der Höhe") singing from the dome at m. 293. Fourthly, as in *Parsifal* Act I the "Communion" is both a cultic meal and nourishing meal. So the opening chorus of the grail scene ("Zum letzten Liebesmahle . . . ")²⁰³ tells us that we are dealing with a "Liebesmahl" and the very title of the 1843 work *Das Liebesmahl* indicates that we are dealing with a rite that is both a cultic "Communion" and a fellowship meal;²⁰⁴ note, however, that there is no actual "Liebesmahl" portrayed in the work.²⁰⁵ Fifthly, *Das Liebesmahl* stresses the mission of the Apostles.²⁰⁶ This corresponds to the final chorus of the grail scene: "Take of the bread . . . to work the Saviour's will. Take of the wine . . . let us fight with holy courage" (*WagPS* 152–53). Sixthly, two musical themes from *Das Liebesmahl* are taken up in *Parsifal*. First the melody of three phrases sung by the first choir (*SW* 335–38: "Kommt her, die ihr hungert, die ihr dürstet" [mm. 125–29]; "Zu stärken euch, opfert' Er sein Fleisch und Blut" [mm. 129–33]; "Da solche Labung uns erquicken soll?" [mm. 141–46]) is taken up in the "Angel Motif" in *Parsifal* (I.575).²⁰⁷ Secondly, the beginning of the phrase "Der uns das Wort, das herrliche, gelehret" (*SW* 16:370–80; mm. 472–515) from the final section of *Liebesmahl* is similar to the chorus of the knights in Act I of *Parsifal*. Note also some common vocabulary (e.g., "Labung"). In view of these similarities, it is more probable that the obvious influence on the grail scene is *Das Liebesmahl* rather than Philo's portrayal of the therapeutae.²⁰⁸

200. *CD* 21 August 1880 relates how Wagner was "moved to tears" by the building.

201. Compare the photographs given in Kirsch, "Biblische Scene," 173–74.

202. Ibid., 167–68.

203. *WagPS* 142–43.

204. Wagner's "Liebesmahl" corresponds to the "agape" of the early church, celebrated through to the middle of the second century (Hauschild, "Agapen I"). Wagner's own Lutheran church would know nothing of this, but it has been introduced into Protestant churches in the 1960s (Niebergall, "Agapen II").

205. Kirsch, "Biblische Scene," 164–65.

206. *PW* 8:282.

207. See *FTG* theme 14.

208. Hartwich himself acknowledges *Das Liebesmahl* as a possible source for

A final argument against the influence of Jewish mysticism is that when Wagner went to see Joukowsky's cover for the grail, he found it "too opulent-looking." Cosima records in her entry for 30 May 1882: "R. expresses his dislike for all Israelite pomp and says that, if people even begin to observe details such as the shrine, etc., then his aim as a dramatist is lost."

Wagner, Hitler, and the Jews

I hesitate to include a discussion of Wagner and Hitler but since many attempts have been made to demonize the composer (and his artwork *Parsifal*) by making associations with Hitler I feel it incumbent upon me to address briefly some key issues.

Hitler was thrilled by Wagner's art[209] but his love of Wagner was not primarily related to the "massive effects," or "pomposity," or "overwhelming hugeness."[210] Rather Hitler was genuinely moved by the works of Wagner. According to the English author Hugh Walpole, while Melchior sang *Parsifal* in Bayreuth "the tears poured down Hitler's cheeks."[211] Even though there may be doubts about the historicity of this observation,[212] it seems to reflect the emotional effect Wagner had on Hitler. In addition, it appears that Hitler did have knowledge of Wagner,[213] although in many respects had little understanding![214]

Wagner's ideas.

209. According to Fest, *Hitler*, 520, he "heard *Tristan* or *Die Meistersinger* more than a hundred times each."

210. Ibid., 50. Fest writes that Wagner's first major composition after *Rienzi* was "a choral work for 1,200 male voices and an orchestra of one hundred." It is worth adding that this work, *Das Liebesmahl der Apostel* (which is not in fact "the first major composition after *Rienzi*") would hardly appeal to Hitler. But the great gathering of crowds in Act III of *Meistersinger* would certainly appeal to him.

211. Hart-Davis, *Walpole*, 263–64.

212. Walpole dated this in 1925 and said he was in the same box as Hitler (this must be the "Mittelloge"). Doubts may arise since Hitler is not mentioned in Walpole's original diary of 1925 and these comments (and others) about Hitler were added in 1940 (Hamann, *Winifred Wagner*, 109). However, Walpole being in the box with Hitler is perfectly plausible, since he was a close friend of Winifred Wagner. There is also the possibility that he did converse with Hitler (as he claims). Although Hitler could not speak English, Walpole did have a knowledge of German. The other possibility is that Winifred acted as an interpreter.

213. Hamann, *Winifred Wagner*, 109, quotes some words of Emmy Krüger, whom Hitler invited to high tea (1925): "He immediately began to talk about my performance, picking out details that astonished me, and I clearly remember thinking 'en passant'— well, this man knows a thing or two about art!"

214. Did he really grasp the "messages" of the *Ring* (power corrupts) and *Parsifal*

A number of works have been published relating links between Wagner and Hitler. The first significant one is that of Gutman (1968) whose prose suggests a clear dislike of the composer and argues almost anything to besmirch his reputation (although he accepts that he was a "great musician").[215] Then, to name a few, came the studies of Fest (1973/ET 1974), Zelinsky (1983, the 100th anniversary of Wagner's death), and Köhler (ET 2000). Fest argued that Hitler was influenced by the personality of Wagner[216] and Köhler argues that Hitler modeled his life and mission on that of Wagner.[217] Such an argument does carry some weight. But what is not quite so clear is whether Hitler was greatly influenced by Wagner's theoretical writings, in particular his political and antisemitic writings. Fest thinks he was influenced by his "political writings,"[218] although no concrete evidence is given. In fact Fest's idea appears to come straight out of Gutman's book, which likewise advances no concrete evidence or argument.[219] Some have specifically said that Hitler was influenced by Wagner's "antisemitic" writings (and I return to this shortly).[220] But there is one major problem: there is simply no evidence in Hitler's writings or recorded utterances that he ever mentions Wagner's antisemitism.[221] Köhler admits that "Hitler never

---

(the centrality of compassion)? Further, *Meistersinger*, a work full of love and joy (and renunciation!) seems to occupy a completely different world to that of the Nuremberg rallies. Note in particular the contrast Wagner draws between "world-overcoming," which all these stage works affirm, and "world-conquering," which Wagner clearly rejects (*On State and Religion* [*PW* 4:25–26; *GSD* 8:21–22], discussed in chapter 11 below).

215. Gutman, *Wagner*, xviii.

216. Fest, *Hitler*, 49. His source for Hitler's view that Wagner was his only forerunner and "the greatest prophetic figure the German people has had" is Rauschning, *Gespräche mit Hitler*, 215–16: "Hitler erkannte keine Vorläufer an. Mit einer Ausnahme: Richard Wagner" (215); "Er sei die größte Prophetengestalt, die das deutsche Volk besessen habe" (216). Although there are grounds for questioning the reliability of the detail, the general thrust may give a truthful picture of Hitler (Zentner and Bedürftig, *Lexikon des dritten Reiches*, 468–69). Note that Rauschning studied "Musikgeschichte."

217. Köhler, *Wagner's Hitler*, 191–208.

218. See Fest, *Hitler*, 56: "Wagner's political writings were Hitler's favorite reading, and the sprawling pomposity of his style unmistakably influenced Hitler's own grammar and syntax."

219. See Gutman, *Wagner*, 426. He asserts that after his fascination with *Lohengrin*, "Hitler moved on to the thick tomes of Wagnerian prose and declared the composer's political writings his favorite reading. Throughout his career he regurgitated their ideas and phraseology, even adopting their convoluted style as his very own."

220. See, for example, Sachs, *Toscanini*, 223: "[Hitler's] love of the composer's music was only matched by his admiration for Wagner's anti-Semitic and other racial writings."

221. See Friedländer, "Erlösungsantisemitismus," 17–18. The *closest possible*

spoke openly about the man who had laid this charge on him." When Hitler "mentioned the name of Wagner he meant either a personal musical preference or the great German cultural revolution." But Köhler then argues that if Hitler really wished to refer to Wagner he would speak of "Providence."[222] This, however, is extremely unlikely.[223] The term "providence" was an abstract term for some sort of "god."

Hitler did receive "inspiration" from Wagner but the precise nature of this is complex. Matters I think are clarified if one speaks of "appropriation" rather than speak of "influence." First of all, I consider the stage works. The two figures of Wagnerian stage works that Hitler identified with were Rienzi and Wotan. In relation to Rienzi he is supposed to have said "I want to become a people's tribune"[224] and drew the lesson that the charismatic figure of Rienzi failed because he did not have the support of a political party and the protection of the security force.[225] The other Wagnerian figure, Wotan, is perhaps not the most obvious figure in the public imagination for Hitler to

---

allusion is telling Hans Frank (1936) of experiencing Siegfried's funeral march and then encountering 'einige mauschelnde Kaftanjuden' on his way home from the Vienna opera: "Ich habe ihn zuerst in Wien gehört . . . Dieses herrliche Mysterium des sterbenden Heros und dieser Judendreck!" (Frank, *Im Angesicht des Galgens*, 213). Note also that although Goebbels did mention Wagner's antisemitism, the reference is vague (presumably because direct quotations from Wagner would hardly promote the Nazi antisemitism). "Was der Jude ist, hat uns Richard Wagner gelehrt. . . . Er sagt uns alles: durch seine Schriften und durch seine Musik, in der jeder Ton deutsches reines Wesen atmet" (*Völkischer Beobachter* 24 July 1937, quoted in Lobenstein-Reichmann, *Chamberlain*, 551).

222. Köhler, *Wagner's Hitler*, 271.

223. As we saw in chapter 2, Köhler uses a similar "labeling" strategy regarding Wagner's use of the word "Schopenhauer," filling the word with his own meaning.

224. According to Paula Kubizek (Hamann, *Hitler's Vienna*, 24).

225. Note, however, that parallels between Hitler and Rienzi have been overplayed. First, although there are occasions when Hitler felt the German people had been unworthy of the aims he had for them (Trevor-Roper, *Last Days*, 54) it is not the case that his "Political Testament" is "nearly a carbon copy of Rienzi's concluding curse on Rome's fickle populace" (Vaget, "Operation Walküre," 10); if anything the Testament acknowledges the sacrifices the German people have made (Noakes and Pridham, *Documents on Nazism*, 678–80). Secondly, the account of August Kubizek, Hitler's fellow Wagnerian and friend from his youth (Paula's husband), that his political vision was born after experiencing a performance of *Rienzi* in Linz is, most likely, a "fabricated account" (Karlsson, "In That Hour It Began," 35). (According to Kubizek, *Young Hitler*, 65, after the performance they climbed to the top of the Freinberg. "Like flood waters breaking their dykes, his words burst forth from him. He conjured up in grandiose, inspiring pictures his own future and that of his people.") However, even if Hitler had not seen *Rienzi* in Linz, it appears he *wanted* to believe that he had seen it and that this had inspired him to "succeed in uniting the German Empire and making it great once more" (Speer, *Spandau*, 88).

fashion himself on.[226] We know that Hitler's close friends (including Sieg-fried and Winifred Wagner) called him "Wolf" and their children to call him "Onkel Wolf,"[227] the reference being to Wotan who between *Das Rhein-gold* and *Die Walküre* roams the world with Wehwalt, his son. Having taken the gold and ring from Alberich, Wotan became an outlaw ("Die Feinde wuchsen ihm viel") and, as Vaget suggests, corresponds to Hitler's "Kamp-fzeit" of 1919 to 1933. Less important than Rienzi and Wotan was Parsifal; it is true that Hitler admired the eponymous hero,[228] but, as we have seen, there is so much in the stage work that contradicts Hitler's ideology.[229]

What about Hitler's appropriation of Wagner's idea through his theo-retical writings? Gutman writes: "Hitler especially revered Wagner's prose works, emulated their turgid style, enthroned him as artistic god of the Third Reich, and carried to their logical and appalling conclusions many of the ideas implicit in the composer's essays and dramas."[230] Further he claims that Hitler "followed the teaching of 'Heldentum' that Jesus was not a Jew."[231] There is, in fact, little evidence that Hitler "revered Wagner's prose works" or "emulated their turgid style." It is instructive to consider one of the few cases where Hitler alludes to the prose writings: Hitler speaking of the link between meat eating and degeneration[232] appears to allude to *Reli-gion and Art*, part III (not exactly the best part of the essay!). However, this does not necessarily mean he read Wagner's essay. In fact the most obvious source for this idea is Chamberlain's book on Wagner, which we know he did possess (and presumably read).[233] This had a long chapter on Wagner's

226. Wotan can certainly be ruthless but he also struggles with his moral dilem-mas. However, the complexity of Wotan's personality can be found in Hitler's. Hitler certainly could suffer from a bad conscience for *certain* things: "I have a bad conscience when I get the feeling that I've not been quite fair to somebody" (Trevor Roper, *Hitler's Table Talk*, 155). Note, however, that these comments are in the context of the dismissal of Julius Streicher, the notorious antisemite of Nuremberg.

227. See the numerous quotations of Winifred in Hamann, *Winifred Wagner*.

228. See chapter 8 above.

229. For example, Hitler had to dismiss what in many ways is the climax of the work: the "Karfreitagszauber" ("Good Friday Magic"). See Rauschning, *Gespräche mit Hitler*, 216.

230. Gutman, *Wagner*, xvii.

231. Ibid., 424 n. 1. As we saw in chapter 6 above, Wagner's view of the non-Jewish Jesus is actually to be found in *Religion and Art* (*PW* 6:233; *GSD* 10:232; *JA* 10:139–40).

232. See Rauschning, *Gespräche mit Hitler*, 215–16. Hitler speaks of Wagner's "Kulturlehre": "Ob ich wüßte, daß Wagner zum Beispiel vieles von unserem kulturellen Verfall auf den Fleischgenuß zurückgeführt habe?"

233. See Zentner, *Hitlers Mein Kampf*, 15, who refers to Ernst Hanfstaengl's recol-lection of Hitler's library before 1923.

"writings and teachings"[234] with a section on diet and a little later a section on degeneration/regeneration.[235] In between these two sections is a page on the inequality of races (which would obviously appeal to Hitler) and then six pages on Jews and Judaism. Of these six pages I suggest that Hitler could take little inspiration.[236] The striking fact is that Hitler never appealed to Wagner to support his antisemitism and one gets the impression that Hitler deliberately ignored Wagner's views in this respect. One reason may be that Wagner's critique of Judaism had a Christian theological rationale and his hope for Jews was that they would come to faith in Christ and be "regenerated."

The upshot of all this is that Hitler did not appear to revere Wagner's prose writings and one wonders whether he actually read them or even possessed them;[237] further he never appealed to Wagner's antisemitism even though such claims are frequently made.[238] Those works that have engaged in a detailed study of Wagner and the Third Reich come rather to the conclusion that Wagner actually played little role in the antisemitism of this period.[239] Further, the basic theological scheme developed by the "German

234. Chamberlain, *Wagner*, 135–304.

235. Ibid., 220–23, 229–41.

236. Ibid., 224–29. The most dangerous parts are Chamberlain's own thoughts on the Jews and his recommendation to study *Know Thyself* (224). But Chamberlain emphasized that many Jews appreciated Wagner and many of his critics were to be found among non-Jews. Further, he pointed out that Wagner was always open to contact and friendship with Jewish people. Chamberlain writes that his *Judaism in Music* is fair and reasonable and that the final word "Untergang" is to be understood in the light of ceasing to be a Jew (228). He says that Wagner is much milder than Luther regarding the Jews. He ends this section by quoting from Micah and from Jesus' words in Luke 23:28: "Weinet nicht über mich, sondern weinet über euch selbst und über eure Kinder." He adds: "Was er die Juden lehrte, war das selbe, was Wagner ihnen jetzt wider zuruft: 'Um gemeinschaftlich mit uns Mensch zu werden, höret auf, Juden zu sein!'" (229).

237. So far there is no evidence for these works being in Hitler's private library.

238. See Weinzierl, "Antisemitismus VII," 161: "Die rassistische Komponente des Antisemitismus wurde von Anfang an von der 'Nationalsozialistischen Deutschen Arbeiterpartei' (NSDAP) unter besonderer Berufung auf Richard Wagner und dessen Schwiegersohn Houston Stewart Chamberlain betont . . ." As regards Wagner this is simply untrue. A closer link can be made between Chamberlain and Hitler but even here there is a gulf between the two. On a similar gulf between Wagner and Chamberlain, see Allen, "Consecration of the House." Such a gulf between the two is often missed. See, e.g., Brearley, "Hitler and Wagner," 4: "Richard Wagner is known to have been the inspiration behind H. S. Chamberlain" (4). The early Chamberlain was certainly influenced by Wagner but the composer is hardly mentioned in the *Grundlagen*. On this see Allen, "Consecration of the House," who provides an English translation of Chamberlain's preface to the 1901 edition, where he explains why Wagner received so little mention: Chamberlain developed his racially inspired historiography independently.

239. See, e.g., Osthövener, "Deutsche Christen," 183, who concludes that "in the

Christians" was quite different to that of Wagner. For whereas "German Christians" stressed "creation" (the first article of the creed) Wagner, as we have seen, stressed redemption and the second article.[240] "German Christians" and Wagner have a completely different understanding of God. A comparison of Hitler and Wagner reveals an even greater gulf. Hitler wrote this: "I believe that I am acting in accordance with the will of the Almighty Creator: *by defending myself against the Jew, I am fighting for the work of the Lord.*"[241] Wagner wrote: "God, the Creator,—he must remain totally unintelligible to the world . . . but the God who suffers, His name is inscribed in our hearts in letters of fire; all the obstinacy of existence is washed away by our immense pain at seeing God suffering."[242] Such a contrast deserves serious reflection.

---

day-to-day business of the Protestant church, and in the day-to-day work of theologians, the work of Wagner played practically no role. Justification for invoking Germanic mythology and for promoting anti-Semitism was largely found in sources other than the work and the 'Weltanschauung' of Richard Wagner" (from the English summary).

240. Osthövener, "Deutsche Christen," 165–66.

241. Hitler, *Mein Kampf,* 70: "So glaube ich heute im Sinne des allmächtigen Schöpfers zu handeln: *Indem ich mich des Juden erwehre, kämpfe ich für das Werk des Herrn.*"

242. *SL* 641 (quoted more fully in chapter 7 above).

10

Theological Reflections V
To What Extent is *Parsifal* a Christian Work?

Introduction

THE QUESTION OF THE extent to which *Parsifal* is a "Christian work" is *related* to the issue of Wagner's own faith, but is ultimately independent of this issue. Just as a case can be made that the atheist Mozart composed music that witnesses to the Christian faith, or that in theory even Judas, Pilate, or Herod can preach Christ,[1] so Wagner, even if one comes to the view he was not a Christian, can still witness to the Christian gospel in his art.

One of the first to express doubts about the Christian character of *Parsifal*, although he later retracted this view, was Houston Stewart Chamberlain who wrote "[t]here is no more Christianity in *Parsifal* than there is paganism in the *Ring* or *Tristan*."[2] More recent arguments put forward that *Parsifal* is not a Christian work can be found in Dahlhaus[3] and Magee[4] and

---

1. See Luther's "Preface to Epistles of James and Jude," quoted in chapter 1 above.

2. Chamberlain, "Notes sur Parsifal," 225: "Il n'y a pas plus de Christianisme dans *Parsifal* qu'il a de Paganisme dans le *Ring* et dans *Tristan*."

3. Dahlhaus, *Music Dramas*, 142–44.

4. Magee, *Wagner and Philosophy*, 278–85.

less measured responses can be found in the *New Catholic Encyclopedia*[5] and in Gutman's work.[6]

Moving to the related issue of Wagner's own faith, Spotts describes Wagner as "an anti-clerical agnostic who despised the Christian church."[7] Gregor-Dellin goes one step further and draws the conclusion that Wagner was actually an atheist.[8] Even Hans Hübner, who believes that Wagner makes an important theological contribution, can write at the conclusion of his book that Wagner in his whole conviction was not a Christian.[9] In assessing to what extent *Parsifal* is a "Christian" work, I turn first to Wagner's own view.

Wagner's Christian Assessment of *Parsifal*

Although many have denied or had doubts about the Christian character of *Parsifal*, Wagner's own essays and letters together with Cosima's diaries affirm that *he* thought it a Christian work and I know of no text or utterance of Wagner's that suggests otherwise (and there is quite a lot of material to draw on!).[10]

5. Beaufils and Evans, "Wagner," 604, find redemption in *Parsifal* to be of a "para-Christian type, in the hero's compassion for all suffering"; more negative is the view that the "'vegetarian' Eucharistic interpretation" is "simply bizarre." Whether the Eucharist is "vegetarian" is another matter (see below). Their judgement on Wagner's *Jesus of Nazareth* is equally negative: Wagner "bends Christian truth to his narcissistic mentality" and Jesus "wills his death because he knows that the world is not worthy of him."

6. Gutman, *Wagner*, 413, concludes: "Despite the sham Christian piety of *Parsifal*, Wagner remained a non-believer to his death," his religion being one of "mock Christianity" (419). In the context of Wagner's antisemitism and his treatment of Levi, he writes: "In such an atmosphere of hate and rancour the 'Christian' drama of *Parsifal* was completed and prepared" (414).

7. Spotts, *Bayreuth*, 80.

8. See Gregor-Dellin, *Wagner*, 743 (missing in the English translation). Likewise, Köhler, *Titans*, 560, considers Wagner a "confirmed atheist."

9. Hans Hübner, *Erlösung*, 124: "Richard Wagner war in seiner ganzen Überzeugung nicht *Christ*."

10. His consistent views on the Christian character of *Parsifal* contrasts with his views of *Lohengrin* where he wished to some extent to disassociate the work from Christianity and give it a more universal basis. See *A Communication to My Friends* (*PW* 1:333–34; *GSD* 4:289; *JA* 6:264): "This 'Lohengrin' is no mere outcome of Christian meditation (Anschauung), but one of man's earliest poetic ideals; just as, for the matter of that, it is a fundamental error of our modern superficialism, to consider the specific Christian legends as by any means original creations. Not one of the most affecting, not one of the most distinctive Christian myths belongs by right of generation to the Christian spirit, such as we commonly understand it: it has inherited them all from the purely human intuitions (Anschauungen) of earlier times, and merely moulded

I start with a number of letters to Ludwig where he expresses the Christian nature of *Parsifal*. In the letter of 11 August 1873 he wrote that he was inspired to write *Parsifal*, the "pinnacle of my achievements," "in order to preserve the world's profoundest secret, the truest Christian faith, nay to awaken that faith anew."[11] Then in a letter of 25 August 1879 *Parsifal* was described as "this most Christian of works of art"[12] and in that of 28 September 1880 he speaks of "a drama in which the most sublime mysteries of the Christian faith are openly presented on stage,"[13] for which reason the work should only be performed in Bayreuth. In addition Wagner gave Ludwig a number of theological commentaries on various parts of the work. His commentary on Kundry's kiss was discussed in chapter 7 above so I turn to his program notes for the prelude to Act I.

"Love—Faith—Hope?"

First theme: "Love."

"Take ye my body take my blood, in token of our love!"

(Repeated in faintest whispers by angel-voices.)

"Take ye my blood, my body take, in memory of me!"—

(Again repeated in whispers.)—

Second theme: "Faith."

Promise of redemption through faith. Firmly and stoutly faith declares itself, exalted, willing, even in suffering.—To the promise renewed Faith answers from the dimmest heights—as on the pinions of the snow-white dove—hovering downwards—usurping more and more the hearts of men, filling the world, the whole of Nature with the mightiest force, then glancing up again to heaven's vault as if appeased. . . . Once more we hear the promise, and—we hope.[14]

---

them to fit its own peculiar tenets." However, Wagner was not exactly to keep to such a derivation of Christian myths.

11. *SL* 823; *KB* 3:21–22.

12. *SL* 897; *KB* 3:158.

13. *SL* 903. *KB* 3:182: "eine Handlung, in welcher die erhabensten Mysterien des christlichen Glaubens offen in Scene gesetzt sind."

14. *Prelude to Parsifal* (*PW* 8:388–89; *DEAP* 45–46; *KB* 3:186–87). The section omitted in this quotation is discussed in chapter 7 above. The two private performances of the prelude for Ludwig took place less than three weeks after writing this program.

This commentary is by no means fanciful. The first theme is well established as the "love feast" or "Communion" theme. Further the words "Take
ye . . ." are sung to this theme in the grail scene of Act I. The faith theme is
likewise well established, and it seems perfectly plausible to say it is first
manifest "[f]irmly and stoutly" and then softly with reference to the dove.[15]
Perhaps more contrived is the idea of hope towards the end of the Prelude.
It could be argued that this program should be dismissed as a concession to
Ludwig.[16] However, the same ideas are expressed in *What Use Is This Knowledge?*. He writes: "The perfect 'likeness' (Gleichniß) of the noblest artwork
would so transport our heart that we should plainly find the archetype, who
'somewhere' must perforce reside within our inner self, filled full with timeless, space-less Love and Faith and Hope."[17] The order of the "virtues" love,
faith, and hope correspond to that of Wagner's program for the prelude to
Act I of *Parsifal*. Wagner explains a little earlier that these "sublime edifices"
("erhabene Gebäude") of love, faith, and hope must be related to the ideality
of the world: "But what an untold boon could we bring to men affrighted
on the one hand by the thunders of the Church, and driven to desperation
by our physicists on the other, could we fit into the lofty edifices of 'Love,
Faith, and Hope' a vivid knowledge of the *ideality* of that world our only
present mode of apperception maps out by laws of Time and Space; then
would each question of the troubled spirit after the 'when' and 'where' of the
'other world' be recognised as answerable by nothing but a blissful smile."[18]

15. Note also its soft use in Kundry's baptism in Act III.

16. That Wagner could take some care in making his theological views sound "orthodox" when writing to Ludwig, see his letter 9 February 1879 where he speaks of the
"sublime symbol of the Holy Trinity that tells how what was once unheard-of has now
become real. We then muse on the theme of the 'Father,' 'Son' and Holy Ghost': and
although it brings a smile to our lips, it is also a source of deep renewal and spiritual
light" (*SL* 888; *KB* 3:144). Contrast Wagner's somewhat unorthodox views on the Trinity discussed below.

17. *PW* 6:261; *GSD* 10:262: "Das vollendete Gleichniß des edelsten Kunstwerkes
dürfte durch seine entrückende Wirkung auf das Gemüth sehr deutlich uns das Urbild
auffinden lassen, dessen 'Irgendwo' nothwendig nur in unserm, zeit- und raumlos von
Liebe, Glauben und Hoffnung erfüllten Innern sich offenbaren müßte." The expression
"the noblest artwork" would most naturally refer to *Parsifal*. The word "Gemüth" (translated by Ellis as "heart" but "mind" would be better) is a term used by Kant (it is rarely
used by Schopenhauer). Note also the Kantian ideas of "time-less" and "space-less."

18. *PW* 6:260; *GSD* 10:261: "Welchen unsäglichen Gewinn würden wir aber
den einerseits von den Drohungen der Kirche Erschreckten, andererseits den durch
unsere Physiker zur Verzweiflung Gebrachten zuführen, wenn wir dem erhabenen
Gebäude von 'Liebe, Glaube und Hoffnung' eine deutliche Erkenntniß der, durch die
unserer Wahrnehmung einzig zu Grunde liegenden Gesetze des Raumes und der Zeit
bedingten, Idealität der Welt einfügen könnten, durch welche dann alle die Fragen des
beängstigten Gemuthes nach einem 'Wo' und 'Wann' der 'anderen Welt' als nur durch

He then argues for the indispensable role of the religious symbol. "But not even the highest art can gain the force for such a revelation while it lacks the support of a religious symbol of the most perfect moral ordering of the world, through which alone it can be made intelligible to the people: only by borrowing from life's exercise itself the likeness of the Divine, can the artwork hold this up to life, and holding, lead us out beyond this life to pure contentment and redemption."[19]

Therefore I do not think that Wagner was being disingenuous in telling Ludwig of the Christian character of *Parsifal*. I am convinced that Wagner himself saw *Parsifal* as a Christian work and this is confirmed by the simple fact that he wished its conductor, Hermann Levi, to be baptized.[20]

This discussion still leaves open the question whether Wagner himself was a Christian. Wagner certainly considered himself a Christian and one of the clearest expressions of his Christian faith and how this related to his creative activity is his response to the question of the French poet Count Philippe-Auguste Villiers de l'Isle-Adam "whether he employed the religious idea simply as a source for theatrical effect." Wagner is reported to have said this:

> [I]f I did not feel in my heart the actual love and light of the Christian faith of which you speak, my works as I give them in evidence . . . would be that of a liar—*of an ape!* . . . My art is my prayer; and, believe me, no true artist creates what he does not believe, speaks of what he does not love, writes of what he does not think. . . . As far as regards me, since you put the question, let me inform you that, before all, *I am a Christian*, and that all the accents in my work which impress you are only inspired and created primarily by that alone.[21]

---

ein seliges Lächeln beantwortbar erkannt werden müßten?" Again note that this is filled with Kantian ideas.

19. *PW* 6:261–62 (modified); *GSD* 10:262: "Nicht aber kann der höchsten Kunst die Kraft zu solcher Offenbarung erwachsen, wenn sie der Grundlage des religiösen Symboles einer vollkommensten sittlichen Weltordnung entbehrt, durch welches sie dem Volke erst wahrhaft verständlich zu werden vermag: der Lebensübung selbst das Gleichniß des Göttlichen entnehmend, vermag erst das Kunstwerk dieses dem Leben, wiederum zu reinster Befriedigung und Erlösung über das Leben hinaus, zuzuführen."

20. See chapter 9 above.

21. Irvine, *'Parsifal' and Wagner's Christianity*, 36–37, who quotes the account given by Hébert, *Sentiment*, 180–82 who in turn quotes (with corrections) from Villiers, "Souvenir," 140–41 (from which I now quote): "si je ne ressentais, EN MON AME, la lumière et l'amour vivants de cette foi chrétienne dont vous parlez, mes œuvres, qui, toutes, en témoignent . . . seraient celles d'un menteur, d'un SINGE? . . . Mon art, c'est ma prière: et, croyez-moi, nul véritable artiste ne chante que ce qu'il croit, ne parle que de ce qu'il aime, n'écrit que ce qu'il pense. . . . Pour moi, puisque vous m'interrogez,

Villiers states that this is precisely the essence of Wagner's response[22] and I see no reason to doubt his testimony. It is one of his strongest confessions and it coheres with many of his other utterances.

More implicit indications of the "Christian" nature of *Parsifal* can be discerned in the music itself. The very first theme is not only understood as a "love-feast" or "Communion" theme but musically is related to the Marian Antiphons of Hermanus Contractus.[23] The next is the "grail" theme, which has an ending taken from the "Dresden Amen," a chord sequence (characterized by rising sixths from the fifth to the octave) composed by Johann Gottlieb Naumann (1741–1801) for the Court Church in Dresden. It became so popular that its use spread to other churches in Saxony, both Lutheran and Catholic. Wagner probably came to know of the theme as he attended church in Dresden and he incorporated a form of it in *Tannhäuser*.[24] It is unlikely that he first came to know of it through Mendelssohn's use in the first movement of his *Reformation Symphony* (at the end of the introduction and before the recapitulation);[25] but can it be a coincidence that Wagner attended a performance of the symphony on 8 February 1876 as he was about to start work on music for *Parsifal*?[26] Although Mendelssohn's use of the Dresden Amen has been understood as rather more "catholic,"[27] Wagner seemed to have understood the symphony as "protestant."[28] Further,

---

sachez QU'AVANT TOUT JE SUIS CHRÉTIEN, et que les accents qui vous impressionnent en mon œuvre ne sont inspirés et créés, en principe, que de CELA SEUL." Villiers dates this to Autumn 1868. However, Westernhagen, *Wagner*, 2:417, places it when Villiers together with Judith and Catulle Mendès visited the Wagner in Tribschen 16–25 July 1869 (see *CD* 16 and 25 July 1869). I assume that he answered Villiers' question in French, a language in which he was fluent.

22. Villiers, "Souvenir," 141: "Tel fut le sense exact de la réponse que me fit, ce soir là, Richard Wagner."

23. See *Alma redemptoris mater*, which could go back to the ninth century. Its melodic shape, like the "love feast," rises up the octave and then descends (see Hiley, *Plainchant*, 107, example II.10.3).

24. In *Tannhäuser* Act III the rising theme does not consistently use the sixths.

25. The first we know of Mendelssohn's plan for this symphony is a letter to his family of 2 September 1829 (it was to commemorate the 300th anniversary of the Augsburg Confession of 1530). It was first performed on 15 November 1832 in Berlin but soon fell into oblivion. However, it was revised and then eventually in 1868 two performances were given in Leipzig.

26. Just three days earlier we read: "R. says if our journey to Berlin were not impending he would start work on *Parzival*" (*CD* 5 February 1876).

27. Deathridge, "Symphony in C," sees the theme "as a sensuous Catholic symbol alongside an austere Lutheran chant."

28. Usually only the first and fourth movements are seen as concerned with reformation issues. But Cosima writes "the second movement makes R. think of Tetzel: 'When the money in the cashbox rings, the soul at once to heaven springs' ('wenn das

Wagner's own musical interpretation of the Dresden Amen often sounds decidedly "protestant."

The third theme ("faith") then sounds remarkably "Lutheran" and the initial instrumentation of brass instruments is reminiscent of the "Posaunen Chor" of the Lutheran Church.[29] Then the development of this theme in the choruses of Act I reminds one of the polyphony of Palestrina,[30] especially appropriate since Wagner thought that Palestrina "brings to our consciousness the inmost essence of Religion free from all dogmatic fictions,"[31] a point I return to in chapter 11.

In addition to such themes from the Prelude to Act I there are other instances of "Christian" music.[32] But perhaps the distinctive aspect of Wagner's portrayal of the Christian faith through his music is the intense sense of pain that is expressed, something he believed witnessed to the suffering Christ,[33] a striking example being the minor key version of the "love feast" as it is repeated in I.25–38, the three oboes adding that distinctive plaintive touch to the melody of violins and trumpet.

Added to the Christian music there is an obvious point that can be too easily overlooked: the profoundly Christian character of Wagner's main source, Wolfram's *Parzival* and the fact that Wagner felt he had Christianized it even more.[34]

Geld im Kasten klingt, die Seele in den Himmel springt')." This relates to Tetzel's sale of indulgences to which Luther objected. Perhaps Wagner was associating the coins dropping in and the souls springing out to the opening dance motif, which falls and then rises. I am unsure of there being an anti-semitic jibe (contrast Deathridge, "Symphony in C," 185).

29. Wagner's use of the "Posaunenchor" has been discussed already in chapter 5 above.

30. Kienzle, *Religion und Philosophie*, 205. In this connection, note that Wagner (and Liszt) supported the "Caecilian Movement," a reform of church music in a polyphonic style, often unaccompanied, and influenced by romantic harmonies (see *NCE* 2:841–42).

31. See his *Beethoven* essay (*PW* 5:79; *GSD* 9:79; *JA* 9:58) discussed in chapter 11 below.

32. See, for example, the "choral" type theme (not named or given in *FGT*) at I.1172–75, 1180–84, 1620–23, 1626–28.

33. See chapter 11 below.

34. See chapter 3 above.

Attempts to Deny the Christian Character of *Parsifal*

Various strategies have been adopted to deny the Christian character of the work. One of them is to argue that Wagner was not a Christian and therefore the artwork cannot be Christian either.

The view that Wagner was not a Christian, indeed that he was an atheist, is often based on Cosima's entry for 20 September 1879: "R. says, 'I do not believe in God, but in [the divine] (godliness), which is revealed in a Jesus *without sin*.'"[35] Two things can be said in response. The first is that the meaning of the utterance depends on what he meant by "God." Since this word is so often associated in Wagner's mind with the creator God or the God of the Old Testament, Wagner may be simply rejecting such a "deity." Secondly, if this were to be Wagner's simple confession of "atheism" (as Gregor-Dellin believes) is seems strange that his pious wife expresses no sense of shock or surprise; rather she simply continues: "Over coffee we talked about the possibility of my father's having come into contact with R. in his youth . . ."[36]

There have been other strategies for denying the Christian character of *Parsifal* that will be considered in relation to Wagner's breach with Nietzsche, but it is striking that directors have to go to some considerable lengths to eradicate the Christian elements from the work and this suggests that the Christianity of *Parsifal* is far from being superficial. Hitler could not deny the Christian character of *Parsifal* and this meant he had to give instructions for non-Christian productions.[37] It is highly significant that many of Hitler's henchmen disliked *Parsifal* because of its Christian character. According to

35. *CD* 20 September 1879 (Cosima's emphasis). I have replaced "godliness" with "the divine" in this translation since it better represents the German "das Göttliche." See *CT* 20 September 1879 n: "R. sagt: An Gott glaube ich nicht, aber an das Göttliche, welches sich im *sündenlosen* Jesus offenbart." This text was added by Cosima on the fourth and fifth pages after her entry for 20 September 1879.

36. *CD* 20 September 1879.

37. See Fröhlich, *Tagebücher Goebbels, II/2*, 344 (22 November 1941): "Den 'Parsifal' will der Führer nicht, wie mir berichtet wurde, allein für Bayreuth reklamieren; er meint nur, daß man die Ausstattung des 'Parsifal' etwas modernisieren sollte. Entweder müssen wir aus diesem christlich-mystischen Stil heraus, oder der 'Parsifal' wird auf die Dauer nicht mehr für den modernen Spielplan zu halten sein. Der Führer gibt mir da eine Reihe von Anregungen, die ich sofort in die Wirklichkeit übersetzen werde." On seeing *Parsifal* in Bayreuth, Goebbels came to the conclusion that the work was "zu fromm. Und zu pathetisch. Nichts für einen alten Heiden. . . . Ich habe lieber, wenn die alten Götter sich zanken und hintergehen. Das ist doch Leben. Natur. Kampf" (*Tagebücher Goebbels, I/3/II*, 136 [21 July 1936]).

Winifred Wagner "the National Socialists thought they had to reject Parsifal as 'ideologically unacceptable.'"[38]

Productions after the Second World War have also had to go out of their way to strip the work of Christian significance. One of the more subtle ways of doing this was Wieland Wagner's production of 1951. He tried to "de-sanctify" the work, which included removing the descent of the dove at the end of the drama;[39] I assume a similar strategy is at work in the production of Nikolaus Lehnhoff who replaced the "grail" as the cup Christ used at the last supper with a "stone."[40] That producers have had to go to such lengths to excise the Christian imagery suggests that *Parsifal* is after all a Christian work.

A final argument for *Parsifal* being a Christian work is that the stage work was one cause if not the cause for the break up of the relationship between Wagner and Nietzsche. But this has become a disputed issue and it is one to which I must now turn.

Wagner's Breach with Nietzsche

The relationship between Wagner and Nietzsche is one of the most significant artistic encounters of all time.[41] Nietzsche first got to know Wagner's art towards the end of his school days when he was around seventeen (1861) by playing through a piano reduction of *Tristan und Isolde* with his friend Gustav Krug[42] and he finally met Wagner in Leipzig at the home of the orientalist Hermann Brockhaus (who was married to Wagner's sister Ottilie).[43] Four weeks later he wrote this: "Wagner, whom I now

38. In addition to Goebbel's objections, neither Rosenberg nor Himmler wanted *Parsifal* staged (Hamann, *Winifred Wagner*, 348). Indeed Hitler told Wieland Wagner that "Himmler is trying to force through a ban on the work!!!" (349).

39. According to Wagner, *Wagners*, 135, shortly before his death in 1966 he confessed to having failed to "demystify" the work. See also chapter 5 above.

40. This rather backfires in that Wolfram's stone or rock can be understood as Christ himself (Horgan, "Grail," 355–65). Although the production attempts to rid the work of Christian imagery, the "synopsis" accompanying the DVD gives a very clear Christian interpretation!

41. Fischer-Dieskau, *Wagner and Nietzsche*, 26, considers that this was "an encounter of the two most important minds of their century."

42. Nietzsche together with Wilhelm Pinder and Gustav Krug formed the *Germania* society at their boarding school, Pforta (Hollingdale, *Nietzsche*, 19–20; *NWSEB* 1:317). The piano reduction was that of Hans von Bülow. The work had to wait until 1865 to be staged.

43. The meeting is described in a letter to Erwin Rohde of 9 November 1868 (Middleton, *Selected Letters*, 35–40).

know from his music, his poetry, his writings on aesthetics and, not least, from happy personal acquaintance with him, is the most vivid illustration of what Schopenhauer calls a 'genius.'"[44] Nietzsche came to be completely overwhelmed by Wagner and his art, and although Wagner had admiration for Nietzsche the relationship between the two "was never even remotely symmetrical."[45] First of all, the intellectual influence was almost entirely one-way, from Wagner to Nietzsche. As Magee puts it, "Nietzsche had no perceptible influence on Wagner's opera, but Wagner was the greatest influence on Nietzsche in the whole of his life."[46] Secondly, for a number of years Wagner completely dominated Nietzsche personally.[47] However, all this was to change: from around 1876 until 1882 there were a series of events that resulted in Nietzsche's absolute adulation for Wagner turning into hatred and abuse of the composer.[48] Somewhere in the rather complex series of events is the issue of Christianity in *Parsifal* and in Wagner's own life, and it is upon this that I now focus.

The young Nietzsche was "surrounded by Lutheran pastors": his father was pastor in the village of Röcken in Saxony and he in turn was the son of Friedrich August Nietzsche, a theologian and superintendent in the Lutheran Church; his mother was the daughter of the pastor of Pobles. Nietzsche had great admiration for his father and felt that he was surrounded by a healthy Christian piety and, as Young points out, this makes his later ferocious attack on Christianity "a biographical puzzle."[49] This puzzle could possibly be solved by considering two things. First, Nietzsche was simply searching for the truth and intellectual integrity simply led him to this. Indeed, he writes in *Ecce homo*: "I have the right to wage war on Christianity because I have never been put out or harmed by it,—the most serious Christians have always been well disposed towards me."[50] A second consideration, one that Young develops, is that there may be some indi-

---

44. Letter to Erwin Rohde, as quoted by Young, *Nietzsche*, 78 (*KGB* 1.2 604; *NWSEB* 1:313).

45. Walter Kaufmann, quoted in Magee, *Wagner and Philosophy*, 288.

46. Magee, *Wagner and Philosophy*, 286. As far as ideas are concerned, Berry, "Positive Influence," highlights Wagner's influence on Nietzsche's will-to-power and issues of morality, social and individual.

47. See Köhler, *Nietzsche and Wagner*.

48. This has been extensively discussed. See, e.g., Newman, *Life IV*, 565–74. Westernhagen, *Wagner*, 2:533–38, is, in the judgment of Kinderman, "Introduction," 2 n. 4, slanted against Nietzsche and he recommends balancing this with Köhler, *Nietzsche and Wagner*, 127–38. See also Fischer-Dieskau, *Wagner and Nietzsche*.

49. Young, *Nietzsche*, 5.

50. Nietzsche, *Anti-Christ Etc*, 83 (*KSA* 6:275).

cations that despite the praise for his father, Nietzsche felt that his father could have had a better life were it not for some of his Christian ideas. To support this, Young quotes a text from *Ecce homo* that says that he owes every privilege to his father except that for "life."[51] This, however, is based on a German edition that has been "edited" by Elizabeth Förster-Nietzsche.[52] A second text Young quotes (from *Twilight of the Idols*) speaks of a "Christian sick house and dungeon atmosphere."[53] This, however, is a free translation of "christliche Kranken- und Kerkerluft,"[54] which can simply be translated "Christian sick and dungeon air/atmosphere." Young points out that from the end of Nietzsche's third year the household was literally a "sick house."[55] But the context of the passage in *Twilight of the Idols* does not seem to suggest a reference to Nietzsche's home.[56] However, Young could well be right in relating the "dungeon atmosphere" to "gothic" elements of his childhood: the frequent contact with death (mortuary, tombstones, black crêpe, funeral biers) and the gloomy church atmosphere with the terrifying figure of St. George.[57] In this connection it is striking that the grail scenes of Act I and III (and of course Titurel's funeral procession) of *Parsifal* could certainly be characterized as having a "dungeon" atmosphere, although it is precisely such elements that initially attracted him to Wagner's art.[58]

51. Young, *Nietzsche*, 6, 11, renders Nietzsche as follows: "I regard it as a great privilege to have had such a father; it seems to me that whatever else of privileges I possess is thereby explained, save for life, the great Yes to life [which is] *not* included."

52. So the 1955 edition gives this text (Nietzsche, "Ecce Homo," 1074). However, the text of *KSA* 6:267–68 (1.3) actually omits these negative words about his father. In fact, it consistently "praises" him and damns his sister and "German blood" (hence the "editing"). See Nietzsche, *Anti-Christ Etc*, 77 (based on *KSA* 6:267–68): "I consider it a great privilege to have had a father like this. . . . And this is where I come to the question of blood, certainly not German blood. When I look to my diametric opposite . . . I always think of my mother and sister,—it would blaspheme my divinity to think that I am related to this sort of *canaille*. The way my mother and sister treat me to this very day is a source of unspeakable horror . . . "

53. Young, *Nietzsche*, 11.

54. *KSA* 6:100.

55. Young, *Nietzsche*, 11.

56. Nietzsche is contrasting the "law of Manu" with Christianity and the New Testament. See Nietzsche, *Anti-Christ Etc*, 184: "You breathe freely again when you leave the Christian atmosphere of disease and dungeon and enter this healthier, higher, more *expansive* world" (Nietzsche's emphasis).

57. See Young, *Nietzsche*, 7–8 (*KGW* 1.1:283 [4 (77)]).

58. In the letter to Erwin Rohde (8 October 1868) written a month before his first meeting, Nietzsche writes that what delights him about Wagner is exactly what delights him about Schopenhauer: "the ethical fragrance, the Faustian atmosphere, cross, death and tomb etc" ("die ethische Luft, der faustische Duft, Kreuz, Tod und Gruft etc" (*NWSEB* 1:308).

But despite this gloomy aspect of the Christian faith, a passage from Nietzsche's *Aus meinem Leben* demonstrates that as a boy of thirteen, "the intensity of his religious feeling is startling."[59] However, once he entered University everything changed. In 1864 he enrolled at the University of Bonn to study theology. But on returning home to Naumberg in Easter 1865[60] he announced he was abandoning theology for philology and he refused to go with his mother to the Sunday service and take Communion.[61] The precise reason for this radical change that led to his atheism is unclear. His reading of Strauß's *The Life of Jesus* could be one cause; however, an aphorism in *Human All Too Human* suggests that he may not have had any clear rational ground for deserting his faith.[62]

Nietzsche's more mature view of Christianity first becomes clear in his first *Untimely Meditation* which concerns Strauß. His focus of criticism is Strauß's second theological book, *The Old Faith and the New* (*Der alte und der neue Glaube*, 1872), not *The Life of Jesus* (*Das Leben Jesu*, 1835). The immediate reason for writing this was because Wagner asked him. Strauß attacked Wagner for persuading Ludwig to dismiss the Court conductor Franz Lachner.[63] Wagner had read *The Life of Jesus* back in 1840s and this probably had *some* impact on his sketches for *Jesus of Nazareth*.[64] But his views towards Strauß later changed; the "sonnets" to Strauß of 1868 show

59. Hollingdale, *Nietzsche*, 17. The passage quoted is as follows: "I have already experienced so much—joy and sorrow, cheerful things and sad things—but in everything God has safely led me as a father leads his weak little child. . . . I have firmly resolved within me to dedicate myself forever to His service. May the dear Lord give me strength and power to carry out my intention and protect me on my life's way. Like a child I trust in His grace: He will preserve us all, that no misfortune may befall us. But His holy will be done! All He gives I will joyfully accept: happiness and unhappiness, poverty and wealth, and boldly look even death in the face, which shall one day unite us all in eternal joy and bliss. Yes, dear Lord, let Thy face shine upon us forever! Amen."

60. He was then aged twenty-one (born 15 October 1844).

61. Young, *Nietzsche*, 58.

62. Nietzsche, *Human*, 330 (2.82): "He who wants to desert a party or a religion believes it is incumbent upon him to refute it. . . . We did *not* attach ourself to this party, or religion, on *strictly rational grounds*: we ought not to *affect* to have done so when we leave it" (*KSA* 2:589).

63. On Wagner's antipathy towards Strauß and Lachner see the three sonnets Wagner composed "To David Strauss" (*BB* 125–26). They were an ironic reply (composed 11–12 March 1868) to the two sonnets Strauß wrote against Wagner.

64. One example of Strauß's influence is that there is no resurrection in Wagner's *Jesus of Nazareth*. See Strauß, *Leben Jesu*, 2:645–63 (Strauss, *Life*, 735–44) for his understanding of the resurrection, the appearances of Jesus being understood as psychological and subjective. A footnote added to the third and fourth editions contrasts this with Weisse's view that the appearances were "objective magical facts" (*Life*, 744 n. 29), a view that I imagine would be more conducive to Wagner.

a disdain towards his Gospel criticism.[65] Then in December 1870, Wagner read Strauß's book on Voltaire[66] that "left a very unpleasant impression through its crudity and affectation."[67] He (and Cosima) found *The Old Faith and the New* "terribly shallow."[68] At a meeting in Strasbourg in November 1872 Wagner persuaded Nietzsche to write against Strauß and that he should receive the work on his sixtieth birthday.[69] The article has been judged to be rather poor[70] but it does highlight Nietzsche's view of what life should be like if Christianity is rejected: "Here was an opportunity to exhibit native courage: for here he ought to have turned his back on his 'we' and boldly derived a moral code for life out of the *bellum omnium contra omnes* [war of all against all] and the privileges of the strong."[71] Already one can perceive why *Parsifal* was to disgust him!

We then see Nietzsche becoming more and more critical of Christianity such that with *Human All Too Human* we find a work that is extremely critical of the Christian faith and which, as we will see, caused great offense to both Wagner and Cosima. But before looking at this I want to trace the way in which Nietzsche slowly broke away from Wagner.

First, it is clear that Nietzsche started to have doubts about Wagner and his musical project in 1874.[72] There are a number of critical comments

65. See the ironic opening of the first sonnet: "O David! Held! Du sträusslichster der Strausse! Befreier aus des Wahnes schweren Ketten! So woll' uns stets von Irr' und Trug erretten, wie du enthüllt der Evangelien Flausse!" (O David! Hero! Straussest of the Strausses! Deliverer from delusion's weighty chains! May us redeem from error and deception your exposé of humbug in the Gospels!") (*BB* 125).

66. Strauß, *Voltaire*.

67. Letter of Cosima to Nietzsche, Dec 1870. See also Cosima's entries for 4–11 December 1870.

68. See *CD* 7 February 1873.

69. Köhler, *Nietzsche and Wagner*, 95.

70. Hans Hübner, *Nietzsche*, 85, quotes from a letter of the Swiss poet Gottfried Keller: "Das knäbische Pamphlet des Herrn Nietzsche gegen Strauß habe ich auch zu lesen begonnen, bringe es aber kaum zu Ende wegen des gar zu monotonen Schimpfstils ohne alle positiven Leistungen und Oasen."

71. Nietzsche, *Untimely Meditations*, 29–30. See also Nietzsche, *Anti-Christ Etc*, 193, where he singles George Eliot: "*G. Eliot.*—They have got rid of the Christian God, and now think that they have to hold on to Christian morality more than ever" (*KSA* 6:113).

72. See, for example, his comments on Wagner's music: "None of our great composers was, at twenty-eight, still so bad a composer as Wagner" ("Keiner unserer grossen Musiker war in seinem 28ten Jahr ein noch so schlechter Musiker wie Wagner"; *KSA* 7:759 (32[15]). Nietzsche's turn against Wagner is well followed through by Young, *Nietzsche*, 185–89. Young emphasizes that although Nietzsche started to have doubts about "the man, thinker, and artist" he remains committed to the "Bayreuth ideal, to the rebirth of the community-gathering theatre of the 'collective artwork'" (189). Further, although Nietzsche's reservations about Wagner increased over the years, he supported

is his notebooks that were either omitted in the 1876 *Untimely Meditations* "Richard Wagner in Bayreuth" or considerably modified.[73] Further, the essay itself, although designed as a homage to Wagner, does not quite read as one.[74]

Further strains were certainly showing in 1876, the year of the first performance of the *Ring*. Wagner was receiving members of high society in Bayreuth and it is highly likely that Nietzsche was feeling neglected.[75] That same sense of neglect can be discerned six years later when we read in a letter to his sister Elizabeth that he would visit the premiere of *Parsifal* if Wagner personally invited him: "But I—forgive me!—will come only on the condition that Wagner personally invites me and treats me as the most honored guest at the festival."[76]

The next stage in their breakdown was their final meetings in Sorrento in Autumn 1876. According to Elizabeth Förster-Nietzsche, on their last walk together, probably 2 November, Wagner "began to speak of his religious feelings and experiences in a tone of the deepest repentance, and to confess a leaning towards the Christian dogmas. For example, he spoke of the delight he took in the celebration of the Holy Communion."[77] However, according to his sister Nietzsche's objection regarded the insincerity of Wagner's Christian confession.[78] And so it was on this "beautiful day" that the breakdown of their relationship was sealed.

---

the "ideal" until the end of his life. It is worth adding that around this time Wagner was also having doubts about Nietzsche. See his critical comments on Nietzsche's second *Untimely Meditation* (*On the Uses and Disadvantages of History for Life*) in *CD* 9 April 1874.

73. See Nietzsche, *Untimely Meditations*, xxvi–xxviii.

74. Ibid., 205: "Wagner's life has, to recall an idea of Schopenhauer's, much of the comedy about it, and markedly grotesque comedy at that." Note also the very ending where he says Wagner is "not the seer of a future, as he would perhaps like to appear to us, but the interpreter and transfigurer of a past" (*KSA* 1:441). There are, however, passages where Nietzsche's admiration for Wagner shines through. See, for example, how he describes *Tristan* as "the actual *opus metaphysicum* of all art" (232; *KSA* 1:479).

75. Magee, *Wagner and Philosophy*, 310–11.

76. Letter of 30 January 1882, Middleton, *Selected Letters*, 181 n. 45.

77. Förster-Nietzsche, *Nietzsche-Wagner Correspondence*, 78.

78. Ibid.: "My brother had the greatest possible respect for sincere, honest Christianity, but he considered it quite impossible that Wagner, the avowed atheist, should suddenly have become a naive and pious believer. He could only regard Wagner's alleged sudden change of heart, as having been prompted by a desire to stand well with the Christian rulers of Germany and thus further the material success of the Bayreuth undertaking."

Doubts have been expressed about this account of their meeting, Ross believing that nothing is right about this account, not even the weather.[79] However, Cosima's description of the weather actually agrees with Elizabeth's description and Nietzsche's letter confirms the conversation about Communion: Wagner was moved "by 'the blood of the redeemer'" and that "there was a moment when he confessed to me the delights that he was able to derive from Holy Communion."[80] But of one thing in Elizabeth's account I do doubt: that Nietzsche's main objection regarded the issue of Wagner's *insincerity*. Regarding Communion she wrote: "Had he had in mind the picturesque ritual of the Catholic church . . . my brother would have had less reason to doubt his sincerity." But of course Wagner had in mind "the rather austere ceremony of the Protestant church." To demonstrate how irrational this argument is, I quote from Wagner's comments two days after Cosima's conversion to the Protestant Church: "R. comes to the subject of our holy event: 'How beautiful it was in that little vestry, how powerful the voice of our dean sounded—like the voice of a lion emerging from a cave! What substitute could there be for the feelings aroused in one when the indescribably moving words "This is my body" are spoken?'"[81]

The next stage in their breakdown was in 1878 and it is here that Nietzsche lashes out at the Christian faith in *Human, All Too Human*. One reason for this was, I suggest, the libretto of *Parsifal*. It was not until 1886, three years after Wagner's death, that he wrote in the preface to the second volume of *Human, All Too Human* (1886) those famous words: "Richard Wagner, seemingly the all-conquering, actually a decaying, despairing romantic, suddenly sank down helpless and shattered before the Christian cross."[82] These words almost certainly refer to *Parsifal*. But already in the

---

79. Ross, *Adler*, 480.

80. *KSA* 15:71: "N schreibt 1886: 'er begann vom 'Blute des Erlösers' zu reden, ja es gab eine Stunde, wo er mir die Entzückungen eingestand, die er dem Abendmahle abzugewinnen wisse . . .'"

81. *CD* 2 November 1872. In fact, Wagner was to speak of the beauty of Protestant services on a number of occasions, sometimes emphasizing their superiority to Catholic ones (see, e.g., *CD* 2 July 1881).

82. Nietzsche, *Human*, 210–11. *KSA* 2:372 (Vorrede to the second volume, 1886): "Richard Wagner, scheinbar der Siegreichste, in Wahrheit ein morsch gewordener, verzweifelnder Romantiker, sank plötzlich, hülflos und zerbrochen, vor dem christlichen Kreuze nieder." This second volume was an addition to the 1878 first edition and comprises "Assorted Opinions and Maxims" ("Vermischte Meinungen und Sprüche") and "The Wanderer and his Shadow" ("Der Wanderer und sein Schatten"). He also changed publisher for this work as he did for *Birth of Tragedy*. This quotation is found again in Nietzsche, *Anti-Christ Etc*, 276 ("romantic" replaced by "decadent") (*KSA* 6:431–32).

first volume (1878) we find caustic criticism of Christianity and of Wagner. The context for this is worth exploring at a little length.

According to Nietzsche's own account the libretto for *Parsifal* and *Human All Too Human* crossed in the post.[83] This, however, is a later dramatization because there was no such "crossing over." There was in fact a period of six months between the libretto reaching Nietzsche and *Human All Too Human* reaching Wagner. A copy of the libretto of *Parsifal* reached Nietzsche on 3 January 1878. The dedication ran as follows: "Cordial greetings and regards to his dear friend Friedrich Nietzsche. Richard Wagner (Senior Church Councillor [Oberkirchenrath]: for kind transmission to Professor Overbeck)."[84] The reference to Overbeck is striking since Wagner actually disliked Overbeck's book *The Christlikeness of Present-day Theology*.[85] But Wagner's intention was to emphasize that the libretto was "unecclesiastical."[86]

Nietzsche's original reaction to the libretto of *Parsifal*, as seen in the letter he sent to Seydlitz the day after receiving the libretto, was not too antagonistic. He writes that the work has more Liszt than Wagner and has the spirit of the counter-reformation ("Geist der Gegenreformation") and that as a lover of the Greeks he finds the work too focused on the Christian world ("Alles [ist] zu christlich zeitlich beschränkt") and referring to the Communion there is far too much blood ("viel zu viel Blut").[87] He is also critical of the idea of actors "praying, trembling, with ecstatically straining throats."[88] But his initial reaction is by no means as violent as it was later to become and indeed he concedes that the poetry is of the highest kind.[89] We will have to tease out why his attitude changed so radically to Wagner.

83. Nietzsche, *Anti-Christ Etc*, 119 (*KSA* 6:327): "When the finished book finally came into my hands—a profound surprise for a very sick man—, I sent two copies to Bayreuth, along with some other things. By some miraculous coincidence, pregnant with meaning, a beautiful copy of the text to *Parsifal* arrived simultaneously at my door, with Wagner's personal inscription, 'for his dear friend, Friedrich Nietzsche, Richard Wagner, Church Counsellor'.—These two books crossing paths—it was as if I had heard some ominous sound. Didn't it sound as if *swords* were crossing? . . . At any rate, that is how we both thought of it: because neither of us said anything.—This was when the first *Bayreuther Blätter* appeared: I saw *what* it was high time for.—Unbelievable! Wagner had become pious . . ."

84. Gregor-Dellin, *Wagner*, 456; *NWSEB* 1:296.

85. For a German summary of this work see Eckert et al., *Lexikon der Theologischen Werke*, 759–60.

86. Westernhagen, *Wagner*, 2:534.

87. *NWSEB* 2:728.

88. *NWSEB* 2:728; Newman, *Life IV*, 566.

89. *NWSEB* 2:728; Newman, *Life IV*, 566.

Further this change to some extent did occur during those first months of 1878 as can be seen in *Human All Too Human.*

When this work appeared, it caused considerable offense to Wagner[90] and Cosima.[91] Not only did it contain personal attacks on them both but, and this is important for our purposes, castigates Wagner for his turn to Christianity. So in Aphorism 109 (in the third section entitled "The Religious Life" ("Das religiöse Leben") we read: "What is certain, however, is that any degree of frivolity or melancholy is better than a romantic retreat and desertion, an approach to Christianity in any form: for, given the current state of knowledge, one can no longer have any association with it without incurably dirtying one's intellectual conscience and prostituting it before oneself and others."[92] One explanation for this outburst may have been that Wolzogen had rejected three articles Peter Gast had submitted for the first issue of *Bayreuther Blätter.* Peter Gast in fact told Joseph Hofmiller that Nietzsche was so incensed by this that he added this especially vitriolic comments to Aphorism 109 (just quoted), aimed not only at Wolgozen but also at Wagner's *Parsifal.*[93] But Wolzogen's rejection of Gast's articles alone is I think insufficient to account for Nietzsche's intemperate words in *Human All Too Human.* I suspect therefore that the libretto of *Parsifal* was one key reason for Nietzsche's change in attitude to Wagner.

However, there is a problem with the suggestion that it was the Christian nature of the libretto that turned him against Wagner. Nietzsche had known of the prose draft of 1865 for some time. Further, he and Cosima had read it together on 25 December 1869[94] and on 10 October 1877 he could still write to Cosima: "The glorious promise of Parcival may comfort us in all things where we need consolation."[95] One therefore wonders

90. See the chapter "From the Souls of Artists and Writers" ("Aus der Seele der Künstler und Schriftsteller"), especially Aphorism 164, "Peril and profit in the cult of the genius" ("Gefahr und Gewinn im Kultus des Genius") (Nietzsche, *Human,* 87–88; *KSA* 2:154–56).

91. See Aphorism 430 in the section "Woman and Child" (Weib und Kind") entitled "Voluntary sacrifice" ("Freiwilliges Opfertier") (Nietzsche, *Human,* 158–59; *KSA* 2:281).

92. Nietzsche, *Human,* 61; *KSA* 2:108–9: "Sicherlich aber ist Leichtsinn oder Schwermuth jeden Grades besser, als eine romantische Rückkehr und Fahnenflucht, eine Annäherung an das Christenthum in irgend einer Form: denn mit ihm kann man sich, nach dem gegenwärtigen Stande der Erkenntnis, schlechterdings nicht mehr einlassen, ohne sein *intellectuales Gewissen* heillos zu beschmutzen und vor sich und Anderen preiszugeben."

93. Westernhagen, *Wagner,* 2:534–35.

94. *CD* 25 December 1869.

95. Borchmeyer, "Wagner and Nietzsche," 338. This was almost a year after the

whether there was something in the final libretto that really offended him, possibly the emphasis that *Christ* is the redeemer and not Parsifal.[96] One could therefore come to the conclusion, held for many years, that the breach is to be understood in terms of the Christian nature of *Parsifal* to which Nietzsche objected. To this one could add that in the last ten years of his life, Wagner became increasingly interested in Christian theology.[97]

But there may have been other forces at work and on this basis some have minimized the possible impact of Christianity on their break up. One of the debated questions is the nature of the "deadly offence" of which Nietzsche writes in later letters. A number of scholars have understood the "deadly offence" in terms of Wagner's correspondence with Otto Eiser, Nietzsche's doctor. Eiser, founder of the Frankfurt Wagner society and a contributor to the *Bayreuther Blätter*,[98] had, together with the ophthalmologist Dr. Krüger, examined Nietzsche (between 3 and 7 October 1877). Among other things they found retinal and inflammatory problems that exacerbated his violent headaches. Wagner came to hear of this via Wolzogen[99] and in a letter to Eiser of 23 October 1877, offered his own diagnosis: Nietzsche's eye problems were the result of what one could term solitary sexual experiences.[100] Dr. Eiser replied to Wagner on 26 October 1877 explaining in some detail his views about Nietzsche's eyesight and his sexual habits.[101]

To work out whether this breach of confidence was significant in their break up, one has to turn to three letters Nietzsche wrote in the months after Wagner's death. The first is to Franz Overbeck (22 February 1883). Here Nietzsche writes about the "deadly offence" ("eine tödliche Beleidigung"):

---

painful meeting in Sorrento.

96. See the discussion in chapter 6 on the changes to Act II.

97. See the discussion in chapter 2 above.

98. His article on *Parsifal* "Andeutungen" is quoted below in relation to "religious pluralism."

99. Wolzogen had moved to Bayreuth as editor of the *Bayreuther Blätter* and had received Eiser's article on the *Ring* ("Richard Wagners Ring des Nibelungen: Ein exegetischer Versuch") via Nietzsche.

100. This was published for the first time (in part) by Westernhagen, *Werk*, 527–29, together with other correspondence with Otto Eiser from October 1877. Note that Wagner speaks only of onanism ("Onanie," 528). He does not write of pederasty as Benders and Oettermann, *Chronik*, 417, suggest. The words "eine Folge unnatürlicher Ausschweifungen mit Hindeutungen auf Päderastie" do *not* come from Wagner's letter but from Nietzsche's letter to Peter Gast (J. Heinrich Köselitz) on 21 April 1883 (see below).

101. See Westernhagen, *Werk*, 529–31. However, Westernhagen decided to omit some parts of Eiser's reply; these were first provided by Gregor-Dellin, *Wagner*, 453–54 (German original published 1980).

"Wagner was by far the *fullest* person I have ever known, and in *this* respect I have had to forgo a great deal for six years. But something like a deadly offence came between us; and something terrible could have happened if he had lived any longer."[102] The question is whether this "deadly offence" is related to this breach of confidence about Nietzsche's sexual practices or to an ideological issue or to neither of these.[103] The second letter, sent to the composer Peter Gast (J. Heinrich Köselitz) on 21 April 1883, may on first appearance support the breach of confidence as the cause of the rift. He writes: "Wagner is rich in malicious ideas, but what do you say to his having exchanged letters on the subject (even with my doctors) to voice his *belief* that my altered way of thinking was a consequence of unnatural excesses, with hints of pederasty?"[104] Köhler takes this at face value: Wagner had accused Nietzsche of "pederasty" (i.e., homosexuality) and adds that onanism in the nineteenth century was a euphemism for homosexuality.[105] Köhler makes the point that "[t]he mere suspicion of . . . homosexuality . . . was enough to destroy a middle-class life and, if proven, would lead to imprisonment" and claims that Wagner was punishing Nietzsche for his apostasy by circulating this rumor.[106] Against Köhler there are three things to bear in mind. First, can one really take those words "with hints of pederasty" at face value? Secondly, would Wagner really be so vindictive in trying to destroy Nietzsche by accusing him of homosexuality?[107] Thirdly, even if

102. Middleton, *Selected Letters*, 209 (quoted in a different translation in Gregor-Dellin, *Wagner*, 455). Nietzsche, "Briefe," 1202–3: "*Wagner* war bei weitem der *vollste* Mensch, den ich kennenlernte, und in *diesem* Sinne habe ich seit sechs Jahren eine große Entbehrung gelitten. *Aber* es gibt etwas zwischen uns beiden wie eine tödliche Beleidigung; und es hätte furchtbar kommen können, wenn er noch länger gelebt haben würde."

103. The context of these comments about Wagner does not settle the issue. In the previous paragraph he writes that he longs for seclusion and speaks of the dangers of "intellectual images and processes." "I mean to find my health by the same means as before, in complete seclusion. My mistake last year was to give up solitude. Through ceaseless contact with intellectual images and processes I have become so sensitive that contact with present-day people make me suffer and forgo incredibly much; eventually this make me hard and unjust—in brief, it does not suit me" (Middleton, *Selected Letters*, 209). The following paragraph parallels what he writes on his relationship to Wagner: "Lou is by far the *shrewdest* (*klügste*) human being I have known. *But* and so on and so on" (209). The reference is to Lou Salomé to whom Nietzsche had unsuccessfully proposed twice the previous Spring (once via Paul Rée, once directly) and who broke off contact with him in November 1882 (Hollingdale, *Nietzsche*, 149, 152).

104. Quoted in Gregor-Dellin, *Wagner*, 455. He notes that Peter Gast omitted this passage in the first edition of Nietzsche's letters which he himself edited (549).

105. Köhler, *Titans*, 527.

106. Ibid., 526.

107. It is true that in private conversation Wagner could be highly critical of

Wagner thought Nietzsche was a homosexual, he would certainly not be vindictive in view of his understanding of and sensitivity towards the sexual orientation of King Ludwig[108] and Paul von Joukowsky.[109]

I would therefore be very doubtful about accusations of homosexuality (never mind that this could be the cause for the rift). But it seems clear Wagner did suggest Nietzsche had problems with onanism and, according to Eugen Kretzer, Eiser did show Wagner's letter to Nietzsche and this caused the break up.[110] The issue would therefore appear to be settled in favor of those such as Gregor-Dellin and Bryan Magee[111] who think that the accusation of onanism caused the rift between the two.

No doubt Wagner's indiscretion was a cause of this breach as Eiser suggests. But to minimize the role Christianity played is seriously mistaken, especially since Wagner's "deadly offence" appears to be linked to his return to the Christian faith. A letter of Nietzsche to Malwida von Meysenbug[112] of 21 February 1883 was first made public by Montinari in 1985 and postdates the books by Gregor-Dellin and Fischer-Dieskau but not that of Magee. Nietzsche writes: "Wagner offended me in a fatal way—I'll say it to you!—his

---

Nietzsche. On looking at a photograph of Nietzsche Cosima records (4 February 1883) that Wagner considered him a "fop" ("Geck"), a "complete nonentity," and that he "has no ideas of his own"; further he has "no blood of his own, it is all foreign blood which has been poured into him."

108. See Dreyfus, *Erotic Impulse*, 196–202. Dreyfus rightly argues that Wagner and Ludwig were in love with each other and concludes: "As for Wagner's own Romantic Friendships with men, so long as sexual intimacy played no role, he was prepared to travel quite some distance" (204).

109. Ibid., 175–81. Joukowsky designed the sets and costumes for *Parsifal* and was an intimate family friend for the last three years of Wagner's life. On Joukowsky's relationship with Pepino, a young Neapolitan folk singer, see *CD* 25 February 1881: "After lunch Jouk's relationship with Pepino discussed in much detail, brought up by a sad amorous incident. I allow myself to be provoked into describing it as *silly*, and I regret that. . . . About the relationship with P., R. said: 'It is something for which I have understanding, but no inclination. In any case, with all relationships what matters most is what we ourselves put into that. It is all illusion.'"

110. Kretzer, "Erinnerungen," 345: "'Warum Nietzsche von Wagner abfiel', meinte Eiser einst:—'ich weiss es allein, denn in meinem Hause, in meiner Stube hat sich dieser Abfall vollzogen, als ich Nietzsche jenen Brief in wohlmeinendster Absicht mitteilte. Ein Ausbruch von Raserei war die Folge. Nietzsche war ausser sich:—die Worte sind nicht wiederzugeben, die er für Wagner fand.—Seitdem war der Bruch besiegelt.' Das müsste im Herbst 1877 geschehen sein."

111. Gregor-Dellin, *Wagner*, 451–56; Magee, *Wagner and Philosophy*, 334–38. A variation of this is Köhler's theory that it was the charge of homosexuality that caused the rift (Köhler, *Titans*, 526–27).

112. Malwida von Meysenbug (1817–1903) was a German writer and political activist and an admirer and friend of both Wagner and Nietzsche.

slow return and creeping back to Christianity and the church I have experienced as a personal insult to me; my whole youth and direction seemed to me mocked, insofar as I had dedicated it to a spirit who was capable of this step. To feel this so strongly—that I have penetrated through to unspoken goals and tasks."[113] In this letter we also find the idea of the "deadly offence" that he also used in the letter to Overbeck (22 February 1883).[114] But in the letter to Malwida von Meysenbug it alludes to Wagner's turn to Christianity. It does *not* refer to Wagner's correspondence with Nietzsche's physician, Dr. Otto Eiser.

But Köhler, who does discuss the letter, remains unconvinced that the "fatal offence" was in fact the "creeping back to Christianity." Köhler believes that had he explained it was to do with onanism this would be acutely embarrassing and this could get back to Cosima.[115] He also argues that if the "creeping back to Christianity" was the real "mortal offence" why did he not explain this in the letter to Overbeck written the following day? Köhler argues that had he explained this, Overbeck, who was critical of the established church, would fully understand.[116] The problem with Köhler's logic is that Overbeck would know all too well that Wagner's "Christianity" was precisely not that of the "established church" and therefore one wonders whether Overbeck would fully "understand." This may be one reason why Nietzsche omitted to explain to Overbeck that the "deadly offence" was Wagner's turn to the Christian faith.

It is perhaps significant that those with an atheist or agnostic agenda wish to pin the breakdown between Wagner and Nietzsche to accusations of onanism[117] or homosexuality;[118] and perhaps I may be accused of supporting the more traditional view that the breach was largely to do with the Christian faith because of my Christian agenda. But there is little doubt in

---

113. Quoted in Borchmeyer, "Wagner and Nietzsche," 338 (for the German see Montinari, "Nietzsche—Wagner im Sommer 1878," 21: "Wagner hat mich auf eine tödliche Weise beleidigt—ich will es Ihnen doch sagen!—sein langsames Zurückgehn und -Schleichen zum Christenthum und zur Kirche habe ich als einen persönlichen Schimpf für mich empfunden: meine ganze Jugend und ihre Richtung schien mir befleckt, insofern ich einem Geiste, der dieses Schrittes fähig war, gehuldigt hatte. Dies so stark zu empfinden—dazu bin ich durch unausgesprochne Ziele und Aufgaben gedrängt."

114. Compare the similar language: "a deadly offence" ("eine tödliche Beleidigung"); "Wagner offended me in a fatal way" ("Wagner hat mich auf eine tödliche Weise beleidigt.")

115. Köhler, *Titans*, 525.

116. Ibid., 525.

117. E.g., Magee, *Wagner and Philosophy*, 335–38.

118. Köhler, *Titans*, 526–28.

my mind that Christianity and its relation to *Parsifal* was a significant cause for the breach if not the main one.

I now return to those words from *Human All Too Human*: "Wagner . . . sank down suddenly, helpless and broken, before the Christian cross."[119] His use of "suddenly" is a dramatization. Borchmeyer rightly points out that Nietzsche could have known of Wagner's move towards Christianity even in his first visits to Tribschen (and that was back in 1868).[120] Thomas Mann puts Wagner's turn to Christianity even earlier; in writing that Wagner fell prostrate at the foot of the cross Nietzsche "overlooks or wishes others to overlook the fact that the emotional atmosphere of *Tannhäuser* anticipates that of *Parsifal* and that the latter is the final, splendidly logical summing up of a life-work at bottom romantic and Christian in its spirit."[121]

It seems difficult to evade the conclusion that it was the Christianity of *Parsifal* to which Nietzsche objected and that this was *a* major cause if not *the* major cause of the break with Wagner. But the issues are rather confused because Nietzsche also criticized *Parsifal* for its Schopenhauerianism, and according to Magee this was his primary objection to the work.[122] It is certainly the case that Nietzsche attacked Wagner for his "life-denial";[123] but although he does directly attack *Parsifal* in this respect[124] he also attacks other works for "life denial."[125] Shortly I will ask whether Nietzsche's criticism of *Parsifal* for world-denial is at all accurate but for now I simply emphasize that during the final stages of the composition of the libretto and music for *Parsifal* Wagner had to some extent moved away from Schopenhauer's aesthetics (and from Nietzsche's as expressed in *Birth of Tragedy*)[126] such that

119. Nietzsche, *Human*, 210–11 (*KSA* 2:372); Nietzsche, *Anti-Christ Etc*, 276 (*KSA* 6:431–32).

120. Borchmeyer, "Wagner and Nietzsche," 338 (a point he makes in relation to his "creeping back to Christianity" in discussing Nietzsche's letter to Malwide von Meysenbug).

121. Mann, "Sufferings and Greatness," 309 (Mann, "Leiden und Größe," 14).

122. Magee, *Wagner and Philosophy*, 318–24.

123. Note also that Nietzsche wished to do away with the phenomenal/noumenal distinction that Wagner held on to (see chapter 8 above).

124. See Nietzsche, *Anti-Christ Etc*, 275–76 (*KSA* 6:430–31).

125. So in ibid., 240 (*KSA* 6:20–21 [4]), he points to Wagner's changing the Feuerbach ending of *Götterdämmerung* (1856) to the Schopenhauerian ending (1856). "Brünnhilde, who, according to the old conception, was to say goodbye with a song in honour of free love, leaving the world to the hope of a socialist utopia where 'all will be well', is now given something else to do. She has to study Schopenhauer first; she has to set the fourth book of the *World as Will and Representation* to verse." It is this fourth book that concerns the denial of the will.

126. Nietzsche was to dissociate himself from this his early "Schopenhauerian" work.

by 1880 he could write that music is "a world-redeeming birth of the divine dogma from the nullity of the phenomenal world itself."[127]

What then were the Christian issues that drove a wedge between Nietzsche and Wagner? The first concerns the assessment of the Jesus himself. In *Human All Too Human* Volume II Part Two ("The Wanderer and His Shadow") Nietzsche placed Socrates above Jesus.[128] Although Wagner does not explicitly reverse this, he does stress in *Religion and Art*, responding to the "doctrine of the Brahmins," that in the Christian religion the "founder was not wise, but divine."[129] This could be seen as an implied criticism of Nietzsche's placing Socrates above Christ.[130]

The second issue, and this is explicit in the writings, is Nietzsche's well-known scorn towards the "savior" Jesus. In the context of criticizing Wagner he speaks of "a god who truly would be a god for the sick, a *savior* ("einen Gott, der ganz eigentlich ein Gott für Kranke, ein *Heiland* ist . . .").[131] And, of course, Jesus is sometimes referred to as the "Heiland" in *Parsifal*,[132] the most frequent term used being "Erlöser" ("redeemer").[133] And whereas in the earlier works the redeemer or savior is a human being, usually a woman,[134] in *Parsifal*, his crowning achievement, the redeemer and savior is Jesus Christ himself.

127. *PW* 6:223 (modified translation); *GSD* 10:222; *JA* 10:129. See chapter 11 below for further discussion of these words from *Religion and Art* (1880).

128. Nietzsche, *Human*, 330–31: "The founder of Christianity was, as goes without saying, not without the gravest shortcomings and prejudices in his knowledge of the human soul" (*KSA* 2:589: "Der Stifter des Christenthums war, wie es sich von selber versteht, als Kenner der menschlichen Seelen nicht ohne die grössten Mängel und Voreingenommenheiten . . ." [Der Wanderer, 83]). See also Nietzsche, *Human*, 332: "Socrates excels the founder of Christianity in being able to be serious cheerfully and in possessing that *wisdom full of roguishness* that constitutes the finest state of the human soul. And he also possessed the finer intellect" (*KSA* 2:592: "Vor dem Stifter des Christenthums hat Sokrates die fröhliche Art des Ernstes und jene *Weisheit voller Schelmenstreiche* voraus, welche, den besten Seelenzustand des Menschen ausmacht. Ueberdiess hatte er den grösseren Verstand" [Der Wanderer, 86]).

129. *PW* 6:214; *JA* 10:119; *GSD* 10:213: "Ihr Gründer war nicht weise, sondern göttlich."

130. See Ellis in *PW* 6:214 n.

131. Nietzsche, *Anti-Christ Etc*, 272 (*KSA* 6:426).

132. Note the two crucial instances in Act III (*WagPS* 194–97). For its use in the Luther Bible see *BBH-K* 394.

133. See the discussion in chapter 7 above on the terms "redeemer," "to redeem," and "redemption."

134. All the works of the Wagnerian canon, with the exception of *Die Meistersinger* (the one non-mythical work) and *Parsifal*, have a female "redeemer figure": Senta, Elisabeth, Elsa, Brünnhilde, Isolde. The figures of Elisabeth, Isolde, and Brünnhilde are especially striking. To some extent there were modeled on Wagner's sister Rosalie,

A third reason Nietzsche despised *Parsifal* was because he saw it as world-denying, something he saw as the Christian flavor of the work. But there is a double misunderstanding here. First, as we saw in chapters 5 and 7 above, it is by no means clear that *Parsifal* is so "world-denying" and secondly it is by no means clear that "world-denial" is the essence of Christianity! So the following attack on *Parsifal* is really a gross misunderstanding. He describes is as "a work of malice, of vindictiveness, of a secret poisoning of the presuppositions of life, a *bad* work.—The preaching of chastity remains an incitement to perversion: I despise anyone who does not regard *Parsifal* as an attempt to assassinate ethics."[135] See also Nietzsche's critique of *Parsifal* in the opening of the third essay "What is the Meaning of Ascetic Ideals?" in *Genealogy of Morals*. Nietzsche finds a contradiction between Wagner's play *Luthers Hochzeit* (characterized by "sensuality"; "Sinnlichkeit") and *Parsifal* (characterized by "chastity"; "Keuschheit").[136] Whereas Wagner used to follow Feuerbach's "dictum of 'healthy sensuality'" ("Wort von der 'gesunden Sinnlichkeit'") Wagner has now finally learned "*something different*": "reversion, conversion, denial, Christianity" ("Umkehr, Bekehrung, Verneinung, Christenthum"), even invoking the "Redeemer's blood."[137]

Such were Nietzsche's objections to the Christian nature of *Parsifal*. Some of these issues arose during Wagner's life as can be seen in Nietzsche's *Human All Too Human* and in Wagner's various responses.[138] But most of

---

considered a saintly figure by both her mother and Wagner. Not only was she saintly but she suffered greatly (she died in childbirth in 1837). Her mother wrote to Wagner: "Rosalie was an angel who was too pure to go to a better world without first being reconciled with you." Wagner himself wrote to his sister Cäcilie: "It was for you all that poor Rosalie suffered" (quoted in Köhler, *Titans*, 29). Köhler adds that when he was writing "his angel had been raised to the level of an inexhaustible archetype who was to inspire him both in real life and in the world of his imagination" (ibid., 29–30). Whereas he felt his mother and sisters had abandoned him, Rosalie remained loyal. Not only did she become a model for the redeeming women of his operas; perhaps she also became a Sieglinde figure to his Siegmund (Siegmund was rejected by all). Note also that he wrote: "you remain my angel, my good, my only Rosalie! Remain so for ever!" (letter of 11 December 1833; quoted in ibid., 30).

135. Nietzsche, *Anti-Christ Etc*, 276 (*KSA* 6:431: "[D]er Parsifal ist ein Werk der Tücke, der Rachsucht, der heimlichen Giftmischerei gegen die Voraussetzungen des Lebens, ein *schlechtes* Werk.—Die Predigt der Keuschheit bleibt eine Aufreizung zur Widernatur: ich verachte Jedermann, der den Parsifal nicht als Attentat auf die Sittlichkeit empfindet." I have discussed the relation of *Parsifal* to chastity and sex in chapter 7 above.

136. Nietzsche, *Genealogy*, 73–74; *KSA* 5:340–41.

137. Nietzsche, *Genealogy*, 74–75; *KSA* 5:342–43.

138. One of these, *Public and Popularity* (*PW* 6:51–81; *GSD* 10:61–90), has been described as "less a statement of aesthetic principles than a voluble invective against his disloyal friend Nietzsche" (Wapnewski, "Literary Works," 93).

Nietzsche's attacks on Wagner's Christianity were to occur after the composer's death.

In addition to the issue of Christianity (and those of "Schopenhauerianism" and "onanism") there were other subsidiary reasons for the break up. First, and this is partly related to Wagner's view of Christianity, is his anti-Judaism and antisemitism. Nietzsche's own views on these issues were complex. Nietzsche divided Jewish history into three periods: the period of the Old Testament, the period of the Second Temple, and the Judaism in the diaspora. He admired the first for its grandeur and third for its rejection of Christianity. The second he despised because of what he perceived as the "slave morality" that led to Christianity.[139] An interesting trace of this can be found in *Nietzsche contra Wagner*: "It was only in the music of Handel that there sounded the best that the soul of Luther and his like contained, the Jewish-heroic impulse that gave the Reformation the character of greatness—the old Testament made into music, *not* the New."[140] By contrast, Wagner did not appreciate the "Jehovah worship" of Handel's oratorios.[141] According to Köhler, a further "Jewish" issue on which they disagreed regarded Paul Rée, a Jewish friend of Nietzsche whom Wagner disliked.[142]

A second additional reason for the rift is that Nietzsche disliked the theatre and one can discern his growing distrust of Wagner, the "Schauspieler" ("play-actor").[143] It is significant that Nietzsche fell in love with *Tristan und Isolde* through the piano reduction and, as Magee highlights, Nietzsche only knew Greek tragedy by *reading* the texts, not by experiencing them in the theatre.[144] Such a view is diametrically opposed to Wagner's view in *Art and Revolution* that what the dramatist creates "becomes an Art-work only

---

139. Yovel, "Nietzsche contra Wagner," 134. For a wider discussion on his complex attitude to Jews and Judaism see Golomb, *Nietzsche and Jewish Culture*.

140. Nietzsche, *Anti-Christ Etc*, 270 (*KSA* 6:423: "Erst in Händel's Musik erklang das Beste aus Luther's und seiner Verwandten Seele, der jüdisch-heroische Zug, welcher der Reformation einen Zug der Grösse gab—das alte Testament Musik geworden, *nicht* das neue"). Note, however, that Nietzsche does praise Dutch Christian art.

141. *CD* 17 February 1876.

142. Köhler, *Nietzsche and Wagner*, 126–27. Köhler quotes from Paul Heinrich Widemann, a friend of Köselitz and early admirer of Nietzsche, who claimed his "relationship with Rée, who was opposed to what Bayreuth stood for, cast a shadow over his relationship with Wagner from the beginning and led to its eventual break-up" (132–33).

143. This also led him to view Wagner as "the sorcerer" ("Der Zauberer"). See *KSA* 4:313–20 and Burnham and Jesinghausen, *Zarathustra*, 175. Zarathustra addresses "the sorcerer" as the "Schauspieler" (*KSA* 4:317).

144. On opportunities to experience Greek tragedy in the theatre in nineteenth century Germany (and elsewhere), see MacIntosh, "Tragedy."

when it enters into open life and a work of dramatic art can only enter life through the theatre."[145]

A third additional reason for the rift (and I admit that this is speculative) is that Amfortas' terrible wound resulting from the sexual encounter with Kundry may have caused Nietzsche to reflect on his own "wound." It may be that the theory that he contracted syphilis as a result of visiting a brothel in Cologne can be discounted[146] but he did have sexual encounters that may have added to his sense of "trauma."

I think this review of Nietzsche's objections to the Christian character of *Parsifal* suggests that for him what happens "on stage" cannot be simply divorced from "real life." Magee criticizes Nietzsche for this, writing that Nietzsche's objection to *Parsifal* "is rather like a militant atheist or a music critic mounting an onslaught on Bach's *St Matthew Passion* on the ground that it is saturated through and through with loathsome religious nonsense, and is for that reason a hateful work." Such a criticism "embodies a fundamental non-comprehension of what art is."[147] I can understand Magee's point. But I wonder whether the "ideology" of an artwork can be simply cast aside in this way, a point I return to in chapter 11 below.

Doctrine of God

I now come to draw together the threads regarding the view of God that can be discerned in *Parsifal* and Wagner's late writings.

The first point to make is that Wagner's understanding of God has to be related to his strong sense of "original sin," which was discussed in chapter 8 above. His strong view of sin was, as we saw, thoroughly Lutheran and the correlate of this pessimistic anthropology is a correspondingly strong view of grace, one that, as we saw in chapter 8 above, is stronger than Schopenhauer's. If Wagner had a strong view of grace one would also expect a high

---

145. *PW* 1:61 (modified); *JA* 5:305. *GSD* 3:37: "Was er schafft, wird zum Kunstwerke wirklich erst dadurch, daß es vor der Öffentlichkeit in das Leben tritt, und ein dramatisches Kunstwerk tritt nur durch das Theater in das Leben." See also the discussion in Mösch, *Weihe, Werkstatt, Wirklichkeit*, 5–6.

146. It has been held that this eventually led to his insanity. However, it is uncertain whether Nietzsche did contract syphilis. He did visit a Cologne brothel, but according to Nietzsche he did not have sex (on this episode see Young, *Nietzsche*, 55–56). According to Otto Eiser Nietzsche claimed not to have been syphilitic, a claim that Young (240) thinks ought to be taken seriously. See the letter to Wagner of 26 October 1877 (Benders and Oettermann, *Chronik*, 417–18). Young, *Nietzsche*, 559–62, argues that Nietzsche's insanity was manic-depression.

147. Magee, *Wagner and Philosophy*, 320.

Christology. We saw in chapter 6 above that some have denied that he had such a Christology and that Jesus was simply special because of his "sinless-ness." But the very fact that Jesus is the "redeemer" who saves human beings from their radical sin and their suffering does point to a higher Christology. Further he can even speak in terms of Jesus' birth as the birth of God.[148] For Wagner divinity is concentrated in the person of Jesus Christ and the "Father" tends to be bracketed out (since he is related to the "creator" and "Jewish" God). But despite this "Christo-monism"[149] the Holy Spirit also has a significant role in that he descends in the form of a dove at the end of *Parsifal*; and at the close of *Jesus of Nazareth* the Holy Spirit inspires Peter to proclaim the fulfillment of Jesus' promise and his words "give strength and inspiration to all."[150] It is also significant that Wagner chose the theme of the giving of the Holy Spirit for his 1843 work *Das Liebesmahl der Apostel*.[151]

This brings us to questions of Wagner's "Trinitarianism." One of Wagner's "orthodox" views of the Trinity can be seen in the work just mentioned, *Das Liebesmahl der Apostel*.[152] But his more adventurous discussions can be found in the sketches for *Jesus of Nazareth*. In the second section of the sketches these words are put in the mouth of Jesus: "God is the Father and the Son and the Holy Ghost: for the father begetteth the son throughout all ages, and the son begetteth again the father of the son to all eternity: this is Life and Love, this is the Holy Spirit."[153] Then a little later in the sketches, Jesus says this in the context of all people being "members of one God": "But God is the father and the son, begetting himself anew forever; in the father was the son, and in the son is the father; as, then, we are members of one body which is God, whose breath is everlasting Love, so do we never die; like as the body, which is God, never dieth, because it is the father and the son, i.e., the constant manifestment of eternal Love itself."[154]

148. See chaper 8 above.

149. See chapter 6 above.

150. *PW* 8:297; *DTB* 246.

151. The basis for the work was Acts 2:1–7 and Wagner stresses the mission to the whole world.

152. Kirsch, "Biblische Scene," 169, points to the musical theme that occurs in a different form at three points in the work, first stressing the Son (m. 28), then the Father (m. 247), and finally the Holy Spirit (m. 470).

153. *PW* 8:300. *DTB* 249: "Gott is der vater u. der sohn u. d. heilige geist: denn der vater zeuget den sohn durch alle zeiten, und der sohn zeuget wieder den vater des sohnes in alle ewigkeit: dies ist das leben, dies ist der heilige geist."

154. *PW* 8:306. *DTB* 252: "Gott aber ist der vater und der sohn, er zeuget sich immer fort neu; im vater war der sohn, und im sohne ist der vater; wie wir nun glieder des eines leibes sind, welcher gott ist und dessen hauch die ewige liebe ist, so sterben wir nie, gleichwie der leib, d.i. gott nie stirbt, da er der vater und sohn ist, das heisset: die

The other significant discussion of the Trinity is in relation to Wagner's reading of Gfrörer. Cosima records: "R. tells me a lot more about what he is reading in Gfrörer's book, which he finds of endless interest: among other things, for example, the definition of the Trinity made shortly before Christ's birth—God the Father, masculine; the Holy Ghost, feminine; the Redeemer as the world stemming from them; will, idea, and world, the world emerging from the division of the sexes."[155] Wagner takes this from the fourth chapter of the first volume of Gfrörer's work. Towards the end of the chapter Gfrörer discusses the "Jewish Trinity" ("Jüdische Dreieinigkeit") and argues that the three forms of Father, Holy Spirit, and Son were related in two possible ways. First, the Father is masculine, the Holy Spirit is feminine, and out of their sexual union comes the Son and with him the world comes into being. Wagner appears to allude to this in the above quotation. The other view is that a man-woman primordial human comes out of God, and then divides into the masculine Son and the feminine Spirit who then together procreate the world.[156] Gfrörer engages in a discussion of Christian sources[157] that speak of "heretical" "Trinitarian" views that, he argues, cannot go back to the New Testament but rather to pre-Christian Jewish views of the "Trinity."[158] He strengthens his case by discussing Jewish texts[159] and

---

stete verwirklichung der ewigen liebe selbst."

155. *CD* 6 January 1875. *CT* 6 January 1875: "Gott, der Vater, männlich; der h. Geist weiblich; der Heiland die Welt, daraus entstanden; Wille, Vorstellung und Welt, die Trennung der Geschlechte als Entstehung der Welt."

156. Gfrörer, *Geschichte I.1*, 332: "Die drei Gestalten wurden in ein eigenthümliches Verhältniß doppelter Art zu einander gesezt. Die eine Partei hielt Gott für männliches, den heil. Geist für ein weibliches Urwesen, aus deren geschlechtlicher Vereinigung der Sohn und mit ihm die Welt entstanden sey. Die andere ließ den mannweiblichen Urmenschen aus Gott strömen, und sich dann zertheilen; der Sohn war ihnen die männliche, der Geist die weibliche Hälfte, beide zusammen zeugten die Welt."

157. Among the sources discussed are the *Recognitions of Clement* 1.69; *Homilies* 16.11; Irenaeus, *Against Heresies,* 1.23.1–2; Justin, *First Apology,* 26; Tertullian, *De Anima,* 34; *Gospel of the Hebrews*; Jerome's commentaries on Isaiah (40.11; 11.2), Micah (7.6) and Matthew (24.5); Epiphanius, *Panarion* (see the references to Elxai) (Gfrörer, *Geschichte I.1*, 325–40).

158. Gfrörer, *Geschichte I.1*, 341: "Also konnten die jüdischen Mystiker, Simon, die Ebioniten, der Verfasser des Klementinen, Elxai und Andere ihre Ansichten nicht aus der Lehre Jesu geschöpft haben. Mit Einem Worte, die Juden befanden sich 3 Jahrhunderte früher in derselben Lage, wie später die christlichen Väter der nicenischen Beschlüsse."

159. I.e., 1 Enoch and Philo. He acknowledges Lawrence, *Enoch*, 43, as finding a Jewish Trinity in his introduction to the book of Enoch. This was the very first translation of the work from Ethiopic into English after its discovery at the end of the eighteenth century in Abyssinia.

finding a trajectory into the later Jewish mystical texts.[160] It is interesting
to see how much of what Gfrörer discusses coheres with Wagner's earlier
"androgeny."[161] Gfrörer writes that the highest God of Jewish mysticism is
a "man-woman double being" ("ein mannweibliches Doppelwesen") that
begets the Son.[162] He then refers to the other tradition whereby out of the
highest original being ("höchste[s] Urwesen") came "Adam Kadmon," the
primordial male-female Adam, who then split into the son and the female
spirit.[163] Such a view he finds in Epiphanius, who writes of the "Ossaeans"
whose prophet Elxai tells of how the Son and Spirit are both of the same
size.[164]

Some of these ideas may have made their way into Wagner's final
libretto (completed 1877) although it is difficult to find clear traces. But we
know that Gfrörer's idea of "God the Father, masculine; the Holy Ghost,
feminine; the Redeemer as the world stemming from them" was interpreted
by Wagner in Schopenhauerian terms, "will, idea, and world, the world
emerging from the division of the sexes."[165] This may be linked in some
way to some of the male/female symbolism in *Parsifal,* particularly the way
"masculine" spear is brought together with the feminine "grail" at the end
of the drama.[166] Hence the final "Erlösung dem Erlöser" may refer to some
extent to the bringing together of the masculine and feminine and over-
coming the "male" principle of the grail community.[167] This would correspond to the re-establishment of the androgynous principle found in Plato's
Symposium.[168]

160. Gfrörer, *Geschichte I.1*, 344–52, discusses sections of two tractates of the Zohar,
Idra Suta, and Idra Rabba.

161. See chapter 7 above.

162. Gfrörer, *Geschichte I.1*, 334. He then speaks of the male as the father, the female as the mother, and the son as the offspring. He finds this reflected in the *Gospel
of the Hebrews,* which refers to the holy spirit as the mother of Jesus (cf. Hennecke,
Schneemelcher, and Wilson, eds., *New Testament Apocrypha I,* 164). Since the idea of
the spirit as mother of Jesus cannot go back to Christian views, he relates it back to
Jewish mysticism.

163. Gfrörer, *Geschichte I.1*, 337.

164. For a convenient translation of the passage (19.4.1–2) see Amidon, *Epiphanius
Panarion,* 57.

165. *CD* 6 January 1875, quoted above.

166. Cf. Kurt Hübner, "Meditationen," 140–41; Borchmeyer, "Erlösung und
Apokatastasis," 320–21.

167. Note that the final chorus, although bringing together male and female voice,
is *not* "the only mixed chorus in the entire work," as Nattiez, *Wagner Androgyne,* 171,
asserts. See I.1204–27; 1404–9; 1440–45.

168. This work was central for Wagner. See, e.g., *CD* 9 April 1870: "R. places this

As a final point about the "doctrine of God," I refer to Cosima's entry for 24 January 1878. Regarding the "Godhead," Cosima says: "'I must believe in it—my unworthiness and my happiness lead me to believe.' He: 'The first part, your unworthiness, you can cross out; Godhead is Nature, the will which seeks salvation and, to quote Darwin, selects the strongest to bring this salvation about.'"[169] This exchange, which at first seems rather obscure, reveals quite a lot about both Richard and Cosima. First Cosima's faith seems very much linked to her sense of guilt ("unworthiness"). Secondly, Wagner can accept that her happiness can lead her to believe, but adds something that looks almost like pantheism: "Godhead is Nature." Nature is then related to the (world) "will" and the key sense in which this world-will is manifest is in Jesus who brings salvation. Bringing together Darwin and Schopenhauer in this way later finds echoes in the work of Teilhard de Chardin and others who have related Christology to evolutionary thought.[170]

Redemption

Much of this work has concerned redemption but here I want to draw some loose ends together, in particular three aspects: first, the redemption of the whole creation; secondly, the redemption without resurrection; thirdly, the question of future eschatology.

After Kundry's baptism we are led straight into the "Good Friday magic" ("Karfreitagszauber"). This passage expresses the renewal of creation through the death of Christ and is fully in line with Rom 8:21.[171] Further, Wagner may be intensifying Romans 8 by making a more organic connection between the redemption of the human being and the redemption of the created order. To explain how, I go back to Schopenhauer. Since the world is my representation and there is a correspondence between subject and object, then what happens to the subject finds a correlate in the object. Schopenhauer's solution was to deny the will such that we get to the position of no will, no representation, no world.[172] But Wagner's version, as we

---

work above everything else: 'In Shakespeare we see Nature as it is, here we have the artistic awareness of the benefactor added; what would the world know of redeeming beauty without Plato?'"

169. *CD* 24 January 1878. The reference is probably to *On the Origin of Species*, published in German translation in 1863.

170. See the summary of Hendry, "Christology," 62–63.

171. See Borchmeyer, *Theory and Theatre*, 395; Kurt Hübner, "Meditationen," 141.

172. Seelig, "Leben," 105.

saw in chapter 8 above, was not to deny the will but possibly even to affirm it. Further, if Wagner believed that the human person was renewed then if the world is their representation that also must be renewed. Therefore the created order is transformed after Parsifal has been installed in his new office and, more significantly, after Kundry has been baptized. In fact the "Good Friday Magic" that "sings" of the new creation follows on directly from Kundry's re-birth of baptism.

This bring me to the striking "mood" of redemption presented in *Parsifal*. In chapter 7 I discussed part of Wagner's letter to Ludwig on 14 April 1865. I want to focus on one aspect of this remarkable letter: the relationship of suffering to the renewal of nature:

> Today is Good Friday again!—O, blessèd day! Most deeply portentous day in the world! Day of redemption! God's suffering!! Who can grasp the enormity of it? . . . A warm and sunny Good Friday, with its mood of sacred solemnity, once inspired me with the idea of writing 'Parzival': since then it has lived on within me and prospered, like a child in its mother's womb. With each Good Friday it grows a year older, and I then celebrate the day of its conception, knowing that its birthday will follow one day . . . I recalled the sunny Good Friday of that first conception . . . the birds were singing, the first flowers gazed up at me . . .[173]

In what I have quoted[174] Wagner here brings together the suffering of Good Friday and the idea of the regeneration of nature in spring. "At the core of *Parsifal* is the overpowering paradox that allows the rite of spring and the divine agony to co-exist in a single day."[175] This is one of the distinctive features of *Parsifal* and determines the theological mood of much of the work. But this idea is also enigmatic especially since Wagner makes this direct link between "God's suffering" on Good Friday and the renewal of nature.

This brings me to the second issue: *Parsifal* appears to offer a redemption without a resurrection. Although there is no specific denial of resurrection, the absence of the resurrection is telling and suggests that this was not an integral part of Wagner's theology of redemption. This could present a puzzle especially for the Christian theologian since for the New Testament witnesses resurrection is usually fully integrated into redemption. Why then does Wagner omit the resurrection?

---

173. *SL* 641–42; Bauer, *Richard Wagner: Briefe*, 432–33; *KB* 1:82.
174. Key elements have been omitted. See the discussion of them in chapter 7.
175. Berlowitz and de Fontenay, "Thoughts," 31.

The first reason may be simply a dramatic consideration. His sketches for *Jesus of Nazareth*, as we saw, ended with the death of Jesus and the giving of the Holy Spirit. The story functions as a sort of tragedy;[176] this is also how he understood John's Gospel.[177] Perhaps we have a link to Bach's St. Matthew and St. John passions (if they can be considered "tragedies") which, by focusing on the death of Christ, have their extraordinary power. Wagner therefore may have omitted the resurrection in that it destroys the "drama." However, there is in addition to the "tragedy" another crucial element: in *Jesus of Nazareth* the disciples have a new mission. "Peter feels himself inspired with the Holy Spirit: in high enthusiasm he proclaims the fulfilment of Jesus' promise: his words give strength and inspiration to all; he addresses the people,—whoever hears him, presses forward to demand baptism (reception into the community).—The end.—"[178] As in *Parsifal* one can say Jesus lives in them through his death.[179]

A second reason for omitting the resurrection is a more theological consideration. For Wagner, once Jesus had died, all that was necessary for atonement of sin and renewal of creation was achieved; a resurrection was theologically unnecessary. Once Jesus dies we read in *Jesus of Nazareth* "He hath fulfilled" ("er hat vollendet").[180] One can compare this to John 19:30: "It is finished" ("Es ist vollbracht").[181]

A third reason for omitting the resurrection concerns the idea that the redeemer figure of *Parsifal* is more mythical than the redeemer of the New Testament and therefore points to a more inner worldly entity. Kurt Hübner

176. *My Life* 387; *Mein Leben* 1:400.

177. See Cosima's entry for 11 February 1875: "In the evening we read Gfrörer with much interest, his interpretation of the Gospel of Saint John very intelligent and engrossing. How utterly sublime the utterances of our Saviour!—When I talk to R. about honorable deaths, he says: 'It is remarkable how frequently they occur; yet one wonders why the death of the Saviour is so incomparably moving, why no martyr's death comes anywhere near it. Probably because he connected his death with the founding of a religion, knowing that only through dying could he do anything for mankind. That is tragedy *par excellence*—that even if he had been acknowledged, Christ could not have prevailed, since the Jews would have demanded political action from him, and unacknowledged, all that remained to him was death."

178. *PW* 8:297. *DTB* 246: "Petrus fühlt sich vom heiligen geist gestärkt: er verkündet in hohem enthusiasmus die erfüllung von Jesus' verheissung; seine wort stärkt und begeistert alles; er redet das volk an,—wer ihn hört, drängt sich hinzu und begehrt die taufe (aufnahme in die Gemeinde.)—Schluss.—"

179. *WagPS* 144–45: "His body, that he gave us strength to purge our sin, lives in us through His death" ("Der Leib, den er zur Sühn' uns bot, er lebt in uns durch seinen Tod").

180. *PW* 8:297; *DTB* 246.

181. See Gfrörer, *Geschichte III*, 254, discussed below.

argues that the redeemer is fully mythical and therefore the redeemer is a *fully* inner worldly figure.[182] He argues that the mythical nature of the redeemer is seen in the fact that the only person to encounter him directly is Kundry who, he argues, belongs to neither space nor time.[183] However, I think the situation is rather more complex. It is precisely *through* Kundry's laughing at Christ that she is *then* condemned to fly through space and time as the "eternal Jew"[184] and she flies both forwards and backwards (primeval witch, Herodias!) in time. But although Hübner's position is rather too extreme there is no doubt that the redeemer of *Parsifal* is more mythical than the redeemer as witnessed to in the New Testament.[185]

A fourth reason for omitting the resurrection is biblical criticism. I mentioned above (and in chapter 2) that Wagner had read Strauß's *Das Leben Jesu* and that this work may have influenced Wagner in omitting the resurrection in *Jesus of Nazareth*. But one does wonder how deep this influence was on *Jesus of Nazareth* and, in view of Wagner's later opposition to Strauß, how much it influenced *Parsifal*? But although Strauß was not congenial to him in his later years, Gfrörer was. Cosima tells us: "R. comes to talk about Renan's and Gfrörer's interpretation of the Resurrection, prefers that of the latter, whom he finds the most sensitive of writers in his handling of religious matters. He observes that one cannot overestimate the burning glow of ecstasy at times when a new religion is emerging."[186] Renan essentially wished to strip the Gospels of any "supernatural elements"[187] and, as Schweitzer puts it, *La Vie de Jésus* was written "by one to whom the New Testament was to the last something foreign."[188] But Gfrörer's view of the resurrection is not much better in that although he is sure that Jesus did appear to the disciples after his crucifixion, he is not so sure that Jesus actu-

---

182. Cf. Kurt Hübner, "Meditationen," 135.

183. Ibid., 141: "Es spielt sich also in einem mythischen Raum und einer mythischen Zeit ab, es ist nirgendwo und nirgendwann; und so ist auch Kundry, die dem Erlöser als einzige der im *Parsifal* auftretenden Personen begegnet ist, eine in keiner Zeit und in keinem Raum lokalisierbare Gestalt."

184. This seems to be clear from Kundry's words in Act II: "I saw Him . . . Him . . . and laughed . . . His gaze fell upon me! Now I seek Him from world to world to meet Him once again" (*WagPS* 198–99).

185. One should note, however, Wagner's interest in the historical Jesus. See, e.g., his letter to Hans von Wolzogen (17 January 1880) where he speaks of the "incomparably and sublimely simple and true redeemer who appears to us in the historically intelligible figure of Jesus of Nazareth" ("unvergleichlich erhaben einfache Erlöser in der historisch erfaßbaren Gestalt des Jesus von Nazareth").

186. *CD* 3 September 1880.

187. Colin Brown, *Jesus in European Protestant Thought*, 236.

188. Schweitzer, *Quest*, 192.

ally died on the cross[189] and even suggests that Jesus, after reviving from his ordeal on the cross, became a hermit or joined the Essenes.[190] But it is the essence of Gfrörer's *theological* view that I imagine struck Wagner: that Jesus saw his mission as completed as he passed away on the cross (cf. John 19:30: "It is finished"); whatever did transpire (resuscitation) was unexpected and did not belong to his plans.[191]

But whatever Wagner's particular view was of the resurrection (and he was clearly skeptical) it is important to stress that in both the sketches for *Jesus of Nazareth* and in *Parsifal* Jesus does "live on" in a way he does *not* in Strauß's book or in the works of Renan or Gfrörer. There may be no "resurrection" for Wagner in the orthodox Christian sense but one gets the impression of a savior who does live on in the community he leaves behind[192] even if, as we have seen, he lives in them "through his death."[193] Further, the sublime music at the end of *Parsifal* does seem to imply a sense of resurrection, certainly something Domingo experiences when he sings the title role: "I feel as if God is about to come on stage, to bless and lift us all up higher, to a kind of Resurrection."[194] Such a sentiment is perhaps not too far away from Wagner's own thinking. It is perhaps significant that, as we saw in chapter 7 above, at a climactic point in *Religion and Art* Wagner quotes Job 19:25: "I know that my redeemer liveth!"[195]

Finally, this brings us to the question whether Wagner's view of redemption is "eschatological" and if so in what sense. The term "eschatology," the "doctrine of the last things," traditionally concerned death, the second coming of Christ, resurrection of the dead, judgement, heaven, and hell. The figure who came to dominate discussion of Jesus' teaching on eschatology was C. H. Weisse, the "direct continuator of Strauss,"[196] who removed eschatology from Jesus' teaching.[197]

189. Gfrörer, *Geschichte III*, 251–52.

190. Ibid., 254–55.

191. Ibid., 254: "Nur so viel scheint mir außer zweifel, daß der Herr Seine Sendung mit dem Verscheiden am Kreuze für vollendet hielt. Was darüber hinaus lag, war Ihm selbst unerwartet, und gehörte nicht zu seinem Plane."

192. For Strauß's discussion of the resurrection see Strauß, *Leben Jesu*, 590–663 (Strauss, *Life*, 709–44).

193. *WagPS* 144–45.

194. Matheopoulos, *Domingo*, 215.

195. *PW* 6:250; *GSD* 10:251; *JA* 10:160.

196. Schweitzer, *Quest*, 122.

197. This was to change after Wagner's death. See ibid., 136: "The whole struggle over eschatology is nothing else than a gradual elimination of Weisse's ideas. It was only with Johannes Weiss that theology escaped from the influence of Christian Hermann

Of the issues of traditional eschatological, the only one that would appear to interest Wagner was death! As we saw in chapter 2 above, it is likely that he was influenced by Weisse in his early life and in the 1840s Feuerbach pushed him in a decisive non-eschatological direction,[198] possibly influencing the sketches for *Jesus of Nazareth*.[199] Such influence is also seen strikingly in *Walküre* Act II where Siegmund decisively rejects the hope of immortality.[200] However, his view of eschatology is complicated by the fact that he did perceive that there is an aspect of the human person that is "eternal," something he no doubt found in Schopenhauer's *World as Will and Representation* and more specifically in his essay "On the Doctrine of the Indestructability of our True Nature by Death."[201] So although the phenomenal body may die (including the intellect since this depends on the brain functions), the thing-in-itself is not subject to time and hence remains.

A more orthodox understanding of "life after death" can be found in his criticism of Judaism as a purely "this-worldly religion." He writes in *Know Thyself*: "Not into the remotest contact is [the Jew] brought with the religion of any of the civilised nations; for in truth he has no religion at all—merely the belief in certain promises of his god which in nowise extend to a life beyond this temporal life of his, as in every true religion, but simply to this present life on earth, whereon his race is certainly ensured dominion over all that lives and lives not."[202] Whatever one may think of these comments, it is the case that most modern forms of Judaism have little clear hope of a future life, even though there are texts in the Hebrew Bible that

---

Weisse."

198. See Feuerbach, *Death and Immortality*.

199. See *PW* 8:313: "The last ascension of the individual life into the life of the whole, is Death, which is the last and most definite upheaval of egoism. The plant grows from *one* germ, which is itself: each evolution of the plant is a manifolding of itself in bloom and seed, and this process of life is a ceaseless progress unto death. Its death is the self-offering of every creature in favour of the maintenance and enrichment of the whole: the creature that fulfils this offering with consciousness, by attuning its free will to the necessity of this offering, becomes a co-creator,—in that it further devotes its free will to the greatest possible moral import of the sacrifice, however, it becomes God himself" (*DTB* 255). However, note the immortality in *PW* 8:306; *DTB* 252, quoted above.

200. *WagRS* 161–62.

201. *PP* 267–82. We know from *CD* 14 June 1880 that he read to Cosima and others the "Short concluding Diversion in the Form and of Dialogue" (279–82). "In the evening R. reads to us Schopenhauer's dialogue about death and life after death. Our starting point had been the sinners who fear Hell (Pascal), whereas a character like Goethe knows nothing of such things!" See the discussion of this entry in chapter 11 below.

202. *PW* 6:271; *GSD* 10:271.

point to a life beyond this one.[203] Wagner's future hope is clearly expressed as Amfortas calls on his deceased father (*WagPS* 230–33):

O you in divine radiance	O! Der du jetzt in göttlichen Glanz
do behold the Redeemer's very self,	den Erlöser selbst erschaust,
entreat of Him that His holy blood,	erflehe von ihm, daß sein heiliges Blut,
if once more today His blessing	wenn noch einmal heut' sein *Segen*
shall revive these my brothers,	die Brüder soll erquicken,
as it gives them new life	wie ihnen neues *Leben*
may at last grant me death!	mir endlich spende den Tod!

If then Titurel attains "paradise," the same is also available for the knights.[204] And although the earlier "Good Friday Magic" ("Karfreitagszauber") is placed in a "mythical present," his hope for a future redeemed creation clearly belongs to a world beyond this one. In fact, he found it difficult to discern anything of authentic Christianity in the present world: "For me Christianity has not yet arrived, and I am like the early Christians, awaiting Christ's return."[205] Perhaps this is where Wagner's "eschatology" is really to be found.

Church and Sacraments

This now brings me to Wagner's view of the church and the related issues of the sacraments of baptism and Holy Communion. We saw in chapter 2 above that as a teenager Wagner lost respect for the clergyman who led his confirmation classes and subsequently often "pre-judged" the clergy.[206] His

---

203. See, e.g., Pss 73:24; 49:15; Isa 26:19; Dan 12:1–2.

204. Cf. what Wolfram (471.1–14) writes about those appointed to the gral (*WolPH* 240): "When they die here in this world, Paradise is theirs in the next."

205. *CD* 15 July 1879.

206. For example, on his visit to London in 1839 (after fleeing Riga) he managed to get into the "strangers' gallery" of the House of Lords. He writes: "The Bishop of London, whom I had also had the chance to hear on this occasion, was the only one among these men whose tone and bearing made an unpleasant impresssion, but possibly this was because of my prejudice against the clergy in general" (*My Life* 167). The bishop was Charles James Blomfield (1786–1857; see *ODCC* 180). The others he heard were Lord Melbourne, leader of the Whigs and prime minister (1834 and 1835–41), and the Duke of Wellington.

main target was the Catholic Church, the "universal pest,"[207] and sometimes he showed utter contempt for her priests.[208] In his letter to Constantin Frantz (14 July 1879) he berates the Catholic Church for exploiting feudalism (he contrasts the fight of the German nation at the time of the Reformation and speaks warmly of the Huguenots). He claims the church has in fact "ruined" Christianity and since religion cannot "guide us along the right path" the only hope is revelation; "Jesus Christ must first be recognized and imitated by us"[209] and must be rescued from the church and religion.[210] But he did hold to the possibility of an "ideal Church" and sometimes the Protestant Church could almost live up to this.[211]

One problem he perceives in having an established church is that Christianity "in its pure form was too fragile to gain ground" and ended up "accommodating itself to the world." "[T]he saviour had no community in the true sense of the word" and "allowed himself to be crucified for the few who committed themselves to him. 'This is sublime,' R. exclaims. . . . R. concluded our evening conversation with the remark that *Parsifal* ought certainly to be his final work, since in these Knights of the Grail he has given

207. *CD* 11 November 1878.

208. See *CD* 23 April 1882 (he was in Venice at the time): "R. asks what priest are for; they are supposed to represent Christianity. Judas has triumphed, he says sorrowfully, and he speaks of Christianity, the relation of man to man—this will be his last work, he says." The choice of the names "Fafner" and "Fasolt" for the giants (with whom the gods were trapped by making contracts) may be a play on "faseln" ("to babble") and "Pfaffen" (priest). See Brearley, "Hitler and Wagner," 20 n. 62. Note that Wolfram's *Parzival* sometimes has an exalted view of priest from which Wagner would no doubt want to distance himself. So in book 9 Trevrizent exhorts Parzival to place his trust in the clergy: "Nothing you see on earth is like a priest. His lips pronounce the Passion that nullifies our damnation" (*WolPH* 255).

209. *SL* 894.

210. There are many cases when he expresses this view. See, e.g., *CD* 13 January 1880 where he despairs that people confuse "church" ("das Kirchliche") with "Christianity" (Christentum).

211. See Cosima's entry for 9–13 December 1873 (these days are entered as one block): "Recalled Fidi's baptism with emotion, R. says he will never forget the occasion, how beautiful, how comforting it had been; how earnest the faces of the people who were present—only in a common faith can people come together like that. Religion is a *bond*, one cannot have religion by oneself." A similar appreciation of "religion" is expressed earlier in the entry: "R. earnestly reproached Malwide for not having her ward baptized. This was not right, he said, not everyone could fashion his religion for himself, and particularly in childhood one must have a feeling of cohesion. Nor should one be left to choose; rather, it should be possible to say, 'You have been christened, you belong through baptism to Christ, now unite yourself once more with him through Holy Communion.' Christening and Communion are indispensable, he said. No amount of knowledge can ever approach the effect of the latter."

expression to his idea of a community."[212] If we relate this "community" to the "church," the drama *Parsifal* actually presents what could be called a "high" view of the "church": redemption on earth can only be achieved by the followers of Christ being faithful to their calling.[213] This is achieved through the preservation of the grail and in Parsifal's "faithfulness" and recovery of the spear. Beckett comments: "The idea that Christ's continuing presence in the world depends, in some sense, upon Christian fidelity is a sound intuition (the church as the body of Christ is an orthodox formulation of it)."[214]

This brings me to the issue of the scope of the "ideal church." His view in the sketches for *Jesus of Nazareth* is that all are members of the "body of God"[215] and within this body there is freedom of will.[216] But nevertheless there is a "community" to which people are invited to join through baptism.[217] In the later Wagner there is a *general* sense in which all are members of the body of God in the sense that there is a correspondence between the suffering of Christ and the suffering of every creature. But, as we saw in chapter 5 above, there is a *special* relationship between the suffering of Christ and of those in the community. Further, as we saw in chapter 8 above, Wagner's thought seems to be more predestinarian (with a stronger emphasis on "sin" and "conversion") in *Parsifal* and in writings such as *Religion and Art*, and this is related to his discovery of Schopenhauer and to his increasing interest in Luther.

Wagner's more positive comments on the church tend to be found in his later life and, together with this, is a stress on the centrality of the sacraments; and of course one needed the church and her priests to administer these. We have already seen how moved he was at Siegfried's baptism.[218] He thought Communion "without doubt the most beautiful sacrament of

212. *CD* 5 April 1882 (the Wednesday of Holy Week).

213. Beckett, *Parsifal*, 140.

214. Ibid.

215. *PW* 8:308; *DTB* 252. Further, "the temple of God is mankind" (*PW* 8:309; *DTB* 253).

216. *PW* 8:308 (*DTB* 252–53): "All men are members of the body of God: each moveth for itself, according to free will; if they strive against each other, however, the body will fall sick, and every several member sicken: but if each one doth bear, support and help the other, the whole body will bloom with living health. This law of life and health ye receive through Love, and whoso keepeth it, what man shall call him slave? for he giveth himself thereby both life and health: but life is freedom, sickness is bondage: Love therefore is the free will of life."

217. *PW* 8:297; *DTB* 246.

218. Also Kundry's baptism in Act III (whereby she dies with Christ) is a fundamental turning point for the final stage of the drama.

Christian worship!"[219] Also, Wagner was "profoundly touched" in receiving Communion with Cosima after she converted to the Protestant faith.[220] It is also striking that the grail scenes are the center pieces of Acts I and III.[221] I discussed the relationship of these grail scenes to Wagner's understanding of the Eucharist in chapter 5 above. An additional element to mention here is that for Wagner the "meal" aspect of Communion was important, something reflected in these grail scenes[222] and in comments he made after visiting St. Mark's cathedral in Venice: "Much did R. say about the need to preserve churches as houses for the poor, places in which love feasts would be celebrated, but without the false pomp of the clerics."[223] It may be that Wagner was also influenced by Thomas à Kempis on the Communion. Cosima certainly treasured his *Imitation of Christ*[224] and there is a little evidence that Wagner had read some of it.[225] There are some striking comments about the Communion in Thomas' work, many of which cohere with the view of Communion in *Parsifal*. These include the idea of union with God in love, eating the bread of immortality, and that the union with Christ in Communion gives not only new spiritual strength but also strengthens the weak body.[226] We know that Cosima certainly sided with Luther in his

---

219. See his letter to Mathilde Wesendonck of 29–30 May 1859 (*SL* 459). Golther, *Mathilde Wesendonk*, 147: "offenbar dem schönsten Sacramente des christlichen Cultus!" Note also the importance placed on Communion in *BB* 202: "If Christ for us is in the end even still merely a most noble poetic fiction, then it is at the same time more realizable than any other poetic ideal,—in the daily communion with wine and bread." The comments about the "noble poetic fiction" have to be placed alongside his comments on the historical Jesus of Nazareth and the significance of Jesus' sacrificial death.

220. See chapter 12 below.

221. On Act I see Cosima's entry for 11 August 1877 (quoted in chapter 11 below).

222. See Cosimas' entry for 16 January 1871: "we come to the subject of the Last Supper and the profound significance of the community *meal*; whereas now the priest performs it, and subtlety has turned bread into wafers, etc."

223. *CD* 25 April 1882.

224. See her entries for 8 June and 17 July 1879.

225. Her entry for 14 January 1881 includes recommending the work to her husband who responds "I am in the clutches of the Devil of art!" However, around four months later we find Wagner quoting him: "Over coffee R. quoted Thomas a Kempis' saying, 'To suffer this, one must be God,' and he thought it right to see godlike qualities in the sufferings of humiliation" (*CD* 20 May 1881). It is also worth adding that for Wagner union with Christ is related to being *imitators* of Christ (cf. Thomas à Kempis, *The Imitation of Christ*). See *Religion and Art* (*PW* 6:214; *GSD* 10:213; *JA* 10:119): "To believe in him, meant to emulate him (ihm nacheifern); to hope for redemption, to strive for union with him." This though was written a year earlier (1880) but at least shows Wagner could have some sympathy with Thomas.

226. See Mertens, "Wagners Gral," 103–4.

controversy with Zwingli over the real presence;[227] it seems highly likely that her husband would adopt the same position.

The Grail

Discussion of the grail has arisen in previous chapters but now I focus on how Wagner developed the grail traditions in a Christian direction. The medieval works on the grail appeared in quick succession. The first extant version may be Robert de Boron[228] writing in 1180 or earlier.[229] Although Wagner appeared to have no firsthand knowledge of the work he would know something of it from Görres,[230] San-Marte,[231] and from Albrecht's *Der Jüngere Titurel* (see below). Robert christianizes the grail traditions, which were originally of pagan Celtic origin,[232] his grail being a "veissel" used at the Last Supper and in which Joseph of Arimathea caught Christ's blood.[233] Wagner may well be alluding to this work when he writes of his "sense of rapture at this splendid feature of Christian mythogenesis."[234]

The next work to consider is the unfinished *Conte du Graal* by the north French Chrétien de Troyes, possibly a Jewish convert to Christianity.[235] The veissel is now a graal, which is in the form of a dish. Wagner would

---

227. See *CD* 26 November 1873: "In the evening read *Luther* with Malwida; the quarrel about the sacrament—how important and significant Luther's decision! And how irreligious of Zwingli to touch on this very point, which can hardly be spoken about! The Bible—that was the thing on which Luther took his stand. Nowadays, when rationalism has so gained the upper hand, he can hardly be comprehended, and yet his decision was such an important one."

228. The text is available in Nitze, *Robert de Boron*.

229. Bayer, "Gralssage," 116. Note, however, that Loomis, *Grail*, 28, and Müller and Eder, "Gral," 200, place Chrétien first.

230. See his "Introduction," XIII–XIV.

231. San-Marte, *Leben und Dichten*, 379, 400–1.

232. Loomis, *Grail*.

233. Note that Robert de Boron suggests that Joseph of Arimathea caught the blood of Christ *after* he was taken down from the cross. See Müller and Eder, "Gral," 204, 206, and Loomis, *Grail*, 229. Wagner would have read of this tradition in San-Marte, *Leben und Dichten*, 2:409. However, Wagner's interpretation was that the blood was collected as Jesus was on the cross.

234. *SL* 459; *SB* 11:107. He does criticize "inferior French chivalric romances" but his target here is clearly Chrétien de Troyes and later French romances.

235. Bayer, "Gralssage," 117, dates the work to 1181; Loomis, *Grail*, 28, gives a range of 1175–90.

have secondhand knowledge of Chrétien from Görres[236] and San-Marte.[237] This is confirmed by Cosima's entry for 5 October 1877, writing that her husband "is busy with the '*laide demoiselle*,' as Kundry is called in Chrétien de Troyes."[238]

Whereas Chrétien works with a salvation historical scheme,[239] Wolfram (c. 1200) works with an inner transformation involving a movement from hearer of the word to doer of the word.[240] The eucharistic graal is replaced by the *lapsit exillîs*.[241] After Wolfram we then have Albrecht's *Der Jüngere Titurel* (dated sometimes before 1272)[242] and the Lancelot Grail prose romances (e.g., *Merlin* and *Quest of the Holy Grail*). Finally the medieval traditions come together with Malory's *Morte d'Arthur*. For Wagner, the only one of these later works to consider is *Der Jüngere Titurel*, which brings together the traditions found in Robert de Boron and Wolfram. Here the gral was originally a precious stone that was then made into a bowl[243] from which Jesus ate on the night before his death, and was kept by Joseph of Arimathea. Then an angel brought it to Titurel in the temple of the gral (details are given for its building). Because of human sin the gral and temple went to India to the Priest Johann (i.e., Prester John, son of Feirefiz). This is a clear christianizing of the gral traditions.[244]

In chapter 3 I discussed Wagner's essential changes to the tradition he knew. For him the gral is no longer a dish (as in Chrétien) or a magic stone (as in Wolfram); it has become the vessel Christ used at the last supper and

236. See his "Introduction," LVIII–LIX.

237. San-Marte, *Leben und Dichten*, 2:397–404.

238. On the previous day she records that her husband "says he has to take care of the *laide demoiselle* [ugly maiden]" (see chapter 3 above on Chrétien's description of this "animal" like creature). Note, however, that he did not have a copy of *Conte du Graal* in his Wahnfried library: he had just one work of Chretien, *Li romans dou Chevalier au Lyon*. Mertens, "Wagners Gral," 92, thinks it unlikely he knew Chrétiens.

239. Perceval's progress is based on a salvation historical scheme of "before law—under law—under grace" (*ante legem—sub lege—sub gratia*). See Bayer, "Gralssage," 117.

240. See Jas 1:22–27; 2:14–26, and their relevance for Wolfram, discussed by Duckworth, *Parzival*, 122–34.

241. See chapter 3 above.

242. Mertens, "Wolfram," 283. This work is based on Wolfram's *Titurel*. Wolfram's short work (173 lines; Lachmann, *Wolfram von Eschenbach*, 389–420) deals with a subsidiary story of *Parzival*: Sigune and her love for Schionatulander who dies. Albrecht's work (assumed in the romantic period to be by Wolfram) fills out and continues the story.

243. This appears to have influenced Wagner's conception of the gral as made out of crystal (and the transparency of this material meant that the blood of Christ can be seen as it miraculously appears in the gral).

244. Mertens, "Wagners Gral," 101.

into which Christ's blood was poured (cf. Robert de Boron). We find him
making this explicit as early as 1853 for program notes for the Prelude to
Act I of *Lohengrin*. The "Holy Grail" is "the precious vase from which the
Saviour once had pledged his farewell to his people, the vessel whereinto his
blood had poured when he suffered crucifixion for his brethren, the cup in
which that blood had been preserved in living warmth, a fountain of imper-
ishable Love."[245] Then in his long letter to Mathilde Wesendonck of 30 May
1859 (part of which is discussed in chapter 3 above), he berates Wolfram
for choosing a grail legend that is "the most meaningless of all."[246] "That this
miraculous object should be a precious stone is a feature which, admittedly,
can be traced back to the earliest sources, namely the Arabic texts of the
Spanish Moors. One notices, unfortunately, that all our Christian legends
have a foreign, pagan origin."[247] Wagner's "Christian" view of the grail is
again clear in his first extant sketch of 1865.[248] Although he would be aware
of some "Christian" element in Wolfram's gral from San-Marte's 1841 work,
which he alludes to in his letter to Mathilde of 30 May 1859, it was not until
1875 that he read San-Marte's study on religion in the works of Wolfram
which emphasizes the Christian significance of the gral in Wolfram.[249] We
know of no comment of Wagner's on this Christian aspect, but Cosima
writes: "in the evening San-Marte on Parcival, R. comes to the conclusion
that the Holy Grail evolved entirely outside the church as a peaceful disen-
gagement from it."[250]

There is one final development in Wagner's understanding of the grail.
Whereas in Wolfram "they received from the Gral meats both wild and
tame: for this man mead, for another wine" (*WolPH* 402), in the 1865 sketch
they received "food and drink,"[251] but in the final libretto they receive from
it only bread and wine, the elements for the Communion. This is the final
stage in Wagner's christianizing Wolfram's gral.

245. *PW* 3:231–32; *JA* 2:201.

246. *SL* 458; *SB* 11:106.

247. *SL* 458–59; *SB* 11:106.

248. See, e.g., *BB* 46–47.

249. San-Marte, *Ueber das Religiöse in den Werken Wolframs von Eschenbach*. In the
second section, "Der heilige Gral und sein Reich" (228–50), he sometimes overempha-
sizes the Christian character of Wolfram's gral: "*In dem Grale ist . . . der dreieinige Gott
der Christenheit gegenwärtig und wirksam*" (233).

250. *CD* 2 September 1875. They continued with the work on 3 September and on
6 September moved on to San-Marte's introduction to Guiot's *Bible* (San-Marte and
Wolfhart, *Guiot von Provins*, 3–27). San-Marte discusses whether Guiot is in fact the
same as Kyot whom Wolfram claimed to be his source for Parzival (see chapter 3 above).

251. *BB* 47.

Related to the grail are two further changes Wagner makes to Wolfram. The first is that whereas the spear in Wolfram is primarily a medical instrument with no Christian connection,[252] in *Parsifal* it is identified with the spear that was thrust into Christ's side. A second change regards Wolfram's whole theological atmosphere, which, as we saw in chapter 3 above, is colored by James and Jewish Wisdom literature. Whereas Wolfram's hero overcomes his "double-mindedness" within such a "Wisdom" tradition, Wagner's Parsifal seems much more dependent on God's grace.[253] Wagner's *Parsifal* could almost be seen as Wolfram's *Parzival* having undergone a Lutheran transformation.

Religious Pluralism

Wagner has been praised for attempting a "synthesis" of Eastern and Christian religions in *Parsifal* thereby initiating an interreligious dialogue that we find today.[254] In particular, it is argued that Wagner presents a "synthesis" of Christianity and Buddhism.[255] In support of this one could appeal among other things to Cosima's entry for 19 September 1882, where she tells of how her husband believes that "by giving much attention to B.[uddha] one learns to understand Christianity, and people were surely now beginning to realize that the greatest heroic power lies in resignation." But although Wagner admired Buddhism (and it certainly helped him cement Christianity and Schopenhauer), he was in no doubt that Christianity was the greatest religion.[256] Comparing the Christian Religion to Buddhism and "Brahminic teachings" he writes in *Religion and Art*: "Its founder was not wise, but divine; his teaching was the deed of free-willed suffering."[257] This is a view Cosima shared.[258]

252. Perhaps it is the spear with which Anfortas was wounded but this is by no means clear. Further, it has a numinous quality in that from its tip drops of blood form.

253. See the discussion in chapter 8 above. In relation to grace and the grail, see Eiser, "Andeutungen," 228.

254. Kienzle, *Religion und Philosophie*, 229.

255. Ibid., 195–201, who focuses on the 1865 sketch.

256. See above and chapter 8.

257. *PW* 6:214; *JA* 10:119. *GSD* 10:213: "Ihr Gründer war nicht weise, sondern göttlich; seine Lehre war die Tat des freiwilligen Leidens."

258. See *CD* 4 December 1873: "The difference between the legends of Buddha and Christ is becoming increasingly clear to me; with Christ one must suffer and be redeemed—that is the religion of the poor; with Buddha one must know—that is the religion of the sages, the educated, which among the common people was bound to degenerate into superstition and the worship of relics." See also *CD* 2 November 1873:

There are Buddhist elements in *Parsifal*, although sometimes it is difficult to discern where these have come from. For example, the emphasis on "Mitleid" ("compassion") could come from Buddhism, but could also come from Schopenhauer, Wolfram, or from the New Testament. Perhaps the clearest case of Buddhist influence regards reincarnation. Wagner writes to Mathilde Wesendonck (early August 1860) of the "beautiful Buddhist doctrine" of "metempsychosis," although Wagner was being highly creative in his interpretation of this doctrine![259] This idea of reincarnation has certainly influenced his portrayal of Kundry.[260] Further, I would not want to exclude the idea that Wagner sometimes brings together Christian and Buddhist ideas.[261] But I find it highly significant that the theologian who has perhaps done more than anyone else to promote dialogue between Christianity and Eastern religions such as Buddhism finds the emphasis on the grace of God in *Parsifal* an unmistakable pointer to it being fundamentally Christian rather than Buddhist.[262] I suspect that were he with us now, Wagner would agree with him.[263]

Wagner did admire Buddhism, but it was a religion of ethics and had no concept of "God." Of all religions it was the one that he found easiest

---

"The only legend which stands above Buddha is that of Christ, since in the latter the action touches the heart—the crib, the supper, the cross; Buddha does not move one, he teaches; Christ teaches by moving us." This corresponds exactly to what her husband wrote in *Religion and Art* (1880).

259. He writes that according to this doctrine "the spotless purity of Lohengrin is easily explicable in terms of his being the continuation of Parzival" (*SL* 499; *SB* 12:236).

260. He the discussion in chapter 5 above.

261. See, e.g., the suggestion of Kienzle, *Religion und Philosophie*, 227, that Wagner may be bringing together nirvâna and Christian eschatology as Kundry falls lifeless to the ground at the end of the *Parsifal*: "Es ist eine Utopie einer Aufhebung von Raum und Zeit, eine bewegte und zugleich stillstehende Ewigkeit: indisches *nirvâna* und christlich-eschatologische Zeitvorstellungen werden eins."

262. See Küng, *Musik und Religion*, 156: "Im 'Parsifal', das ist eindeutig unbuddhistisch, erlöst sich der Mensch nicht selbst, sondern wird erlöst. Letzte Erlösung durch Glauben: darauf läuft nach Wagner der 'Parsifal' hinaus! Ganz unbefangen wird in diesem mittelalterlichen Kontext schon am Anfang Gott angerufen. Nicht genug, so scheint es, kann Wagner von Versuchung, Sünde und Schuld reden. 'Die Wunde ist's, die sich nie schließen will'. Nicht genung kann er auch von Gnade and Glauben sprechen: von 'des Heilands Huld' und dem von daher ermöglichen Glauben: 'der Glaube lebt, die Taube schwebt, des Heilands holder Bote.'"

263. Note especially the view of Eiser, "Andeutungen," 228, published in the *Bayreuther Blätter* just a year after Wagner had completed his poem. He likens the "Buddhist" view of self-help in the *Ring* (where Siegfried has to offer his own life) to that in *Parsifal*: "Hier tritt als letzte und höchste Konsequenz jenes grossen Weltgedankens die christliche Idee *der Gnade* hinzu, welche durch des Heilands Kreuzestod die Erlösung Aller erbarmend vermitteln lässt."

to relate to Christianity since there was no conflict of "concepts of God." When it came to other religions that did have a concept of God, he seemed to despise what one could term "religious pluralism." Such religious pluralism could range from there being some truth in other religions to their even offering a way of salvation. Although there are occasions when he saw truth in other religions, even in Judaism,[264] his general attitude is summed up in his aversion to the religious pluralism in Lessing's *Nathan the Wise*. He considered this work to have "a very superficial conception of religion" with "not a trace of profundity."[265] Cosima relates how on Maundy Thursday (Grün Donnerstag), which in 1874 fell on the Jewish Passover, "R. was . . . very indignant over the way the Jews were strutting about here in their best clothes, because today is their Easter festival. 'I shall put my foot in it again when I become a town councilor one day; to offend the feelings of the people like that, by walking around in festive garb on our days of mourning! That's what Lessing bequeathed to us—the idea that all religions are good, even stupid Mohammedanism.'"[266] Although Wagner may be accused of intolerance, some have (rightly, I think) seen serious problems in Lessing's view of religious pluralism, especially regarding the ring parable: "Hat von / Euch jeder seinen Ring von seinem Vater: / So glaube jeder sicher seinen Ring / Den echten" ("Each of you has a ring from your father; have faith that it is the true one").[267] Lessing's concern was the three Abrahamic faiths, and it is telling that current interreligious dialogue for Christians focuses precisely on such faiths. Wagner's rejection of such religious pluralism is, I suggest, worth serious consideration.

Wagner's dislike of religious pluralism is found not only in his many utterances on the issue but also in the way representatives of non-Christian

264. See chapter 9 above.

265. *CD* 8 September 1879 and 18 December 1881. Cosima, on the other hand, seemed to like the play, believing it contained "a peculiarly German kind of humanity." See also her positive comments in *CD* 29 January 1875 (this and *CD* 31 January tells us she was reading it with her children). In this context it is interesting to read of this positive comment of Cosima's about Judaism on 30 January 1975: "In the evening Gfrörer's *Primitive Christianity*, in which a saying of the Jews makes a deep imprint on my mind: 'One should pray for a good eye, a humble spirit, and a soul free from desire.'"

266. *CD* 2 April 1874.

267. Göpfert, *Lessing Werke II*, 279–80. Kurt Hübner, *Wettstreit*, 143–44, makes the point that in Lessing's "Ring-parable" the rightness of a religion (he is thinking here of Judaism, Christianity, and Islam) can simply be judged by the moral consequences. Such consequences, Hübner rightly argues, are not the primary aspect with which to judge a religion (a point Wagner often makes, e.g., *On State and Religion* [*PW* 4:26]). Also Hübner criticizes Lessing for speaking of the impossibility of distinguishing between the religions. Nathan speaks simply of a "blind tradition" ("blinde Überlieferung") (see Act II Scene 7, *Lessing Werke*, 278).

religions are negatively portrayed in his dramas such as *Parsifal*. This contrasts starkly with Wolfram who, although believing pagans can only be saved by being converted to the Christian faith, nevertheless gives an extremely sympathetic view of their life and customs.[268] If Wolfram's "pagans" are usually Muslims, it may be that Wagner's "target" in *Parsifal* it is not so much Judaism but more likely Islam.[269] We saw in chapter 2 that Wagner had contempt for this religion, a view strengthened by Schopenhauer. One *possible* way of interpreting an aspect of the drama of Act II of *Parsifal* is to see the victory of "Christianity" over "Islam." Whereas the "domain and castle ('Monsalvat') of the Guardians of the Grail" is in a landscape "in the style of the northern Mountains of Gothic Spain" (*WagPS* 106–7), Klingsor's magic castle is "on the southern slope of the same mountain range, facing Moorish Spain" (*WagPS* 156–57). Klingsor's magic garden has "a rich Arabian style of terraces" and the Flower Maidens are "clad in soft-coloured veils" (*WagPS* 166–67). Kundry, on appearing to Parsifal in Act II, is "on a couch of flowers, wearing a light, fantastic, veil like robe of Arabian style" (*WagPS* 188–89). This kingdom, which Klingsor (in Arabic costume!)[270] rules, is the destroyed at the end of Act II as Parsifal makes the sign of the cross with the holy spear. This sign of the cross may point back to "Monsalvat" in a quite literal way since it can mean not only "mountain of salvation" (mons salvationis) but also "*hill* of salvation"![271]

Wagner shared the view of St. Paul that those of non-Christian religions are following a counterfeit religion and the natural desire of the Christian is to see them convert to the Christian faith. In Wolfram we saw the conversion of Feirefiz, a "pagan" who appears to be a "Muslim."[272] To some extent Kundry's conversion and baptism in *Parsifal* is modeled on this, but

268. This is true of both *Parzival* (especially the figure of Feirefiz) and of *Willehalm* (see *WolWGJ* 25, 273–79).

269. This seems to be missed by Weiner, *Imagination*, 237–49, who relates everything "oriental" to Judaism.

270. See the photograph of Anton Fuchs as Klingsor from the first performances of 1882 (*DEAP* 251). As noted in chapter 3 above, Klingsor is partly modeled on the "pagan" (i.e., Muslim) who inflicted the wound on Anfortas in Wolfram (*WolPH* 244).

271. Cf. Brian Murdoch, "Fallen Man," 151, who makes a point about Munsalvaesche as the "hill of redemption" upon which is the "Rood-tree."

272. Wolfram seems to relate Islam to paganism, even polytheism. So in *Willehalm*, the pagans worship "Apolle and Tervigant and the deceitful Mahmete" (*WolWGJ* 25). In *Parzival* he tells of a "heathen" (i.e., a Muslim) Flegetanis "who worshipped a calf as though it were his god" (*WolPH* 232). Also Feirefiz is a polytheist ("All my gods are forsworn"), his gods including Jupiter and Juno (*WolPH* 372–74). Likewise "heathenish" appears to be Arabic (*WolPH* 213–14; 232). Portraying Muslims as idolaters was common in medieval literature (Daniel, *Islam*, 309).

her conversion is genuine and one from within (we saw that Feirefiz had mixed motives for wanting to become a Christian). It is a conversion involving a union with Christ and a death with him in baptism; and her union with Christ is consummated in those final moments of the drama when she falls to the ground "entseelt" (indicating the departure of her soul).

Often in this work I have stressed the ambivalence often found in Wagner's art. However, when it comes to aspects of redemption, Wagner can be remarkably unambivalent. As his great granddaughter puts it: "Everything is ultimately forced into the unequivocal unity of Christian redemption, blessed by above." And she adds that in *Parsifal* we have "an ideological crusade . . . conducted in the name of the Cross."[273] The only difference between our positions is that Nike Wagner finds such things as "problems"[274] and I see them as strengths.

Ethics

It has been widely recognized that Wagner's ethical system was influenced by Schopenhauer. Many of his writings and of course *Parsifal* point to the centrality of Schopenhauerian "compassion" ("Mitleid"). In his *Open Letter to Herr Ernst von Weber* he writes: "In our days it required the instruction of a philosopher who fought with dogged ruthlessness against all cant and all pretence, to prove the *pity* deeply-seated in the human breast the only true foundation of morality."[275] He continues: "It was mocked at, nay, indignantly repudiated by the senate of a learned Academy; for virtue, where not enjoined by Revelation, was only to be based on Logic (Vernunfts-Erwägung)."[276] The "learned Academy" here is the Royal Danish Society of Sciences, which ran an essay competition concerning the basis of ethics. Although Schopenhauer's essay "On the Basis of Morals" was the only entry it was turned down.[277]

273. Wagner, *Wagners*, 134.

274. Ibid., 135: "the dominance of the Cross over the imagery of *Parsifal* exerts a fundamentally anti-emancipatory effect. It undermines the piece's claims to aesthetic autonomy, and has the effect of stifling the imagination, associating it forever with the same fixed ideas." I imagine the same "criticism" could be leveled at Bach's St. Matthew Passion.

275. *PW* 6:197; *GSD* 10:196.

276. *PW* 6:197; *GSD* 10:196.

277. For the text of the essay which he later entitled "Prize Essay on the Basis of Morals not awarded the prize by the Royal Danish Society of Sciences, at Copenhagen on 30 January 1840," see Schopenhauer, *Ethics*, 121–271. The judgement of the Society ended thus: ". . . when the writer attempted to show that the basis of ethics consists in

Although Schopenhauer's moral philosophy has had its supporters,[278] many have pointed to its inadequacies regarding altruism[279] and "Mitleid."[280] Although both these aspects can be found in Wagner,[281] he gives a fundamental correction in his emphasis on love, "the light which gave eyes to will, and redeemed it from its fatal bias and curse."[282]

It perhaps has not been sufficiently recognized that the basis of Wagner's ethics was the New Testament with its emphasis on the "new commandment." Just as I appealed to Nietzsche to underline the Christian nature of *Parsifal*, so I appeal again to him to suggest that Wagner's ethics were Christian (even if he failed to live up to it). In the Epilogue to *The Case of Wagner* Nietzsche contrasts "*master-morality*" ("*Herren-Moral*") and the "morality of *Christian* value concepts" ("Moral der *christlichen* Wertbegriffe"): "In the narrower sphere of so-called moral values you will not find a greater contrast than between *master-morality* and the morality of *Christian* value concepts: this last having grown on soil that is morbid through and through (—the Gospels present exactly the same physiological types that you find described in Dostoevsky's novels); on the other hand, master morality ('Roman', 'heroic', 'classical', 'Renaissance') is the sign language of a sound constitution, of *ascending* life, of the will to power as the principle of life."[283]

---

compassion, he neither satisfied us with the form of his discussion, nor in fact proved that this basis is sufficient; rather, he was forced to admit the opposite himself. Nor should it go unmentioned that several supreme philosophers of recent times were so indecently mentioned, that it caused just and grave offence" (272). The "supreme philosophers" were Hegel (Schopenhauer speaks of "the gross, mindless charlatan Hegel" [160]) and Fichte ("a buffoon," 189).

278. E.g., Murdoch, *Metaphysics*, 63.

279. See Young, *Schopenhauer*, 182–83. He points out that for Schopenhauer the actions of the altruist have moral worth whereas those of the egoist do not. But altruism is a disguised form of egoism because the altruist is kind to others and avoids harming others because in the world of the noumenon he cannot be distinguished from others since there is no principle of individuation!

280. Forsyth, "Pessimism," 236–37: "Many who are swift to compassion are slow to righteousness. . . . Something else than pity is needed to guide pity, and something more real than emotion must be the ground of action on the large and beneficient scale."

281. Schopenhauer's view of altruism is reflected in Sach's "Wahn" monologue in *Meistersinger* Act III Scene 1 (Magee, *Wagner and Philosophy*, 252).

282. Forsyth, "Pessimism," 239–40.

283. Nietzsche, *Anti-Christ Etc*, 261. *KSA* 6:50: "In der engeren Sphäre der sogenannten moralischen Werthe ist kein grösserer Gegensatz aufzufinden, als der einer *Herren-Moral* und der Moral der *christlichen* Werthbegriffe: letztere, auf einem durch und durch morbiden Boden gewachsen (– die Evangelien führen uns genau dieselben physiologischen Typen vor, welche die Romane Dostoiewsky's schildern), die

Concluding Thoughts on the Christian
Nature of *Parsifal*

Throughout this work we have seen that Wagner's Christian faith, judged by the general tenor of Christian tradition, was rather "unorthodox." Some have accused him of reinventing a faith "that held out the promise of redemption to him" and his own "godlike saviour."[284] Others, however, have positively endorsed Wagner's version of Christianity because, it is claimed, he gets to the very core of the Christian faith, and that the churches have offered a "parody."[285] Wagner's own view was that through his art he could revitalize the Christian faith,[286] and that through a work such as *Parsifal* Christ crucified was being proclaimed, an idea I will pursue in the following chapter.

Two key figures who tried to continue Wagner's religious program were Wolzogen and Chamberlain. Chamberlain, as we saw above, initially denied the Christian character of *Parsifal*, but he, through Wolzogen, came to see *Parsifal* as a profoundly Christian work.[287] In fact, the whole Bayreuth circle developed a Christian understanding of *Parsifal*, which in many respects faithfully follows Wagner's theological intentions. This is especially significant since whilst Wagner was still alive a number of articles appeared in the *Bayreuther Blätter* that related Wagner's art to the Christian faith,[288]

Herren-Moral ('römisch', 'heidnisch', 'klassisch', 'Renaissance') umgekehrt als die Zeichensprache der Wohlgerathenheit, des *aufsteigenden* Lebens, des Willens zur Macht als Princips des Lebens."

284. Köhler, *Titans*, 560. He then supports this with a reference to Nietzsche's *Nachgelassene Fragmente* (Autumn 1887). The full text is: "Wagner, ein Stück Aberglaube schon bei Lebzeiten, hat sich inzwischen so in die Wolken des Unwahrscheinlichen eingewickelt, daß in Bezug auf ihn nur das Paradoxe noch Glaube findet" (*KSA* 12:399).

285. Irvine, *"Parsifal" and Wagner's Christianity*, 44.

286. Cf. Field, *Evangelist of Race*, 162.

287. Chamberlain, *Mensch und Gott*, 282: "Den entscheidenden Schritt zur Vermählung der Kunst mit der Religion tat jedoch erst Richard Wagner, dessen Bühnenwerke alle . . . in irgendeiner Beziehung zum Erlösungsgedanken stehen." Further he writes: "Nannte ich nur den Erlösungsgedanken, so füge ich jetzt hinzu, daß dieser—wo er christlich auftritt—gar nicht zur Darstellung gebracht werden kann ohne die begleitenden christlichen Auffassungen von Glauben, Gnade, Liebe, Hoffen, Entsagen, Aufopfern" (283). Concerning *Parsifal* he writes: "Ein solches Werk gehört offenbar ganz und gar in das Gebiet der Religion und sollte ausschließlich im Dienste der religiösen Überzeugung, der es sein Entstehen verdankt, aufgeführt werden" (285).

288. See, e.g., Eiser, "Andeutungen."

providing a bridge between Wagner's own theology and the later "patristic theology" developed by Wolzogen and Chamberlain.[289]

---

289. To some extent their work parallels the way the church fathers reflected on the New Testament: distortions did occur (and often one can account for these), but the main message was often faithfully propagated.

11

Revealing the World and the Divine through *Parsifal*

Introduction

REFLECTING ON THE 1882 *Parsifal* performances Wagner wrote this: "Whoever had the mind and eye to seize the character of all that passed within the walls of that house during those two months, both the productive and the receptive, could not describe it otherwise than as governed by a consecration that shed itself on everything without the smallest prompting."[1]

Wagner clearly believed that as *Parsifal* was being performed something profound was being disclosed in his theatre in Bayreuth;[2] and those who experience performances there and elsewhere can (but not always) also sense that something quite "out of this world" is happening. Writers, philosophers, musicians, and poets have struggled to express the transcendent quality of music[3] and in *Parsifal* we have sublime music and a drama that has the capacity to transform the human person. This chapter brings us to the question of "revelation" through *Parsifal* and there are two aspects

---

1. *PW* 6:303; *GSD* 10:297.

2. Köhler, *Titans*, 115, writes: "For Wagner, the theatre became a place where the different forms of reality that eluded our everyday understanding could be summoned into existence. . . . [T]he theatre was neither an educational institution . . . nor a place of entertainment . . . but a 'demonic abyss containing within it the potential for all that is most base and most sublime'" (Köhler quoting from von Wolzogen, *Bayreuth*, 3).

3. For example, Herbert von Karajan is reported to have said that music comes "from another world," indeed comes "from eternity" (Osbourne, *Karajan*, 469).

to consider: first, how Wagner through composing could be disclosing the fundamental nature of the world and even acting as a "prophet" in that he speaks God's "word"; secondly, how a work such as *Parsifal* can reveal something of the world and God to those who experience it.

For this investigation I will initially use a Kantian-Schopenhauerian framework for relating "subject" and "object." Such a system is particularly apposite since it is the framework within which Wagner himself worked (although as we shall see he did depart from it in key respects). Just as one can say a biblical text should be understood as it understands itself,[4] so I think it is with Wagner (and any artwork). But in this exercise we are not only engaged in a hermeneutical enterprise but also delving into questions of what is actually happening as music is composed and experienced. In view of this one has to reckon with the fact that a Kantian-Schopenhauerian framework has its drawbacks. There are a range of philosophical problems relating to space, time, and causation; also there is the issue whether it can deal with revelation of "the divine."[5] But despite such problems there are a remarkable number of insights such a framework can offer;[6] after all, it has been developed by Kant, the greatest philosopher of modern times, and by his disciple Schopenhauer, one of the most discerning writers on art.[7]

Wagner's own thought was shot through with Kant and Schopenhauer as seen in his discussions of space and time. For example, in a letter to Mathilde Wesendonck (early August 1860) he writes: "In this way, all the terrible tragedy of life would be attributable to our dislocation in time and space: but since time and space are merely *our* way of perceiving things, but otherwise have no reality, even the greatest tragic pain must be explicable to those who are truly clear-sighted as no more than an individual error."[8] Wagner continued to grapple with questions of space and time[9] as can be

---

4. See Gese, "Der auszulegende Text," 269: "Es muß als hermeneutische Grundregel gelten, daß der Text so zu verstehen ist, wie er verstanden sein will, d.h. wie er sich selbst versteht."

5. I use quotation marks simply to leave open what "the divine" could possibly be.

6. Such a framework was used in Bell, *Deliver Us from Evil*.

7. Schopenhauer has enjoyed a renaissance in the last fifty to sixty years and has found admirers even in unexpected quarters. See the conclusions of an analytic philosopher, Jacquette, *Schopenhauer*, 261–64, on Schopenhauer's philosophical achievement: "it is difficult not to exaggerate the brilliance of his philosophy" (261) and that "[h]e offers penetrating insight into some of philosophy's deepest and most longstanding problems" (263). Also there is a clarity in his thinking and writing such that "[w]e can generally see where we think he may have taken a false step, and the criticisms it would be useful to raise" (263).

8. *SL* 499; *SB* 12:236.

9. According to a reading of *CD* 19 January 1881, Melderis, *Raum*, 7, writes that

seen from two further examples from twenty years later (when he was completing *Parsifal*). First, one regarding the nature of time: "He relates various things from Schopenhauer regarding time, the reflected image of which lies in ourselves; in the same way that one can discern a moving object only by reference to a stationary one, so within ourselves we carry the reflected image of time."[10] Secondly, some comments on more existential concerns: "In the evening R. reads to us Schopenhauer's dialogue about death and life after death. Our starting point had been the sinners who fear Hell (Pascal), whereas a character like Goethe knows nothing of such things!"[11] In this dialogue[12] "Philalethes" explains that although the individual "which manifests itself in the form of time and accordingly has a beginning and an end," "the true essence-in-itself does not know either time, beginning, end, or the limits of a given individuality" and it is in this sense that one is indestructible.[13] "You as an individual end at your death";[14] but you should "give up a fear that would seem to you to be childish and utterly ridiculous if you knew thoroughly and to its very foundation your own nature, namely as the universal will-to-live, which you are."[15] This is the "fear" that Cosima had interpreted as Pascal's fear of hell.

Although Wagner was Schopenhauer's most celebrated "evangelist" in the second half of the nineteenth century, we have also seen ways in which he has distanced himself from Schopenhauer, and one wonders whether he would fully agree with Schopenhauer's dialogue on life after death. One would at least have to question whether Tristan and Isolde lose their individuality when they die.[16] But despite these differences there is one aspect of Schopenhauer that Wagner held on to: his distinction between the phenomenal and noumenal worlds. Schopenhauer was in many ways Kant's most faithful "disciple" in holding to this distinction[17] and since this is central for

---

Wagner considered time and space to be "ein verfluchtes Thema" ("an accursed subject"). However, the reference appears to be to the Jewish people!

10. *CD* 14 May 1880. Two days previously he had been reading Schopenhauer's *Parerga* (*CD* 12 May 1880). See volume 2 § 29 (concerning the "ideality of time") and § 30 (concerning the "ideality of space") (*PP* 2:38–45; *ASSW* 5:49–57).

11. *CD* 14 June 1880.

12. It is the concluding section of *Parerga*, volume 2, chapter 10 ("On the Doctrine of the Indestructability of our True Nature by Death.")

13. *PP* 2:279; *ASSW* 5:330.

14. *PP* 2:279; *ASSW* 5:330.

15. *PP* 2:282; *ASSW* 5:333.

16. Cf. Scruton, *Death-Devoted Heart*, 190, and the discussion in chapter 2 above.

17. Wagner, in a letter to Liszt of 16 December 1854, described Schopenhauer as "the greatest philosopher since *Kant*, whose ideas—as he himself puts it—he is the first

Wagner's philosophy and theology of music, I turn to discuss whether this distinction is at all credible today.

The Phenomenal/Noumenal Distinction

This distinction between the phenomenal and noumenal worlds came about because of Kant's "Copernican revolution," which occurred around 1770 and was developed in what is one of the greatest works on philosophy, Kant's *Critique of Pure Reason*. It is upon this, especially the first edition (1781), that Schopenhauer developed his own philosophical system. This phenomenal/noumenal distinction is so bold and so ground breaking that inevitably it came to be questioned. Does it seem at all reasonable to claim, as Schopenhauer does, that "[t]he world is my representation"[18] and that space, time, and causation are imposed on our experience? How can such radical idealism be defended today?

Over the last 200 years since Kant and Schopenhauer developed their transcendental[19] idealism there have been two major scientific revolutions which have fundamentally changed how we understand space, time, and causation: Special and General Relativity, and Quantum Theory. However, rather than debunking transcendental idealism, such theories have been interpreted in some quarters so as to confirm some of Kant's and Schopenhauer's insights,[20] although inevitably suggestions have had to be made as to how their views should be modified.[21] Philosophical reflection has also suggested that the "two-tiered" world of phenomena and noumena is a

---

person to think through to their logical conclusion" (*SL* 323; *SB* 6:298).

18. *WWR* 1:3; *ASSW* 1:31.

19. The word "transcendental" has often been confused with "transcendent" but these terms point in opposite directions. The etymology of both words is "to climb over" (*trans* over *scandere* climb) and both mean "exceeding experience." But whereas a transcendent object exceeds experience in that it is beyond experience and remote, a transcendental structure exceeds experience because it is a precondition for experience. See Ellington, *Prolegomena*, 373 n. 48.

20. See Bitbol, Kerszberg, and Petitot, "Introduction"; Bitbol, "Reflective Metaphysics"; Pringe, *Quantum Power of Judgment*. See also my lecture "Mind and Matter: The World as Representation in Quantum Theory" delivered to the Faraday Institute in Cambridge on 20 October 2011 and available on their website.

21. One example is the issue of non-Euclidean geometry (see Bell, *Deliver Us from Evil*, 123–25).

simplification, and that the world should be viewed as three-tiered[22] or even multi-tiered.[23]

If the views of Kant and Schopenhauer have to be modified, sometimes fairly drastically, does Wagner's own philosophy and theology of music, based on this 200 year old transcendental idealism, have anything other than historical interest? Despite advances made in natural science and philosophy, I think there are still good reasons for maintaining that there is more to the world than the "phenomena" together with "information": one of these reasons is the mystery of the human person and another is the nature of great art. And it is precisely through self-knowledge and art that one can access deeper levels of reality.

In what follows, I explain how Schopenhauer (via Kant) came to such views, and how Wagner subsequently developed them.

Accessing the Thing-in-Itself through Self-Knowledge and through Art

For Kant the thing-in-itself was truly unknown, being a "limiting concept" ("Grenzbegriff").[24] However, Schopenhauer, in opposition to Kant, argued that we can approach the noumenal world and the rather confusing term he used for this is the "will" ("Wille"). One of the key things to bear in mind is that for Schopenhauer there is as much "will" in the fall of a stone as there is in human action.[25] One way to approach this thing-in-itself is through self-knowledge. But in order to understand this, it is necessary to step back to consider his view of the subject and the self.

Schopenhauer's understanding of the subject, based on Kant's, was that it is a spaceless and timeless entity. But it imposes time upon the mental states and the mental states in turn impose time and space upon the outer world. The subject thus orders the world of representation according to space, time, and causality. But in self-knowledge we are confronted by that which cannot be known as representation since this transcendental subject is the source of all such representation. Although some self-knowledge does

---

22. Young, *Schopenhauer*, 202, makes a distinction between the Schopenhauerian thing-in-itself (the "will," see below) and the Kantian thing-in-itself which is truly unknown and inaccessible.

23. This could be an inference of the work of Bohm, *Implicate Order*.

24. Kemp Smith, *Critique of Pure Reason*, 272 (A 255, B 310–11).

25. See *WWR* 2:299; *ASSW* 2:387 (2.23). Schopenhauer actually has three senses of "will": 1. the act of will; 2. the manifestation of desires; 3. the ultimate will, the "thing-in-itself." See Bell, *Deliver Us from Evil*, 217–18.

pass through our senses, much of it does not. We then have direct non-sensory knowledge from inside. Schopenhauer writes: "Consequently, a way *from within* stands open to us to that real inner nature of things to which we cannot penetrate *from without*. It is, so to speak, a subterranean passage, a secret alliance, which, as if by treachery, places us all at once in the fortress that could not be taken by attack from without."[26] On the basis of this, some have argued that Schopenhauer believed that through self-knowledge one can have direct knowledge of the thing-in-itself. However, the context suggests that there is no direct knowledge of the noumenon because in the next paragraph but one he writes that self-knowledge is free in respect to space and causality but not free in respect to time since, as I noted above, the timeless subject imposes time upon the mental states.[27]

Schopenhauer argued that knowledge of the thing-in-itself can be gained not only by self-knowledge but also through the arts. Schopenhauer here introduces the "Platonic Ideas"[28] and a careful reading reveals what I think is a convincing use of the Ideas.

The first thing one must make clear is that for Schopenhauer (and Kant) the "noumenal" is not used in its Platonic sense.[29] We are not talking about a world of ideas and ideals and reason. Rather for Schopenhauer the "Platonic Ideas" come in on the interface between the phenomenal and noumenal worlds. One way they come to have this intermediate status is as follows. Since the "Ideas" are plural and knowable they cannot belong to the noumenon (which for Schopenhauer is an undifferentiated whole). But they are not phenomenal either. Although they are manifested in the phenomenal world they are not to be equated with it. Such is the case with

---

26. *WWR* 2:195; *ASSW* 2:253.

27. He writes that "even the inward observation we have of our own will still does not by any means furnish an exhaustive and adequate knowledge of the thing-in-itself. . . . [I]nner knowledge is free from two forms belonging to outer knowledge, the form of *space* and the form of *causality* which brings about all sense-perception. On the other hand, there still remains the form of *time*, as well as that of being known and of knowing in general. Accordingly, in this inner knowledge the thing-in-itself has indeed to a great extent cast off its veils, but still does not appear quite naked. In consequence of the form of time which still adheres to it, everyone knows his *will* only in its successive individual *acts*, not as a whole, in and by itself. . . . Yet the apprehension in which we know the stirrings and acts of our own will is far more immediate than is any other. It is the point where the thing-in-itself enters the phenomenon most immediately" (*WWR* 2:196–97).

28. He makes a crucial distinction between "Idea" ("Idee") and "concept" (Begriff") (*WWR* 1:233–36; *ASSW* 1:328–32).

29. Janaway, *Schopenhauer*, 26–27, points out that around 1813 Schopenhauer came to see that "revealing the nature of the thing in itself and clarifying the 'better' Platonic consciousness were two distinct enterprises."

scientific laws.[30] These, like all "Platonic Ideas," are the "deep grammar" via which the noumenal finds expression in the phenomena.[31]

But the Ideas operate in a special way in the arts. Schopenhauer introduces the Platonic Ideas in book three of *The World as Will and Representation*, which concerns "The Representation Independent of the Principle of Sufficient Reason."[32] So in the arts we are still dealing with "representation" but, unlike the natural sciences, it *does not have to be* according to "the principle of sufficient reason," the principle that governs ordinary experience. So the Platonic Idea is still "representation" but it is "the most *adequate objectivity* possible of the will"[33] and is therefore a means of accessing it. Schopenhauer in his aesthetics distinguishes between ordinary consciousness and aesthetic consciousness. In ordinary consciousness we are "egocentric" but in the aesthetic state we lose ourselves in the object:[34] "[w]e *lose* ourselves entirely in this object . . . we forget our individuality, our will, and continue to exist only as pure subject, as clear mirror of the object, so that it is as though the object alone existed without anyone to perceive it, and thus we are no longer able to separate the perceiver from the perception, but the two have become one, since the entire consciousness is filled and occupied by a single image of perception."[35] And so the subject becomes the "*pure* will-less, painless, timeless *subject of knowledge*"[36] and "no longer follows relations in accordance with the principle of sufficient reason."[37]

---

30. Magee, *Confessions*, 413.

31. Ibid., 414.

32. The term "principle of sufficient reason," introduced by Leibniz, is central for Schopenhauer (see Magee, *Schopenhauer*, 28). His doctoral dissertation was devoted to it and he employs it in place of Kant's transcendental proof (Gardner, *Kant*, 341). Essentially it is the principle that governs ordinary experience and reasoning.

33. *WWR* 1:175; *ASSW* 1:253.

34. This is still "representation" but the object is transformed and representation is not according to the principle of sufficient reason (*WWR* 1:179–80; *ASSW* 1:257).

35. *WWR* 1:178–79; *ASSW* 1:257. As Young, *Schopenhauer*, 111, puts it: "In ordinary consciousness . . . I am *in* the world of my experience as an 'object among objects,' indeed *the* object to which all others are related as the world's centre. In the moment of aesthetic entrancement, however . . . [t]he 'I' vanishes from the scene (which therefore becomes 'decentred' . . .)."

36. *WWR* 1:179 *ASSW* 1:257.

37. *WWR* 1:178; *ASSW* 1:256. Concerning independence of the principle of sufficient reason, note that the third book of this work is entitled "The World as Representation, Second Aspect: The Representation Independent of the Principle of Sufficient Reason: The Platonic Idea: The Object of Art" ("Der Welt als Vorstellung, zweite Betrachtung: Die Vorstellung, unabhängig vom Satze des Grundes: Die platonische Idee: Das Objekt der Kunst").

What may seem remarkable is that in this aesthetic state "simultaneously and inseparably"[38] the object is also transformed: "the perceived individual thing is raised to the Idea of its species, and the knowing individual to the pure subject of will-less knowing, and now the two, as such, no longer stand in the stream of time and of all other relations."[39] So since space and time are the principles of individuation (*principia individuationis*), the object ceases to belong to the world of individuals, occupying its own place in space-time and becomes instead the "Platonic idea." So "at one stroke the individual thing becomes the Idea of its species and the perceiving individual the pure subject of knowing."[40] Great art involves seeing the Platonic universal.[41]

Schopenhauer writes that the genius sees "the universal in the particular";[42] he perceives the idea not *instead* of the individual; rather he perceives the individual *as* idea.[43] If great art is "universal" it has this extraordinary ability to be contemporary (see, e.g., the contemporary nature of Wagner's *Ring* or *Parsifal* or Shakespeare's *Hamlet*). If great art involves finding the "universal" it explains why it is able to address every generation. Related to this "universal" is that great art deals with disassociated emotion. In great art the will is not aroused. So "painted fruit" (i.e., "still life") can be beautiful without our desiring to eat it (i.e., it does not arouse our will).[44] On the other hand, lower forms of art, if they can be considered art, provoke the will. So what makes *Parsifal* "high art" and Mel Gibson's film *The Passion of Christ* "low art"? The latter arouse one to acts of will; the former could be said to deal with disassociated emotion.[45] Or to take another example, what distinguishes the flowers maidens' attempted seduction of Parsifal or the

38. *WWR* 1:197; *ASSW* 1:280.

39. *WWR* 1:197; *ASSW* 1:281.

40. *WWR* 1:179; *ASSW* 1:257.

41. Young, *Schopenhauer*, 124, writes: "This idea that the great artist expresses our joys, fears and sorrows, the lesser one his joys, fears and sorrows, captures, perhaps something of the difference between Goethe and Paul McCartney."

42. *WWR* 2:379; *ASSW* 2:489.

43. Young, *Schopenhauer*, 132. So Nietzsche, influenced by Schopenhauer, speaks of the artist idealizing the object. See Nietzsche, *Anti-Christ Etc*, 196: "The essential thing about intoxication of the will is the feeling of fullness and increasing strength. This feeling makes us release ourselves onto things, we *force* them to accept us, we violate them,—this process is called *idealizing*." *KSA* 6:116: "Das Wesentliche am Rausch ist das Gefühl der Kraftsteigerung und Fülle. Aus diesem Gefühle giebt man an die Dinge ab, man *zwingt* sie von uns zu nehmen, man vergewaltigt sie,—man heisst diesen Vorgang *Idealisieren*" ("Streifzüge eines Unzeitgemässen," 8).

44. *WWR* 1:208; *ASSW* 1:295.

45. This claim about *Parsifal* will be examined further below.

"Venusberg Baccanale" of *Tannhäuser* from a pornographic film? Again the latter excites the erotic instinct whereas the former reveals the "universal" (even though in both instances there may be the same absence of clothing). One deals with "the alluring" ("das Reizende");[46] the other deals with dis-associated emotion. In many respects Schopenhauer's analysis can help in working out what distinguishes "great art" from "lesser art" but we will see that Wagner himself found it necessary to correct his system.

The Thing-in-Itself and Music

Schopenhauer presents a hierarchy of arts. He had a view of the will's self-objectification in the world of phenomena going from the lowest grade, inorganic matter,[47] through to plant life, animal life, and finally human life. Correspondingly he graded the arts.[48] The equivalent of the highest form of the will's objectification, human life, is drama and of drama he placed tragedy at the top. Tragedy, the "summit of poetic art,"[49] was most able to *access* this noumenal world. However, within this hierarchy there was no place for music. Music came to have a completely different status and before considering Schopenhauer's view, I want to make some general comments about music and its relationship to "nature."

Magee, who largely supports Schopenhauer's aesthetics of music, argues that music "is not arbitrary in the sense that language is. Language is entirely a human creation; but music is rooted in the nature of things."[50] To defend this position one could go back to Pythagoras. He discovered that the basic intervals of the octave, the fifth and the fourth have the ratios 2:1, 3:2, and 4:3 respectively. Schopenhauer observed that the chords we find attractive have ratios "expressible in small numbers."[51] One can go further and develop a circle of fifths to produce each note of the chromatic scale: C G D A E B F#/Gb Db Ab Eb Bb F C. If one were to try this on a piano one would then be rising by fifths twelve times and this would correspond to seven octaves, which would appear to confirm the mathematical nature of musical tones. However, there is a slight problem. If the steps of fifths are

---

46. *WWR* 1:207; *ASSW* 1:294.

47. Magee, *Schopenhauer*, 176: "Platonic ideas characteristically inherent in this [lowest grade] include those of mass, extension, light, water, stone."

48. Magee, *Schopenhauer*, 177.

49. *WWR* 1:252; *ASSW* 1:353.

50. Magee, *Schopenhauer*, 187.

51. *WWR* 2:450; *ASSW* 2:577.

taken strictly as a ratio of 3:2, twelve fifths does not equal seven octaves,[52] the difference being the "Pythagorean comma." It is only by the rather artificial development of "equal temperament" that the twelve fifths corresponds to the seven octaves. Nevertheless, it does seem remarkable that twelve fifths is almost the same the seven octaves.

Another argument used to argue that the key system of Western music does reflect the basic patterns in nature is considering the harmonic series. A string can vibrate at the base frequency (let us say C) but also can produce a series of harmonics: C' (2), G' (3), C'' (4), E'' (5), G'' (6). Such a harmonic series has given us the octave, fifth, and third. However, the seventh harmonic lies between A and Bb. Bernstein says it is a "sort-of-A,"[53] but it is in fact closer to Bb.[54] The eighth in the series is C''' (so in the case of a vibrating string we have it divided into eight) and, rather remarkably, the ninth is D'''. From this last step one can then derive the interval of the tone. So it appears that to a great extent the harmonic series shows that our Western scale is related to nature and mathematics.

Therefore music *does* have a relationship to nature and mathematics,[55] and it is certainly so related in a way other arts are not. I now turn to Schopenhauer's next stage in the argument. He contends that whereas other arts approach the noumenal via the Platonic ideas, music is not a "copy" ("Abbild") of anything in the phenomenal world. After writing of tragedy being the summit of his hierarchy of arts, he writes: "After this, we find that there is yet another fine art that remains excluded, and was bound to be excluded, from our consideration, for in the systematic connection of our discussion there was no fitting place for it; this art was *music*. It stands quite apart from all the others. In it we do not recognize the copy, the repetition, of any Idea of the inner nature of the world."[56]

Schopenhauer came to this fundamental understanding of the role of music in this way. He felt that music is a "language" that reflects something in nature; yet because it is abstract it does not represent anything in the phenomenal world. To what then is it related? Schopenhauer came to the

---

52. One can do a simple calculation. (2/1) to the power 7 gives 128; (3/2) to the power 12 gives 531441/4096 = 129.74633. As Professor John Hunton pointed out to me, this must happen for any exponents. If n fifths were to equal m octaves, we would be saying $(3/2)^n = 2^m$, i.e., $3^n = 2^{n+m}$. This cannot be true since the left hand side is odd and the right is even.

53. Bernstein, *Question*, 27.

54. Storr, *Music*, 60–61.

55. Ibid., 51–64, is rather missing the obvious in denying the links between nature and music (perhaps overreacting to Bernstein's confidence is rooting music in nature).

56. *WWR* 1:255–56; *ASSW* 1:357.

view that it must be related directly to the noumenon, the will. Whereas other arts approach the noumenal via the Platonic Ideas, music is a direct "copy" ("Abbild") of the noumenon. His essential argument is thus:

> As our world is nothing but the phenomenon or appearance of the Ideas in plurality (Erscheinung der Ideen in der Vielheit) through entrance into the *principium individuationis* . . . music, since it passes over the Ideas, is also quite independent of the phenomenal world, positively ignores it, and, to a certain extent, could still exist even if there were no world at all, which cannot be said of the other arts. Thus music is as *immediate* an objectification and copy of the whole *will* as the world itself is . . . (Die Musik ist nämlich eine so *unmittelbare* Objektivation und Abbild des ganzen *Willens*, wie die Welt selbst es ist . . .). Therefore music is by no means like the other arts, namely a copy of the Ideas, but a *copy of the will itself* (*Abbild des Willens selbst*). . .[57]

Schopenhauer argued that not all music reflects the noumenon. There are cases where "music does not express the inner nature of the will itself, but merely imitates its phenomenon inadequately."[58] He gives the examples of Haydn's *The Seasons* and *Creation* and his battle pieces.[59] And although he did not know the music, he would have to include passages from Wagner's *Ring* (e.g., the use of anvils in *Das Rheingold* and *Siegfried*; the representation of thunder storms in *Das Rheingold* and *Die Walküre*; the forest murmurs and the woodbird in *Siegfried*) and of course the bells of Monsalvat! But ignoring such cases where music imitates the phenomena, Schopenhauer asserts this: "The inexpressible depth of all music, by virtue of which it floats past us as a paradise quite familiar and yet eternally remote, and is so easy to understand and yet so inexplicable, is due to the fact that it reproduces all the emotions of our innermost being, but entirely without reality and remote from its pain."[60]

Schopenhauer, rightly I believe, thought that music "is such a great and exceedingly fine art, its effect on man's innermost nature is so powerful, and it is so completely and profoundly understood by him in his inner most being as an entirely universal language" such that one has to go beyond the dictum of Leibniz: music is "an unconscious exercise in arithmetic in which

---

57. *WWR* 1:257; *ASSW* 1:359. In chapter 6 above I compared this to Wagner's view in *Religion and Art* that Christ is an "Abbild" of the divine (*PW* 6:217; *GSD* 10:215; *JA* 10:121). See also the discussion below.

58. *WWR* 1:263; *ASSW* 1:367-68.

59. *WWR* 1:263-64; *ASSW* 1:368.

60. *WWR* 1:264; *ASSW* 1:368.

the mind does not know it is counting."[61] Schopenhauer parodying this gave his higher view of music: "Music is an unconscious exercise in metaphysics in which the mind does not know it is philosophizing."[62]

Many philosophers have not accepted the view that music is a copy of the noumenon. However, some modification can be made. Scruton argues that if, according to Schopenhauer, self-knowledge accesses the will and if music does the same, why not "divide through" by the will[63] and say that when we hear music we are acquainted with *the very same thing* we encounter in self-knowledge. "So music presents subjective awareness in objective form. In responding to expressive music, we are acquiring a 'first-person' perspective on a state of mind that is not our own—indeed which exists unowned and objectified, in the imaginary realm of musical movement."[64] A related approach is offered by Anthony Storr who also seems to "divide through" by the will although he does not put it that way. He actually rejects Schopenhauer's philosophical approach but finds he is nevertheless able to account for the link between music and physiological arousal.

> Schopenhauer's idea that our experience of our own bodies gives a pointer to an underlying reality which we can only otherwise obtain through music is surely connected with his view that music is unlike other arts in that it is a "copy of the will itself." For if music is rooted in the body, and closely connected with bodily movement . . . then Schopenhauer's view that both our experience of the body and our experience of music possess a depth, an immediacy, and an intensity which cannot be obtained in other ways becomes comprehensible and persuasive.[65]

We will see that a related idea is put forward by Wagner in his *Beethoven* essay.

Schopenhauer's view of music does presents problems but there are insights and one of them is precisely this parallel between music and first person knowledge that Scruton suggests. This parallel can also be found in relation to time. As we saw, Schopenhauer did pay attention to time in

---

61. Quoted in *WWR* 1:256; *ASSW* 1:357: music is "*exercitium arithmeticae occultum nescientis se numerare animi.*" Schopenhauer references the Korholt edition of Leibniz's letters (epistula 154).

62. *WWR* 1:264; *ASSW* 1:369: "*Musica est exercitium metaphysices occultum nescientis se philosophari animi.*"

63. He compares Wittgenstein, *Philosophical Investigations*, 1.293 (the "beetle" in the box).

64. Scruton, *Death-Devoted Heart*, 77.

65. Storr, *Music*, 149.

relation to self-knowledge. He also addresses the issue briefly at the end of his discussion of music (section 52), which forms the end of book 3:

> I might still have much to add on the way in which music is perceived, namely in and through time alone, with absolute exclusion of space, even without the influence of the knowledge of causality, and thus of the understanding. For the tones make the aesthetic impression as effect, and this without our going back to their causes, as in the case of perception.[66]

From this one can perceive a parallel between his approach to the noumenon in self-knowledge and in music. So in both self-knowledge and in music the subject is imposing time. But many would object to the idea of a timeless subject imposing time within themselves or on experienced music or, of course, on the outer world generally. Taking the instance of music, is this not *given* to us. Of course, our subjective experience varies in that some music seems interminably long and some feels like a passing moment and such experiences can come to an extreme when experiencing Wagner! But what is interesting is that our experiences of time in relation to our inner life parallels our experiences of time in music. And it could be said that in both music and self-knowledge time is "experienced" in a special way: it is not time-less and neither is one in time "according to the principle of sufficient reason."[67]

So there are some fundamental loose ends in Schopenhauer's understanding of music, not only in regard to time but also to the will of the subject. Further he does not seem to discuss the question of the "aesthetic state" in listening to music. Is such a state now redundant since one no longer needs the Platonic Ideas to access the noumenon? Also what does one say about music with words (songs and oratorios) or with movement (ballet), or with words and action (opera)? For if music is an "Abbild," a "copy" of the noumenon, if it gives us immediate knowledge of the ultimate (or penultimate) reality of the world, then the addition of words and action would seem at best an irrelevance and at worst a serious distraction. "In Platonic terms, if music takes us directly to the sunlit world of reality, what possible interest could one have in trying to decipher the nature of that world by looking at the flickering shadows in the cave?"[68]

For now I address this last set of problems for which there are two possible solutions. The first is to say that the finest songs, operas, and oratorios

---

66. *WWR* 1:266; *ASSW* 1:371.

67. Perhaps it could be described as a "semi-aesthetic experience."

68. Young, *Schopenhauer*, 154.

give a stereoscopic view of the world-will.[69] They point to an inner *and* outer view of the world. So Schopenhauer writes: "the effect of music is so very much more powerful and penetrating than is that of the other arts, for these others speak only of the shadow, but music of the essence. However, as it is the same will that objectifies itself both in the Ideas and in music, though in quite a different way in each, there must be, not indeed an absolutely direct likeness, but yet a parallel, an analogy, between music and the Ideas, the phenomenon of which in plurality and in incompleteness is the visible world."[70] This stereoscopic nature of music with words or with action is at its highest when there is an appropriate combination of words and music. *Parsifal* is full of such instances as we have seen in chapters 5 and 7 above.

Schopenhauer's philosophy of music, for all its defects, is nevertheless highly suggestive. But can Wagner's theories take us any further? Schopenhauer argues that music takes us to the essence of the world. Can Wagner develop this and indeed tell us whether his music dramas can reveal something of God or the "divine"? And how does he deal with the interaction of music, text, and drama? And how can this be related to a revelation of "the divine"?

Wagner on Music, Text, Drama, and the Thing-in-Itself, and God

The issue of "revelation" in a work such as *Parsifal* is very much tied up with the question of how the various elements, music, text, "dance," etc., relate to the "drama." Wagner's 1850–51 extended "essay" *Opera and Drama* argued that music should serve the drama[71] and it could be said that such a theory is worked out in the next stage work he composed, *Das Rheingold*. In *Opera and Drama* he likens poetry (discussed in Part I) to the male and music (discussed in Part II) to the female.[72] The drama then comes about by the sexual union of the two;[73] or, using a term from Christology, one could speak of a "hypostatic union."

---

69. Cf. ibid., 155.

70. *WWR* 1:257–58; *ASSW* 1:359–60.

71. On the sense of drama see Dahlhaus, *Music Dramas*, 156.

72. Note that Luther understands music as feminine ("Frau Musika [spricht] . . .") in his preface to "Lob und Preis der löblichen Kunst Musica: durch H. Johann Walter" (Fausel, *Leben II*, 69–70). Note especially the lines "hie bleibt kein Zorn, Zank, Haß noch Neid, / weichen muß alles Herzeleid."

73. See Dyson, "Sea, Mirror, Woman, Love."

Wagner, however, changed his mind concerning the relationship of these various elements partly as a result of reading Schopenhauer. In *Tristan und Isolde* it is the music that is primary, "giving birth" to the drama. *Tristan*, together with Wagner's *Beethoven* essay and Schopenhauer's aesthetics,[74] was to inspire Nietzsche's *The Birth of Tragedy from the Spirit of Music* (1872).

In Wagner's operas written after his discovery of Schopenhauer (1854), we not only have an intricate combination of music, drama, text, and visual (his so-called "Gesamtkunstwerk," "total artwork") but the idea that drama grows out of the music. Music, an abstract art, manifests itself in the drama (as the noumenon manifests itself in the phenomenon). Perhaps in Wagner's mature stage works, music really does "gives birth" to the tragedy; they are not simply a musical setting of a text. Support for such a view is given by Wagner himself in his essay *On the Name Musikdrama* (1872) where he described his dramas as *"deeds of music that have become visible"* (*"ersichtlich gewordene Thaten der Musik"*)[75] And even looking back at *Das Rheingold* (which was composed before his discovery of Schopenhauer) he writes that the drama was conceived by the Eb major chord.[76] And going back even further I noted in chapter 2 his idea that it was the "music within the heart" that was the driving force.[77] The question though is whether this is simply a romantic view put forward by the "Wort-Ton Künstler" that has little bearing on the realities of his composition.

When we come to *Parsifal*, it appears that its genesis was not so much a musical inspiration but rather the atmosphere of "Good Friday." And when we look at the mechanism by which Wagner composed, the words were written first and the details of the music had to fit that.[78] An exception that proves the rule is his composition of "Nehmet hin mein Blut" ("Take this

---

74. Compare *WWR* 1:263 (*ASSW* 1:367), on the relation of music to text: concepts are *universalia post rem*; music gives the *universalia ante rem*. See also *WWR* 2:449; *ASSW* 2:575–76.

75. *PW* 5:303 (modified); *GSD* 9:306; *JA* 9:276.

76. See *My Life* 499 (*Mein Leben* 2:512), recounting an event that is supposed to have taken place in Spezia: "I sank into a kind of somnambulistic state, in which I suddenly had the feeling of being immersed in rapidly flowing water. Its rushing soon resolved itself for me into the musical sound of the chord of E flat major, resounding in persistent broken chords." Millington, *Sorcerer*, 193, now believes "it may just be that he did indeed have some hallucinatory experience on that couch in La Spezia" (contrast his earlier sceptical view, Millington, *Wagner*, 198–99).

77. *PW* 1:365; *GSD* 4:318–19; *JA* 6:297.

78. See Deathridge, "Reviews," 83, in critical comments on Robert Bailey and Curt von Westernhagen: "There is not one scrap of evidence proving that Wagner's musical ideas were anything but rudimentary when he was writing his librettos."

my blood"),[79] especially significant because it goes back to one of the earliest sketches Wagner made for the work.[80] Cosima's entry for 11 August 1877 records this "revelation": "R. tells me he wrote it down shortly before my return, with his hat and coat on, just as he was about to go out to meet me. He has had to alter the words to fit it, he says; this scene of Holy Communion will be the main scene, the core of the whole work; with the 'Prize Song' in *Die Meistersinger*, too, the melody came first, and he had adapted the words to it."

Although in his "workshop" the text usually came first and was then "set" to music, a case could still be made that the music was the fundamental driving force and was ontologically prior. This would certainly cohere with the crucial role of music in Wagner's understanding of "revelation." I now turn to three essays that in one way or another deal with this question: first, his *Beethoven* essay, which deals especially with music's revelatory role; secondly, his essay *On State and Religion,* which offers an important theological supplement to *Beethoven*; finally, *Religion and Art,* which is especially important for understanding how the "divine" is revealed in *Parsifal*.

In his *Beethoven* essay of 1870, "the major aesthetic work of Wagner's later years,"[81] there are views expressed that contradict those in *Opera and Drama*. It is especially valuable for discussing *Parsifal* since there is an intense discussion not only about music but also about its relationship to other arts. As Wagner explains in the preface,[82] his contribution to the centenary of Beethoven's birth is an imaginary speech delivered "at an ideal feast in honour of the great Musician" and goes beyond the music of the composer, conducting the reader "through a more searching inquiry into the nature of

---

79. *WagPS* 148–49.

80. Kinderman, "Genesis," 149–54. The very first sketch was Parzival's appearance in Act 3 of *Tristan*, the date of which is disputed (144–45). It is significant that it contains elements that were to form the grail motif. However, this sketch was abandoned. The first music written specifically for *Parsifal* is the chorus for the flowermaidens "Komm! holder Knabe!" (146–48). See also the earlier study of Voss, "Klage in der Wonne," 227–30. He establishes that this sketch (from 9 February 1876, further developed a week later, 16 February) gives the foundational key of the whole work (Ab major) and from this one can derive the grail theme (the rising from the fifth to the octave with the parallel sixths). He also makes suggestions as to how other themes were developed from the music of Act II Scene 2 (228–30).

81. Kühnel, "Prose Writings," 619. This work was in fact to become the inspiration of *Birth of Tragedy*. See Nietzsche's Preface: "you will recall that I was collecting myself to frame these thoughts at the same time as you were composing your magnificent celebratory essay on Beethoven . . ." (Nietzsche, *Tragedy*, 13).

82. The work consists of a preface (*PW* 5:59–60) and three roughly equal sections without headings (61–81, 81–113, 113–26).

Music, and thus to submit to the consideration of men of serious culture a contribution to the Philosophy of Music."[83]

He takes over the essence of Schopenhauer's aesthetics that music speaks "a language immediately intelligible by everyone" since it is not mediated by "concepts" ("Begriffe"). In poetry, on the other hand, concepts are essential, employed by it to visualize the *Idea* ("zur Veranschaulichung der *Idee*").[84] It is such Platonic ideas "that constitute the 'object' of the fine arts." But whereas the poet "interprets these Ideas to the visual consciousness (dem anschauenden Bewusstsein)" through "rationalistic concepts," in music we have an idea of the world itself ("eine Idee der Welt").[85]

He accepts Schopenhauer's view that to seize an idea there must be temporary preponderance of intellect over will.[86] He then employs his crucial distinction between two sides of human consciousness, taken from Schopenhauer: "consciousness of *one's own self*" and "consciousness of *other things*." The former is the "self-knowledge" discussed above by which one can approach the "will"; the latter is "a consciousness of *other things*, and chiefly then a *visual* knowledge of the outer world, the apprehension of objects." Then, quoting Schopenhauer: "The more the one side of the aggregate consciousness comes to the front, the more does the other retreat."[87]

He then engages in a contrast between these two forms of consciousness, one directed inwards to the "will," the other directed outwards to "objects." Building on Schopenhauer's "Dream-theory," he suggests that "inward-facing consciousness," as in dreams, attains "actual power of sight" ("wirkliche(r) Hellsichtigkeit") whereas the "waking daylight consciousness feels nothing but a vague impression of the midnight background of our will's emotions." Ironically, then, one has more profound "sight" through dreams and the "night" than through the "day" (a view that is supported by both *Tristan* and *Parsifal*). Thus he comes to contrast the

---

83. *PW* 5:59; *GSD* 9:61; *JA* 9:38. Köhler, *Titans*, 518, comments that the commemorative essay "dealt less with the subject of the centennial celebrations than with Beethoven's role within the metaphysical framework of Wagner's thinking. Like both *Opera and Drama* and Nietzsche's 1872 study, it examined the question of the conditions that make art possible, together with its origins and decline. In short, it could equally well have been called not *Beethoven* but *The Birth of Tragedy from the Spirit of Music.*"

84. *PW* 5:65; *GSD* 9:66; *JA* 9:43.

85. *PW* 5:65; *GSD* 9:66; *JA* 9:43–44.

86. *PW* 5:66–67; *GSD* 9:67; *JA* 9:45.

87. *PW* 5:67; *GSD* 9:68; *JA* 9:45. The reference to Schopenhauer can be found in *WWR* 2:367 (2.30).

"sound-world" ("Schallwelt") and "light-world" ("Lichtwelt"), the former accessing the "Will" whereas the latter is a mere perception of "appearance" ("Erscheinung").[88]

And so Wagner compares music to "plastic art" ("die bildende Kunst"). In plastic art there is the possibility of "pure Beholding" where the object is "raised to an Idea."[89] In music, however, "the world immediately displays its essence" and does not have to pass through "the medium of understanding (das Erkennen)."[90]

We now come to a point where Wagner appears to be deviating from Schopenhauer in relation to questions of the "will." In "pure beholding" the "individual will" is silenced. This is thoroughly Schopenhauerian.[91] But for the musician, the "universal Will" is aroused.

> Hence the great difference in the mental state of the concipient musician and the designing artist; hence the radically diverse effects of music and of painting; here the profoundest stilling, there utmost excitation of the will.... This prodigious breaking-down the floodgates of Appearance must necessarily call forth in the inspired musician a state of ecstacy wherewith no other can compare; in it the will perceives itself the almighty Will of all things: it has not mutely to yield place to contemplation, but proclaims itself aloud as conscious World-Idea.[92]

Such an approach to music coheres very well with Storr's approach discussed above[93] and both Wagner and Storr are taking a different path to that of Schopenhauer.[94]

For Wagner only the state of the "saint" ("der Heilige") surpasses that of the experience of music. This is because whereas "the clairvoyant ecstasy of the musician has to alternate with a perpetually recurrent state of individual consciousness, which we must account the more distressful the higher has his inspiration carried him above all bounds of individuality," in the case of the "saint" there is a "permanence and imperturbability."[95] Wagner would appear to be saying that for the saint the "being taken out of oneself" is

---

88. *PW* 5:68; *GSD* 9:68; *JA* 9:46.

89. *PW* 5:72; *GSD* 9:72; *JA* 9:50.

90. *PW* 5:72; *GSD* 9:72; *JA* 9:50.

91. See Schopenhauer's example of still life quoted above (*WWR* 1:208).

92. *PW* 5:72; *GSD* 9:73; *JA* 9:50–51.

93. See Storr, *Music*, 149.

94. Cf. *WWR* 2:451 (*ASSW* 2:579), where Schopenhauer argues that music does not excite the will: "Therefore the affectations of the will itself ... must not be excited ..."

95. *PW* 5:72; *GSD* 9:73; *JA* 9:51.

permanent, but for the musician it is temporary.[96] For Wagner, the musician has to suffer "as a penalty for the state of inspiration," and as a consequence should be held "in higher reverence than other artists," indeed he should be afforded the rank of "holy."[97] "For his art, in truth, compares with the communion of all the other arts as *Religion* with the *Church*."[98]

Wagner then returns to comparing the world of dreams to the "representations (Vorstellungen) of the waking brain."[99] The former corresponds to music and the latter to the plastic arts where space and time are applicable. In the world of music, harmony, he claims, belongs to neither space nor time; but in rhythmic sequences, "the musician (as a teacher) reaches forth a hand, so to speak, to strike a compact with the waking world of semblances."[100] This parallels the way in which we are able to form a bridge between the images of dreams and the "outer incidents of actual life."[101] He continues: "So the musician makes contact with the plastic world through the *rhythmic* ordering of his tones, and that in virtue of a resemblance to the laws whereby the motion of visible bodies is brought to our intelligence."[102] He then makes a comment that clarifies his earlier writings where he discusses "dance":[103] "Human Gesture (Die menschliche Gebärde), which seeks to make itself intelligible in Dance through an expressive regularity of changeful motion, thus seems to play the same part toward Music as bodies, in their turn, toward Light: without refraction and reflection, Light would not shine; and so we may say that without rhythm, Music would not be observable."[104] So "dance" as one of the three key arts is actually related to the wider issue of "gesture."

---

96. On the issue of existential displacement, something central for Luther, see Bell, *Deliver Us from Evil*, 248–49. See also the closing discussion in chapter 12 below.

97. *PW* 5:72–73; *GSD* 9:73; *JA* 9:51.

98. *PW* 5:73; *GSD* 9:73; *JA* 9:51.

99. *PW* 5:75 (modified); *GSD* 9:76; *JA* 9:54.

100. *PW* 5:75 (modified). This is a free translation of a clause almost impossible to translate ("reicht der nun bildende Musiker der wachenden Erscheingungswelt durch die *rhythmische* Zeitfolge seiner Kundgebungen gleichsam die Hand zur Verständigung"; *GSD* 9:76; *JA* 9:54).

101. *PW* 5:75–76; *GSD* 9:76; *JA* 9:54.

102. *PW* 5:76; *GSD* 9:76; *JA* 9:54–55.

103. In *The Art-Work of the Future* Wagner presents the "most high-born Muses of artistic man" of "*Dance*, of *Tone*, and *Poetry*." They are "the three primeval sisters," the "trinitarian utterance of human Art" (*PW* 1:95). Section 3 is devoted to "The Art of Dance" (*PW* 1:100–10).

104. *PW* 5:76; *GSD* 9:76; *JA* 9:55. One could question whether this comment is illuminating!

Wagner then turns to the aesthetic judgement ("Urteil") of music, warning that if music represses her fundamental nature, she functions merely for "turning her outmost side to our delectation," i.e., simply to reinforce other arts.[105] Further, music should be judged solely "by . . . the category of the *sublime*" ("nach der Kategorie des *Erhabenen*") "for as soon as she [i.e., "die Musik"] engrosses us, she transports us to the highest ecstacy of the consciousness of our infinitude."[106] To this he adds a comment on "beauty" (where the intellect is released from any recollection of the "will"):[107] in plastic art, the experience of beauty is a sequel to the temporary liberation of the intellect from the will, but in music it comes at her very first entry. "Consequently our verdict (Urteil) on any piece of music should be based upon a knowledge of those laws whereby the effect of Beauty (Wirkung der schönen Erscheinung), the very first effect of Music's mere appearance, advances the most directly to a revelation of her truest character through the effect of the Sublime (durch die Wirkung des Erhabenen)."[108]

This section is crucially important since it demonstrates that although music is a direct copy of the world-will, some music is better than others; and for Wagner "our great *Beethoven*" was "the true archetype of the Musician."[109] How then does one come to compose such great music?

Music, he suggests, is incited by an inmost vision ("von einer innersten Schau angeregt") and to convey that vision to the outer world a special organ "analogous to the Dream-organ" is required, "a kind of eye, when it faces inwards, that becomes an ear when directed outwards."[110] The manifestation of the inmost dream-image into the outer world can be clearly seen in Palestrina's church music. "Here rhythm is nowhere traceable save through the play of harmonic sequences. . . . Succession (Zeitfolge) is still so rigidly bound to that timeless, spaceless essence, Harmony, that we can-

105. Wagner seems to have moved on from his position put forward in *The Artwork of the Future*: "The true Drama is only conceivable as proceeding from a *common urgence of every art* (aus dem *gemeinsamen Drange aller Künste*) towards the most direct appeal to a *common public*. In this Drama, each separate art can only bare its utmost secret to their common public through a mutual parleying with the other arts; for the purpose of each separate branch of art can only be fully attained by the reciprocal agreement and co-operation of all the branches in their common message" (*PW* 1:184; *GSD* 3:150; *JA* 6:127).

106. *PW* 5:77; *GSD* 9:78; *JA* 9:56. Contrast Schopenhauer's discussion of music in *WWR* which does not bring in the category of the sublime.

107. On the distinction between the sublime and the beautiful see Bell, *Deliver Us from Evil*, 158–61.

108. *PW* 5:78 (modified); *GSD* 9:78; *JA* 9:57.

109. *PW* 5:79; *GSD* 9:79; *JA* 9:57–58.

110. *PW* 5:79; *GSD* 9:79; *JA* 9:58.

not as yet employ the laws of Time to aid us in the understanding of such music."[111] We are given an image that is "almost as timeless as it is spaceless, an altogether spiritual revelation."[112] He adds: "and the reason why it moves us so indicibly is that, more plainly than all other things, it brings to our consciousness the inmost essence of Religion free from all dogmatic fictions (frei von jeder dogmatischen Begriffsfiktion)."[113] Wagner, I think, has put his finger on why a work such as *Parsifal* can have such a profound effect; even if one considers the final words theologically dubious ("Redemption to the Redeemer"), the music of those closing moments is so exalted as to bring to our consciousness "dogma free" Christian truth.

He concludes the first section by pointing to cases where "plastic" elements enter in "dance music" (e.g., in orchestral symphonic movement).[114] "Music developed along these lines has very properly been given the name of 'secular' ('weltlich'), in opposition to that 'spiritual' ('geistlichen')."[115] But there is a danger here. If music is too closely linked with the "outer" world, then music loses her "state of lofty innocence";[116] "she loses her power of redeeming from the curse of Appearance: no longer is she the prophetess of the Essence of things, but herself becomes entangled in the illusive show of things outside us."[117] For this music "one wants to *see* something as well, and that something to-be-seen becomes the chief concern." Such is the case in "Opera." He clearly has his sights on "Grand Opera" (especially Meyerbeer) "where spectacle, ballet, and so forth make out the lure, the main attraction, and visibly enough proclaim the degeneracy of the music there employed."[118]

Section two begins by considering the "evolution of Beethoven's genius," starting with a discussion of the "practical maturing" of his style.[119] In the course of this discussion he speaks of the degeneration of music. He speaks of a "Vernunft" ("reason") that formed the "operatic aria," "the stringing together of operatic numbers," "the logic that made Haydn chain his genie to an everlasting counting of his rosary-beads."[120] He adds: "For

---

111. *PW* 5:79; *GSD* 9:79; *JA* 9:58. Note his point above that harmony is "timeless."

112. *PW* 5:79; *GSD* 9:79; *JA* 9:58.

113. *PW* 5:79; *GSD* 9:80; *JA* 9:58.

114. *PW* 5:79–80; *GSD* 9:80; *JA* 9:58.

115. *PW* 5:80; *GSD* 9:80; *JA* 9:59.

116. *PW* 5:80; *GSD* 9:81; *JA* 9:59.

117. *PW* 5:80; *GSD* 9:81; *JA* 9:59.

118. *PW* 5:80–81; *GSD* 9:81; *JA* 9:59–60.

119. *PW* 5:81; *GSD* 9:81; *JA* 9:60.

120. *PW* 5:83–84; *GSD* 9:84; *JA* 9:63.

Religion had vanished from the Church with Palestrina's music, and the artificial formalism of Jesuit observance had counterformed Religion and Music alike."[121]

Towards the end of this second section he then returns to the aesthetic themes that occupied much of section one, and focuses on the relationship between music and "poetry" and "drama." One of his striking comments, and this shows a clear departure from his view in *Opera and Drama* Part 3, is that "the relation of Music to *Poetry*" is "a sheer illusion (ein durchaus illusorisches)."[122] This is seen by the fact that "music loses nothing of its character even when the most diverse texts are laid beneath it" and that in the union of music and poetry, the latter is subordinated.[123]

Now for Wagner, "Drama towers above the bounds of Poetry," and he offers a philosophical analysis of the relationship of music and drama: "Seeing that Music does not portray Ideas inherent in the world's phenomena, but is itself an Idea of the World, and a comprehensive one, it naturally includes the Drama in itself; as Drama, again, expresses the only world's-Idea proportionate to Music."[124] As a result of this he then develops his philosophy of music's relationship to drama:

> We consequently should not go far astray, if we defined Music as man's qualification *a priori* for fashioning the Drama. Just as we construct for ourselves the world of semblances through application of the laws of Time and Space existing *a priori* in our brain, so this conscious representation of the world's Idea in Drama would thus be foreordained by those inner laws of Music, operating in the dramatist equally unconsciously with the laws of Causality we bring into employment for apperception of the phenomenal world.[125]

Wagner then applies his theory to Shakespeare who "remained entirely beyond comparison" until his counterpart, Beethoven, appeared. Wagner

121. *PW* 5:84; *GSD* 9:84; *JA* 9:63.

122. *PW* 5:104; *GSD* 9:103; *JA* 9:85. On this departure, see Kühnel, "Prose Writings," 621.

123. *PW* 5:104; *GSD* 9:103; *JA* 9:85. This is a view which is in tune with Schopenhauer (e.g., *WWR* 1:263). Again Wagner's comments makes sense of experiencing the close of *Parsifal*.

124. *PW* 5:106; *GSD* 9:105; *JA* 9:87.

125. *PW* 5:106–7; *GSD* 9:106; *JA* 9:87. Although many may consider Wagner's claim for music excessive (he also seems to retract this somewhat in *GSD* 9:108; *PW* 5:108, quoted below), a more modest proposal could be that music provides the "grammar" for drama rather as natural theology provides a grammar for revealed theology (cf. Torrance, *Reality*, 32–63).

here does not discuss the process of "fashioning the Drama"; rather he makes the point that "[i]f we take the whole impression left by Shakespeare's world of shapes upon our inner feeling . . . and uphold it to the sum-total of Beethoven's world of motives . . . we cannot but see that the one of these worlds completely covers the other . . ."[126] As an example he gives the overture to Coriolanus.[127]

He therefore sees music as "the revelation of the inner vision of the Essence of the world (die Offenbarung des innersten Traumbildes vom Wesen der Welt), and Shakespeare we might term a Beethoven who goes on dreaming though awake. What holds their spheres asunder, are the formal conditions of the laws of apperception obtaining in each."[128] He thinks the "perfect art-form would therefore have to take its rise from the point where those respective laws could meet."[129] Since Shakespeare and Beethoven are counterparts, "we perhaps may gain the clearest notion of that point where their two spheres would touch, or melt into each other, if we take our philosopher once more for guide, and proceed to the goal of his Dream-theory, his hypothesis of ghostly apparitions."[130] We know that Wagner was reading Schopenhauer's "Versuch über das Geistersehn"[131] as he conceived of *Tristan*.[132] Using this framework Wagner calls Beethoven, a kind of "clairvoyant," "the hidden motor of Shakespeare the ghost-seer."[133] An "Artwork" such as the Ninth Symphony is "the most perfect Drama" and the "drama," not the "dramatic poem," is the visible counterpart of music; in "drama," "word and speech belong no more to the poet's thought, but solely to the action."[134]

Wagner's philosophical analysis finishes with the close of this second section of the essay. His analysis of music, text, and drama is certainly thought provoking; but is he correct? He has been accused of exploiting "a

126. *PW* 5:107; *GSD* 9:107; *JA* 88.

127. *PW* 5:107–8; *GSD* 9:107; *JA* 9:88–89. Although Beethoven was "[a]n enthusiastic reader of Shakespeare in A. W. Schlegel's translation" (Daverio, "Chamber Music," 152), the overture was written for Heinrich Joseph von Collin's tragedy "Coriolan," not for Shakespeare's Coriolanus (Bekker, *Wagner*, 409). In fact Beethoven named none of his works after Shakespeare (the name "The Tempest" for the Piano Sonata no. 17 in D minor does not go back to Beethoven).

128. *PW* 5:108; *GSD* 9:108; *JA* 9:89–90.

129. *PW* 5:108; *GSD* 9:108; *JA* 9:90.

130. *PW* 5:109; *GSD* 9:108; *JA* 9:90.

131. *PP* 1:225–309; *ASSW* 4:273–372.

132. Deathridge, "Postmortem on Isolde," 265 n. 17.

133. *PW* 5:110; *GSD* 9:110; *JA* 9:92.

134. *PW* 5:112; *GSD* 9:111; *JA* 9:93.

facile dichotomy between the inner world and the outer world, in order to privilege music and the ear over and against the plastic arts and the eye,"[135] and Bekker also questions this dichotomy since the "sound-world" ("Schall-welt") is just as subject to the senses as the "light-world" ("Lichtwelt").[136] In defense of Wagner one could make the point that the senses function in quite different ways in these two "worlds." In the case of the "light-world," electro-magnetic waves actually form an "image" on the retina, although the way the brain interprets this (in terms of shape, color, and movement) is complex (and quite "Schopenhauerian").[137] But in the case of the "sound-world" the air vibrations produce no corresponding "image" in the hearing mechanism and the "noise" or "tone" or "music" appears to be a product of the human brain/mind. Perhaps Wagner is not so fanciful when he writes, "[a]s the world of dreams can only come to vision through a special op-eration of the brain, so Music enters our consciousness through a kindred operation."[138]

Wagner's dichotomy between the outer world where objects are given to us in a certain way (according to space, time, and causation) and the inner world where we have an immediate consciousness is partly based on Schopenhauer who has certainly had his defenders on this point.[139] Further, Wagner, it could be said, has "corrected" Schopenhauer in relating music to excitation of the will.[140] But to judge the essay in terms of its "philosophical rigor" is perhaps to miss the point. Although Wagner claims to be offering a "philosophy of music" the whole work seems to be more about Wagner reflecting on his own creative processes,[141] rather as a prophet may try to explain what is going on in his consciousness as he speaks God's "word." Also, the whole thrust of Wagner *and* philosophy is not so much a phi-losophy *of* music but doing philosophy *through* music. Likewise, although he does engage in a theology *of* music, the emphasis is on doing theology *through* music.

The final thing to note about the Beethoven essay is that Wagner does have positive things to say about Christianity. In the third and final section

---

135. Burnham, "Beethoven," 278.

136. Bekker, *Wagner*, 406.

137. Zeki, *Vision of the Brain*; Zeki, *Splendors and Miseries of the Brain*, 1–128.

138. *PW* 5:68; *GSD* 9:69; *JA* 9:46.

139. E.g., Magee, *Schopenhauer*, 119–36.

140. See *PW* 5:72. He is perhaps less successful in arguing that music functions rather like the categories for drama (*PW* 5:106–7).

141. Cf. Bowie, *Music*, 218. Also Bekker, *Wagner*, 411, despite his criticisms, finds value in the essay as "primarily a work of art" in that Wagner discloses "the nature of his own creative activity."

of his essay he writes: "As Christianity stepped forth amid the Roman civilisation of the universe, so *Music* breaks forth from the chaos of modern civilisation."[142] Further: "It was the spirit of Christianity that rewoke to life the soul of Music (Der Geist des Christenthums war es, der die Seele der Musik neu wieder belebte)."[143] And it was this music which inspired the Italian painters.[144] These are ideas which he later developed in *Religion and Art*, discussed below.

The *Beethoven* essay demonstrates that music certainly reveals the "essence" ("Wesen") of the world. This parallels his view on revelation of "the divine" in that music "brings to our consciousness the inmost essence (Wesen) of Religion."[145] In order to tease out his thoughts on divine revelation more fully, I turn to his slightly earlier essay *On State and Religion*, written privately for Ludwig in 1864 but not published until 1873.[146] Wagner explains to Ludwig how his views on state and religion have changed since his writings of 1849–51.[147] What concerns us here are his comments on theological epistemology, which deserve closer attention. Roughly half way through the essay he moves from a discussion of state to religion, two contrasting entities. "To the religious eye (der religiösen Vorstellung) . . . there must be another world than this."[148] One needs to "perceive the nullity of all the world" for which we need a "wonder-working representation" ("diese wunderwirkende Vorstellung")[149] that "must have a source so sublime" which can only be recognized "from this its supernatural effect (aus dieser übernatürlichen Wirkung)."[150]

142. *PW* 5:120; *JA* 9:103; *GSD* 9:121.

143. *PW* 5:121; *GSD* 9:121; *JA* 9:104.

144. *PW* 5:121: "And Music lit the eye of the Italian painter, inspiring it to penetrate the veil of things and reach their soul, the Christian spirit, fast decaying in the Church." *GSD* 9:121 (*JA* 9:103): "Sie verklärte das Auge des italienischen Malers, und begeisterte seine Sehkraft, durch die Erscheinung der Dinge hindurch auf ihre Seele, den in der Kirche andererseits verkommenen Geist des Christenthums zu dringen."

145. *PW* 5:79; *GSD* 9:79; *JA* 9:58, quoted above.

146. Ellis comments: "Undoubtedly to its intimate character we owe those deeper glimpses into Wagner's inmost thought, such as we meet so often in his private correspondence" (*PW* 4:4).

147. Wagner downplays his part in the Dresden uprising of May 1849 claiming that whoever assigned him "the role of political revolutionary" really knows nothing about him (*PW* 4:6; *GSD* 8:4; *JA* 8:218)!

148. *PW* 4:24; *GSD* 8:20; *JA* 8:236.

149. Ellis in *PW* 4:25 translates "Vorstellung" with "intuition"; the latter is usually a rendering of "Anschauung."

150. *PW* 4:25; *GSD* 8:21; *JA* 8:237.

Wagner emphasizes "voluntary suffering and renunciation" and being "relieved from all representations of Space and Time" ("der in Raum und Zeit befangenen Vorstellung enthoben").[151] A "superhuman strength" is needed to suffer voluntarily, this being the "measurelessly lofty joy of world-overcoming (Weltüberwindung), compared wherewith the empty pleasure of the world conqueror (des Welteroberers) seems downright null and childish."[152] This points us to the "Divine Wahn" (obviously Wahn used in its positive sense), which cannot be reduced to "*our* conceptual method."[153]

The essence of religion is not in its moral law, since the root principles of all morality can be found in even the most imperfect religion. Wagner obviously thinks Christianity is the only authentic religion. "As Religion's highest force proclaims itself in *Faith*, its most essential import lies within its Dogma" ("Wie die höchste Kraft der Religion sich im *Glauben* kundgiebt, liegt ihre wesentlichste Bedeutung in ihrem *Dogma*").[154] Such knowledge of the divine can only come to the religious person through what one would call revelation; but this is almost impossible to articulate to the profane person. So the "immediate vision seen by the Religious (unmittelbare Wahrnehmung des Religiösen), to the ordinary human apprehension remains entirely foreign and unconveyable, in respect of both its substance and its form. What, on the other hand, is imparted thereof and thereon to the layman (den Profanen), to the people, can be nothing more than a kind of allegory."[155] Hence "allegory" for Wagner is an inferior form of communication (whereas for Schopenhauer it was the only form whereby religion could communicate).[156] "In this sacred allegory an attempt is made to transmit to worldly minds (der weltlichen Vorstellung) the mystery of the divine revelation: but the only relation it can bear to what the Religious had immediately beheld, is the relation of the day-told dream to the actual dream of night."[157] The inferiority of allegory is again stressed by Wagner: "If, then, the record left upon our mind by a deeply moving dream is strictly nothing but an allegorical paraphrase, whose intrinsic disagreement with the original remains a trouble to our waking consciousness; and therefore if the knowledge reaped by the hearer can at bottom be nothing but an

151. *PW* 4:25 (modified); *GSD* 8:21; *JA* 8:237.

152. *PW* 4:25–26; *GSD* 8:21–22; *JA* 8:237. This distinction between "world-over-coming" and "world-conquering" is crucial as we saw in chapter 9 above.

153. *PW* 4:26; *GSD* 8:22; *JA* 8:238.

154. *PW* 4:26; *GSD* 8:22; *JA* 8:238.

155. *PW* 4:27; *GDS* 8:22; *JA* 8:239.

156. Schmidt, *Wahrheit*, 12. Note the way in which myth can pass over to allegory in apocalyptic eschatology (see Bell, *Deliver Us from Evil*, 58–60).

157. *PW* 4:27; *GSD* 8:23; *JA* 8:239.

essentially distorted image of that original: yet this [allegorical] message, in the case both of the dream and of the actually received divine revelation (göttlichen Offenbarung), remains the only possible way of proclaiming the thing received to the layman (den Laien)."[158]

It is from this allegory that dogmas come. "Upon these lines is formed the Dogma; and this is the revelation's only portion cognisable by the world, which it therefore has to take on authority, so as to become a partner, at least through Faith, in what its eye has never seen."[159] He continues: "Hence is Faith so strenuously commended to the Folk (Volk): the Religious, become a sharer in salvation through his own eye's beholding (durch eigene Anschauung), feels and knows that the layman, to whom the vision (die Anschauung) itself remains a stranger, has no path to the knowledge of the Divine except the path of Faith."[160] Wagner makes the fundamental distinction between "the Religious" ("der Religiöse)" (who receives special revelation) and the "people" ("Volk") or "laymen" ("Laien") who are entirely dependent on "faith." This faith to be effective "must be sincere, undoubting and unconditional."

Such "faith" may appear at first sight to be a "blind faith"; but it is more likely to be a genuine faith, which does not conform to the usual rules of "rationality." Hence the "intrinsic distortion of Religion's fundamental essence" comes about when "the Dogma's nature is dragged before the tribune of common causal apprehension (kausale Erkenntniß)." Religion is vitiated when the "dogma," which blesses "through an inward Faith," has to be defended "against the assaults of common human apprehension (gegen die Angriffe der gemeinen menschlichen Erkenntniß zu verteidigen)."[161] This is especially problematic when religion "which has its primal fount within the deepest chasms of the world-fleeting heart" comes in relation to the state.[162]

Wagner contrasts two modes of religious knowing. In the one case "religious Dogma" is understood "by laws of cause-and-effect deduced from the phenomena of natural and social life." This occurred partly through the church clutching "at the weapons of State-jurisdiction." The second mode of knowing, one that demonstrates that "Religion" has not ceased, is where it truly does live, "but only at its primal source and sole true dwelling-place, within the deepest, holiest inner chamber of the individual (im tiefsten, heiligsten Innern des Individuums)."[163]

158. *PW* 4:27; *GSD* 8:23; *JA* 8:239.

159. *PW* 4:27–28; *GSD* 8:23; *JA* 8:239.

160. *PW* 4:28; *GSD* 8:23; *JA* 8:239–40.

161. *PW* 4:28; *GSD* 8:24; *JA* 8:240.

162. *PW* 4:28; *GSD* 8:24; *JA* 8:240.

163. *PW* 4:29; *GSD* 8:25; *JA* 8:240–41.

What he now writes about true religion parallels what he writes about music: "For *this* is the essence of true Religion: that away from the cheating show of the day-tide world, it shines in the night of man's inmost heart, with a light quite other than the world-sun's light, and visible nowhence save from out that depth."[164] As Ellis notes, this is an unmistakable reference to *Tristan*.[165]

Thus with the usual means of perception[166] "we cannot possibly perceive the basis for the Oneness of all being (den Grund der Einheit aller Wesen)."[167] This is only possible "solely by the new cognitive faculty that is suddenly awoken in us, as if through Grace (einzig durch das neue Erkenntnißvermögen, welches uns plötzlich wie durch Gnade erweckt wird)."[168] Wagner here would seem to be affirming Luther's view that true faith is not "speculative" or "theoretical" but "practical."[169] Had he not tried to flatter Ludwig (by introducing the idea of "example"), I think Wagner could have produced a much more powerful theological treatise.[170]

By comparing *Beethoven* and the best aspects of *On State and Religion*, we discern a clear similarity between music and theology. Composing music and coming to theological insight both involve immediate revelation and both are associated with the realm of dreams and of the "night."[171] But this immediacy of the "night" is lost if one has to resort to allegories in conveying revelation to the "layman" or "profane person." Wagner brings music and theological revelation much closer together in his *Religion and Art*, an essay written as he was composing the music for *Parsifal*, and it is to this essay that I now turn.

164. *PW* 4:29–30; *GSD* 8:25; *JA* 8:241.

165. He quotes Tristan's words from Act II: "da erdämmerte mild / erhabner Macht / im Busen mir die Nacht / mein Tag war da vollbracht" ("then there gently spread / within my breast / the noble sway of night / for me day was at an end") (*WagTS* 114). Many other examples lines from *Tristan* could make the same point.

166. Wagner does not explicitly mention this, but it is what Schopenhauer calls "the principle of sufficient reason."

167. *PW* 4:30 (translation modified); *GSD* 8:25; *JA* 8:242.

168. *PW* 4:30; *GSD* 8:25; *JA* 8:242.

169. Bell, *Deliver Us from Evil*, 245–58.

170. Wagner I think spoils his argument by understanding the "practical" in terms of example. "The saint, the martyr, is therefore the true mediator of salvation" (*PW* 4:30; *GSD* 8:25; *JA* 8:242) and if the "attribute of true religiousness" dwells in the king, then this "becomes the only revelation, of profit to both State and Religion, that can bring the two into relationship" (*PW* 4:31; *GSD* 8:26; *JA* 8:243). Hence the key is through the example of the saint (and possibly the king if he is a Christian).

171. Note the frequent use of dreams and visions in revelatory moments in the Bible (e.g., Daniel; Revelation; Acts 10:9–16; 2 Cor 12:1–10).

The opening paragraphs of this essay have been discussed already in chapter 8 and I now want to focus on those parts that deal with how music can be a means of revealing the "divine," in particular the Christian faith. Wagner in fact argues that music is the best possible medium to reveal the Christian faith and we see him clearly departing from the philosophical framework of Schopenhauer (and of Nietzsche).[172]

Already in *Beethoven* Wagner argues that music is more than a simple cognitive exercise. In *Religion and Art* he argues the same for the Christian religion. In chapter 8 we saw that Wagner maintains that Christianity is not a religion of knowing in the sense of the elitism of the "Brahmins" but was a religion for the "poor in spirit."[173] Indeed it is a religion of the miraculous, of revelation, and this is related to the person of Christ with whom one seeks union.[174] After those five paragraphs discussed in chapter 8, Wagner then turns to the superiority of Christianity over Greek religion. Their *individual* gods may be personal but not *the God*!

> Of Greek belief in gods it may be said that, in touch with the artistic instinct of the nation, it always clung to anthropomorphism. Their gods were figures with distinctive names and plainest individuality; their names were used to mark specific groups of things, just as the names of various coloured objects were used to denote the colours themselves, for which the Greeks employed no abstract terms like ours: "gods" were they called, to mark their nature as divine; but the Divine itself the Greeks called *God*, "ὁ θεός." Never did it occur to them to think of "God" as a Person, or give to him artistic shape as to their named gods; he remained an idea, to be defined by their philosophers, though the Hellenic spirit strove in vain to clearly fix it—till the wondrous inspiration of poor people spread abroad the incredible tidings that the "Son of God" had offered himself on the cross to redeem the world from deceit and sin.[175]

172. Hartwich, "Religion und Kunst," 299.

173. *PW* 6:214; *GSD* 10:212; *JA* 10:118.

174. *PW* 6:214–15; *GSD* 10:213; *JA* 10:119.

175. *PW* 6:216–17 (modified); *JA* 10:121. *GSD* 10:215: "Von dem Götterglauben der Griechen ließe sich sagen, daß er, der künstlerischen Anlage des Hellenen zu Liebe, immer an den Anthropomorphismus gebunden sich erhalten habe. Ihre Götter waren wohlbenannte Gestalten von deutlichster Individualität . . . Götter hießen sie nur, um ihre Natur als eine göttliche zu bezeichnen; das Göttliche selbst aber nannten sie: *der Gott*, 'ὁ θεός.' Nie ist es den Griechen beigekommen, 'den Gott' sich als Person zu denken und künstlerisch ihm eine Gestalt zu geben wie ihren benannten Göttern; er blieb ein ihren Philosophen zur Definition überlassener Begriff . . .—bis von wunderbar begeisterten armen Leuten die unglaubliche Kunde ausging, der 'Sohn Gottes' habe, für die Erlösung der Welt aus ihren Banden des Truges und der Sünde, sich am Kreuz

Whereas the one "God" of the Greeks was what one could call "impersonal" Wagner makes the point that "[t]he very shape of the Divine had presented itself in anthropomorphic guise." This was "the body of the quintessence of all pitying Love, stretched out upon the cross of pain and suffering."[176] Wagner questions whether this body of Christ is a religious "symbol." In fact he stresses that he was rather an image, a real replica ("Bild, wirkliches Abbild") of the divine.[177] Christ being an "Abbild" of the divine parallels Schopenhauer's idea that music in an "Abbild" of the world-will. Christ crucified is *not* a symbol depicting reality; he is reality itself;[178] and this reality is "preached" through music. This, I think, counts as Wagner's key insight regarding theology *through* music and theology *of* music.[179]

Through Christ being such an "Abbild" and through "its effect on the human heart," the church "soon made the Graeco-Roman world her own."[180] But the mistake the church made was to trace this divinity upon the cross ("dieses Göttlichen am Kreuze") to the Jewish "creator of heaven and earth."[181] This "wrathful God of Punishment . . . seemed to promise greater power than the self-offering, all loving Saviour of the Poor."[182] Wagner then writes:

> As though impelled by an artistic need, leaving Jehova as "Father" to rest, Belief (der Glaube) devised the necessary miracle of the Saviour's birth by a *Mother* who, not herself a goddess, became divine through her virginal conception of a son without

---

geopfert.'" Wagner's point that the Greek did not have abstract views of colors as we do is broadly correct. For a summary of scholarship of Greek color usage see Bradley, *Colour*, 14–17.

176. *PW* 6:217; *GSD* 10:215; *JA* 10:121.

177. *PW* 6:217; *GSD* 10:215; *JA* 10:121. Cf the discussion chapter 6 where I argued that Christ was *not* one of the mythical symbols of which Wagner speaks at the beginning of *Religion and Art*.

178. Compare the way in which in myth we come into contact with reality itself, whereas in metaphor or symbol we just depict reality.

179. Cf. Grätzel, "Ethik," 144.

180. *PW* 6:217; *JA* 10:121–22. *GSD* 10:215: "In ihm und seiner Wirkung auf das menschliche Gemüth liegt der ganze Zauber, durch welchen die Kirche sich zunächst die griechisch-römische Welt zu eigen machte." The antecedent of "ihm" could be the previous sentence ("In this, and its effect upon the human heart" as in the translation of Ellis [*PW* 6:217]) or Christ himself ("In him and his effect upon the human heart"), but most likely it is the "Bild" and "wirkliches Abbild."

181. *PW* 6:217; *GSD* 10:216; *JA* 10:122. On the problems Wagner found in this "Jewish God" see the discussion in chapter 9 above.

182. *PW* 6:217; *GSD* 10:216; *JA* 10:122. Again see chapter 9 above about the Jewish God being "doomed by art."

human contact, against the laws of Nature. . . . [T]he mystery of motherhood without natural fecundation can only be traced to the greater miracle, the birth of the God himself (die Geburt des Gottes selbst ergründlich): for in this the Denial-of-the-world is revealed by a life prefiguratively offered up for its redemption. As the Saviour himself was recognised as sinless, nay, incapable of sin, it followed that in him the Will must have been completely broken ere ever he was born, so that he could no more suffer, but only feel for others' suffering; and the root hereof was necessarily to be found in a birth that issued, not from the Will-to-live, but from the Will-to-redeem (Willen zur Erlösung).[183]

Ellis compares this to elements in Schopenhauer's *Parerga* §167: "The woman's share in generation is, in a certain sense, more innocent than the man's, in so far as the man gives to the being to be procreated the *will* that is the first sin and hence the source of all wickedness and evil, whereas the woman gives *knowledge* which opens up the way to salvation. The act of generation is the world-knot, for it states: 'The will-to-live has affirmed itself anew.'"[184] Again he says a little later: "From the father the child receives the will, the character; from the mother, the intellect. The latter is the redeeming principle, the former the binding."[185] However, it is important to stress that Wagner is going well beyond Schopenhauer in speaking of the "Will-to-redeem."

Wagner now moves to his appraisal of painting, looking at the virgin birth, last judgement, and crucifixion. As we have just seen, he understands the virgin birth as a way of circumventing "Jehovah," the "Father."[186] He warns that it is possible to misinterpret this miracle and to make it "artificial" (künstlich),[187] such an example being the portrayal above the porch of St. Kilian at Würzburg.[188] But the Virgin Birth has been wonderfully portrayed by artists such as Raphael just as Michelangelo's "prodigious painting" has shown "God fulfilling his terrible work."[189] We have then these two dogmas, virgin birth and final judgement, that have offered themselves "to

183. *PW* 6:217–18; *GSD* 10:216; *JA* 122–23.

184. *PP* 2:316–17; *ASSW* 5:373.

185. *PP* 2:317; *ASSW* 5:374.

186. Again compare Brünnhilde's putting Wotan to rest at the end of *Götterdämmerung* (*WagRS* 349: "Rest now, rest now, you god!").

187. Again see the opening of his article: "One might say that where Religion becomes artificial (künstlich) . . ." (*PW* 6:213; *GSD* 10:211; *JA* 10:117).

188. Here we see a "bas-relief of God the Father transmitting the embryo of the Saviour to the body of Mary by means of a blow-pipe" (*PW* 6:219; *GSD* 10:217; *JA* 10:123).

189. *PW* 6:220; *GSD* 10:219; *JA* 10:125.

the artist's phantasy."[190] Wagner's appraisal of painting is striking in that he has an exalted view of its theological potential. Whereas poetry is limited in that it is bound up with the formulation of dogmas,[191] painting has a higher status, for here one can represent allegories and symbols without dogmatic concepts. For Wagner, the best painting is religious painting. "Now, in respect of plastic art it is palpable that its ideally creative force diminished in exact proportion as it withdrew from contact with religion."[192] He continues: "Betwixt those sublimest revelations of religious art, in the godlike birth of the Redeemer and the fulfilment of the work of the Judge of the world, the saddest of all pictures, that of the Saviour suffering on the cross, had likewise attained to its height of perfection."[193]

Although painting has this exalted status, the highest art for expressing Christian belief is music. "Through the art of Tone did the Christian Lyric thus first become itself an art: the music of the Church was sung to the words of the abstract dogma; in its effect however, it dissolved those words and the ideas they fixed, to the point of their vanishing out of sight; and hence it rendered nothing to the enraptured Feeling save their pure emotional content."[194] He then continues is the next paragraph with this striking sentence: "Speaking strictly, the only art that fully corresponds with the Christian belief is Music; even as the only music which, now at least, we can place on the same footing as the other arts, is an exclusive product of Christianity."[195] Since music has the effect of dissolving words (as in church

190. *PW* 6:219; *GSD* 10:218; *JA* 10:124.

191. So Dante, for example, is at his best "where he can hold the visionary world aloof from dogma (wo er die anschauliche Welt von der Berührung mit dem Dogma fernhalten kann)" (*PW* 6:221; *GSD* 10:219; *JA* 10:126).

192. *PW* 6:221; *JA* 10:126. *GSD* 10:220: "Im Betreff der bildenden Kunst bleibt es nun auffällig, daß ihre ideal schaffende Kraft in dem Maaße abgenommen hat, als sie von ihrer Berührung mit der Religion sich entfernte."

193. *PW* 6:221; *JA* 10:126. *GSD* 10:220: "Zwischen jenen erhabensten kunst-religiösen Offenbarungen der göttlichen Herkunft des Erlösers und der schließlichen Werk-Vollbringung des Welten-Richters, war das schmerzlichste aller Bilder, das des am Kreuze leidenden Heilandes, ebenfalls zur höchsten Vollendung gelangt."

194. *PW* 6:223; *JA* 10:128. *GSD* 10:221: "Erst durch die Tonkunst ward die christliche Lyrik daher zu einer wirklichen Kunst: die kirchliche Musik ward auf die Worte des dogmatischen Begriffes gesungen; in ihrer Wirkung löste sie aber diese Worte, wie die durch sie fixirten Begriffe, bis zum Verschwinden ihrer Wahrnehmbarkeit auf, so daß sie hierdurch den reinen Gefühlsgehalt derselben fast einzig der entzückten Empfindung mittheilte."

195. *PW* 6:223; *JA* 10:128. *GSD* 10:221: "Streng genommen ist die Musik die einzige dem christlichen Glauben ganz entsprechende Kunst, wie die einzige Musik, welche wir, zum mindesten jetzt, als jeder anderen ebenbürtige Kunst kennen, lediglich ein Produkt des Christenthums ist."

music) Wagner argues that "we must recognise that Music reveals the in-most essence of the Christian religion with definition unapproached (daß die Musik das eigenste Wesen der christlichen Religion mit unvergleichli-cher Bestimmtheit offenbart)."[196] He then likens the relationship of music to religion as that between the child of God and the virgin Mother: "wherefore we may figure it as bearing the same relation to Religion which that picture of Raphael's has shewn us borne by the Child-of-god to the virgin Mother."[197] Music therefore has the same mediatorial status as Christ.[198] Again we see Wagner's parallel between music and Christ, both functioning as an "Ab-bild." Wagner then adds: "for, as pure Form of a divine Content entirely freed from all concepts, we may regard [music] as a world-redeeming birth of the divine dogma from the nullity of the phenomenal world itself."[199] And so we arrive at a Christianized version of Schopenhauer's escape from the world of phenomena. The "Schopenhauerian night" of *Tristan* becomes in *Parsifal* the "Christian night" of the Holy Communion.[200] In this connection it is interesting that Wagner uses an image from the Communion disagree-ments of the sixteenth century to contrast the different roles of visual art and music. Whereas for the former we have "that signifies" ("das bedeutet"), for music we have "that is" ("das ist"), "for she stops all strife between reason and feeling, and that by a tone-shape completely removed from the world of appearance, not to be compared with anything physical, but usurping our heart as by act of Grace (weil sie jeden Zwiespalt zwischen Begriff und Emp-findung aufhebt, und dies zwar durch die der Erscheinungswelt gänzlich abgewendete, dagegen unser Gemüth wie durch Gnade einnehmende, mit nichts Realem vergleichliche Tongestalt)."[201]

---

196. *PW* 6:223; *JA* 10:129; *GSD* 10:222.

197. *PW* 6:223; *GSD* 10:222; *JA* 10:129.

198. As Hartwich, "Religion und Kunst," 305, interprets Wagner as referring to "ab-solute music": "Die absolute Musik schließlich weist als bild- und begrifflose Form eine strukturelle Analogie zum transzendenten Prinzip der Einheit auf und hat insofern denselben medialen Status wie Christus, der als unmittelbare Emanation der Gottheit gedacht wird. Insofern kann Wagner die Musik 'sinnbildlich in dasselbe Verhältnis zur Religion setzen . . . wie den Gottesknaben zur jungfräulichen Mutter'" (quoting *Religion und Kunst*; I have added minor corrections, cf. *GSD* 10:222).

199. *PW* 6:223 (modified); *JA* 10:129. *GSD* 10:222: "denn als reine Form eines gän-zlich vom Begriffe losgelösten göttlichen Gehaltes, darf sie uns als eine welterlösende Geburt des göttlichen Dogmas von der Nichtigkeit der Erscheinungs-Welt selbst gelten." Note that "Dogma" is used in a positive sense.

200. We have noted elsewhere the significance of the darkness on the stage in the Communion scene in Act I. Note that the Communion scene of Act I is central for the stage work. See Kinderman, "Genesis," 150.

201. *PW* 6:224; *GSD* 10:222; *JA* 10:129.

Wagner finishes Part I of *Religion and Art* by saying that only the "final severance from the decaying church could enable the art of Tone to save the noblest heritage of the Christian idea (das edelste Erbe des christlichen Gedankes)."[202] He indicates that the continuing discussion will concern the affinity of the Beethoven Symphony to the blossoming religion that comes from the Christian revelation.[203] However, first he says he must examine the downfall of even the most exalted religions. In fact, he spends much of Parts II and III writing about "degeneration" and little concerning "Religion and Art," but at the end he does return to this theme. He writes:

> The Redeemer himself has bidden us sound and sing our long-ing, faith and hope. Its noblest legacy the Christian Church has left us in the all-uttering, all expressing soul of the Christian religion: wafted beyond the temple-walls, the holy strains of Music fill each sphere of Nature with new life, teaching redemp-tion-starved mankind a second speech in which the Infinite can voice itself with clearest definition.[204]

He exhorts the reader: "after celebrating in our daily meal (Speise-Mahle) the Will's sure triumph over itself through knowledge wrung from manhood's fall, we might view the plunge into the waves of those symphonic revelations as a religious act of hallowed cleansing."[205] These symphonies are those of Beethoven, especially the last four. The "daily meal" seems to be the Communion and he speaks of knowledge gained from humankind's fall, a central theme of Wagner's.[206] He ends this section by contrasting the severe limitations of the poet regarding the theological enterprise to the revela-tions possible through music.

> "Divin'st thou thy Creator, World? (Ahnest Du den Schöpfer, Welt?)"—so cries the Poet, obliged to hazard an anthropomor-phic metaphor for That which words can ne'er convey. But above all possibility of concrete thought, the Tone-poet Seer reveals to us the Inexpressible: we divine, nay, feel and see that this

---

202. *PW* 6:224; *GSD* 10:222; *JA* 10:129.

203. *PW* 6:224; *JA* 10:129–30. *GSD* 10:223: "die Affinitäten einer Beethoven'schen Symphonie zu einer reinsten, der christlichen Offenbarung zu entblühenden Religion, ahnungsvoll nachzuweisen, soll unsere Aufgabe für den Fortgang dieser begonnenen Darstellung sein."

204. *PW* 6:249; *GSD* 10:250; *JA* 10:159.

205. *PW* 6:250; *GSD* 10:250; *JA* 10:160.

206. See the discussion in chapter 7 above.

insistent World of Will is also but a state that vanishes before the
One: "I know that my redeemer liveth!"[207]

The final quotation from Job 19:25 suggests that the idea of resurrection was
not totally absent from Wagner's theological reflection.[208]

Revelation of God through *Parsifal*

The above analysis of these three essays demonstrates that although Wagner
employs many ideas of Schopenhauer he actually goes well beyond him.
Schopenhauer writes of the possibility of accessing deeper levels of reality
through art. Although this is something I will later appeal to, Wagner takes
us much further, to the revelation of the divine. In *Beethoven* he writes of
the inmost vision that music provides such that the essence of religion is
brought to our consciousness. In *On State and Religion* he writes of how
knowledge of the divine can only come through revelation. In *Religion and
Art* he argues that "the only art that fully corresponds with the Christian
belief is Music"[209] and that "music" and "Christ" both have a key mediatorial
role: music is an "Abbild" of the world as Christ is an "Abbild" of the divine.

Wagner in many respects was not a systematic thinker and no doubt
contradictions can be found in his "theology of music" just as they can be
found in his *Ring*! In his thinking he was more of a Martin Luther than
a John Calvin; and he was a poet rather than a philosopher. But what he
presents in these essays can I think be developed to suggest ways in which a
knowledge of "God" can be disclosed through *Parsifal*.

Wagner quite rightly in my view writes of Christ being an "Abbild"
of the divine. One can add that he was also an "Abbild" of the most perfect
human being, this cohering with Wagner's stress on Christ's sinlessness.
Wagner does not have a traditional view of the "pre-existence" of Christ and
indeed writes of "the birth of God himself" through his virgin mother.[210]
An idea of "pre-existence" though could be found in his eternal soul in the
noumenal world. As Abbild of both the divine and human Christ then spans
both the divine and the world. Wagner's view of art could be developed
in two possible ways to suggest that Christ can be revealed through *Parsifal*. The first, suggested above in the discussion of *Religion and Art*, is that

207. *PW* 6:250; *GSD* 10:250–51; *JA* 10:160.

208. As noted in chapter 7, these words are commonly applied to the resurrection
of Jesus (e.g., as in Handel's *Messiah*).

209. *PW* 6:223; *GSD* 10:222; *JA* 10:128.

210. *PW* 6:217–18; *GSD* 10:216; *JA* 10:122.

if music is an "Abbild" of the "thing-in-itself" and if with Schopenhauer we assume this noumenal world is an undifferentiated whole, then music in witnessing to this suffering world-will also reveals the suffering Christ who, according to Wagner, encompasses the suffering of the whole world. A second approach questions whether the thing-in-itself is in fact an un-differentiated whole and we saw that *Tristan* puts a question mark against this Schopenhauerian view.[211] Whereas Schopenhauer conceives of a kind of "world soul," Wagner I suggest could conceive of individual souls in the noumenal realm. My own view expressed elsewhere that the body should be considered a manifestation of the soul in the phenomenal world[212] coheres with Wagner's understanding of the human person. Wagner considered Jesus of Nazareth to be a historical person, and I add that his supra-temporal soul was manifest in the "space-time" historical events that culminated in his death in Jerusalem around AD 30. One of the weaknesses of Schopenhauer's philosophy of music is that there is no clear differentiation between "good" and "bad" music; there are only distinctions between music that is "abstract" and that which can represent something in the phenomenal world (e.g., birdsong). Wagner does introduce some distinctions in his *Beethoven* essay and to this I add that music such as that of *Parsifal* has a greater capacity to "reveal" Christ's soul (in the noumenon) than other music; further, certain performances and productions of *Parsifal* have a greater capacity to reveal Christ than others.[213]

If *Parsifal* can witness to Christ's soul in the noumenon, then we have the possibility of revealing "God" since we have the hypostatic union of his humanity and divinity. This union of the two "natures" would be highly conducive for Wagner in view of his sympathy for Luther's theology and particularly his understanding of the Eucharist.[214] Those theologians who hold the two nature together tend to have a high view of the Eucharist (Cyril of Alexandria; Luther) whereas those who hold them apart tend to have a low view (Nestorius; Zwingli).[215]

If Wagner's artwork can reveal Christ's soul it may be that it can also witness to a resurrected Christ, even if this goes beyond Wagner's intention. The supra-temporal soul of Christ once manifested itself in the phenomenal world as his "earthly body" but a believer holds that it is now manifest as his

211. See chapter 2 above.

212. Bell, *Deliver Us from Evil*, 206–8.

213. Reviews of *Parsifal* recordings sometimes highlight those (e.g., Eugen Jochum and Herbert von Karajan) that have a "spiritual" aspect.

214. I noted in chapter 10 Cosima's definite preference for Luther over Zwingli regarding the Eucharist, a view which I imagine her husband would share.

215. On Cyril's response to Nestorius, see Kelly, *Doctrines*, 317–23.

"resurrection body," a new phenomenal realm. Perhaps this explains how Domingo is able to perceive the resurrected Christ in the closing moments of *Parsifal* (see below).

We can then be confronted by Christ through this artwork: and it is the Son who speaks to us, not the "humanless" Father in heaven (whether God the Father is really bypassed is discussed below). But it is one thing to be confronted by Christ's soul; it is quite another to be in union with him. Putting it in this way, Kundry comes to faith in Christ not through an "aesthetic experience," not through a fusion of subject and object, but in union with Christ, in dying with him. The aesthetic experience is not the same as having faith; the former concerns the subject on the boundary of the world; the latter involves the soul which is in the depths of the world.[216]

There is, I believe, a way forward. *Parsifal* can offer not just an aesthetic experience; it can also bring about a union with Christ, and it can do this through music and myth. Putting it very generally, both these can bring about a participation in the drama. Music has a unique capacity to bring together the "I" of Christ and the "I" of the human being. Further, myth if received positively has the capacity to embed the person in a reality outside themselves. Let me explain with reference to Paul's myth of Adam and Christ. In Rom 5:12–21 he develops the myth of the "fall" of Adam as found in Genesis 3, elaborating it by means of other ancient Jewish traditions.[217] But most important of all, he was developing this Adam myth in the light of the death of Christ. The most significant element he introduced was that just as the Christian participated in the death of Christ, so he participated in the sin of Adam. Although Paul was developing the myth as found in Genesis 3, this was not the activity of a "free invention"; mythogenesis is more a "discovery" than an "invention." Likewise when Wagner was "working on" his myths (whether pagan or Christian) he was not involved in a free invention.[218] In the case of *Parsifal* he was taking Wolfram (which is not "mythology" but nevertheless has mythological elements), "baptizing" it in the sense that he is adding Christian elements (although as I argued in chapter 3 above, Wolfram already had many Christian elements) and developing

216. See Bell, "Mind," 207–16, for my understanding of the relationship of subject to soul.

217. See especially Wis 2:23–24: "For God created us for incorruption, and made us in the image of his own eternity, but through the devils' envy death entered the world, and those who belong to his company experience it." Although Adam is not named the reference to him is clear.

218. This point was made well by Eiser, "Andeutungen," 225–26. Any element of "invention" ("Erfindung") is concerned with creating elements of the "artwork," not the fundamental "work on myth." Cf. Borchmeyer, "Eigensinn," 184.

his mythology of the grail, spear, blood, Kundry, etc. He was doing his own mythogenesis.[219]

Now one reason myth is so important in Christian theology is that through it one can undergo an existential displacement. If the myth is received positively it has the power to take us into another reality. In the case of *Parsifal* the fundamental reality is Christ himself who is manifest in various ways but especially through his blood, which appears in the grail. We are presented with a reality into which we can be embedded. Therefore the union that is achieved on the stage, Kundry's union with Christ, is something that can be achieved for anyone in the theatre who receives the myth positively.

The fundamental way then in which "the divine" is revealed in *Parsifal* is through the art-work witnessing to the soul of Christ; thereby the human person is confronted by Christ, and even unified with him, all this coming about by Wagner's remarkable marriage of music and mythology. But there is another way in which the "divine" could be revealed, although Wagner may have objected to this. If there is some sort of correspondence between God and the world, a not unreasonable assumption if God is considered the creator of the world, then if music tells us something about the fundamental reality of the world, in theory it can also tell us something of the reality of God. One can then possibly develop a "natural revelation" through music. Music, if it is a copy of the thing-in-itself, could speak more powerfully than the cosmological and teleological arguments since these appeal to the mere phenomenal world.[220]

Experiencing the Divine in the Theatre?

The discussion in this chapter about the possibilities of revealing deeper levels of reality and even "the divine" through *Parsifal* may appear to be highly idealistic and so I want to conclude this chapter by asking whether what one experiences in the theatre corresponds at all to what Wagner expresses in his various writings.

The first thing to say is that although some performances are enthralling, many can leave one disappointed and frustrated. The Wagners also knew of disappointments. Cosima tells her husband

---

219. See his letter to Mathilde Wesendonck of 29–30 May 1859, discussed in chapter 3 above.

220. One complicating factor here is whether there could be a natural revelation through music but no actual knowledge of God. See the problems St. Paul raises about "natural theology" (Bell, *No One Seeks for God*, 90–118).

how curious is was that all performances (5th Symphony, *Tristan*, *Meistersinger*), no matter how good, leave me to a certain extent cold, but I feel ecstatic when R. talks to me about Beethoven, when he tells me of his first conceptions; I cannot put myself in the position of the audience but, rather, feel as if the work becomes disassociated from me as soon as it takes on an outer form. R. says he feels exactly the same way, and he knows that we shall regard our *Nibelungen* theater with cold pleasure, watching and observing. "For ourselves we do not need it, our pleasures lie in the idea (unsere Freuden liegen in der Idee)."[221]

In relation to *Parsifal* Cosima notes these words of her husband: "'Oh, I hate the thought of all those costumes and grease paint! When I think that characters like Kundry will now have to be dressed up, those dreadful artists' balls immediately spring into my mind. Having created the invisible orchestra, I now feel like inventing the invisible theater! And the inaudible orchestra,' he adds concluding his dismal reflections in humourous vein."[222] This depressing outlook on *Parsifal* probably reflects the disasters that accompanied the *Ring* in 1876.[223] But in the event, the production of *Parsifal* was successful, as Wagner's own comments at the beginning of this chapter attest.

Interestingly Nietzsche seems, like Cosima, to be unmoved by stage productions of Wagner.[224] So he writes about purely orchestral music as in the Overture *Meistersinger*[225] or the Prelude to *Parsifal* Act I (which he heard in Monte Carlo); even his speaking of *Tristan* Act III in *Birth of Tragedy* suggests an intellectual reading of the text. Magee adds: "It may be pertinent to remember that the plays of his beloved Greeks were known to him only through reading."[226]

In view of these practical problems with productions a revelation of the divine may better come through concert performances or through listening to the CDs. But there *are* occasions when the stage performances do

221. *CD* 21 May 1871.

222. *CD* 23 September 1878. Regarding the last two sentences, Deathridge, "Reviews," 89 (on Westernhagen's Wagner biography) comments: "Instead of the completely serious remark it is often taken to be, it is actually a perfect example of the sardonic humour seldom appreciated by Wagner's admirers."

223. See, e.g., Richard Fricke's description of the inconsolable Wagner after the first performance of *Das Rheingold* (Spencer, *Wagner Remembered*, 248).

224. Magee, *Wagner and Philosophy*, 327.

225. See *Beyond God and Evil* § 240 (*KSA* 5:179).

226. Magee, *Wagner and Philosophy*, 327.

reveal something of the "divine," even if one cannot articulate precisely what this is. Domingo says this about the very ending of *Parsifal*:

> As for the finale of this Act, where Parsifal brings back the Spear to the knights, heals Amfortas and is able to unveil the Grail and once more bestow its blessing on the knights, it is such a mystical moment that I don't know that I can find words to describe it. I feel as if God is about to come on stage, to bless and lift us all up higher, to a kind of Resurrection. I *feel* the presence of God coming down to touch us for a moment. And at the moment Parsifal bestows this blessing I find myself wishing it could reach out, embrace and bring peace to everyone, the audience and the whole world. It's a profoundly emotional experience.[227]

The words "Redemption to the redeemer" as we have seen can present some theological problems. But I suggest that such an exalted ending points to the overpowering revelation of the divine through music. And a sense of the divine is perhaps better achieved through this music with the questionable words than through the poor musical settings of "orthodox" doctrine.

---

227. Matheopoulos, *Domingo*, 215.

12

Wagner in the Pew and Pulpit

Wagner, the "Christian" in the Pew

NOT MANY WOULD EXPECT to find Wagner sitting in the church pew
on Sunday; and it is the case that his church attendance was sporadic.
Also not many would describe the composer as a Christian. However, we
have seen that on occasions he did so describe himself and I have no doubt
that he was sincere in his belief that in Jesus of Nazareth we see the God
of suffering atoning for the sins of humanity and that through union with
him the whole of creation can be renewed. Paul's words in Rom 10:9 are
often taken as a "definition" of a Christian: "If you confess with your lips
that Jesus is Lord (*kyrios*) and believe in your heart that God raised him
from the dead, you will be saved." Although Wagner did believe in *some*
sense that Jesus was "divine" (Jesus as *kyrios*)[1] he certainly had doubts about
the resurrection and if one takes this text from Romans as the criterion for
being a Christian then one has to say he does not meet it (as many others
would not who call themselves Christians). However, if one recognizes that
one is not saved by believing in "correct doctrine" but rather through faith
in Christ (which entails union with him), then one can certainly consider
Wagner to be Christian: so many of his utterances reflect precisely such faith
and union with him.[2]

---

1. Note, however, that Paul probably had in mind believing in the full divinity of
Christ, *kyrios* being used for the divine name (YHWH) in the Greek Old Testament.

2. In debates as to whether Wagner was a Christian, these words of Nietzsche,
Anti-Christ Etc, 262, are often quoted: "If Wagner was a Christian, well then maybe

Despite this faith one has to say Wagner did not share "a highly religious constitution (eine eminente religiöse Natur)"[3] which we find in Cosima. Nevertheless he had a piety, often fed by Cosima herself, which is not easy to dismiss.[4] I take just two examples to illustrate this. The first is taken from Cosima's entry for 31 October 1872. On this "Reformation Day" when she converted to Protestantism, she tells how she went to the dean's house[5] where her conversion was recorded in front of Friedrich Feustel[6] and the mayor as witnesses. Then she received the sacrament with her husband in the vestry:

> a deeply moving occasion, my whole soul trembles, our dean speaks from the depths of his heart. R. is profoundly touched. What a lovely thing religion is! What other power could produce such feelings? We are all in a state of sublime and solemn devoutness (Wir sind alle in gehobener feierlicher Andacht). "God is love," the dean says once again. Oh, could I but die in such a spirit, could one remain in it to the end of one's life! As we embraced, R. and I, I felt as if our bond had only now been truly sealed, that now we were united in Jesus Christ.[7]

As a second example, Cosima's in her entry for 14 May 1878 tells how her husband "reads to me with his splendid delivery the First Epistle to the Corinthians in Luther's translation." One suspects that First Corinthians

---

Liszt was a Church Father! (Wenn Wagner ein Christ war, nun dann war vielleicht Liszt ein Kirchenvater!)" (*KSA* 6:51). This is a strange utterance since Liszt became an abbé (of the Franciscans) and for some time lived at the monastery of Santa Francesca Romana. As an abbé he was able to carry out certain church duties but not preside at Communion. It was therefore a lesser order which corresponded to that of the deacon. According to this logic, if Liszt was to some extent a church father then perhaps to some extent Wagner could be recognized as a Christian!

3. Scholz, *Antisemitismus*, 110.

4. Ibid., describes him as "ein sehr realitätsbewußter, sinnlich-diesseitiger Künstler (und nicht etwa Theologe, Politiker oder Kultur-Philosoph)." I hope to show that this is not an accurate description.

5. This is Dr. Dittmar, dean of Bayreuth, who died in 1877 and was a close personal friend of the Wagners. Cosima often refers to him and nearly always in very glowing terms. His one fault seemed to be that he had not read Schopenhauer (*CD* 1 January 1873)! The record of her conversation with the dean (*CD* 26 November 1873) is an interesting window on the Protestant Church and their feelings toward it. The dean bemoans the state of the church especially that the clergy act as "officials" ("Beamte") rather than "pastors" ("Pastoren") and fail to influence "children, the poor, and the sick."

6. Feustel was a banker and chair of the town council of Bayreuth and fundamental for the establishing of the Bayreuth festival.

7. *CD* 31 October 1872.

had a special appeal for Wagner in view of Paul's writing on the "word concerning the cross" in chapters 1–3 and chapter 13 on love.[8]

However, despite this piety, generally speaking Wagner kept his distance from the church (as a great number of men still do!) and Cosima's diaries indicate the general pattern that she attended church with her children while her husband remained at home.[9] But it is striking that Wagner was happy to speak about Jesus Christ in everyday contexts. One remark he makes in his autobiography still has resonance for the Britain of today (which in many respects is more "secular" than Germany). Wagner recollects the first concert he gave in London in 1855: "For my prelude to *Lohengrin* I had written a program note, but the words 'Holy Grail' and 'God' were solemnly excised, on the grounds that this sort of thing was not appropriate for secular concerts."[10] Another example of his Christianity in every day is that although it seems he did not go to church regularly for Communion, every meal for him had a "sacred" significance.[11]

Wagner in the Pulpit: An Assessment of *Parsifal*'s Theological Contribution

Many would not want to see Wagner set loose in the pulpit. However, a case can be made for allowing his artwork *Parsifal* to preach to us. In this work (and in some of his writings) we see the development of a rich theology. Some of it may be considered "unorthodox," but one could say that he was simply exercising his "evangelische Freiheit" (often translated as "evangelical freedom" but more accurately "Protestant freedom") thereby being true to his Lutheran heritage; and although he exercised his freedom in a way that would probably engender Luther's displeasure,[12] he was not simply a theo-

8. I have noted many instances where Wagner speaks of the triad love, faith, and hope (e.g., in his commentary to the Prelude to Act I, *DEAP* 45–46).

9. Just to take an example, on Maundy Thursday 1882 the children go to church (*CD* 6 April 1882). Then on Good Friday Cosima goes to church with the children whilst her husband stays at home reading the "Classical Walpurgnis Night" (*CD* 7 April 1882). Such a pattern is repeated, with Wagner going to Church on only few occasions. It is perhaps ironic that Wagner thinks *Parsifal* will be his final work "since in these Knights of the Grail he has given expression to his idea of a community" (*CD* 5 April 1882).

10. *My Life* 516; *Mein Leben* 2:529.

11. See chapter 11 above on the "daily meal" (*PW* 6:250; *GSD* 10:250). It is likely that for the early Christian, every meal also had this sacred character, especially so for the disciples who shared in Jesus' final meal.

12. Although in theory Luther held firmly to the freedom of a Christian (see especially his ground breaking 1520 treatise *On the Freedom of a Christian*, *LW* 31:333–77), in practice he could be as intolerant as his Catholic contemporaries (consider his

logical anarchist for he did hold positive views of the Protestant church[13] and respected Christian tradition.[14] But what then was Wagner's distinctive theological contribution?

The first is that for Wagner divinity was concentrated in the person of Jesus.[15] With Jesus' birth from the virgin Mary, God was born. His divinity is seen in his sinlessness and in his suffering. Wagner does not necessarily exclude a Trinitarian God but his starting point is the historical figure of Jesus of Nazareth and from there he works out in concentric circles to include the Holy Spirit and perhaps even God the Father. Wagner's emphasis is that divinity cannot be divorced from humanity and that God can only be known through Christ.[16]

Secondly, Wagner's stress is on Christ as the God who suffers, and he tends to understand the creator God rather like Luther's hidden God (*deus absconditus*).[17] Not only is Christ's suffering the converse of the suffering of the world and vice versa,[18] but he fully identifies with the world's suffering. In the pain of cancer patients, in the misery of war and human conflict, even in the fall of every sparrow to the ground, Christ also suffers. His suffering is projected into our suffering and our suffering is projected into his.

Thirdly, Christ's suffering is redemptive. Wagner shares the view of the New Testament witnesses that Christ's death atones for sins. But there is an added element which is related to Kant and Schopenhauer and by which he manages to offer a theology for a "scientific age." Wagner, unlike the New

---

treatment of Anabaptists).

13. See chapter 10 on "Church and Sacraments" and the discussion in the previous section.

14. See, e.g., *CD* 17 January 1880: "Less and less can R. tolerate mocking references to Christianity."

15. Such a view obviously is not going to help those who wish to bring the three Abrahamic faiths together.

16. Wagner would fully agree with the quotation Chamberlain gives on the title page of *Mensch und Gott* (part of a letter of Oliver Cromwell to his son Richard, 2 April 1650): "Das Antlitz Gottes kannst du nirgends finden noch betrachten außer in Christo zu erkennen; darum strebe Gott in Christo zu erkennen. Denn das wahre Wissen von Gott wird weder durch Wortweisheit noch durch Denken erreicht, vielmehr handelt es sich um einen inneren Vorgang, der den Geist gottwärts umwandelt." The original English is as follows: "You cannot find nor behold the face of God but in Christ; therefore labour to know God in Christ, which the Scripture make to be the sum of all, even life eternal. Because the true knowledge is not literal or speculative, but inward, transforming the mind to it" (Carlyle, *Cromwell*, 2:53–54). There is no reason to believe Wagner knew this letter, but he did have great admiration for Cromwell (see the various references to him in Cosima's diaries).

17. See *SL* 641–42; *KB* 1:82, discussed in chapter 7.

18. Cf. Mösch, *Weihe, Werkstatt, Wirklichkeit*, 42.

Testament authors, had to face the grim realities of Darwinian evolution. This has been a major challenge to Christian theology and I mention just two issues. First, Darwin demonstrates that suffering was always in the world; there has never been a period of "paradise." Secondly, if there was no "paradise" how do we relate the suffering in the world to the sin of humanity if there was no literal "Adam and Eve in the garden of Eden"? One way Wagner deals with this is by making the distinction between the phenomenal and noumenal worlds, something explored in chapter 11 above.[19] Often Wagner does this by speaking of the world of "appearance" ("Erscheinung"). Toward the end of part III of *Religion and Art* Wagner speaks of the "simplest and most touching of religious symbols"[20] which brings to us knowledge of the need of redemption.[21]

> In the solemn hour when all the world's appearances dissolve as in a prophet's dream (wie im ahnungsvollen Traume), we seem already to partake of this redemption in advance: no more then tortures us the memory of that yawning gulf (die Vorstellung jenes gähnenden Abgrundes), the gruesome monsters of the deep (der grausenhaft gestalteten Ungeheuer der Tiefe), the reeking litter of the self-devouring Will (aller der süchtigen Ausgeburten des sich selbst zerfleischenden Willens), which Day—alas! the history of mankind, had shown us: then pure and peace-desiring sounds to us the cry of Nature, fearless, hopeful, all-assuaging, world-redeeming. United in this cry, by it made conscious of its own high office of Redemption of the whole like-suffering Nature (mit-leidenden Natur), and the soul of Manhood rises from the abyss of appearances (Erscheinungen), and, loosed from all that awful causality of becoming and fading (grauenhaften Ursächlichkeit alles Entstehens und Vergehens), the restless Will feels fettered by itself alone, but from itself set free.[22]

There is then no doubt as to what is the basis of this "redemption." "The redeemer himself has bidden us sound and sing our longing, faith and hope. Its noblest legacy the Christian Church has left us in the all-uttering,

19. I have also made my own attempt to deal with the problem of the "fall" using this distinction (Bell, "Adam and his 'Fall'").

20. *PW* 6:248; *GSD* 10:249; *JA* 10:158.

21. *PW* 6:248–49; *GSD* 10:249; *JA* 10:158. The religious symbol could be Communion. There is a rough parallel two paragraphs later where he writes of "celebrating in our daily meal the Will's sure triumph over itself through knowledge wrung from manhood's fall" (*PW* 6:250; *GSD* 10:250; *JA* 10:160).

22. *PW* 6:249 (modified); *GSD* 10:249; *JA* 10:158–59.

all-expressing soul of the Christian religion: wafted beyond the temple-walls, the holy strains of Music fill each sphere of Nature with new life, teaching redemption-starved mankind a second speech in which the Infinite can voice itself with clearest definition."[23] He then writes that "the plunge into the waves of [Beethoven's] symphonic revelations"[24] is "a religious act of hallowed cleansing."[25] What Wagner writes about experiencing Beethoven he could just as well write about his own works (and most probably he is implying his own art also): being plunged into those music dramas is "a religious act of hallowed cleansing." His works have a profound spiritual message and many are those who have experienced this.[26]

Fourthly, if Wagner's theology and philosophy of music (discussed in the previous chapter) has any element of truth, then as *Parsifal* is being performed, the Christian gospel is preached. This preaching is not restricted to a mediation through the "words" or "concepts" found in the libretto; in the most fundamental way the gospel is preached in that the music speaks of the suffering world-will, such suffering being summed up in the passion of Jesus Christ.[27] Wagner therefore makes his fundamental contribution by bringing together Kant, Schopenhauer, the New Testament, and a great deal of Christian tradition.

Fifthly, not only does Wagner preach Christ crucified by bringing together in a remarkable mix the power of Shakespeare and Beethoven, but he also offers a profound therapy. His art can bring succor to those facing crises in work and relationships, those facing serious illness, and those facing our "final enemy" death.

Finally, Wagner offers a spiritual Christian message to those who either feel their spiritual needs are not met by the churches or to those who find it impossible to accept certain dogmas the churches consider non-negotiable. I know many who cannot accept the resurrection not because they are "unspiritual" or "obtuse" but simply because they feel they have intellectual problems in accepting it.[28] For them Wagner offers a spiritual message that Christ, even if he did not rise from the dead, lives in us "through his death."

---

23. *PW* 6:249; *GSD* 10:250; *JA* 10:159.

24. He has in view symphonies 6, 7, 8, and 9.

25. *PW* 6:250; *GSD* 10:250; *JA* 10:160.

26. E.g., Gabriel Fauré on experiencing the *Ring* in 1896 writes that the work "is penitence in the noblest meaning of the word[;] it is almost contrition" (Hartford, *Bayreuth*, 223).

27. See the example I gave in chapter 10 above (I.25–38).

28. For the record I should say that I do believe in the resurrection. I briefly addressed the issue of the resurrection appearances in *Deliver us from Evil*, 330–31.

In an interview made just a few months before he died in April 2013 Sir Colin Davis was asked whether he was a religious man. He explained that he would not count himself a believer but when he conducts a piece of Christian music he does believe the Christian message *so long as the music lasts*. If I am right that *Parsifal* preaches Christ crucified, then receiving it as it is meant to be received brings one in touch with the redeemer and savior and, who knows, perhaps it will even have a spiritual effect once the music ceases.

Bibliography

Musical Scores and Sketches of *Parsifal*

Autographe Partitur. Richard-Wagner-Archiv, Bayreuth.
Kompositionsskizze. Richard-Wagner-Archiv, Bayreuth.
Orchesterskizze. Richard-Wagner-Archiv, Bayreuth.
Partitur-Abschrift Ernst Hausburgs. Richard-Wagner-Archiv, Bayreuth.
Klindworth, Karl, editor. *Parsifal: A Stage-Consecration Festival-Play.* New York: G.
    Schirmer, 1904.
Voss, Egon, and Martin Geck, editors. *Parsifal: Ein Bühnenweihfestspiel.* 3 vols. SW 14.
    Mainz: B. Schott's Söhne, 1972.

Versions of the Bible used by Wagner

*Das neue Testament, unseres Herrn und Heilandes Jesu Christi. Leipziger Jubelausgabe,
    nach der letzten Ausgabe Dr. Martin Luthers (vom Jahre 1545) revidiert von Hofrath
    Dr. Gersdorf und Dr. K. A. Espe.* Leipzig: Verlag von Im. Tr. Möller, n.d.
*Evangelische Deutsche Original-Bibel. Das ist: Die gantze Heilige Schrift; Altes und Neues
    Testaments, dergestalt eingerichtet, daß der hebräische oder griechische Grundtext u.
    die dt. Uebers. Martin Luthers neben einander erscheinen, die Blätter aber mit den
    Seiten der so gemein gewordenen Cansteinischen Bibel übereintreffen / mit reichen
    Summarien, richtigen Parallelen, einer kurtzen Biblischen Chronologie, Harmonie
    der Evangelisten, u. andern dienlichen Stücken versehen; nebst einer Vorrede Johann
    Muthmanns.* 2 vols. Züllichau: Frommann, 1741.
*Novum Testamentum griech. u. lat. in antiquis testibus textum versionis vulgatae latinae
    indagavit lectionesque variantes Stephani et Griesbachii; notavit v. S. Jager in
    consilium adhibito Constantius Tischendorf.* Paris: Didot, 1861.

Secondary literature

Abbate, Carolyn. "*Parsifal*: Words and Music." In *Parsifal, Richard Wagner*, 49–67.
    Richmond, VA: Oneworld Classics, 2011.

Aberbach, Alan David. *Richard Wagner's Religious Ideas: A Spiritual Journey*. Lewiston. NY: Mellen, 1996.

Adorno, Theodor. *In Search of Wagner*. Translated by Rodney Livingstone. New York: Verso, 2005.

Ahrens, Christian. "Posaunenchor." In *MGG* 7 (Sachteil): 1751–56.

Allen, Roger. "*Die Weihes des Hauses* (The Consecration of the House) Houston Stewart Chamberlain and the Early Reception of *Parsifal*." In *A Companion to Wagner's Parsifal*, edited by William Kinderman and Katherine R. Syer, 245–76. Rochester, NY: Camden House, 2005.

Althaus, Paul. *Die christliche Wahrheit. Lehrbuch der Dogmatik*. 3rd ed. Gütersloh: Bertelsmann, 1952.

———. *Die Theologie Martin Luthers*. 6th ed. Güterloh: Güterloher Verlaghaus Gerd Mohn, 1983.

———. "Ur-Offenbarung." *Luthertum* 46 (1935) 4–24.

Amidon, Philip R., editor. *The Panarion of St. Epiphanius, Bishop of Salamis*. Oxford: Oxford University Press, 1990.

Audin, Jean M. *Geschichte des Lebens, der Lehren und Schriften Dr. Martin Luther's*. 2 vols. Augsburg: Rieger, 1843.

Barr, James. *The Garden of Eden and the Hope of Immortality*. London: SCM, 1992.

Barth, Herbert, Dietrich Mack, and Egon Voss, editors. *Wagner: A Documentary Study*. Translated by P. R. J. Ford and Mary Whittall. London: Thames and Hudson, 1975.

Barth, Karl. *From Rousseau to Ritschl*. LPT. Translated by Brian Cozens. London: SCM, 1959.

———. *Die protestantische Theologie im 19. Jahrhundert: Ihre Vorgeschichte und ihre Geschichte*. Zürich: Zollikon, 1947.

Bauer, Bruno. *Kritik der evangelischen Geschichte der Synoptiker*. 3 vols. 2nd ed. Leipzig: Wigand, 1848.

———. "Luther's Pessimismus und Optimismus." *Bayreuther Blätter* 4 (Oktober-November 1881, Doppelstück Erste Hälfte) 285-90.

Bauer, Hans-Joachim, editor. *Richard Wagner: Briefe*. Stuttgart: Reclam, 1995.

Bayer, Hans. "Gralssage." In *TRE* 14:116–18.

Beaufils, M., and M. E. Evans. "Wagner, Richard." *NCE* 14:603–4.

Beckett, Lucy. *Parsifal*. COH. Cambridge: Cambridge University Press, 1981.

———. Review of *A Companion to Wagner's Parsifal*, edited by William Kinderman and Katherine Syer. *Music and Letters* 87 (2006) 453–57.

Beckh, Hermann. *Die Sprache der Tonart in der Musik von Bach bis Bruckner*. Stuttgart: Urachhaus, 1937.

Bekker, Paul. *Richard Wagner: His Life in His Work*. Translated by M. M. Bozman. London: Dent, 1931.

Bell, Richard H. "The Corrupt Mind and the Renewed Mind: Some Qualifications on the Grandeur of Reason from Pauline, Kantian and Schopenhauerian Perspectives." In *The Grandeur of Reason: Religion, Tradition and Universalism*, edited by Peter M. Chandler Jr. and Conor Cunningham, 197–217. London: SCM, 2010.

———. *Deliver Us from Evil. Interpreting the Redemption from the Power of Satan in New Testament Theology*. WUNT 216. Tübingen: Mohr/Siebeck, 2007.

———. *The Irrevocable Call of God: An Inquiry into Paul's Theology of Israel*. WUNT 184. Tübingen: Mohr/Siebeck, 2005.

———. "The Myth of Adam and the Myth of Christ." In *Paul, Luke and the Graeco-Roman World: Essays in Honour of Alexander J. M. Wedderburn,* edited by Alf Christofersen, Carsten Claussen, Jörg Frey, and Bruce Longenecker, 21–36. JSNTSup 217. Sheffield, UK: Sheffield Academic, 2002.

———. *No one seeks for God: An Exegetical and Theological Study of Romans 1.18—3.20.* WUNT 106. Tübingen: Mohr/Siebeck, 1998.

———. *Provoked to Jealousy: The Origin and Purpose of the Jealousy Motif in Romans 9–11.* WUNT 2.63. Tübingen: Mohr/Siebeck, 1994.

———. "Reading Romans with Arthur Schopenhauer: Some First Steps towards a Theology of Mind." *Journal for the Study of Paul and his Letters* 1 (2011) 41–56.

———. "Sacrifice and Christology in Paul." *JTS* 53 (2002) 1–27.

———. "Science and the Bible: Adam and His 'Fall' as a Case Study." In *The Bible: Culture, Community, Society,* edited by Angus Paddison and Neil Messer, 31–46. London: T. & T. Clark, 2013.

———. "The Transfiguration: A Case Study in the Relationship between 'History' and 'Theological Symbol' in the Light of Pope Benedict's Book." In *The Pope and Jesus of Nazareth: Christ, Scripture and the Church,* edited by Adrian Pabst and Angus Paddison, 159–75. London: SCM, 2009.

Benders, Raymond J., and Stephan Oettermann, editors. *Friedrich Nietzsche: Chronik in Bildern und Texten.* München: Hanser, 2000.

Bergfeld, Joachim, editor. *The Diary of Richard Wagner 1865–1882: The Brown Book.* Translated by George Bird. London: Gollancz, 1980.

Berlowitz, Béatrice, and Elisabeth de Fontenay. "Some Thoughts about *Parsifal.*" *Booklet Accompanying Wagner's Parsifal Conducted by Daniel Barenboim* (1990) 31–37.

Bernstein, Leonard. *The Unanswered Question.* Cambridge: Harvard University Press, 1976.

Berry, Mark. "The Positive Influence of Wagner upon Nietzsche." *Wagner Journal* 2.2 (2008) 11–28.

Bertram, Johannes. *Der Seher von Bayreuth. Deutung des Lebens und Werkes Richard Wagners.* Berlin: Büchergilde Gutenberg, 1943.

Bethge, Eberhard. *Dietrich Bonhoeffer: Eine Biographie.* 8th ed. Darmstadt: Wissenschaftliche Buchgesellschaft, 2004.

Beyschlag, Karlmann. *Grundriss der Dogmengeschichte, Band II: Gott und Mensch. Teil 1: Das christologische Dogma.* Grundrisse 3.1. Darmstadt: Wissenschaftliche Buchgesellschaft, 1991.

Bitbol, Michel. "Reflective Metaphysics: Understanding Quantum Mechanics from a Kantian Standpoint." *Philosophica* 83 (2010) 53–83.

Bitbol, Michel, Pierre Kerszberg, and Jean Petitot. "Introduction." In *Constituting Objectivity: Transcendental Perspectives on Modern Physics,* edited by Michel Bitbol, Pierre Kerszberg, and Jean Petitot, 1–29. Dordrecht: Springer, 2009.

Bohm, David. *Wholeness and the Implicate Order.* 1980. Reprint. London: Routledge & Kegan Paul, 1981.

Borchmeyer, Dieter. "Ahasvers Wandlungen: *Der fliegende Holländer* und seine Metamorphosen." In *Richard Wagner. Ahasvers Wandlungen,* 117–42. Frankfurt am Main: Insel, 2002.

———. "Eigensinn und Sinnenteignung des Mythos. Wagners Wirkung im Widerspruch von Poesie und Politik." In *Zukunftsbilder: Richard Wagners*

Revolution und ihre Folgen in Kunst und Politik, edited by Hermann Danuser and Herfried Münkler, 179–91. Schliengen, Germany: Argus, 2002.

———. "Erlösung und Apokatastasis: *Parsifal* und die Religion des späten Wagner." In *Richard Wagner. Ahasvers Wandlungen*, 308–34. Frankfurt am Main: Insel, 2002.

———. "Heinrich Heine—Richard Wagner." In *Richard Wagner und die Juden*, Juden, 20–34. Stuttgart: Metzler, 2009.

———. "Kundrys Lachen, Weinen und Erlösung. Eine Betrachtung zu Richard Wagners Parsifal." *Internationale katholische Zeitschrift 'Communio'* 20 (1991) 445–51.

———. "The Question of Anti-Semitism." In *Wagner Handbook*, edited by Ulrich Müller, Peter Wapnewski, and John Deathridge, 166–85. Cambridge: Harvard University Press, 1992.

———. "Recapitulation of a Lifetime." In *Parsifal: Richard Wagner*, 9–15. London: Overture, 2011.

———. *Richard Wagner: Theory and Theatre*. Translated by Stewart Spencer. Oxford: Clarendon, 2002.

———. "Richard Wagners Antisemitismus." *Aus Politik und Zeitgeschichte* 63 (2013) 23–29.

———. "Wagner and Nietzsche." In *Wagner Handbook*, edited by Ulrich Müller, Peter Wapnewski, and John Deathridge, 327–42. Cambridge: Harvard University Press, 1992.

Bornkamm, Günther. "The Letter to the Romans as Paul's Last Will and Testament." In *The Romans Debate*, edited by Karl P. Donfried, 16–28. 2nd ed. Peabody, MA: Hendrickson, 1991.

Bornkamm, Heinrich, editor. *Luthers Vorreden zur Bibel*. 3rd ed. Göttingen: Vandenhoeck & Ruprecht, 1989.

Bowie, Andrew. *Music, Philosophy, and Modernity*. Cambridge: Cambridge University Press, 2007.

Bradley, Mark. *Colour and Meaning in Ancient Rome*. CCS. Cambridge: Cambridge University Press, 2009.

Brakelmann, Günter. "Stoecker, Adolf." In *TRE* 32:194–95.

Brandon, S. G. F. *The Trial of Jesus of Nazareth*. London: Batsford, 1968.

Brearley, Margaret. "Hitler and Wagner: The Leader, the Master and the Jews." *Patterns of Prejudice* 22.2 (1988) 3–21.

Brecht. "Daumer, Georg Friedrich." In ²*RGG* 1:1794–95.

Breckenridge, James. "Compassion and Knowledge in Wagner's *Parsifal*." *Perspectives in Religious Studies* 15 (1988) 47–56.

Breig, Werner. "The Musical Works." In *Wagner Handbook*, edited by Ulrich Müller, Peter Wapnewski, and John Deathridge, 397–482. Cambridge: Harvard University Press, 1992.

Brown, Colin. *Jesus in European Protestant Thought, 1778–1860*. Grand Rapids: Baker, 1988.

———. *Miracles and the Critical Mind*. Grand Rapids: Eerdmans, 1984.

Brown, Raymond E. *The Gospel according to John, Volume 2 (XIII–XXI)*. AB. 1966. Reprint. London: Chapman, 1978.

Bultmann, Rudolf. "The Question of Wonder." In *Faith and Understanding: Collected Essays*, translated by Louise Pettibone Smith, 247–61. London: SCM, 1969.

Burnham, Douglas, and Martin Jesinghausen, editors. *Nietzsche's Thus Spoke Zarathustra*. EPG. Edinburgh: Edinburgh University Press, 2010.

Burnham, Scott. "The Four Ages of Beethoven: Critical Reception and the Canonic Composer." In *Cambridge Companion to Beethoven*, edited by Glenn Stanley, 272–91. Cambridge: Cambridge University Press, 2000.

Busch, Eberhard. *Karl Barth: His Life from Letters and Autobiographical Texts.* Translated by John Bowden. Grand Rapids: Eerdmans, 1976.

Carlyle, Thomas, editor. *The Letters and Speeches of Oliver Cromwell.* 3 vols. London: Methuen, 1904.

Cartwright, David E. *Schopenhauer: A Biography.* Cambridge: Cambridge University Press, 2010.

Chamberlain, Houston Stewart. *Mensch und Gott: Betrachtungen über Religion und Christentum.* 1921. Reprint. München: Bruckmann, 1933.

———. "Notes sur Parsifal." *Revue wagnérienne* 2.7 (August 1886) 220–26.

———. *Richard Wagner.* 6th ed. München: Bruckmann, 1919.

Cicora, Mary A. "Medievalism and Metaphysics: The Literary Background of *Parsifal.*" In *A Companion to Wagner's* Parsifal, edited by William Kinderman and Katherine R. Syer, 29–53. Rochester, NY: Camden House, 2005.

Clines, David J. A. *Job 1–20.* WBC 17. Dallas: Word, 1989.

Colson, F. H., editor. *Philo IX.* LCL 363. 1941. Reprint. Cambridge: Harvard University Press, 1985.

Conway, David. *Jewry in Music: Entry to the Profession from the Enlightenment to Richard Wagner.* Cambridge: Cambridge University Press, 2012.

———. "Jews, Music and Wagner." *Wagner Journal* 6.1 (2012) 4–14.

Cooke, Deryck. "Wagner's Musical Language." In *The Wagner Companion*, edited by Peter Burbidge and Richard Sutton, 225–68. London: Faber and Faber, 1979.

Cormack, David. "An Abduction from the Seraglio: Rescuing Jessie Laussot." *The Wagner Journal* 6.1 (2012) 50–63.

———. "Faithful, All Too Faithful." *The Wagner Library* 4.9 (2002) 1–86.

Dahlhaus, Carl. *Richard Wagner's Music Dramas.* Translated by Mary Whittall. Cambridge: Cambridge University Press, 1979.

Daniel, Norman. *Islam and the West: The Making of an Image.* Edinburgh: University, 1960.

Danuser, Hermann. "Tristanakkord." In *MGG* 9 (Sachteil) 832–44.

Darwin, Charles. *The Descent of Man, and Selection in Relation to Sex.* 2nd ed. London: John Murray, 1896.

Daumer, Georg Friedrich. *Kaspar Hauser.* Regensburg: Coppenrath, 1873.

———. *Das Wunder: seine Bedeutung, Wahrheit und Nothwendigkeit, den Herren Strauß, Frohschammer, Lang, Renan, Reinkens & c. gegenüber ins Licht gesetzt; nebst thatsächlichen Belegen aus Geschichte und Ueberlieferung.* Regensburg: Coppenrath, 1874.

Daverio, John. "Beethoven's Chamber Music for Strings." In *Cambridge Companion to Beethoven*, edited by Glenn Stanley, 147–64. Cambridge: Cambridge University Press, 2000.

Deathridge, John. "Mendelssohn and the Strange Case of the (Lost) Symphony in C." In *Wagner Beyond Good and Evil*, 178–88. Berkeley: University of California Press, 2008.

———. "Postmortem on Isolde." In *Wagner Beyond Good and Evil*, 133–55. Berkeley: University of California Press, 2008.

————. "Reviews of A.D. Sessa, *Richard Wagner and the English*; J. L. DiGaetani (ed.), *Penetrating Wagner's Ring*; P. Burbidge and R. Sutton (ed.), *The Wagner Companion*; C. von Westernhagen, *Wagner: A Biography.*" *19th Century Music* 5 (1981–82) 81–89.

————. "Strange Love, Or, How We Learned to Stop Worrying and Love *Parsifal.*" In *Wagner Beyond Good and Evil*, 159–77. Berkeley: University of California Press, 2008.

Deines, Roland. "Jesus der Galiläer: Traditionsgeschichte und Genese eines antisemitischen Konstrukts bei Walter Grundmann." In *Walter Grundmann. Ein Neutestamentlicher in Dritten Reich*, edited by Roland Deines, Volker Leppin, and Karl-Wilhelm Niebuhr, 43–131. Leipzig: Evangelische Verlagsanstalt, 2007.

Dennett, Daniel C. "Intentionality." In *The Cambridge Dictionary of Philosophy*, edited by Robert Audi, 441. Cambridge: Cambridge University Press, 1999.

Dreyfus, Laurence. "Hermann Levi's Shame and *Parsifal's* Guilt: A Critique of Essentialism in Biography and Criticism." *COJ* 6.2 (1994) 125–45.

————. *Wagner and the Erotic Impulse.* Cambridge: Harvard University Press, 2010.

Duckworth, David. *The Influence of Biblical Terminology and Thought on Wolfram's Parzival.* Göppingen: Kümmerle, 1980.

Dühring, Eugen. *Die Judenfrage als Racen-, Sitten- und Culturfrage.* Karlsruhe, Germany: Reuther, 1881.

Dyson, Michael. "Sea, Mirror, Woman, Love: Some Recurrent Imagery in 'Opera and Drama.'" *Wagner Journal* 5.3 (2011) 16–33.

Eckert, Michael, Eilert Herms, Bernd Jochen Hilberath, and Eberhard Jüngel, editors. *Lexikon der Theologischen Werke.* Darmstadt: Wissenschaftliche Buchgesellschaft, 2003.

Eichholz, Georg. *Die Theologie des Paulus im Umriß.* 5th ed. Neukirchen-Vluyn: Neukirchener, 1985.

Eiser, Otto. "Andeutungen über Wagners Beziehung zu Schopenhauer und zur Grundidee des Christentums." *Bayreuther Blätter* 1 (August 1878, Achtes Stück) 222–29.

————. "Richard Wagners Ring des Nibelungen: Ein exegetischer Versuch." *Bayreuther Blätter* 1 (August 1878, Elftes Stück) 309–17.

Ellington, James W., editor. *Immanuel Kant: Prolegomena to any Future Metaphysics.* Indianapolis: Hackett, 1977.

Ellis, William Ashton. "Richard Wagner's Prose." *Proceedings of the Musical Association* 19 (1892–93) 13–30.

Emslie, Barry. "Wagner: Race, Nation, Culture." *Wagner Journal* 2.1 (2008) 3–19.

Eschenbach, Wolfram von. *Parzival. Mittelhochdeutscher Text nach der Ausgabe von Karl Lachmann. Übersetzung und Nachwort von Wolfgang Spiewok.* 2 vols. Suttgart: Reclam, 1994.

Eschenbach, Wolfram von. *Parzival und Titurel. Rittergedicht; übersetzt und erläutert von Karl Simrock.* 3rd ed. Stuttgart: Cotta, 1857.

Evans, Donald D. *The Logic of Self-Involvement.* London: SCM, 1963.

Fausel, Heinrich. *D. Martin Luther. Sein Leben und Werk, Band 2, 1522–1546.* 2nd ed. Neuhausen-Stuttgart: Hänssler, 1996.

Fee, Gordon D. "The New Testament and Kenosis Christology." In *Exploring Kenotic Christology: The Self-Emptying of God*, edited by C. Stephen Evans, 25–44. Oxford: Oxford University Press, 2006.

Fest, Joachim. *Hitler.* Translated by Richard and Clara Winston. London: Weidenfeld and Nicolson, 1974.

Feuerbach, Ludwig. *Thoughts on Death and Immortality.* Translated by James A. Massey. Berkeley: University of California Press, 1980.

———. *Das Wesen des Christentums.* Leipzig: Wigand, 1841.

Field, Geoffrey G. *Evangelist of Race: The Germanic Vision of Houston Stewart Chamberlain.* New York: Colombia University, 1981.

Fischer, Jens Malte. "Richard Wagners Das Judentum in der Musik." In *Richard Wagner und die Juden,* edited by Dieter Borchmeyer, Ami Maayani, and Susanne Vill, 35–54. Stuttgart: J. B. Metzler, 2000.

———. *Richard Wagners 'Das Judentum in der Musik'.* Frankfurt am Main: Insel, 2000.

Fischer, Johannes. "Über die Beziehung von Glaube und Mythos." *ZThK* 85 (1988) 303–28.

Fischer-Dieskau, Dietrich. *Wagner and Nietzsche.* Translated by Joachim Neugroschel. London: Sidgwick and Jackson, 1978.

Forsyth, P. T. "Richard Wagner and Pessimism." In *Religion in Recent Art,* 209–51. London: Hodder & Stoughton, 1901.

———. "Wagner's 'Parsifal.'" In *Religion in Recent Art,* 252–316. London: Hodder & Stoughton, 1901.

Förster-Nietzsche, Elizabeth. *The Nietzsche-Wagner Correspondence.* Translated by Caroline V. Kerr. Memphis: General Books, 2012.

Frank, Hans. *Im Angesicht des Galgens: Deutung Hitlers und seiner Zeit auf Grund eigener Erlebnisse und Erkenntnisse.* München-Gräfeling: Friedrich Alfred Beck, 1953.

Frey, Christofer. "Quietismus." *EKL* 3:1416–17.

Friedländer, Saul. "Bayreuth und der Erlösungsantisemitismus." In *Richard Wagner und die Juden,* edited by Dieter Borchmeyer, Ami Maayani, and Susanne Vill, 8–18. Stuttgart: J. B. Metzler, 2000.

Friend, Lionel. "Thematic Guide." In *Parsifal: Richard Wagner,* 95–104. London: Overture, 2011.

Fröhlich, Elke, editor. *Die Tagebücher von Joseph Goebbels, I/3/II (März 1936 bis Februar 1937).* München: Saur, 2001.

———. *Die Tagebücher von Joseph Goebbels, II/2 (Oktober bis Dezember 1941).* München: Saur, 1996.

Gardner, Sebastian. *Kant and the Critique of Pure Reason.* RPG. 1999. Reprint. London: Routledge, 2004.

Gay, Peter. "Wagner aus psychoanalytischer Sicht." In *Richard Wagner und die Juden,* edited by Dieter Borchmeyer, Ami Maayani, and Susanne Vill, 251–61. Stuttgart: J. B. Metzler, 2000.

Gese, Hartmut. "Der auszulegende Text." In *Alttestamentliche Studien,* 266–82. Tübingen: J.C.B. Mohr (Paul Siebeck), 1990.

———. "Das biblische Schriftverständnis." In *Zur biblischen Theologie,* 9–30. 1977. Reprint. Tübingen: J.C.B. Mohr (Paul Siebeck), 1989.

Gfrörer, August Friedrich. *Geschichte des Urchristenthums I: Das Jahrhundert des Heils.* Stuttgart: Schweizerbart, 1838.

———. *Geschichte des Urchristenthums II: Die heilige Sage. Zweite Abteilung.* Stuttgart: Schweizerbart, 1838.

————. *Geschichte des Urchristenthums III: Das Heiligtum und die Wahrheit.* Stuttgart: Schweizerbart, 1838.

————. *Kritische Geschichte des Urchristentums: Philo und die jüdisch-alexandrinische Theosophie.* 2 vols. 2nd ed. Stuttgart: Schweizerbart, 1835.

Gobineau, Arthur. *Essai sur l'inégalité des races humaines.* 4 vols. Paris: Didot, 1853–55.

Gobineau, Arthur de. *The Inequality of the Human Races.* Translated by Adrian Collins. New York: Fertig, 1967.

Golomb, Jacob, editor. *Nietzsche and Jewish Culture.* London: Routledge, 1997.

Golther, Wolfgang, editor. *Richard Wagner an Mathilde Wesendonk: Tagebuchblätter und Briefe 1853–1871.* Berlin: Duncker, 1904.

Göpfert, Herbert G., editor. *Gotthold Ephraim Lessing Werke, Zweiter Band.* Darmstadt: Wissenschaftliche Buchgesellschaft, 1996.

Görres, Joseph von, editor. *Lohengrin: Ein altdeutsches Gedicht nach der Abschrift des Vaticanischen Manuscriptes von Ferdinand Gloeckle.* Heidelberg: Mohr/Zimmer, 1813.

Görres, Joseph von. *Die christliche Mystik, 5 vols.* Regensburg: Manz, 1836–42.

Grätzel, Stephan. "Musikalische Ethik bei Schopenhauer und Wagner." In *Musik als Wille und Welt: Schopenhauers Philosophie der Musik,* edited by Matthias Koßler, 139–47. Würzburg: Königshausen & Neumann, 2011.

Gregor-Dellin, Martin. *Richard Wagner: His Life, His Work, His Century.* Translated by J. Maxwell Brownjohn. London: Collins, 1983.

————. *Richard Wagner: Sein Leben, sein Werk, sein Jahrhundert.* Munich: Piper, 1980.

Groos, Arthur. *Romancing the Grail: Genre, Science, and Quest in Wolfram's Parzival.* Ithaca, NY: Cornell University Press, 1995.

Gutman, Robert W. *Richard Wagner: The Man, His Mind, and His Music.* London: Secker & Warburg, 1968.

Haas, Frithjof. *Zwischen Brahms und Wagner: Der Dirigent Hermann Levi.* Zürich: Atlantis, 1995.

Hamann, Brigitte. *Hitler's Vienna: A Dictator's Apprenticeship.* Translated by Thomas Thornton. Oxford: Oxford University Press, 1999.

————. *Winifred Wagner: A Life at the Hearts of Hitler's Bayreuth.* Translated by Alan Bance. London: Granta, 2005.

Hamp, Petrus. *Ein Blick in die Geisteswerkstatt Richard Wagners. Von einem alten geistlichen Freunde des Meisters von Bayreuth zur Erinnerung an dessen Schwanengesang – den 'Parzival'.* Berlin: Böhler, 1904.

Handel, George Frederick. *Der Messias/The Messiah.* London: Eulenburg, 1963.

Harries, Richard. *After the Evil: Christianity and Judaism in the Shadow of the Holocaust.* Oxford: Oxford University Press, 2003.

Hart-Davis, Rupert. *Hugh Walpole.* London, 1952.

Hartenstein, G., editor. *Immanuel Kant's Kritik der reinen Vernunft.* Leipzig: Voss, 1868.

Hartford, Robert, editor. *Bayreuth: The Early Years.* London: Gollanz, 1980.

Hartwich, Wolf-Daniel. "Jüdische Theosophie in Richard Wagners 'Parsifal'. Vom christlichen Antisemitismus zur ästhetischen Kabbala." In *Richard Wagner und die Juden,* edited by Dieter Borchmeyer, Ami Maayani, and Susanne Vill, 103–22. Stuttgart: Metzler, 2000.

————. "Religion und Kunst beim späten Wagner. Zum Verhältnis von Ästhetik, Theologie und Anthropologie in den 'Regenerationsschriften'." *Jahrbuch der deutschen Schillergesellschaft* 40 (1996) 297–323.

Hauschild, Wolf-Dieter. "Agapen I." In *TRE* 1:748–53.

Hayum, Andrée. *The Isenheim Altarpiece: God's Medicine and the Painter's Vision.* Princeton: Princeton University Press, 1989.

Heer, Hannes, Jürgen Kesting, and Peter Schmidt, editors. *verstummte stimmen. Die Bayreuther Festspiele und die 'Juden' 1876 bis 1945.* Berlin: Metropol, 2012.

Hegel, G. W. F. *Aesthetics: Lectures on Fine Art.* Translated by T. M. Knox. Oxford: Clarendon, 1975.

Hendry, George S. "Christology." In *DCT*, 51–64.

Hengel, Martin. *The Johannine Question.* Translated by John Bowden. London: SCM, 1989.

Hennecke, Edgar, Wilhelm Schneemelcher, and R. McL. Wilson, editors. *New Testament Apocrypha.* 2 vols. London: SCM, 1963–64.

Heydorn. "Daumer, Georg Friedrich." In *1RGG* 1:1985–86.

Hébert, Marcel. *Le Sentiment Religieux dans l'Œuvre de Richard Wagner.* Paris: Librairie Fischbacher, 1895.

Hiley, David. *Western Plainchant.* Oxford: Clarendon, 1993.

Hilmes, Oliver. *Herrin des Hügels. Das Leben Cosima Wagner.* München: Pantheon, 2008.

Hitler, Adolf. *Mein Kampf.* München: Franz Eher, 1936.

Hofius, Otfried. "Ist Jesus der Messias? Thesen." In *Jahrbuch für Biblische Theologie* 8 (1993) 103–29.

Hollingdale, R. J. *Nietzsche: The Man and His Philosophy.* 2nd ed. Cambridge: Cambridge University Press, 1999.

Hollinrake, Roger. "Philosophical Outlook." In *The Wagner Compendium: A Guide to Wagner's Life and Music,* edited by Barry Millington, 143–46. London: Thames and Hudson, 1992.

Holloway, Robin. "Experiencing Music and Imagery in *Parsifal.*" In *Parsifal: Richard Wagner,* 31–48. London: Overture, 2011.

Horgan, A. D. "The Grail in Wolfram's *Parzival.*" *Mediaeval Studies* 36 (1974) 354–81.

Hübner, Hans. *Erlösung bei Richard Wagner und im Neuen Testament.* Neukirchen-Vluyn: Neukirchener, 2008.

———. *Nietzsche und das Neue Testament.* Tübingen: Mohr/Siebeck, 2000.

Hübner, Kurt. *Das Christentum im Wettstreit der Weltreligionen: Zur Frage der Toleranz.* Tübingen: J.C.B. Mohr (Paul Siebeck), 2003.

———. "Meditationen zu Wagners Schrift 'Religion und Kunst.'" In *Richard Wagner—Der Ring des Nibelungen,* edited by Udo Bermbach and Dieter Borchmeyer, 129–42. Stuttgart: J. B. Metzler, 1995.

———. "Wagners mythisches Christentum." In *Getauft auf Musik: Festschrift für Dieter Borchmeyer,* edited by Udo Bermbach and Hans Rudolf Vaget, 275–90. Würzburg: Königshausen & Neumann, 2006.

———. *Die Wahrheit des Mythos.* München: C. H. Beck, 1985.

Hübscher, Arthur. *Arthur Schopenhauer: Gesammelte Briefe.* Bonn: Bouvier Verlag Herbert Grundmann, 1978.

———. *Denker gegen den Strom.* Bonn: Bouvier Verlag Herbert Grundmann, 1973.

Idigoras, J. Ignacio Tellechea. "Molinos, Miguel de." In *TRE* 23:203–5.

Irvine, David. *'Parsifal' and Wagner's Christianity.* London: Grevel, 1899.

Jacobs, Joseph. "Wandering Jew." *JE* 12:462–63.

Jacquette, Dale. *The Philosophy of Schopenhauer.* CEP. Chesham, UK: Acumen, 2005.

Jager, S., and C. Tischendorf, editors. *Novum Testamentum in antiquis testibus textum versionis vulgatae latinae indagavit lectionesque variantes Stephani et Griesbachii.* Paris: Didot, 1861.

Janaway, Christopher. *Schopenhauer: A Very Short Introduction.* 2nd ed. Oxford: Oxford University Press, 2002.

Jefferson, Alan. *Elisabeth Schwarzkopf.* London: Gollanz, 1996.

Jones, Martin. "The Significance of the Gawan Story in *Parzival.*" In *A Companion to Wolfram's* Parzival, edited by Will Hasty, 37–76. Rochester, NY: Camden House, 1999.

Jüngel, Eberhard. "Anthropomorphismus als Grundproblem neuzeitliche Hermeneutik." In *Wertlose Wahrheit: Zur Identität und Relevanz des christlichen Glaubens. Theologische Erörterungen III.* BevTh 107, 110–31. München: Kaiser, 1990.

———. *Gott als Geheimnis der Welt: Zur Begründung der Theologie des Gekreuzigten im Streit zwischen Theismus und Atheismus.* 5th ed. Tübingen: J.C.B. Mohr (Paul Siebeck), 1985.

———. *Paulus und Jesus. Eine Untersuchung zur Präzisierung der Frage nach dem Ursprung der Christologie.* HUTh 2. 6th ed. Tübingen: J.C.B. Mohr (Paul Siebeck), 1986.

———. "Quae supra nos, nihil ad nos: Eine Kurzformel der Lehre vom verborgenen Gott – im Anschluß an Luther interpretiert." In *Entsprechungen: Gott—Wahrheit—Mensch,* 202–51. München: Kaiser, 1986.

Kant, Immanuel. *Religion within the Boundaries of Mere Reason and Other Writings.* Edited and translated by Allen Wood and George di Giovanni. Cambridge: Cambridge University Press, 1998.

Karlsson, Jonas. "'In That Hour It Began'? Hitler, *Rienzi,* and the Trustworthiness of August Kubizek's *The Young Hitler I Knew.*" *Wagner Journal* 6.2 (2012) 33–47.

———. "Wagner-Stoecker-Wagner." In *Wagnerspectrum: Bayreuther Theologie,* 219–32. Würzburg: Königshausen & Neumann, 2009.

Katz, Jacob. *The Darker Side of Genius: Richard Wagner's Anti-Semitism.* Hanover, NH: University Press of New England, 1986.

———. *From Prejudice to Destruction: Anti-Semitism, 1700–1933.* Cambridge MA: Harvard University Press, 1980.

Kelly, J. N. D. *Early Christian Doctrines.* 5th ed. London: A. & C. Black, 1977.

Kemp Smith, Norman, editor. *Critique of Pure Reason, Immanuel Kant (with a New Introduction by Howard Caygill).* Basingstoke, UK: Palmgrave Macmillan, 2003.

Kemp, W. "Götter, heidnische." In *LchI* 2:170–79.

Kern, Udo. "Eckhart, Meister." In *TRE* 9:258–64.

Kienzle, Ulrike. *. . . daß wissend würde die Welt! Religion und Philosophie in Richard Wagners Musikdramen.* Wagner in der Diskussion 1. Würzburg: Königshausen & Neumann, 2005.

———. "*Parsifal* and Religion: A Christian Music Drama?" In *A Companion to Wagner's Parsifal,* edited by William Kinderman and Katherine R. Syer, 81–130. Rochester, NY: Camden House, 2005.

Kinderman, William. "The Genesis of the Music." In *A Companion to Wagner's Parsifal,* edited by William Kinderman and Katherine R. Syer, 133–75. Rochester, NY: Camden House, 2005.

————. "Introduction: The Challenge of Wagner's *Parsifal*." In *A Companion to Wagner's Parsifal*, edited by William Kinderman and Katherine R. Syer, 1–26. Rochester, NY: Camden House, 2005.

Kirsch, Winfried. "Richard Wagners Biblische Scene *Das Liebesmahl der Apostel*." In *Geistliche Musik: Studien zu ihrer Geschichte und Funktion im 18. und 19. Jahrhundert*, edited by Constantin Floros, Hans Joachim Marx, and Peter Petersen, 157–84. Laaber, Germany: Laaber, 1985.

Kniese, Julie. *Der Kampf zweier Welten um das Bayreuther Erbe: Julius Knieses Tagebuchblätter aus dem Jahre 1883*. Leipzig: Weicher, 1931.

Köhler, Joachim. *Nietzsche and Wagner: A Lesson in Subjugation*. Translated by Ronald Taylor. New Haven: Yale University Press, 1998.

————. *Richard Wagner: The Last of the Titans*. Translated by Stewart Spencer. New Haven: Yale University Press, 2004.

————. *Wagner's Hitler: The Prophet and His Disciple*. Translated by Ronald Taylor. Oxford: Polity, 2000.

Kretzer, Eugen. "Erinnerungen an Dr. Otto Eiser." In *Begegnungen mit Nietzsche*, edited by Sander L. Gilman, 344–45. Bonn: Bouvier Verlag Hebert Grundmann, 1981.

Kubizek, August. *The Young Hitler I Knew*. Translated by Geoffrey Brooks. London: Greenhill, 2006.

Kühnel, Jürgen. "Parsifal 'Erlösung dem Erlöser': Von der Aufhebung des Christentums in das Kunstwerk Richard Wagners." In *Richard Wagner und sein Mittelalter*, edited by Ursula Müller and Ulrich Müller, 171–227. Salzburg: Müller-Speiser, 1989.

————. "The Prose Writings." In *Wagner Handbook*, edited by Ulrich Müller, Peter Wapnewski, and John Deathridge, 565–651. Cambridge: Harvard University Press 1992.

Kümmel, Werner Georg. *The New Testament: The History of the Investigation of Its Problems*. Translated by S. McLean Gilmour and Howard C. Kee. London: SCM, 1973.

Küng, Hans. *Musik und Religion: Mozart–Wagner–Bruckner*. 3rd ed. München: Insel, 2007.

————. "Wagner's *Parsifal*: A Theology for Our Time." *Michigan Quarterly Review* 23 (1984) 311–33.

Lachmann, Karl, editor. *Gotthold Ephraim Lessing's sämtliche Schriften*. 12 vols. Berlin: Voß'sche, 1838–40.

————, editor. *Gotthold Ephraim Lessing's sämtliche Schriften*. 12 vols. Leipzig: Göschen, 1853–57.

————, editor. *Wolfram von Eschenbach*. 2nd ed. Berlin: Reimer, 1854.

————, editor. *Wolfram von Eschenbach*. 6th ed. Berlin/Leipzig: Walter de Gruyter 1926.

Laurence, Dan H., editor. *Shaw's Music: The Complete Musical Criticism of Bernard Shaw, Volume 3, 1893–1950*. 2nd ed. London: Bodley Head, 1989.

Lawrence, Richard, editor. *The Book of Enoch the Prophet*. Oxford: Oxford University Press, 1821.

Lewin, David. "Amfortas's Prayer to Titurel and the Role of D in *Parsifal*: The Tonal Spaces of the Drama and the Enharmonic Cb/B." *19th Century Music* 7.3 (1984) 336–49.

Lévi-Strauss, Claude. "From Chrétien de Troyes to Richard Wagner." In *The View from Afar*, 219–34. Translated by Joachim Neugros. Oxford: Blackwell, 1985.

Lobenstein-Reichmann, Anja. *Houston Stewart Chamberlain: Zur Textlichen Konstruktion einer Weltanschauung*. Berlin: Walter de Gruyter, 2008.

Loomis, Roger Sherman. *The Grail: From Celtic Myth to Christian Symbol*. Cardiff: University of Wales, 1963.

Lorenz, Alfred. *Der Musikalische Aufbau von Richard Wagners 'Parsifal'*. Das Geheimnis der Form bei Richard Wagner 4. 1933. Reprint. Tutzing, Germany: Schneider, 1966.

Luther, Martin. *Die gantze Heilige Schrift Deudsch, Wittenberg 1545, herausgegeben von Hans Volz*. 2 vols. München: Rogner & Bernhard, 1972.

———. *Passional Christi und Antichristi mit Bildern v. Lucas Cranach d. Aelteren; auf's Neue aufgelegt mit den Briefe d. Papstes Pius IX u. der Antwort Sr. Majestät d. Kaisers Wilhelm vermehrt*. Leipzig: Hoffmann, n.d.

Luz, Ulrich. *Das Evangelium nach Matthäus (Mt 1–7)*. EKK 1.1. 5th ed. Düsseldorf: Benziger/Neukirchen-Vluyn: Neukirchener, 2002.

McConnell, Winder. "Otherworlds, Alchemy, Pythagoras, and Jung: Symbols of Transformation in *Parzival*." In *A Companion to Wolfram's Parzival*, edited by Will Hasty, 203–22. Rochester, NY: Camden House, 1999.

MacIntosh, Fiona. "Tragedy in performance: nineteenth- and twentieth-century productions." In *The Cambridge Companion to Greek Tragedy*, edited by P. E. Easterling, 284–323. Cambridge: Cambridge University Press, 1997.

Mack, Michael. *German Idealism and the Jew: Inner Anti-Semitism of Philosophy and German Jewish Responses*. Chicago: University of Chicago Press, 2003.

Magee, Bryan. *Aspects of Wagner*. 2nd ed. Oxford: Oxford University Press, 1988.

———. *Confessions of a Philosopher*. London: Weidenfeld & Nicolson, 1997.

———. *The Great Philosophers*. Oxford: Oxford University Press, 1987.

———. *The Philosophy of Schopenhauer*. 2nd ed. Oxford: Oxford University Press, 1997.

———. *Wagner and Philosophy*. London: Penguin, 2001.

Mann, Thomas. "Leiden und Größe Richard Wagners (1933)." In *Thomas Mann, Essays, Band 4: Achtung, Europa!* 11–72. Frankfurt am Main: Fischer, 1995.

———. "Sufferings and Greatness of Richard Wagner." In *Essays of Three Decades*, translated by H. T. Lowe-Porter, 307–52. London: Secker & Warburg, n.d.

Marr, Wilhelm. *Der Sieg des Judenthums über das Germanenthum—Vom nichtconfessionaellen Stadnpunkt aus betrachtet*. Bern: Costenable, 1879.

Matheopoulos, Helena. *Placido Domingo: My Operatic Roles*. London: Little, Brown and Company, 2000.

Mehlhausen, Joachim. "Bauer, Bruno (1809–1882)." In *TRE* 5:314–17.

Melderis, Hans. *Raum—Zeit—Mythos: Richard Wagner und die modernen Naturwissenschaften*. Hamburg: Europäische Verlagsanstalt, 2001.

Meredith, Anthony. "Quietismus." In *TRE* 28:41–45.

Merleau-Ponty, Maurice. *The Phenomenology of Perception*. 1962. Reprint. London: Routledge, 2002.

Mertens, Volker. "Wie christlich ist Wagners Gral?" In *Wagnerspectrum: Der Gral*, 91–115. Würzburg: Königshausen & Neumann, 2008.

———. "Wolfram von Eschenbach." In *TRE* 36:281–84.

Mertens, Völker. "Wagner's Middle Ages." In *Wagner Handbook*, edited by Ulrich Müller, Peter Wapnewski, and John Deathridge, 236–68. Cambridge: Harvard University Press, 1992.

Meurer, Moritz. *Luther's Leben aus den Quellen erzählt.* 3rd ed. Leipzig: Naumann, 1870.

Meyer, Rudolf. *Zum Raum wird hier die Zeit: Die Gralsgeschichte.* 3rd ed. Stuttgart: Urachhaus, 1980.

Mickisch, Stefan. *Parsifal: Einführungsvortrag Bayreuther Festspiele 2004.* Himmelkron, Germany: Fafnerphon, 2005.

———. *Tonarten und Sternzeichen.* Himmelkron, Germany: Fafnerphon, 2005.

Middleton, Christopher, editor. *Selected Letters of Friedrich Nietzsche.* Chicago: University of Chicago Press, 1969.

Millington, Barry, editor. *The Wagner Compendium: A Guide to Wagner's Life and Music.* London: Thames and Hudson, 1992.

———. "The Music." In *The Wagner Compendium: A Guide to Wagner's Life and Music*, edited by Barry Millington, 269–324. London: Thames and Hudson, 1992.

———. *Richard Wagner: The Sorcerer of Bayreuth.* London: Thames & Hudson, 2012.

———. *Wagner.* MM. 1984. Reprint. Oxford: Oxford University Press, 2000.

Montinari, Mazzino. "Nietzsche–Wagner im Sommer 1878." *Nietzsche-Studien* 14 (1985) 13–21.

Mösch, Stephan. *Weihe, Werkstatt, Wirklichkeit: Parsifal in Bayreuth 1882–1933.* Suttgart: J. B. Metzler, 2009.

Murdoch, Brian. "*Parzival* and the Theology of Fallen Man." In *A Companion to Wolfram's Parzival*, edited by Will Hasty, 143–58. Rochester, NY: Camden House, 1999.

Murdoch, Iris. *Metaphysics as a Guide to Morals.* New York: Allen Lane, 1992.

Mühlen, Patrik von zur. *Rassenideologien: Geschichte und Hintergründe.* Bonn: Dietz, 1977.

Müller, Ulrich, and Annemarie Eder. "Wer ist der Gral?" In *Ring und Gral*, edited by Ulrich Müller and Oswald Panagl, 199–237. Würzburg: Königshausen & Neumann, 2002.

Nattiez, Jean-Jacques. *Wagner Androgyne: A Study in Interpretation.* Translated by Stewart Spencer. Princeton: Princeton University Press, 1993.

Neill, Stephen. *The Interpretation of the New Testament, 1861–1961.* London: Oxford University Press, 1964.

Neumann, Angelo. *Personal Recollections of Wagner.* Translated by Edith Livermore. London: Constable, 1909.

Newman, Ernest. *The Life of Richard Wagner, Volume II: 1848–1860.* London: Cassell, 1947.

———. *The Life of Richard Wagner, Volume IV: 1866–1883.* London: Cassell, 1947.

———. *A Study of Wagner.* 1899. Reprint. New York: Vienna House, 1974.

Nicosia, Francis R. *The Third Reich and the Palestine Question.* 1985. Reprint. New Brunswick: Transaction, 2000.

Niebergall, Alfred. "Agapen II." In *TRE* 1:753–55.

Nietzsche, Friedrich. *The Anti-Christ, Ecce Homo, Twilight of the Idols and Other Writings.* CTHP. Edited by Aaron Ridley and Judith Norman. 2005. Reprint. Cambridge: Cambridge University Press, 2012.

―――. *The Birth of Tragedy and Other Writings*. CTHP. Edited by Raymond Geuss and Ronald Speirs. Cambridge: Cambridge University Press, 1999.

―――. "Briefe." In *Friedrich Nietzsche: Werke in drei Bänden, Dritter Band*, edited by Karl Schlechta, 927–1352. Darmstadt: Wissenschaftliche Buchgesellschaft, 1997.

―――. *Daybreak: Thoughts on the Prejudices of Morality*. CTHP. Edited by R. J. Hollindale. 1997. Reprint. Cambridge: Cambridge University Press, 2012.

―――. "Ecce Homo. Wie man wird, was man ist." In *Friedrich Nietzsche: Werke in drei Bänden, Zweiter Band*, edited by Karl Schlechta, 1063–1159. Darmstadt: Wissenschaftliche Buchgesellschaft, 1997.

―――. *Human, All Too Human: A Book for Free Spirits*. CTHP. Translated by R. J. Hollindale. 1996. Reprint. Cambridge: Cambridge University Press, 2012.

―――. *On the Genealogy of Morality*. CTHPT. Edited by Keith Ansell-Pearson. Translated by Carol Diethe. Cambridge: Cambridge University Press, 1994.

―――. *Untimely Meditations*. Edited by R. J. Hollingdale. Cambridge: Cambridge University Press, 1983.

―――. *Untimely Meditations*. TGP. CTHP. Edited by Daniel Breazeale. Translated by R. J. Hollingdale. 1997. Reprint. Cambridge: Cambridge University Press, 2001.

Nitze, William A., editor. *Robert de Boron: Le roman de l'estoire dou graal*. Les classiques français du moyen age. Paris: Librarie ancienne honoré champion éditeur, 1927.

Noakes, Jeremy, and Geoffrey Pridham, editors. *Documents on Nazism, 1919–1945*. London: Jonathan Cape, 1974.

Novak, David. *Talking with Christians: Musings of a Jewish Theologian*. RTrad. London: SCM, 2006.

Nygren, Anders. *Agape and Eros*. Translated by Philip S. Watson. Philadelphia: Westminster, 1953.

Oberman, Heiko A. *The Dawn of the Reformation*. 1986. Reprint. Grand Rapids: Eerdmans, 1992.

Osbourne, Richard. *Herbert von Karajan: A Life in Music*. London: Pimlico, 1999.

Osthövener, Claus-Dieter. "Bayreuther Theologie und Deutsche Christen: Zur Wirkungsgeschichte des Bayreuther Kreises." In *Wagnerspectrum: Bayreuther Theologie*, 157–83. Würzburg: Königshausen & Neumann, 2009.

Otto, Werner. *Richard Wagner: Ein Lebens- und Charakterbild in Dokumenten und zeitgenössischen Darstellungen*. Berlin: Der Morgen, 1990.

Oxenford, John. "Iconoclasm in German Philosophy." *Westminster and Foreign Quarterly Review* 3.2 (1853) 388–407.

Passow, Franz, Chr. F. Rost, and Fr. Palm. *Handwörterbuch der griechischen Sprache*. 2 vols. 5th ed. Leipzig: Vogel, 1841–57.

Pedersen, Johs. *Israel: Its Life and Culture, I–II*. Translated by Johs. Pedersen and Aslaug Møller. 1926. Reprint. London: Cumberlege, 1946.

Porges, Heinrich. "Levi." *Musikalisches Wochenblatt* (1900) 334–36.

Pott, August F. *Die Ungleichheit menschlicher Rassen: hauptsächlich vom sprachwissenschaftlichen Standpunkte, unter besonderer Berücksichtigung von des Grafen von Gobineau gleichnamigem Werke; mit einem Ueberblicke über die Sprachverhältnisse der Völker; ein ethnologischer Versuch*. Lemgo/Detmold, Germany: Meyer, 1856.

Pound, Marcus. *Žižek: A (Very) Critical Introduction*. Interventions. Grand Rapids: Eerdmans, 2008.

Prawer, S. S. *Heine, the Tragic Satirist: A Study of the Later Poetry 1827–56*. Cambridge: Cambridge University Press, 1961.

Pretzel, Ulrich, and Wolfgang Bachofer. *Bibliographie zu Wolfram von Eschenbach*. BdLdM 2. Berlin: Schmidt, 1968.

Pringe, Hernán. *Critique of the Quantum Power of Judgment: A Transcendental Foundation of Quantum Objectivity*. Kantstudien 154. Berlin: de Gruyer, 2007.

Rad, Gerhard von. *Genesis*. OTL. Translated by John H. Marks. London: SCM, 1972.

Rauschning, Hermann. *Gespräche mit Hitler*. Zürich: Europa, 1940.

Renan, Ernest. *The Life of Jesus*. London: Dent, 1927.

Rengstorf, Karl Heinrich, and Siegfried von Kortzfleisch, editors. *Kirche und Synagoge: Handbuch zur Geschichte von Christen und Juden. Darstellung mit Quellen*. 2 vols. 1968–70. Reprint. München: DTV, 1988.

Roberts, Neil. *George Eliot: Her Beliefs and Her Art*. London: Elek, 1975.

Rose, Paul Lawrence. *Wagner: Race and Revolution*. London: Faber, 1992.

———. "Wagner und Hitler—nach dem Holocaust." In *Richard Wagner und die Juden*, edited by Dieter Borchmeyer, Ami Maayani, and Susanne Vill, 223–37. Stuttgart: J. B. Metzler, 2000.

Rosenberger, Veit. *Griechische Orakel. Eine Kulturgeschichte*. Darmstadt: Wissenschaftliche Buchgesellschaft, 2001.

Rosenkranz, Karl, and Friedrich W. Schubert, editors. *Immanuel Kant's sämmtliche Werke*. Leipzig: Voss, 1838–40.

Ross, Werner. *Der ängstliche Adler: Friedrich Nietzsches Leben*. Stuttgart: Kastell, 1998.

Roukema, Riemer. *Gnosis and Faith in Early Christianity*. Translated by John Bowden. London: SCM, 1999.

Rudolph, Kurt. *Gnosis: The Nature and History of Gnosticism*. Translated by Robert McLachlan Wilson. Edinburgh: T. & T. Clark, 1983.

Sachs, Hans. *Die Wittenbergisch Nachtigall: Reformationsdichtung*. 1974. Reprint. Stuttgart: Reclam, 1998.

Sachs, Harvey. *Toscanini*. London: Weidenfeld and Nicolson, 1978.

Saebo, Magne. "Yahweh as Deus absconditus: Some Remarks on a Dictum by Gerhard von Rad." In *Shall Not the Judge of All the Earth Do What is Right? Studies on the Nature of God in Tribute to James L. Crenshaw*, edited by D. Penchansky and P. L. Redditt, 43–55. Wiona Lake, IN: Eisenbrauns, 2000.

San-Marte, editor. *Leben und Dichten von Wolfram von Eschenbach*. 2 vols. Magdeburg: Creutz, 1836–41.

———, editor. *Ueber das Religiöse in den Werken Wolframs von Eschenbach und die Bedeutung des heiligen Grals in dessen 'Parcival.'* Parcival-Studien 2. Halle: Buchhandlung des Waisenhauses, 1861.

San-Marte, and Johann Friedrich Wolfhart, editors. *Des Guiot von Provins bis jetzt bekannte Dichtungen*. Parcival-Studien 1. Halle: Buchhandlung des Waisenhauses, 1861.

Sartre, Jean-Paul. *Being and Nothingness: An Essay on Phenomenological Ontology*. Translated by Hazel E. Barnes. 1958. Reprint. London: Routledge, 1991.

Schelling, Friedrich Wilhelm Joseph von. *Einleitung in die Philosophie der Mythologie*. Edited by Karl Friedrich August Schelling. Sämmtliche Werke 11. Stuttgart: Cotta'scher, 1856.

Schmidt, Alfred. *Die Wahrheit im Gewande der Lüge*. München: Piper, 1986.

Scholder, Klaus. *The Churches and the Third Reich, Volume 2: The Year of Disillusionment 1934, Barmen and Rome*. Translated by John Bowden. London: SCM, 1988.

Scholz, Dieter David. *Richard Wagners Antisemitismus: Jahrhundertgenie im Zwielicht— Eine Korrektur*. Berlin: Parthas, 2000.

Schopenhauer, Arthur. *The Two Fundamental Problems of Ethics*. Translated by David E. Cartwright and Edward E. Erdmann. Oxford: Oxford University Press, 2010.

Schreckenberg, Heinz. *The Jews in Christian Art: An Illustrated History*. Translated by John Bowden. London: SCM, 1996.

Schweitzer, Albert. *Denken und Tat: Zusammengetragen und dargestellt von Rudolf Grabs*. Hamburg: Meiner, 1952.

———. *Geschichte der Leben-Jesu-Forschung*. 9th ed. Tübingen: J.C.B. Mohr (Paul Siebeck), 1984.

———. *J. S. Bach*. 2 vols. Translated by Ernest Newman. London: A. & C. Black, 1908.

———. *The Quest of the Historical Jesus: A Critical Study of Its Progress from Reimarus to Wrede*. Translated by W. Montgomery. London: Black, 1945.

Scruton, Roger. *Death-Devoted Heart: Sex and the Sacred in Wagner's Tristan and Isolde*. Oxford: Oxford University Press, 2004.

———. "A Quest for Truth." *Literary Review* (April 2006) 15.

Seelig, Wolfgang. "Leben und Erlösung: Über das Leiden und den Erlösungsgedanken bei Schopenhauer und Wagner." *Schopenhauer-Jahrbuch* 64 (1983) 101–10.

Sellin, Gerhard. "Mythologeme und mythische Züge in der paulinischen Theologie." In *Mythos und Rationalität*, edited by Hans Heinrich Schmid, 209–23. Gütersloh: Gütersloher Verlagshaus Gerd Mohn, 1988.

Skinner, John. *A Critical and Exegetical Commentary on Genesis*. ICC. Edinburgh: T. & T. Clark, 1917.

Soden, Michael von, editor. *Richard Wagner: Lohengrin*. Frankfurt am Main: Insel, 1980.

Sohn, Joseph. "Levi, Hermann." *JE* 8:32.

Speer, Albert. *Spandau: The Secret Diaries*. Translated by Richard and Clara Winston. New York: Macmillan, 1976.

Spencer, Stewart. "Letters." In *The Wagner Compendium: A Guide to Wagner's Life and Music*, edited by Barry Millington, 190–93. London: Thames and Hudson, 1992.

———. *Wagner Remembered*. London: Faber and Faber, 2000.

Spencer, Stewart, and Barry Millington, translators and editors. *Selected Letters of Richard Wagner*. New York/London: W.W. Norton, 1987.

Spotts, Frederic. *Bayreuth: A History of the Wagner Festival*. New Haven: Yale University Press, 1994.

Steinacker, Peter. *Richard Wagner und die Religion*. Darmstadt: Wissenschaftliche Buchgesellschaft, 2008.

Stevens, Adrian. "Wolfram's *Parzival* and Its Narrative Sources." In *A Companion to Wolfram's Parzival*, edited by Will Hasty, 99–123. Rochester, NY: Camden House, 1999.

Storr, Anthony. *Music and the Mind*. 1992. Reprint. London: HarperCollins, 1997.

Stöcker, Adolf. "Hofprediger Stöcker Über 'Parsifal' und Bayreuth." *Musikalisches Wochenblatt* 25 (1894) 454–55.

Strauss, David Friedrich. *The Life of Jesus Critically Examined*. Translated by George Eliot. London: SCM, 1973.

Strauß, David Friedrich. *Das Leben Jesu.* Tübingen: Osiander, 1835.

———. *Das Leben Jesu kritisch bearbeitet (mit einer Einleitung von Werner Zager).* 2 vols. Darmstadt: Wissenschaftliche Buchgesellschaft, 2012.

———. *Voltaire: sechs Vorträge.* 2nd ed. Leipzig: Hirzel, 1870.

Syer, Katherine R. "Wagner's Shaping of the Grail Scene of Act 1." In *A Companion to Wagner's Parsifal,* edited by William Kinderman and Katherine R. Syer, 177–214. Rochester, NY: Camden House, 2005.

Tanner, Michael. "The Total Work of Art." In *The Wagner Companion,* edited by Peter Burbidge and Richard Sutton, 140–224. London: Faber and Faber, 1979.

———. *Wagner.* London: Harper Collins, 1996.

Taylor, Ronald. *Richard Wagner: His Life, Art and Thought.* London: Elek, 1979.

Torrance, Thomas F. *Reality and Scientific Theology.* TSFK 1. Edinburgh: Scottish Academic, 1985.

Trevor-Roper, Hugh, editor. *Hitler's Table Talk.* London: Phoenix, 2000.

———. *The Last Days of Hitler.* 2nd ed. London: Macmillan, 1950.

Vaget, Hans Rudolf. "'Operation Walküre': The Movie and the History." *The Wagner Journal* 5.1 (2011) 4–16.

Villiers de l'Isle-Adam, Philippe-Auguste, "Souvenir." *Revue Wagnérienne* 3.5 (Juin 1887) 139–41.

Voss, Egon. "Die Möglichkeit der Klage in der Wonne." In *'Wagner und kein Ende': Betrachtungen und Studien,* 222–33. Zürich: Atlantis, 1996.

Wackernagel, Philipp, editor. *Martin Luthers geistliche Lieder mit den zu seinen Lebzeiten gebräuchlichsten Singweisen.* Stuttgart: Liesching, 1848.

Wagner, Friedelind. *Nacht über Bayreuth: Die Geschichte der Enkelin Richard Wagners.* Berlin: List, 2002.

Wagner, Gottfried. *He Who Does Not Howl with the Wolf: The Wagner Legacy.* Translated by Della Couling. London: Sanctuary, 1998.

Wagner, Nike. *The Wagners: The Dramas of a Musical Dynasty.* Translated by Ewald Osers and Michael Downes. London: Weidenfeld & Nicholson, 2000.

Wagner, Richard. *Briefwechsel zwischen Wagner und Liszt, Erster Band: Vom Jahre 1841 bis 1853.* Leipzig: Breitkopf und Härtel, 1887.

Walker, Alan. *Hans von Bülow: A Life and Times.* Oxford: Oxford University Press, 2010.

Wapnewski, Peter. "The Operas as Literary Works." In *Wagner Handbook,* edited by Ulrich Müller, Peter Wapnewski, and John Deathridge, 3–95. Cambridge: Harvard University Press, 1992.

———. *Der traurige Gott. Richard Wagner in seinen Helden.* München: Deutscher Taschenbuch, 1982.

———. *Wolframs Parzival: Studien zur Religiosität und Form.* Heidelberg: Winter, 1955.

Weiner, Marc A. *Richard Wagner and the Anti-Semitic Imagination.* Lincoln, NE: University of Nebraska Press, 1995.

Weingartner, Felix. *Lebenserinnerungen.* Wien: Wiener Literarische Anstalt, 1923.

Weininger, Otto. *Geschlecht und Charakter: Eine prinzipielle Untersuchung.* München, 1903.

Weinzierl, Erika. "Antisemitismus VII." In *TRE* 3:155–65.

Weischedel, Wilhelm, ed. *Kritik der reinen Vernunft, erster Teil. Immanuel Kant: Werke in Zehn Bänden.* Band 3. 1956. Reprint. Darmstadt: Wissenschaftliche Buchgesellschaft, 1983.

————, ed. *Kritik der reinen Vernunft, zweiter Teil. Immanuel Kant: Werke in Zehn Bänden. Band 4.* 1956. Reprint. Darmstadt: Wissenschaftliche Buchgesellschaft, 1983.

————, editor. *Schriften zur Anthropologie, Geschichtsphilosophie, Politik und Pädagogik, erster Teil: Immanuel Kant. Werke in Zehn Bänden. Band 9.* 1964. Reprint. Darmstadt: Wissenschaftliche Buchgesellschaft, 1983.

Weisse, Christian Hermann. *Die evangelische Geschichte kritisch und philosophisch bearbeitet.* 2 vols; Leipzig: Breitkopf und Härtel, 1838.

Westermann, Claus. *Genesis 1–11: A Commentary.* Translated by John J. Scullion. London: SPCK, 1984.

Westernhagen, Curt von. *Richard Wagner. Sein Werk, sein Wesen, seine Welt.* Zürich: Atlantis, 1956.

————. *Richard Wagners Dresdener Bibliothek 1842 bis 1849.* Wiesbaden: Brockhaus, 1966.

————. *Wagner: A Biography.* 2 vols. Translated by Mary Whittall. Cambridge: Cambridge University Press, 1978.

Wittgenstein, Ludwig. *Philosophical Investigations.* Edited by G. E. M. Anscombe. 3rd ed. Oxford: Blackwell, 2001.

Wolzogen, Hans von. *Bayreuth.* Leipzig: Siegel, n.d.

————. "Beiträge zur Kritik des modernen Kunstgeschmackes, v: Bühnenweihfestspiel." *Bayreuther Blätter* 1 (1878, Zehntes Stück) 295–302.

Young, Julian. *Friedrich Nietzsche: A Philosophical Biography.* Cambridge: Cambridge University Press, 2010.

————. *Schopenhauer.* London: Routledge, 2005.

Yovel, Yirmiyahu. "'Nietzsche contra Wagner' und die Juden." In *Richard Wagner und die Juden,* edited by Dieter Borchmeyer, Ami Maayani, and Susanne Vill, 123–43. Stuttgart: Metzler, 2000.

Zegowitz, Bernd. *Richard Wagners unvertonte Opern.* HBzdL 8. Frankfurt am Main: Peter Lang, 2000.

Zeki, Semir. *Splendors and Miseries of the Brain: Love, Creativity, and the Quest for Human Happiness.* Oxford: Wiley-Blackwell, 2009.

————. *A Vision of the Brain.* Oxford: Blackwell, 1993.

Zelinsky, Hartmut. "Die 'Feuerkur' des Richard Wagner oder die 'neue Religion' der 'Erlösung' durch 'Vernichtung.'" In *Wie antisemitisch darf ein Künstler sein?* edited by Heinz-Klaus Metzger and Rainer Riehn, 79–112. München: Text + Kritik, 1978.

————. *Richard Wagner—ein deutsches Thema. Eine Dokumentation zur Wirkungsgeschichte Richard Wagners.* München: Zweitausendeins, 1976.

Zentner, Christian, editor. *Adolf Hitlers Mein Kampf: Eine kommentierte Auswahl.* 17th ed. München: List, 2004.

Zentner, Christian, and Friedemann Bedürftig, editors. *Das grosse Lexikon des dritten Reiches.* München: Sudwest, 1985.

Index of Authors

Index of Biblical Texts

↬

II NEW TESTAMENT

Index of Wagner's Works

II WRITINGS

Index of Subjects and Names

G

U

Uhlig, Theodor, 193

V

Verlaine, Paul, 84, 179
Villiers de l'Isle-Adam, Philippe-
    Auguste, 227–28
Virgin Birth,
    and causation, 117, 176, 302–3
    and history, 115
    as birth of God, 307, 316
    as miracle, 117, 176, 302–3
    in painting, 303–5
    Schopenhauer on, 167
virginal conception
    Wagner on, 114, 176, 302, 303
Virgin Mary
    assumption of, 162–63, 179
    in art, 162–63, 303–5
    relationship to Child-of-God,
        305
vivisection
    in training of medical students,
        210
    Schopenhauer on, 210
    Wagner on, 122, 210
Voltaire (François-Marie Arouet),
    173, 192, 215, 235

W

Wagner, Adolf (uncle), 21–22
Wagner, Adolph (economist), 204
Wagner, Cäcilie (half-sister), 23, 246
Wagner, Cosima, see also Index of
    Authors
    and Isolde von Bülow, 9
    antisemitism of, 182, 202–3
    conversion to Protestantism,
        237, 261, 314
    faith of, 21, 43, 175–76, 198,
        208, 230, 235, 252, 265, 267,
        275, 308, 314–15
    marriage to von Bülow, 6–7

marriage to Wagner, 6–7, 9–10,
    156
sense of guilt of, 7, 252
Wagner, Luise (sister), see
    Brockhaus, Luise,
Wagner, Ottilie (sister), see
    Brockhaus, Ottilie
Wagner, Siegfried, 5, 208
    baptism of, 259, 260
Wagner, Richard
    and Angelo Neumann, 131,
        201–2, 182
    and Hermann Levi, 8, 136,
        181–82, 196, 204–8, 212,
        224, 227
    and Joseph Rubinstein, 8, 182,
        203, 208
    and Lilli Lehmann, 182
    anti-Judaism of, 33, 36, 133,
        182–85, 188–90, 198, 210–
        11, 247
    antisemitism of, 3–4, 6–8, 10,
        124, 182–84, 191–92, 198–
        99, 200–204, 209, 218–19,
        221, 224, 247
    as agnostic, 224
    as "atheist," 2, 172, 224, 230, 236
    as Christian, 9, 20, 22, 63, 131,
        224–25, 227–31, 236–40,
        242–44, 271, 313–19,
    as father, 9
    as Marcionite, 12
    as "prophet," 274
    copy of New Testaments, 24, 39,
        43, 93, 109, 137, 194, 320
    copy of Luther Bible, 43, 150,
        320
    death of, 65
    discovery of Schopenhauer, 19,
        22, 28–32, 37, 151, 198, 260,
        287
    Dresden library of, 24, 39, 45,
        62, 113
    experience of Communion, 21,
        104, 206, 236–37, 259–61,
        306, 315
    humor of, 10, 181–82, 311
    ill health of, 65, 177, 179

Lightning Source UK Ltd.
Milton Keynes UK
UKOW02f1848090816

280321UK00001B/2/P